NEW CENTURY BIBLE COMMENTARY

General Editors

RONALD E. CLEMENTS
(Old Testament)

MATTHEW BLACK
(New Testament)

Isaiah 1-39

THE NEW CENTURY BIBLE COMMENTARIES

Other titles in preparation

NEW CENTURY BIBLE COMMENTARY

Based on the Revised Standard Version

ISAIAH 1-39

R. E. CLEMENTS

WM. B. EERDMANS PUBL. CO., GRAND RAPIDS

MARSHALL, MORGAN & SCOTT PUBL. LTD., LONDON

Copyright © Marshall, Morgan & Scott (Publications) Ltd. 1980
First published 1980

Printed in the United States of America
for
Wm. B. Eerdmans Publishing Company
255 Jefferson Ave. S.E., Grand Rapids, Mich. 49503
and
Marshall, Morgan & Scott
A Pentos company
1 Bath Street, London EC1V 9LB
ISBN 0 551 00828 8

Library of Congress Cataloging in Publication Data
Clements, Ronald Ernest, 1929-
Isaiah I-39.

(New century Bible commentaries)
Bibliography: p. xii.
Includes indexes.
1. Bible. O. T. Isaiah I-XXXIX — Commentaries.
I. Bible.   O.T. Isaiah I-XXXIX.   English.
Revised standard. 1980. III. Series: New century Bible commentary.
BS1515.3.C57   1980   224'.1077   80-20905
ISBN 0-8028-1841-2

CONTENTS

PREFACE

My own interest in the great pre-exilic prophets of the Old Testament arose whilst I was undertaking research into the history and theology associated with the temple of Jerusalem. At that time I had no intention of developing this further into a special study of chapters 1–39 of the book of Isaiah, even though this might have seemed appropriate. However, when I was asked to take over responsibility for the editorial planning of the Old Testament volumes in the New Century Bible series I quickly found myself without a contributor for the book of Isaiah. Professor H. H. Rowley had intended that, like the original contribution by O. C. Whitehouse to the Century Bible, the entire commentary should be produced by a single scholar. Since that earlier two-volume work was published, however, a good many writers have felt it more appropriate to divide the book into the two sections comprising chapters 1–39 and 40–66. Professor R. N. Whybray of the University of Hull kindly agreed to write the commentary on the later chapters, and with his characteristic industry was able to publish his work in 1975. My interest in the earlier chapters led me to undertake to write the commentary upon them, but unfortunately other pressures have held up their completion until now. I hope that the delay has not occasioned too great a disparity between the two volumes, which are certainly intended to be seen as interrelated.

For me, however, the delay has not been entirely without its advantages, and I hope that this may prove to be true for the reader also. The great and masterly work by H. Wildberger in the *Biblische Kommentar* series has continued to appear, and I have had access to the published sections as far as chapter 32 of the book. So too I have greatly profited by having available the work of Hermann Barth on the Josianic Redaction of Isaiah's prophecies through his kindness in making available to me a copy of his original Hamburg Dissertation of 1974. Its subsequent publication has made it possible to refer to the more widely available edition of his research. My own indebtedness to these two works in particular will be evident in the following pages, as well as to all those other works on Isaiah 1–39 which I have been able to consult. I am certainly very conscious that I have done no more than direct the attention of students of Isaiah to some of the major studies that are available.

In the past two decades the study of these chapters of the book of Isaiah has been heavily influenced by a particular theory concerning the supposed influence upon the prophet of the 'Zion Tradition' of Jerusalem. This is especially associated with the work of G. von Rad. I began with a belief in the existence of such a tradition, and with the conviction that many of the complex tensions in the book could be understood in the light of it. I came, however, decisively to reject such a view, and my reasons and counter-proposals are set out in the study *Isaiah and the Deliverance of Jerusalem*, which I hope to be able to publish separately. That study may certainly serve to clarify some of the positions adopted in the present commentary and to set them in a wider perspective.

It remains for me finally to thank the Publishers for their patience with my delays, and the many friends who have assisted me for their support. In particular I wish to express my indebtedness to Professor J. A. Emerton for his encouragement, and especially for his help in making available much of the extensive literature which is important for the modern study of Isaiah. I am also very much indebted to my colleague Dr G. I. Davies who has kindly given of his time to read through the typescript for me. For the rest I am more conscious than ever that the writing of commentaries is an art full of compromises. To be too long is to be unhelpful to the novice, yet to be too short is to disappoint the expert scholar. I may well have fallen down somewhere between the two extremes, but I have tried to blend a modest survey of the work of others with some researches and conclusions of my own.

R. E. Clements
May 1979

ABBREVIATIONS

BIBLICAL

OLD TESTAMENT (*OT*)

Gen.	Jg.	1 Chr.	Ps.	Lam.	Ob.	Hag.
Exod.	Ru.	2 Chr.	Prov.	Ezek.	Jon.	Zech.
Lev.	1 Sam.	Ezr.	Ec.	Dan.	Mic.	Mal.
Num.	2 Sam.	Neh.	Ca.	Hos.	Nah.	
Dt.	1 Kg.	Est.	Isa.	Jl	Hab.	
Jos.	2 Kg.	Job	Jer.	Am.	Zeph.	

APOCRYPHA (*Apoc.*)

1 Esd.	Tob.	Ad. Est.	Sir.	S 3 Ch.	Bel	1 Mac.
2 Esd.	Jdt.	Wis.	Bar.	Sus.	Man.	2 Mac.
			E. Jer.			

NEW TESTAMENT (*NT*)

Mt.	Ac.	Gal.	1 Th.	Tit.	1 Pet.	3 Jn
Mk	Rom.	Eph.	2 Th.	Phm.	2 Pet.	Jude
Lk.	1 C.	Phil.	1 Tim.	Heb.	1 Jn	Rev.
Jn	2 C.	Col.	2 Tim.	Jas	2 Jn	

DEAD SEA SCROLLS (DSS)

1QIs^a First Isaiah Scroll
1QIs^b Second Isaiah Scroll

GENERAL

AfO   *Archiv für Orientforschung*
ANEP   *The Ancient Near East in Pictures Relating to the Old Testament*, edited by J. B. Pritchard, 2nd edn, Princeton, 1969
ANET   *Ancient Near Eastern Texts Relating to the Old Testament*, edited by J. B. Pritchard, 3rd edn, Princeton, 1969
AR   Assyrian Redaction (Barth)
Aram.   Aramaic
ASTI   *Annual of the Swedish Theological Institute*
ATANT   *Abhandlungen zur Theologie des Alten und Neuen Testaments*

AV	*Authorised Version* (King James Version), 1611
BDB	*Hebrew and English Lexicon of the Old Testament*, ed. by F. Brown, S. R. Driver and C. A. Briggs, Oxford, 1906
BHH	*Biblisch-historisches Handwörterbuch*, edited by L. Rost and Bo Reicke, 3 vols, Göttingen, 1962–6
BHS	*Biblia Hebraica Stuttgartensia*, edited by K. Elliger and W. Rudolph, Stuttgart, 1977
BWANT	*Beiträge zur Wissenschaft vom Alten und Neuen Testament*
BZ	*Biblische Zeitschrift*
BZAW	*Beihefte zur Zeitschrift für die Alttestamentliche Wissenschaft*
CahRB	*Cahiers de Revue Biblique*
CBQ	*Catholic Biblical Quarterly*
ExpT	*Expository Times*
ET	English translation
EvTh	*Evangelishe Theologie*
FRLANT	*Forschungen zur Religion und Literatur des Alten und Neuen Testaments*
G-K	*Gesenius' Hebrew Grammar*, as edited and enlarged by E. Kautzsch and revised by A. E. Cowley, 2nd edn, London, 1910
GNB	*Good News Bible*, 1971
Heb.	Hebrew
HTOT	*The Hebrew Text of the Old Testament*, L. H. Brockington, Oxford/Cambridge, 1973
JAOS	*Journal of the American Oriental Society*
JBL	*The Journal of Biblical Literature*
JNES	*Journal of Near Eastern Studies*
JSS	*Journal of Semitic Studies*
JTS	*Journal of Theological Studies*
K-B	*Hebräisches und Aramaisches Lexikon zum Alten Testament*, by L. Köhler and W. Baumgartner, 3rd edn edited by W. Baumgartner, 2 vols, Leiden, 1967–74
LXX	The Greek Septuagint Version
MS, MSS	manuscript(s)
MT	The Massoretic Text of the Old Testament
NEB	*New English Bible*, 1970
NF	Neue Folge
ns	new series; nouvelle série
POTT	*Peoples of Old Testament Times*, edited by D. J. Wiseman, London, 1973
RB	*Revue Biblique*
RSV	*Revised Standard Version*, 1952, 1973
SANT	*Studien zum Alten und Neuen Testament*
Syr.	Syriac
Targ.	Targum
TB	*Theologische Bücherei*
TDNT	*Theological Dictionary of the New Testament*, edited by

	G. Kittel and J. Friedrich, ET by G. W. Bromiley, Grand Rapids, 1964–74
THAT	*Theologisches Handwörterbuch zum Alten Testament*, edited by E. Jenni and C. Westermann, 2 vols., Zürich/Munich, 1971–6
TWAT	*Theologisches Wörterbuch zum Alten Testament*, edited by H. Ringgren and G. J. Botterweck, Stuttgart, 1970–
VT	*Vetus Testamentum*
VT Supp.	*Supplements to Vetus Testamentum*
Vulg.	Vulgate
WMANT	*Wissenschaftliche Monographien zum Alten und Neuen Testament*
ZAW	*Zeitschrift für die Alttestamentliche Wissenschaft*
ZDMG	*Zeitschrift der deutschen Morgenländischen Gesellschaft*
ZDPV	*Zeitschrift des Deutschen Palästinavereins*
ZThK	*Zeitschrift für Theologie und Kirche*

An asterisk (*) against a Bible reference indicates that not all verses are included.

SELECT BIBLIOGRAPHY

COMMENTARIES (*cited in text by author's name only*)

P. Auvray, *Isaie 1–39* (*Sources bibliques*), Paris, 1972.

B. Duhm, *Das Buch Jesaja* (*Handkommentar zum Alten Testament*), 5th edn, Göttingen, 1968 (= 4th edn, 1922).

W. Eichrodt, *Der Heilige in Israel. Jesaja 1–12* (*Die Botschaft des Alten Testaments*), Stuttgart, 1960.

W. Eichrodt, *Der Herr der Geschichte. Jesaja 13–23, 28–39* (*Die Botschaft des Alten Testaments*), Stuttgart, 1967.

G. Fohrer, *Das Buch Jesaja* (*Zürcher Bibelkommentare*), 2nd edn, Zürich/Stuttgart, Bd. I, chs. 1–23, 1966; Bd. II, chs. 24–39, 1967.

G. B. Gray, *Isaiah I–XXVII* (*International Critical Commentary*), Edinburgh, 1912.

A. S. Herbert, *The Book of the Prophet Isaiah, 1–39* (*Cambridge Commentary on the New English Bible*), Cambridge, 1973.

V. Herntrich, *Der Prophet Jesaja. Kapitel 1–12* (*Das Alte Testament Deutsch*), Göttingen, 1954.

O. Kaiser, *Isaiah 1–12* (*Old Testament Library*), ET by R. A. Wilson, London, 1972.

O. Kaiser, *Isaiah 13–39* (*Old Testament Library*), ET by R. A. Wilson, London, 1974.

K. Marti, *Das Buch Jesaja* (*Kurzer Hand-Kommentar zum Alten Testament*), Tübingen, 1900.

J. Mauchline, *Isaiah 1–39* (*Torch Bible Commentaries*), London, 1962.

O. Procksch, *Jesaja I.* (*Kommentar zum Alten Testament*), Leipzig, 1930.

A. Schoors, *Jesaja* (*De Boeken van het Oude Testament*), Roermond, 1972.

R. B. Y. Scott, *The Book of Isaiah* (*The Interpreter's Bible 5*), New York/Nashville, 1956, pp. 149–381.

L. A. Snijders, *Jesaja Pt. I* (*De Prediking van het Oude Testament*), Nijkerk, 1969.

H. Wildberger, *Jesaja 1–12* (*Biblische Kommentar*), Neukirchen-Vluyn, 1965–72.

H. Wildberger, *Jesaja 13–27* (*Biblische Kommentar*), Neukirchen-Vluyn, 1974–8.

H. Wildberger, *Jesaja 28–39* (*Biblische Kommentar*), Neukirchen-Vluyn, 1978– .

SPECIAL STUDIES (*cited in text by author's name only*)

H. Barth, *Die Jesaja-Worte in der Josiazeit* (*WMANT* 48), Neukirchen-Vluyn, 1977.

W. Dietrich, *Jesaja und die Politik (Beiträge zur evangelischen Theologie* 74), Munich, 1976.

H. Donner, *Israel unter den Völkern (VT Supp.* 11), Leiden, 1964.

H. W. Hoffmann, *Die Intention der Verkündigung Jesajas (BZAW* 136), Berlin/New York, 1974.

F. Huber, *Jahwe, Juda und die anderen Völker beim Propheten Jesaja (BZAW* 137), Berlin/New York, 1976.

W. H. Irwin, *Isaiah 28–33. Translation with Philological Notes (Biblica et Orientalia* 30), Rome, 1977.

J. Vermeylen, *Du prophète Isaïe à l'apocalyptique (Études bibliques)*, 2 vols., Paris, 1977.

Other Special Studies

J. Bright, *Covenant and Promise. The Future in the Preaching of the Pre-exilic Prophets*, London, 1977.

M. Cogan, *Imperialism and Religion: Assyria, Judah and Israel in the Eighth and Seventh Centuries B.C.E. (SBL Monographs Series* 19), Missoula, 1974.

I. Engnell, *The Call of Isaiah. An Exegetical and Comparative Study*, Uppsala, 1949.

R. Fey, *Amos und Jesaja. Abhängigkeit und Eigenständigkeit des Jesaja (WMANT* 12), Neukirchen-Vluyn, 1963.

N. K. Gottwald, *All the Kingdoms of the Earth. Israelite Prophecy and International Relations in the Ancient Near East*, New York/Evanston/London, 1964.

G. F. Hasel, *The Remnant. The History and Theology of the Remnant Idea from Genesis to Isaiah (Andrews University Monographs* 5), Berrien Springs, 1972.

W. Janzen, *Mourning Cry and Woe Oracle (BZAW* 125), Berlin/New York, 1972.

P. Jensen, *The Use of tora by Isaiah. His Debate with the Wisdom Tradition (CBQ Monograph Series* 3), Washington, 1973.

Th. Lescow, 'Jesajas Denkschrift aus der Zeit des syrisch-ephraimitischen Krieges', *ZAW* 85 (1973), pp. 315–31.

W. McKane, *Prophets and Wise Men (SBT* 44), London, 1965.

S. Mowinckel, *Jesaja-Disiplene. Profetien fra Jesaja til Jeremia*, Oslo, 1926.

H.-P. Müller, 'Glauben und Bleiben. Zur Denkschrift Jesajas Kapitel vi.1–viii.18', *Studies on Prophecy (VT Supp.* 26), Leiden, 1974, pp. 25–54.

H.-P. Müller, *Ursprünge und Strukturen alttestamentlicher Eschatologie (BZAW* 109), Berlin, 1969.

H. D. Preuss, *Jahweglaube und Zukunftserwartung (BWANT* 87), Stuttgart/Berlin/Cologne/Mainz, 1968.

O. H. Steck, 'Bemerkung zu Jesaja 6', *BZ* NF 16 (1972), pp. 188–206.

O. H. Steck, 'Beiträge zum Verständnis von Jesaja 7,10–17 und 8,1–4', *ThZ* 29 (1973), pp. 161–78.

O. H. Steck, 'Rettung und Verstockung. Exegetische Bemerkungen zu Jesaja 7,3–9', *EvTh* 33 (1973), pp. 77–90.

J. W. Whedbee, *Isaiah and Wisdom*, Nashville/New York, 1971.

The Immanuel Prophecy of 7: 10–17 and the Royal Prophecies of 9: 2–7; 11: 1–9

A. Alt, 'Jesaja 8, 23–9,6. Befreiungsnacht und Krönungstag', in *Festschrift A. Bertholet*, Tübingen, 1950, pp. 29–49 (= *Kleine Schriften*, II, Munich, 1953, pp. 206–25).

A. Bentzen, *King and Messiah*, 2nd edn, edited by G. W. Anderson, Oxford, 1970.

K. Budde, 'Das Immanuelzeichen und die Ahaz-Begegnung Jesaja 7', *JBL* 52 (1933), pp. 22–54.

K. Budde, 'Jesaja und Ahaz', *ZDMG* NF 9 (1930), pp. 125–38.

P. J. Calderone, *Dynastic Oracle and Suzerainty Treaty*, Manila, 1966.

H. Gese, 'Natus ex virgine', in *Probleme biblischer Theologie (Festschrift G. von Rad)*, Munich, 1971, pp. 73–89 (= *Vom Sinai zum Zion*, Munich, 1974, pp. 130–46).

H. Gese, 'Der Davidsbund und die Zionserwählung', *ZThK* NF 61 (1964), pp. 10–26 (= *Vom Sinai zum Zion*, pp. 113–29).

N. K. Gottwald, 'Immanuel as the Prophet's Son', *VT* 8 (1958), pp. 36–47.

H. Gressmann, *Der Messias (FRLANT* NF 26), Göttingen, 1929.

E. Hammershaimb, 'The Immanuel Sign', *Studia Theologica* 3 (1949), pp. 124–42.

A. R. Johnson, *Sacral Kingship in Ancient Israel*, 2nd edn, Cardiff, 1967.

R. Kilian, *Die Verheissung Immanuels. Jes.7.14 (SBS* 35), Stuttgart, 1968.

L. Köhler, 'Zum Verständnis von Jesaja 7,14', *ZAW* 67 (1955), pp. 48–50.

Th. Lescow, 'Das Geburtsmotiv in den messianischen Weissagungen bei Jesaja und Micha', *ZAW* 79 (1967), pp. 172–207.

Th. Lescow, 'Jesajas Denkschrift aus der Zeit des syrisch-ephraimitischen Krieges', *ZAW* 85 (1973), pp. 315–31.

J. Lindblom, *A Study of the Immanuel Section in Isaiah. Isa. vii,1–ix,6*, Lund, 1958.

W. McKane, 'The Interpretation of Isaiah vii, 14–25', *VT* 17 (1967), pp. 208–19.

F. L. Moriarty, 'The Immanuel Prophecies', *CBQ* 19 (1957), pp. 226–33.

S. Mowinckel, *He That Cometh*, ET by G. W. Anderson, Oxford, 1956.

L. G. Rignell, 'Das Immanuelszeichen. Einige Gesichtspunkte zu Jes. vii', *Studia Theologica* 11 (1957), pp. 99–119.

M. Saebø, 'Formgeschichtliche Erwägungen zu Jes. 7,3–9', *Studia Theologica* 14 (1960), pp. 54–69.

K. Seybold, *Das davidische Königtum im Zeugnis der Propheten* (*FRLANT* 107), Göttingen, 1972.

J. J. Stamm, 'La Prophétie d'Emmanuel', *Revue de Theologie et de Philosophie* 32 (1944), pp. 97–123.

J. J. Stamm, 'Die Immanuel-Weissagung. Ein Gespräch mit E. Hammershaimb', *VT* 4 (1954), pp. 20–33.

J. J. Stamm, 'Neuere Arbeiten zum Immanuel-Problem', *ZAW* 68 (1956), pp. 46–53.

W. Vischer, *Die Immanuel-Botschaft im Rahmen des königlichen Zionsfestes* (*Theologische Studien* 45), Zürich, 1955.

H. Wildberger, 'Die Thronnamen des Messias. Jes. 9,5b', *ThZ* 16 (1960), pp. 314–32.

E. Würthwein, 'Jesaja 7,1–9. Ein Beitrag zu dem Thema: Prophetie und Politik', *Festschrift K. Heim*, Hamburg, 1954, pp. 47–63 (= *Wort und Existenz*, Göttingen, 1970, pp. 127–43).

Sennacherib's Invasion in 701 BC

J. Bright, *A History of Israel*, 2nd edn, London, 1972.

B. S. Childs, *Isaiah and the Assyrian Crisis* (*SBT*, Second Series, 3), London, 1967.

W. Dietrich, *Prophetie und Geschichte. Eine redaktionsgeschichtliche Untersuchung zum deuteronomistischen Geschichtswerk* (*FRLANT* 108), Göttingen, 1972.

W. Dietrich, *Jesaja und die Politik* (*Beiträge zur evangelischen Theologie* 74), Munich, 1976.

J. H. Hayes and J. Maxwell Miller (eds.), *Israelite and Judean History*, London, 1977.

L. L. Honor, *Sennacherib's Invasion of Palestine. A Critical Source Study* (*Contributions to Oriental History and Philology* 12), New York, 1926.

D. D. Luckenbill, *The Annals of Sennacherib* (*Oriental Institute Publications* 2), Chicago, 1924.

H. H. Rowley, 'Hezekiah's Reform and Rebellion', *Bulletin of the John Rylands Library* 44 (1961–2), pp. 395–461; reprinted in *Men of God. Studies in Old Testament History and Prophecy*, London/Edinburgh, 1963, pp. 98–132.

W. Zimmerli, 'Jesaja und Hiskia', *Wort und Geschichte. Festschrift K. Elliger*, Neukirchen-Vluyn, 1973, pp. 199–208 (= *Ges. Aufsätze*, II (*TB* 51), 1974, pp. 88–103).

The Religious Traditions of Jerusalem

R. E. Clements, *God and Temple. The Idea of the Divine Presence in Ancient Israel*, Oxford, 1965.

H. J. Kraus, *Worship in Israel*, ET by G. Buswell, Oxford, 1966.

H.-M. Lutz, *Jahwe, Jerusalem und die Völker. Zur Vorgeschichte von Sach. 12,1–8 und 14,1–5* (*WMANT* 27), Neukirchen-Vluyn, 1968.

N. Poulssen, *König und Tempel im Glaubenszeugnis des Alten Testaments* (*Stuttgarter Biblische Monographien* 3), Stuttgart, 1967.

J. J. M. Roberts, 'The Davidic Origin of the Zion Tradition' *JBL* 92 (1973), pp. 329–44.

K. Rupprecht, *Der Tempel von Jerusalem* (*BZAW* 144), Berlin/New York, 1976.

J. Schreiner, *Zion-Jerusalem. Jahwes Königsitz* (*SANT* 7), Munich, 1963.

Th. C. Vriezen, 'Essentials of the Theology of Isaiah', *Festschrift J. Muilenburg*, edited by B. W. Anderson and W. Harrelson, London, 1962, pp. 128–46.

The Prophecies Against Foreign Nations

J. Begrich, 'Jesaja 14, 28–32', *ZDMG* 86 (1933), pp. 66–79 (= *Ges. Stud. zum A.T.* [*TB* 21], 1964, pp. 121–31).

R. E. Clements, *Prophecy and Tradition*, Oxford, 1975.

S. Erlandsson, *The Burden of Babylon. A Study of Isaiah 13,2–14* (*Coniectanea Biblica. O.T. Series* 4), Lund, 1970.

J. H. Hayes, 'The Usage of Oracles against Foreign Nations in Ancient Israel', *JBL* 87 (1968), pp. 81–92.

D. R. Hillers, *Treaty-Curses and the Old Testament Prophets* (*Biblica et Orientalia* 16), Rome, 1964.

G. Quell, 'Jesaja 14:1–23', in *F. Baumgärtel Festschrift*, Erlangen, 1959, pp. 131–57.

W. Rudolph, 'Jesaja 23:1–14', in *F. Baumgärtel Festschrift*, Erlangen, 1959, pp. 166–74.

M. F. Unger, *Israel and the Aramaeans of Damascus*, London, 1957.

A. H. van Zyl, *The Moabites*, Leiden, 1960.

The Apocalypse of Isaiah

G. Fohrer, 'Der Aufbau der Apokalypse des Jesajabuches (Is. 24–27)', *CBQ* 25 (1963), pp. 34–35.

M.-L. Henry, *Glaubenskrise und Glaubensbewährung in den Dichtungen der Jesajaapokalypse* (*BWANT* 86), Stuttgart, 1966.

J. Lindblom, *Die Jesaja-Apokalypse. Jes. xxiv–xxvii*, Lund, 1938.

E. S. Mulder, *Die teologie van die Jesaja-apokalipse*, Groningen/Djakarta, 1954.

B. Otzen, 'Traditions and Structures of Isaiah xxiv–xxvii', *VT* 24 (1974), pp. 196–206.

O. Plöger, *Theocracy and Eschatology*, ET by S. Rudman, Oxford, 1968.

W. Rudolph, *Jesaja 24–27* (*BWANT* 62), Stuttgart, 1933.

J. Vermeylen, *La composition littéraire de l'apocalypse d'Isaïe* (*Ephemerides Theologicae Lovanienses* 50), Louvain, 1974, pp. 5–38.

INTRODUCTION
to
Isaiah 1–39

A. THE STRUCTURE AND COMPOSITION OF ISAIAH 1-39

I. The Present Divisions of the Book

In his commentary of 1775 J. C. Doederlein argued that chs. 40–66 of the book of Isaiah were to be distinguished from chs. 1–39 and ascribed to a prophet of a later time. Since that time this view, which in fact had been anticipated earlier, has come to be the prevalent consensus of scholarship. See the Commentary on chs. 40–66 by R. N. Whybray (*New Century Bible*, 1975, pp. 20ff.). There is justification, therefore, for considering chs. 1–39 separately from the later chapters and recognising them as a section of the book which has a distinctive origin and character of its own. They are not, however, completely independent of chs. 40–66, so that questions of the nature of the connection, and of the many important links which exist between the two major parts of the book must be considered separately. Whether the two major parts ever existed as totally independent collections remains questionable, and is, in any case, not an issue which can be easily determined. Nonetheless there are certainly major reasons for recognising the separateness of chs. 1–39 and for noting that a major division occurs at this point. All that is now contained in chapters 40ff. certainly dates from the sixth century BC and later.

Within chs. 1–39, however, there are also clear signs of a structure which can be quite readily seen, and which is important for the study of the book. This appears as follows:

(1) Chapter 1: An introduction to the preaching of Isaiah

(2) Chapters 2–12: Prophecies of Isaiah concerning Judah and Jerusalem

(3) Chapters 13–23: Prophecies concerning foreign nations and cities

(4) Chapters 24–27: The 'Apocalypse' of Isaiah

(5) Chapters 28–33: Further prophecies concerning Judah and Jerusalem

(6) Chapters 34–35: The 'Little Apocalypse' of Isaiah

(7) Chapters 36–39: Narratives concerning Isaiah, Hezekiah and Jerusalem

It quickly becomes clear that the organization of the material of the prophecies into separate sections in this way is the consequence of editorial work that took place relatively late in the history of the book. In part it represents a planned and imposed grouping of prophecies according to the subject matter and in part a reflection of the way in which the separate prophecies had been collected together and formed into longer sections. Ch. 1, for example, which is for the most part built up from authentic prophecies of Isaiah, has nonetheless been used as a kind of summary of the prophet's preaching and a guide to the way in which the book as a whole is to be read. The narratives of chs. 36–39 have, apart from some small changes and one major addition, been taken over from the parallel account which is now to be found in 2 Kg. 18:17–20:19. This section has certainly been incorporated into the book of Isaiah at a very late stage, evidently to provide a more comprehensive collection of material relating to Isaiah, even though actual prophecies ascribed to him take only a minor place in the narratives. In two of the present sections of the book nothing at all of the actual words of the prophet Isaiah has been preserved. These are the 'Apocalypse' of chs. 24–27 and the 'Little Apocalypse' of chs. 34–35. Nevertheless, in spite of the late origin of the contents of these sections (probably from the fifth century BC), there is no doubt that their 'message' was felt to have a direct bearing on the earlier prophecies of Isaiah, and, for this reason to belong to the proper interpretation of these. There is no question, therefore, of their being regarded as 'spurious', or in some other way irrelevant, or unrelated, to the central structure of the book. This has not grown up out of a desire to preserve the words of Isaiah the prophet alone, unaffected by other sayings or teaching, but rather to preserve the message of Isaiah, and to interpret it in the light of the subsequent history of Israel, Judah and Jerusalem. Nowhere is this more evident than in the third of the major sections of the book, that of chs. 13–23 containing prophecies against foreign nations. Here, as for example in the prophecies concerning Babylon (chs. 13–14), a long period of historical dealings between Judah and Babylon is reflected in the prophecies, most of which cannot have come from Isaiah in the eighth century. In fact only some of the contents of these chapters derive from Isaiah. Similarly, in the section comprised of chs. 28–33, none of the contents of chs. 32–33 can have come directly from Isaiah, and even those of chs. 28–31 have undergone some addition. Yet here too the intention of interpreting and supplementing the authentic prophecies of Isaiah in the light of subsequent events becomes readily apparent. This means therefore that the primary collection of Isaiah's prophecies is to be found in chs. 2–12, with an important supplementary collection, almost all of which relate to the years 705–701 BC, in chs. 28–31(33).

II. Traces of Earlier Collections

On closer examination it can be seen that there are clear signs of earlier collections having existed in the history of the collection and transmission of Isaiah's prophecies. In part this reveals itself through the ordering and structure of various sections within the larger collections, and in part through the treatment of certain themes in a comprehensive way. All in all, therefore, we are presented with the undoubted fact that the present book of Isaiah has acquired its extant shape as a result of a very extended process of transmission-history, the course of which we can only hope to reconstruct in bare outline by looking at the various sections of the book as we come to them. However, it must be noted that the process of recording and preserving prophecies, and even of interpreting them in relation to particular historical events, began in Isaiah's own lifetime. There is no reason whatsoever, therefore, for supposing that a long period of oral transmission occurred during which original words of the prophet became so buried within their repeated interpretation by disciples as to render them irrecoverable. On the contrary, we may rest assured that the very foundation of the book of Isaiah began in the prophet's own lifetime with the composition of a memoir (German *Denkschrift*) recorded by him of prophecies uttered during the period of the Syro-Ephraimite crisis (735–733 BC). This memoir was almost certainly composed after the resolution of that crisis with the arrival of the Assyrians in Damascus and Samaria in 733 BC, and is now to be found preserved in 6:1–8:18*. It has undoubtedly undergone subsequent expansion. Furthermore, 30:8 reports a command to Isaiah to record a further prophecy in 'a book'. This may have been only a short inscription, containing a cryptic message, or it may relate to a larger collection of Isaiah's prophecies. If so, this must point to a collection, made by the prophet himself, of his preaching during the years of Judah's revolt against Sennacherib in 705–701. There are very strong reasons, therefore, for accepting that a significant body of written prophecies from Isaiah came into being during the prophet's own lifetime. That these were edited and collected together with other prophecies before the prophet's death is then a reasonable assumption.

It had frequently been concluded that Isaiah established a band of 'disciples' who would have been responsible for the preservation and transmission of his prophecies. However, we hear nothing whatever about the existence and work of these 'disciples' in the book, and the oft-repeated interpretation of 8:16 as a reference to them must be set aside. The allusion here is quite clearly to the two witnesses, Uriah and Zechariah, referred to in 8:2, who are those who were instructed by the prophet as to the meaning of the mysterious sign-name inscribed on the tablet in 8:1. There is no reason for thinking of a large and organised body of disciples of Isaiah, therefore, who may be assumed to have remained in being after his death in order to preserve his prophecies. It is pointless and gratuitous to reconstruct the existence of such a hypothetical body of 'disciples', continuing after the prophet himself had died. However, it is clear that the prophet did not stand entirely alone, and that his preaching and prophesying aroused an important band of hearers and followers. After his death a collection of his prophecies was established in writing for others to reflect upon and interpret in the light of events. Where this took place, and by whom, can only be a matter of conjecture, but it is certain that this activity of preserving and developing written prophecies to form larger collections proceeded during the period after the prophet himself had ceased to be the controlling influence upon them. It is virtually impossible for us now, therefore, to determine how the written collection of a particular group of prophecies looked at a given period of time. Perhaps in recent years the tendency has been for scholars to allow too little of this development to have occurred during the prophet's lifetime, and for most of it to be ascribed to a much later time.

Certainly in the book of Isaiah we can discern the compilation of groups of prophecies, and this process of collection most probably began with the prophet himself. Hence we can see now that Isaiah's memoir has been set in the centre of a larger collection which extends from 5:1 to 14:27*. This large and very central collection cannot, on the evidence of the material within it, have been given its present shape before Josiah's time, yet it nevertheless contains an overwhelmingly large preponderance of authentic prophecies. A similar collection of prophecies, all of them threatening to Judah and Jerusalem, can be found in 2:6–4:1, and a further important collection has already been noted as having been set in 28–31*. The shaping of the book of Isaiah into its present form of sixty-six chapters can therefore be seen as the end-result of a long history of collection, redaction and interpretation. It is in effect as though a series of prophecies, together with a commentary upon them, have been blended into a very elaborate whole. It is unlikely that we shall ever be able with complete confidence to reconstruct the entire process. Nevertheless it is not difficult to unearth the major phases of this remarkable literary history.

III. The Redaction in Josiah's Reign

One of the most constructive features in the scholarly study and interpretation of the book of Isaiah in recent years has been the discovery that a major stage in the redactional history of the book took place during Josiah's reign (640–609 BC). This has been set out with great clarity and persuasiveness by Hermann Barth in his study *Die Jesaja-Worte in der Josiazeit* (*WMANT* 48), Neukirchen-Vluyn, 1977. A related view, that there was a significant editorial redaction made of Isaiah's prophecies during Josiah's reign is also to be found in the work by J. Vermeylen, *Du prophète Isaïe à l'apocalyptique* (*Études bibliques*), 2 vols., Paris, 1977. I have found Vermeylen's reconstructions of the literary structure very much less convincing than those of Hermann Barth, and have consequently been unable to make more than a very limited use of them in the present commentary. The case advocated by Barth, however, is so strong as to be largely convincing, and I have considered most of his arguments carefully, without always agreeing with them. Barth has termed this redaction in the reign of Josiah the *Assur-Redaktion* (AR), since its primary concern was to show that Yahweh, the God of Israel, would shortly overthrow the Assyrians by a mighty demonstration of his power. Since I have not always agreed with Barth on all the passages concerned, it has appeared to me fairer to describe this redaction as the Josianic Redaction of the book, in order not to prejudge the ascription of the material which Barth designates as originating from AR. The main structure of this Josianic Redaction is to be found in chs. 2–32, and Barth sets out a full reconstruction of this (*op. cit.*, pp. 311–36).

The clear delineation of this redactional stage as belonging to the reign of Josiah is provided by two factors. The first is the obvious fact that Assyria had not yet fallen as a world-power, which means that this expectation belongs before the fall of Nineveh in 612 BC. On the other side the hope of the downfall of Assyria is sufficiently strong as to appear imminent, and the sense that the grip of Assyria upon Judah is now almost non-existent, so that the century of vassaldom which began in the reign of Ahaz was almost over, is much in evidence. Judah no longer has anything to fear from Assyria (cf. 10:24–27; 30:27–33). This situation did not arise until the early years of Josiah's reign.

On two major points I have ventured to disagree with Barth's conclusions regarding this redaction. The first concerns the question of the authenticity of the very important prophecy of 9:2–7 (Heb. 8:23b–9:6), which he ascribes to AR, but which I have claimed as authentic to Isaiah. Furthermore it appears to me most probable that the Josianic Redaction originally commenced with 5:1ff., and that the prefacing of the threats to Judah and Jerusalem (2:6–4:1) to this took place later, in the wake of the disasters of 598 and 587 BC. There are also some other passages where I have sought a rather different interpretation from his. Overall, therefore, I have found the hand of this Josianic Redaction in the following passages: 7:20–25; 8:9–10; 10:16–19, 20–23, 24–27, 33–34; 14:24–27; 17:12–14; 28:23–29; 29:5–8; 30:27–33; 31:5, 8–9; 32:1–5, 15–20.

More particularly I have endeavoured to show in my forthcoming study *Isaiah and the Deliverance of Jerusalem* that the original formation of the narrative of Jerusalem's deliverance from Sennacherib in 701 (chs. 36–37) emanated from the same basic circle to which we must ascribe this Josianic Redaction. In fact a major feature in the theological structure of this narrative is the development of the conviction that what took place in 701 was the first step in the overthrow by God of the power of Assyria (see below pp. 18f.). Not all of this Josianic Redaction can be ascribed to a single hand, but there is a marked similarity of method, which is basically that of building up a midrashic type of exegesis upon the basis of authentic words and images used by Isaiah. The two basic 'sources' of this imagery are to be found in the prophecies of exaltation of Israel under a Davidic ruler (9:2–7) and the overthrow of Assyria (10:5–15*).

IV. Subsequent Redactional History

From the time of the Josianic Redaction of Isaiah's prophecies it is possible to recognise that something resembling a 'book' of Isaiah's preaching had come into being. It is also evident that a great many further additions have been made subsequent to that time. An attempt to trace the major features of this development is to be found in H. Barth, pp. 285ff., and also in the work of J. Vermeylen. In the case of some recent interpretations of the book of Isaiah the view has been widely canvassed that this process of addition and further expansion was quite prolific and extended down into the period of the second century BC, reflecting the further tensions of the Seleucid oppressions. Such a view is most notable in the commentary by O. Kaiser on Isaiah 13–39 (ET by R. A. Wilson, London, 1974), who finds the vast bulk of the contents of those chapters to derive from the post-exilic era, most of them from the Hellenistic period. Such is not the view advocated here, and it is necessarily to be admitted that in many cases decisive criteria by which to establish a certain date for several of the prophecies simply do not exist. A broad probability only can be sought, and a general picture arrived at.

In the present commentary it has seemed to me very unlikely that any of the prophetic units preserved in the book, save for a few isolated sayings, derive from as late as the Hellenistic era. In general it appears that two main phases of further addition and redaction can be discerned, after that set in Josiah's reign. The first of these occurred after 587 BC, when Jerusalem was captured by the Babylonians and much of the city, including the temple, destroyed. Not only does it appear that the threats uttered by Isaiah against the city and its rulers in 2 : 6–4 : 1 were felt to have found a new meaning at this time, but other threats also were related to what had happened in that tragic year. We may compare Jer. 26 : 18f. for a similar awareness of a new vitality given to the prophetic word of Micah in the eighth century (Mic. 3 : 12) at this time. The additions to Isaiah made after 587 would appear to be *post eventum* additions interpreting the fall of Jerusalem and its aftermath in the light of Isaiah's prophecies, and especially ascribing the catastrophe to the idolatrous behaviour of the inhabitants. To such a redactional development we may ascribe such passages as 2 : 18–19; 5 : 14–17; 6 : 12–13; 8 : 19–22; 17 : 7–9; 22 : 4, 5–8a, 8b–11, 24f.; 32 : 9–14. This period of redaction in the wake of the disaster of 587 was evidently quite essential in view of the very confident expectations that were generated by the Josianic Redaction in regard to the future of Judah and Jerusalem (cf. 32 : 1–5, 15–20). At the same time the future of the monarchy, which was so closely bound up with the Davidic dynasty and the belief in Yahweh's special commitment to it, was placed in question. As a consequence Isaiah's own assurances regarding the promises associated with the Davidic monarchy (especially 9 : 2–7), which had been further enhanced in the Josianic Redaction (32 : 1; cf. 37 : 35), required a new perspective. It is to this immediate situation, which arose in the latter half of the sixth century, that we should ascribe the promise concerning the Davidic monarchy in 11 : 1–5. This is a carrying-forward of the original Isaianic promise into the situation which arose with the ending of the long period of more than three centuries during which the Davidic monarchy had reigned in Jerusalem. This hope of restoring the Davidic monarchy, which became a prominent feature of the hope of the exilic age, finds what was perhaps its earliest expression in 11 : 1–5 (cf. also 33 : 17).

There was undoubtedly also a further stage of development and elaboration of the preaching of Isaiah in the period of the fifth century, very possibly extending over quite a considerable period. Most of all the 'apocalyptic' material of chs. 24–27 and 34–35 would appear to belong to this age, although these particular chapters have proved notoriously difficult to date with any degree of confidence at all. Some commentators would clearly prefer to ascribe them to a considerably later age, stretching into the Hellenistic era. Certainty is impossible, but the fifth century appears to me to be very plausible. In any case it seems likely that the three great prophetic collections of Isaiah, Jeremiah and Ezekiel were all in something very close to their present shape by the fourth century BC.

So far as the development of Isaiah's prophecies is concerned one feature stands out very prominently, and concerns quite directly the present structure of the book as a whole. This is the undoubted use of prophecies and promises derived from chs. 40–55 in the earlier chapters. Such developments are to be seen in 11:12–16; 18:7; 19:23 and 27:13. Most strikingly of all, ch. 35, which some earlier scholars have sought to associate with the 'Deutero-Isaiah' of chs. 40–66 (so H. Graetz, C. C. Torrey), can be seen to be a veritable catena of words, images and themes drawn from chs. 40–55. So close are the verbal similarities, and so evidently secondary are these distinctive sayings now included in chs. 1–35 to those of chs. 40ff., that there can be no doubt that the former are dependent upon the latter. Why this took place, and what bearing it has upon the placing of chs. 40ff. after 1–39, must be considered separately. There can be no doubt, however, that in its present form the book of Isaiah shows a number of significant connections of theme and prophetic expectation which stretch across the division between chs. 1–39 and 40–66.

B. ISAIAH THE PROPHET

I. The Historical Background

The superscription in Isa. 1:1 asserts that Isaiah prophesied during the days of Uzziah, Jotham, Ahaz and Hezekiah, kings of Judah. Such a broad introductory note quite clearly has been composed at a relatively late stage in the literary growth of the book, as the presence of an earlier heading in 2:1 shows. How much reliance can be placed on the information given in 1:1 therefore is questionable since it is not a contemporary note, but rather an editor's inference drawn from the contents of the book. Since Isaiah did not receive his call to be a prophet until 'the year that king Uzziah died' (6:1), it is in any case evident that little could have derived from that same year and none at all if, as is most probable, Uzziah was already dead when the call came. For the rest there is considerable dissension among scholars concerning the precise dates to which we should ascribe the reigns of the kings mentioned, as reference to the comparative chronological table set out in *Israelite and Judean History* (eds. J. H. Hayes and J. M. Miller, London, 1977), p. 683, shows. The chronology adopted in the present commentary is essentially that of J. Begrich, (*Die Chronologie der Könige von Israel und Juda und die Quellen des Rahmens der Königsbucher (BHTh* 3), Stuttgart, 1929), as modified by A. Jepsen (A. Jepsen and R. Hanhart, *Untersuchungen zur israelitisch-jüdischen Chronologie (BZAW* 88), Berlin, 1964; cf. also E. Kutsch in *RGG*³, III, cols. 942–4). This gives the following dates for the kings with which we are immediately concerned:

Uzziah (Azariah)	787–736
Jotham (co-regent)	756–741
Ahaz (co-regent)	741–736
Ahaz (sole ruler)	736–725
Hezekiah	725–697

An important consequence of the adoption of this chronology for the understanding of Isaiah's prophecies is that it precludes the dating of any of them to the reigns of either Uzziah or Jotham. The fact of the co-regencies during Uzziah's long illness (2 Kg. 15:5) has evidently contributed to the confusion of dating during this period. Nevertheless it appears to be fully borne out by the contents of Isa. 1–39 that there are no prophecies which belong to the reign of Jotham, nor any belonging to that of Uzziah. Effectively, therefore, all are to be placed in the years of Ahaz and Hezekiah.

Unfortunately yet another major point of uncertainty over dating emerges with regard to the year in which Hezekiah came to the throne. The evidence of 2 Kg. 18:1f., 9, asserts that Hezekiah had already assumed the throne of Judah for some years when Samaria fell to the Assyrians in 722 BC. This conflicts with the evidence of 2 Kg. 18:13 that it was only the fourteenth year of Hezekiah when Sennacherib marched into Judah and attacked Jerusalem, an event which we can confidently place in 701. Several scholars in recent years (W. F. Albright, J. Bright, S. Herrmann) have preferred the conclusion that Hezekiah's accession did not take place until 715 BC. This appears to me to be the less probable resolution of what is, on any reckoning, a complex and difficult issue. I have preferred, therefore, to work on the assumption that Ahaz's death probably occurred in 726/5 and that Hezekiah's accession took place in 725. From these conclusions we can then proceed to locate Isaiah's prophesying between these two reigns. The prophet's call may be located in 736 BC, and the latest prophecies which have been preserved from him in the year 701, or very shortly thereafter (1:4–8[9]; 22:1–4, 12–14).

The major political events which affect the entire period of Isaiah's activity were those occasioned by the military and political threat posed to Israel and Judah by the Assyrians. It is useful, therefore, to note briefly the reigns of the four great rulers of the neo-Assyrian empire whose imperial ambitions impinged so directly upon the affairs of Israel and Judah:

Tiglath-pileser III	744–727
Shalmaneser V	726–722
Sargon II	721–705
Sennacherib	704–681

The presence of Assyrian forces in Syria can be placed as far back as 738, when Tiglath-pileser III was undoubtedly campaigning there. After this a series of major incursions and campaigns brought Judah and Israel directly under Assyrian domination, and this fact provides the determining political consideration for the entire period of Isaiah's preaching. We may note four major periods of such Assyrian activity, and the corresponding moves and counter-moves which were provoked by this Assyrian pressure.

The first of these covers what we may refer to as the Syro-Ephraimite crisis and extends from the time of Uzziah's death in 736 to 733, or possibly the following year (732). 2 Kg. 15:37 would locate the beginning of the Syro-Ephraimite conflict even earlier than this, in Jotham's reign. There is, however, undoubtedly some foreshortening of perspective here, although the basic insight that as far back as Jotham's time relations between the two sister kingdoms of Israel and Judah became strained is probably correct. When Uzziah died Ahaz was bent upon pursuing a more compliant policy towards Assyria, whereas his northern neighbours, Syria and Israel, were determined to force a firmer and more solid alliance against Assyrian control. In pursuit of this goal these latter kingdoms sought to force Judah into line, with the intention of deposing Ahaz and replacing him with a certain 'ben Tabeel' (7:6). Ahaz was determined to invite Assyrian support to protect him from this threat, and to send a large tribute to Tiglath-pileser in order to solicit his attention. He was willing to pay the price of vassaldom to Assyria in order to secure his own position, and in the process to invite brutal destruction upon his sister kingdom of Israel. Although Ahaz appears to have delayed sending the tribute as long as possible, he eventually did so, and Assyria responded to it. Indeed the Assyrian response may already have moved ahead of Ahaz's vacillations and delays, since Samaria was entered and overthrown by Tiglath-pileser in 733 and Damascus in the following year. As a consequence of the punitive treatment meted out by the Assyrians, only a rump-state of Ephraim was left (see below on 9:1).

Both Judah and Israel now became vassals of Assyria, but this eventually led to further rebellion on the part of the Northern Kingdom of Ephraim-Israel. A siege of Samaria took place and the city fell in 722 BC, so that this event marks the second major period of Assyrian activity. As a result of the settlement imposed by the Assyrians, the erstwhile Northern Kingdom lost all separate identity as a political power and was administered as an internal province of the Assyrian empire. The important differences which this brought in the subsequent political history of this region, when contrasted with Judah which, though a vassal-kingdom, retained a native (Davidic) ruler, are shown by M. Cogan, *Imperialism and Religion. Assyria, Judah and Israel in the Eighth and Seventh Centuries B.C.E. (S.B.L. Monograph Series* 19, Missoula, 1974).

Understandably Judah did not remain entirely quiet under the suzerain control of Assyria, and naturally looked for support among the neighbouring kingdoms which shared a comparable distaste for payment of the yearly tribute to so demanding a master. A third period of Assyrian interference in the affairs of Judah was then occasioned by a revolt led by the Philistine city of Ashdod in the years 713–711 BC (cf. Isa. 20). Judah was certainly pressed into joining this revolt against Assyria, and it is very probable that a much wider, and more concerted, withdrawal of allegiance, in which Egypt was also expected to take part, was contemplated. If so, then it is most likely that the negotiations between Judah and Egypt, which form the background to the prophecies of 18 : 1–5 and 19 : 1–15, belong to this time. How far the revolt spread is not clear, but it was promptly put down by Sargon II, and Judah was fortunate to escape without becoming more deeply implicated.

The temptation to rebellion was a strong one, however, and how heavily the hand of Assyrian control was felt in Judah can only be guessed at. In 705 Hezekiah was himself at the centre of a carefully planned attempt at withdrawing allegiance to Assyria and establishing his independence. In this a central foundation of the proposed rebellion was an alliance with Egypt, in which the promise of Egyptian military aid, should this become necessary, formed a basis of supposed security. No doubt also the internal situation in Assyria following Sargon's death gave hope that that power would be too pre-occupied with other matters to bother with the distant kingdom of Judah. Such a calculated risk, however, proved ill-judged, and in 701 the fourth period of Assyrian intervention in the affairs of Israel-Judah brought further disaster. The Assyrian records of Sennacherib provide a full picture of the horror that was brought upon Judah (*ANET*, pp. 287f.), and in 701 BC, after virtually every town and fortress in Judah had suffered destruction, Hezekiah surrendered (2 Kg. 18 : 13–16). The fact that the narrative preserved in Isa. 36–37 now looks back upon this event in a rather different light calls for further separate discussion (see below pp. 277ff.). The year 701, in any case, marks the close of the activity of the prophet Isaiah. Whether he prophesied further, but his words have failed to be preserved, can only be a matter of speculation. Most likely his own death took place soon afterwards, and there is no evidence that he continued to prophesy into the second decade of the seventh century.

II. Isaiah the Man

It is beyond question that behind chs. 1–39 of the book of Isaiah there stands one of the greatest figures of the religious and political story of ancient Israel. Equally clear, however, is the fact that we have very little positive information about this man and the personal circumstances in which he lived and worked. The very desire for some biographical details about so remarkable a figure may tempt us into drawing firmer conclusions than we are entitled to do, on the basis of the evidence given to us. So prominent is the reality that those who have preserved a knowledge concerning him have done so with an interest in his message, rather than in the man himself, that it is now very difficult for us to reconstruct what kind of person he was. We are left entirely to a process of making inferences from incidental features preserved in his sayings. The manner, style and contents of his speech are all that we have to go on in attempting to make deductions about him. It is not surprising therefore that very markedly divergent pictures have been drawn of him, and we can do little more than note the factors which have led to the various individual reconstructions of his person and life.

Isaiah was called to be a prophet in the year of Uzziah's death (736 BC), which also effectively marked the beginning of the Syro-Ephraimite crisis. His father was a certain 'Amoz', who is not to be confused with the prophet of a similar sounding name. The fact that his call took place during a service in the Jerusalem temple is an illuminating circumstance, although even this point has not been universally conceded. In consequence some attempts have been made to place the call in a more domestic setting, with the divine throne representing a vision of the heavenly throne of God, and not that associated with the symbolism of the temple. However, this temple setting appears to be assured. Beyond this, Isaiah clearly had a wife, who is called a prophetess (8:3), and at least three children (8:18). He was known to the king (cf. 7:3), and was evidently familiar with the work and planning of the king. Beyond this he was well known to the rulers and priests of Jerusalem (cf. 28:7, 14), and appears to have had remarkably prompt and full information about the most intimate details of the thinking and planning that took place in the inner circles of government in Jerusalem (cf. especially 29:15). From him little that was important in the plans and aims of the court appears to have remained hidden.

This deep insight into the inner life of government and the court has given rise to a widely adopted theory concerning the person of Isaiah: that he was himself a nobleman of high birth and high education among the wealthy and aristocratic leaders of his people. In more recent years this belief in the special connection between Isaiah and the circles of the court has given place to the suggestion that he was himself a scribe, brought up among the official administrative classes in Jerusalem, where a training in the skills of rhetoric, writing and administration was especially nurtured. Cf. J. Fichtner, 'Jesaja unter den Weisen', *TLZ* 74 (1949), pp. 75–80 (= *Gottes Weisheit. Gesammelte Studien zum Alten Testament*, ed. K. D. Fricke (*Arbeiten zur Theologie* II,3), Stuttgart, 1965, pp. 18–26); J. W. Whedbee, *Isaiah and Wisdom*, New York/Nashville, 1971. Such a view, however, begs too many questions. The first relates to the obvious fact that Isaiah could not address himself to political issues without using the technical vocabulary of politics. Hence the arguments based on vocabulary and speech-forms associated with Wisdom cannot carry much weight. More than this, however, it remains unclear to what extent Wisdom could be regarded as in any sense a unique possession of the administrative classes in Jerusalem. It evidently had a much wider and more popular currency, as the various facets of ancient Israel's folk-wisdom reveal to us. Isaiah was undoubtedly a highly educated man, with an expert mastery of the skills of rhetoric and persuasion. No other figure of Old Testament literature shows so commanding a control of the use of irony and subtle word-play. Equally he shows himself to have been a master of hyperbole, and to have possessed great skill in presenting circumlocutions which give to his sayings an air of mystery whilst robbing them of none of their clarity and sharpness. Yet all of these skills could have been accessible to a well-educated citizen, and especially to a prophet whose skills in rhetoric were endemic to his calling. So, too, the fact that Isaiah could write (cf. 30:8) proves little in the way of linking him directly with a special court circle of scribal activity or government administration, in which Wisdom might be held to have been a specially nurtured expertise. The comparisons between Isaiah's prophecies and other speech-forms associated with Wisdom falls far short, therefore, of proving very much that is tangible about the upbringing which Isaiah received, or the background to which he belonged. Evidently he was a highly literate and well-educated man, but this leaves us still lacking in firm information concerning how this distinguished him from other citizens, and prophets, in Jerusalem.

In contrast with these attempts to find a uniquely aristocratic, or scribal, setting for the life and work of Isaiah, there are other features which have led to the assumption that he was brought up and trained in the Jerusalem cultus. The arguments here are of two kinds: the first drawing heavily upon the fact that Isaiah's call took place in the Jerusalem temple (Isa. 6), and the second relating more broadly to issues concerning the identity and function of those who were called *nābi'*. Broader discussion of these issues is to be found in my earlier study *Prophecy and Tradition* (Oxford, 1975). The knowledge that Isaiah had of the Jerusalem prophets and priests, together with their knowledge of him (cf. Isa. 28:7), may also help to point in this direction, as also may the fact that his wife is called a 'prophetess' (8:3). This latter point, however, remains with some measure of ambiguity, since it is possible that she acquired this title through association with Isaiah. Yet this is unlikely, and the possibility that she too was involved in some form of cultic activity in Jerusalem cannot be ruled out. Yet, against this linking of Isaiah with the temple personnel of Jerusalem, there is the obvious fact that he says little about the daily life of the temple, and his vocabulary shares little of the strong priestly colouring that we find, for example, in Ezekiel. The case for a special cultic background for Isaiah, therefore, with the claim that he may himself have been among the cult-personnel of Jerusalem, remains lacking in decisive evidence.

Overall, therefore, we must note these different approaches to the problem of identifying the immediate day-to-day setting in which we should see Isaiah, and admit their lack of conclusiveness. We must be honest in recognising that we do not know as much as we should like. If a choice must be made, I should myself incline more closely to the belief in some direct cultic setting for the prophet, but this can be no more than an interesting hypothesis.

When we come to consider the specific influences which are detectable in the prophet's preaching we are essentially faced with the same problem that we have already noted. That there are important connections with the language and speech-forms of Wisdom is certainly to be conceded. So too the influence of the Jerusalem cult is very strong, and in some ways stronger than in the case of any other of the prophets of the Old Testament. We detect through the sayings of Isaiah many of the themes, imagery and ideas of the old Jerusalem temple cult that would otherwise have been lost to us. Thus, for instance, it is he alone who reflects the belief in the heavenly Seraphim, the mysterious serpent guardians of the divine throne (6:2, 6). It is he, too, who records the fact, which comparative evidence has now corroborated in great measure, that Yahweh, the God of Israel, was venerated in the cultus by the title Melek—King (6:5). So, too, Isaiah's call records for us the details of a strange ritual which finds no parallel elsewhere in the Old Testament (6:6f.). There stands behind the preaching of Isaiah, therefore, a very full and rich world of cultic life, imagery and tradition, of which we elsewhere read little in the Old Testament.

A third area of particular importance to the prophet was the royal court, and the distinctive traditions associated with the Davidic dynasty assume a very special prominence with him. It appears strongly in the prophecies relating to the Syro-Ephraimite crisis, and most strongly of all in the well-known 'messianic' prophecy of 9:2–7. In the present commentary I have argued for the authenticity of this oracle to Isaiah, although I am very conscious that many scholars, in the past and the present, have doubted this. Nevertheless it does appear that Isaiah was deeply committed to the royal Davidic tradition, even though he may have interpreted some of its features in a rather different way from his contemporaries. The possibility that he himself contemplated, or even directly prophesied, the ending of the long period of Davidic rule from Jerusalem (cf. 7:9), must be considered. There is certainly no intrinsic reason why he should have precluded this eventuality altogether, but, nonetheless he does appear to have shared the conviction that the Davidic house had a special divinely given role to play for all Israel. In the present commentary I have argued the case for Isaiah's acceptance of this Davidic kingly rule as God's gift to all Israel, and not to Judah alone. Part of the prophet's deep antipathy to Ahaz's action in appealing to Assyria, therefore, was engendered by the abandonment of such expectations on the part of the king. In the prophet's eyes, it was the king who was abandoning the historic promise and responsibility of the Davidic line of kings, not God.

Two other areas of religious and cultural background have been discerned by scholars as particularly affecting the prophet Isaiah. The first of these, in the Holy War traditions of ancient Israel (cf. G. von Rad, *Old Testament Theology*, vol. II, Edinburgh/London, 1965, pp. 159f.), is difficult either to prove, or disprove. This is because it is exceedingly hard to distinguish what ideas and themes belonged to an exclusive 'Holy War' tradition, and what were more widely accepted religious assumptions and beliefs among the people. Thus the idea that 'faith' was a distinctive 'Holy War' requirement appears to me to be an over-restriction of a major religious theme to one rather limited sphere of activity.

The other major influence upon Isaiah which recent scholarship has thought to discern, has been found in the preaching of the prophet Amos (cf. especially R. Fey, *Amos und Jesaja*, *WMANT* 12, Neukirchen-Vluyn, 1963). Admittedly there are several important similarities, both in the form of the prophecies (especially the 'Woe'-oracles), and in the content of the specific criticisms levelled by the prophets against their contemporaries, which link Isaiah with Amos. The case is an attractive one, and there is nothing intrinsically against it, either from a historical or religious point of view. Yet, in the end of the day, the assumption of such a direct dependence of Isaiah upon Amos, tells us little about either man. Furthermore there are many factors which suggest that both Amos and Isaiah were drawing upon a prophetic tradition which was older than both of them. The recognition of the similarities which each of these prophets shared between their own outlook and that of a much older tradition of folk-wisdom has served to highlight still more the recognition that the common elements in their preaching can be explained in more than one way. The degree of Isaiah's familiarity with a collection of Amos's prophecies appears, therefore, to be very unclear and ill-defined. For this reason the hypothesis, though attractive, sheds only a small amount of light upon Isaiah and his background.

In the pages of the Old Testament we find that Isaiah had a major contemporary in the prophet Micah of Moresheth-gath. There are some important connections which link the preaching of the two prophets with each other, and there are some fundamental perspectives in which they differ. It would seem highly unlikely that the two men should have remained ignorant of the existence of each other, and certainly those circles who preserved their respective prophecies are likely to have associated them in various ways. Yet beyond this there are few passages where a direct comparison with the prophecies of Micah can shed very much light upon the preaching of Isaiah. A comparison between the work of the two men, therefore, is scarcely a very practicable undertaking. Certainly Micah reveals little of the intimate knowledge of court and governmental affairs that figure so prominently in Isaiah.

Behind the prophecies of Isaiah there lies hidden a person about whom we should obviously like to know a great deal more. To study the remarkable prophecies he has left to us stimulates an interest which we should naturally wish to pursue further. Yet in reality he remains quite surprisingly hidden, and would evidently point us to his message about the work of God in his days rather than to his own personality. This is so, even when we consider his own account of his prophetic call.

III. The Theology and Preaching of the Prophet

A study of the background to the preaching of the prophet has already raised a number of matters concerning his particular theology. That he was a citizen of Jerusalem, born and brought up in the city, has clearly pointed us to the main setting of his understanding of God and his relationship to Israel. His favourite title for God is 'the Holy One of Israel' (1:4, etc.), and this immediately draws our attention to a major feature of his whole outlook. Yahweh was the God of 'Israel', and by this the prophet quite evidently understood both kingdoms, Ephraim and Judah, to be referred to (cf. 5:7; 8:14), so that no narrow interpretation of the prophet as concerned with Judah alone, or more narrowly still with Jerusalem, can properly grasp the breadth of his thought. Isaiah began his ministry at a time when the relationship between Israel (Ephraim) and Judah was more strained and hostile than at any time since the two kingdoms had fallen apart after Solomon's death (cf. 7:17). He found himself confronted with a king, Ahaz, who was bent on betraying this historic unity between the two kingdoms still further by appealing to Assyria to rescue him from the sister kingdom in the north. Beyond this, he lived through years in which the Northern Kingdom of Ephraim was first broken up, leaving only a rump-state, and finally destroyed altogether as a political entity. The land, that historic gift of God to the nation's ancestors, had been ravaged and torn, until only a very small part of it was left (cf. 6:11). By this not only the land of Judah can have been meant, but the whole land as it had once been held, even if only precariously, in the great days of the United Kingdom.

It is not surprising therefore that Isaiah should have felt able to affirm that the people whom God had once owned as 'my people' had become a band of rebels, whom he could only describe as 'this people' (cf. 6:9). Even the reigning king of Judah, in whose days he began to prophesy, had forsaken the traditional claim and responsibility that belonged to the Davidic heritage of ruling with a regard for all Israel. He played politics against the interests of God's people. Especially was this true of Ahaz, whom Isaiah regards as having betrayed the very foundation of the throne of David. He had greater hopes for Hezekiah (cf. 9:2–7), although these were destined never to be realised so far as the remains of the Northern Kingdom were concerned (cf. 9:8ff.). Nonetheless, the sense that in God's eyes both 'houses' of Ephraim and Judah formed only one people Israel established a basis for all Isaiah's preaching. In his eyes the royal claims of the Davidic family belonged within this 'all Israel' perspective. So far as this side of Isaiah's preaching is concerned the Josianic redactors of his prophecies appear to have reflected accurately and faithfully his own outlook.

It is within this broader perspective that we must understand the special significance which both the temple of Jerusalem and the Davidic royal dynasty had for Isaiah. They were institutions which belonged to the entire nation. At no point does Isaiah appear to have considered either of them to be entirely indispensable to the purposes of God with Israel. So we must dismiss completely any suggestion that he regarded Jerusalem as inviolable on account of the presence of God in the temple there, or the Davidic dynasty as irreplaceable. They each fulfilled a purpose in the plans of Yahweh, but this was open to the realities of each historical situation, as God made his intentions known regarding it.

A comparable openness must be understood to have motivated the great hostility which Isaiah's prophecies display towards the making of foreign alliances. First, Isaiah sharply condemned Ahaz for his plan to seek an alliance with Tiglath-pileser of Assyria to protect him from the Syro-Ephraimite coalition. Subsequently he vigorously opposed the negotiations which Hezekiah entered into at the time of the Ashdodite rebellion, and which would have led to the withdrawal of allegiance to Assyria. Later he repeatedly denounced as disastrous the treaty with Egypt upon which Hezekiah relied for his rebellion in the years 705–701 (Isa. 28 : 14–22; 30 : 1–5). It is impossible to suppose that this opposition stemmed simply from a belief that such treaties would involve Judah in forbidden religious practices. Nor should we attempt to account for it on the basis of some kind of Utopian expectation that God would act more directly to secure Judah from whatever threats should emerge. Isaiah was too firm a political realist, and too conscious of the harsh experiences of the past, to resort to any such doctrinaire rigidity. The reason why these alliances were in opposition to the 'plan' of Yahweh as Isaiah saw it, was because they simply would not work, and would not offer anything other than a totally spurious security. Ahaz's appeal to Assyria would rebound upon him to his own ruin (cf. 8 : 8, 14), which it clearly did. So, too, the reliance upon Egypt for military aid was both bad military strategy as well as bad religion. In Isaiah's eyes it would prove no greater a protection to Judah than it had for the citizens of Philistia (cf. Isa. 20). There is no justification at all, therefore, for regarding Isaiah as a far-sighted, if Utopian, visionary who believed that faith in God could provide an alternative to effective political policies. The truth of the matter, as Isaiah saw it, was that the policies that were being forced on a perplexed and long-suffering people were disastrous in conception and horrifying in their consequences. All that we know of the events of his period of ministry fully bears this out. Within the space of less than forty years, from the time of Uzziah's death in 736 to that of Jerusalem's surrender to Sennacherib in 701, Israel had been cut to pieces and reduced to a single city, with little else (1 : 4–8[9]). Even then, far from mourning the ruin and destruction which decades of misrule and the pursuit of political illusions had brought, we find Isaiah at the end rebuking the people of Jerusalem for their crass insensitivity in celebrating their own personal survival from the sufferings which the rest of the nation had endured, and to which most of it had fallen victim (22 : 1–4; 12–14). Throughout those painful years Isaiah's preaching had pointed a way back to God, and to a more realistic, if more humble, willingness to remain obedient to him (cf. 30 : 15).

IV. The Historical Crisis of 701 BC

A problem of a quite unusual character exists for the interpreter of Isaiah over the question of the events of the year 701 BC, and the attitude of the prophet to them. According to 2 Kg. 18:13–16 Hezekiah surrendered to Sennacherib after most of Judah had been conquered, and before a full-scale siege of Jerusalem began. This agrees with the account of this campaign recorded in Sennacherib's Annals, and which has been available to the student of the Old Testament in an English translation for a century and more. Yet the narratives contained in Isa. 36–37 (= 2 Kg. 18:17–19:37) ascribe the failure of Sennacherib to take the city of Jerusalem to a more direct act of God's power (Isa. 37:36) in which the Assyrian army experienced some kind of unexpected reverse. A variety of theories have been put forward to explain what appears to be a very different outcome to Hezekiah's rebellion from that which we have so far noted.

The historical problem is a primary factor, and has led to the suggestions that, either Sennacherib subsequently attempted to take Jerusalem a second time in the year 701, but failed to do so, or came back to the city in the course of some later campaign (688 BC?). Neither of these suggestions can be regarded as credible, nor do they pay proper regard to the nature of the narrative account preserved in Isa. 36–37. As I have sought to show elsewhere in my study *Isaiah and the Deliverance of Jerusalem*, the narrative now set out in Isa. 36–37 is a late reflection on the events of the year 701, written in the light of Isaiah's preaching. It has the benefit of a knowledge of the way in which Judah thereafter survived the miseries of Manasseh's reign until the time of Josiah witnessed the weakening of Assyrian control in Judah, and its eventual complete breakdown. Judah came to a new period of freedom, and this historical circumstance provides the background to the work of the Josianic Redaction of Isaiah's prophecies. It is undoubtedly to the same circle of scribes that we owe the composition of the narrative (which is in fact a composite narrative, see below *in loc.*) of chs. 36–37. They have viewed the failure of Sennacherib to take Jerusalem as an anticipation and foretaste of the way in which it was believed that the Assyrians would be overthrown. The earlier versions of this narrative account made no mention of the overthrow of the Assyrian army by the 'angel of Yahweh', but simply pointed to the fact that Sennacherib would not take Jerusalem, and would be compelled to return home 'by the way that he came'. Only at a late stage in the growth of the tradition has the idea entered that some more dramatic misfortune befell the Assyrian forces. There is no likelihood, therefore, that the account contained in Isa. 36–7 was originally intended to refer to some other campaign than that of 701 BC. Nor does it indicate that some other attempt was made by Sennacherib upon Jerusalem after Hezekiah had surrendered.

The picture that we have given above of the grim experience which marks the close of Isaiah's prophetic ministry therefore does not need to be supplemented by the supposition that, subsequently, some more triumphant victory for Judah and Jerusalem took place to lift the reputation of Hezekiah. It was only in retrospect that Hezekiah's surrender, and the fact that he did not, as a punishment for his rebellion, lose his throne nor jeopardise the continued succession of the Davidic dynasty, came to be seen in a more hopeful light.

The question arises, however, concerning the preaching of Isaiah during the year 701, and the possibility that he may, at the last moment, have turned from his castigation of Hezekiah's foolish rebellion, to assure him of Yahweh's protection. The belief that Isaiah did make such a change has been argued by a number of scholars (cf. J. Bright, *Covenant and Promise*, London, 1974, pp. 100f.), or it has been argued that he affirmed that Yahweh would deliver him, if he showed a genuine repentance (so G. Fohrer). Yet in fact Isaiah made no such turnaround in his preaching, and the passages that appear to suggest that he did so are to be ascribed to the Josianic Redaction (see above, pp. 5f.). Their original purpose was not to promise that the defeat of the Assyrians would take place whilst Jerusalem was under siege, but at some more indeterminate stage in the future. Yet the belief came to be accepted that the failure of Sennacherib to take Jerusalem did mark the first step in the overthrow of the Assyrians, and this has reflected itself back into the way in which the prophecies have been developed and preserved (see below, especially on 29 : 5–8 and 31 : 5, 8f.). The much used assumption that Isaiah himself developed this message regarding the overthrow of the Assyrians on the basis of a supposed Zion tradition which he inherited from the temple-cultus of Jerusalem must be discounted. Such a 'Zion tradition' is largely a construction which emerged in Josiah's reign, although it was built upon much earlier elements of the royal Davidic court tradition. Behind this, it evidently was related to more widespread beliefs about the divine protection afforded to dynasties of kings whom the gods had chosen. It came, however, to flourish briefly in Josiah's reign, although its unrealistic claims quickly necessitated a considerable degree of modification, as the narratives preserved in Isa. 38–39 (= 2 Kg. 20) show. From neither a historical nor a theological perspective, therefore, can it be said that the crisis of the year 701 faces us with insuperable difficulties for the interpretation of the book of Isaiah.

C. THE TEXT AND INTERPRETATION OF ISAIAH 1–39

I. The Text and Versions

The text of Isa. 1–39 must be regarded as extraordinarily well preserved in view of its immense antiquity. The discovery of major scrolls of the book of Isaiah at Qumran (especially 1QIs[a]) has brought remarkable confirmation of the excellent degree of reliability which belongs to the transmission of the text. This does not mean, however, that the extant tradition of the Heb. text is in all points to be followed, since the more recent evidence reveals that there are a number of

places where some corruption has occurred. Besides this, there are a
great many passages which can only be regarded as extremely obscure,
and where the inherent likelihood is that some damage to the original
form of the text has occasioned this. It is certain, therefore, that
throughout the entire book of Isaiah there are numerous passages
where a more correct rendering or reconstruction of the original must
be striven for.

For the modern scholar three major avenues of research may assist
the reconstruction of what may be held as a truer rendering of the
original Heb. text. The first of these can be found in the study of the
great mass of Heb. MSS, as collected and collated since the eighteenth
century. To this the incomparable value of the variant readings of the
Heb. MSS from Qumran can now be added. In addition to these
resources, it is of value to consult the ancient versions, especially that
of the ancient Greek (LXX). Since the present commentary is not
primarily intended as a fresh examination of the text, the variants
considered in it have been restricted almost exclusively to those noted
in the *Biblia Hebraica Stuttgartensia* (*BHS*). The examination of the
Heb. MS tradition, even when supplemented by additional evidence
drawn from the ancient versions, does not bring us back directly to
anything resembling an original prototypical text of the book of
Isaiah. Indeed it is inherently probable that a number of confusions
and misinterpretations occurred during the stage of redaction in
which the present book was being formed. The striving for an
original 'pure' and uncorrupted form of the text must consequently
remain something of an ideal. In many instances it is probable that
errors arose at a time when the original Heb. reading was no longer
understood, or was incorrectly understood, as a result of changes
within the use of the Heb. language itself. In recent years, therefore, a
great deal of additional effort has been expended upon the study of
Heb. vocabulary and grammar, especially in the light of the greatly
increased resources for a comparative study of these from neighbouring cognate languages, and from Semitic lexicography more broadly.
Where important suggestions have been made from this direction
towards a better understanding of the Heb. text of Isaiah it has been
felt valuable to notice the most significant of them.

The English text upon which the present commentary is based is,
in company with other volumes in the series, that of the *RSV*. In view
of the ready availability of the *NEB*, and the fact that this has, in
particular, endeavoured to explore much more fully than other
contemporary renderings have done the resources of Heb. lexicography, I have felt it valuable to note the major points where this differs.
The availability of a volume noting the places where the *NEB* has
deviated from the standard (received) text (*HTOT*) has made it
possible in numerous instances to refer to this, rather than to set out
too many notes of relatively minor Heb. variants. Where there are
major deviations from the traditional understanding, based upon the
evidence of comparative philology and lexicography, I have endeavoured to draw attention to sources where a treatment of these can be

found. It has not been felt appropriate to make allusion to other modern versions, save in certain instances where they highlight certain difficulties inherent in the text by the manner in which they have endeavoured to overcome them.

II. The Relationship to Chapters 40–66

It has already been noted above (pp. 2, 8) that the relationship between chs. 1–39 and 40–66 is a very complex one. Undoubtedly all of the material now preserved in chs. 40–66 belongs to a time from the sixth century BC, or later. It has often been assumed therefore that the reason for the connection of these later chapters with 1–39 was a pragmatic one, concerned only with literary convenience. Yet this can scarcely be correct, in view of the fact that there are a significant number of passages in chs. 1–39 where undoubted allusion is made to ideas, images and themes which originally belonged first in chs. 40ff. Similarly there are certainly passages in chs. 40ff. where an allusion back to a major theme of the earlier chapters appears to be intended (cf. 42:18f.; 44:18 with 6:9f.; and then further 29:18; 35:5). If the directness of the allusions in chs. 40ff. to earlier themes and ideas appears questionable and uncertain, this cannot be said to be so for the quite direct summaries made in 11:16; 27:12f., of the central theme of chs. 40–55. Most strikingly of all 35:1–10 consists entirely of a citation of condensed themes and images drawn from chs. 40–55. The evidence is clear, therefore, that an inherent connection of theme and message links together the main divisions of the book of Isaiah (chs. 1–39; 40–66). It would seem to be a clear deduction from this that some association of the contents of chs. 1–35 with those of 40–55(66) took place quite early. There are certainly then a great many additional places where some linking of the message of the two halves of the book appears to be intended (as in the 'Babylon' prophecies of 13:1–22).

The fact that ch. 35 must once have marked the close of the collection of chs. 1–35 strongly suggests that this was intended to round-off the message of the original book of Isaiah by giving a kind of 'digest' of the more hopeful themes which are to be found in chs. 40ff. If this is so, then it would strongly point in the direction of some association of the contents of chs. 1–35 with those of 40–55 having been established at an early time.

III. From Prophecy to Apocalyptic

The original prophecies of the eighth-century Isaiah of Jerusalem speak frequently of the direct action of God in history (cf. 5:25; 8:7, etc.). It is clear from these, and the many similar passages that are to be found, that the prophet was using conventional prophetic imagery and was referring to actions which would be brought about through human agency. The hand of God was to be seen in action, working in and through the hands of men (cf. especially 10:5). The events which the prophet foretold, therefore, were to possess a peculiar character since they revealed the mind and purposes of God. They did not, however, refer to a totally new world order which God would initiate and which would replace the existing order of natural and historical activity. In the presentation of God's action in the Josianic Redaction of Isaiah's prophecies a quite special point has been made of the affirmation that God would act to overthrow the forces of Assyria, by his own hand, and not through the hands of human agents (cf. 10:16, 33; 29:6; 31:8). Even here, however, it does not appear that the redactors were seeking to foretell a completely supernatural event that would overtake the Assyrians, and that would lie entirely outside the natural order. The traditional language of a theophany has been developed in a unique way, but the main point appears to be to assert that God would act in some way other than through a human army.

In a number of later passages in the book of Isaiah, especially in the 'apocalyptic' chs. 24–27, 34–35, the action of God that is foretold has taken on a more emphatically supernatural character, so that what is foretold is to mark the end of the existing world order, and to replace this by a new divine world order. In this way the assumptions of 'prophecy' have passed over into the contentions of 'apocalyptic'. Alongside these sections we find others which point to a similar coming New Age, in which a complete transformation of the political and natural life of the world will be changed (cf. 30:19–26; 34:1–4). This development from prophecy to apocalyptic forms one of the most striking features in the literary growth of the book of Isaiah. Not only has an elaborate pattern of development and elaboration of the original core of Isaianic prophecies taken place, but alongside this there has gone a progressive change in the way in which the prophetic word of God has been understood. We find a similar development of understanding and interpretation when comparing the contents of chs. 56–66 with those of 40–55 (cf. P. D. Hanson, *The Dawn of Apocalyptic*, Philadelphia, 1975, pp. 32ff.). A prominent aspect of this change in the understanding of the prophetic imagery and message is a changed understanding of history to which it bears witness. The original prophetic 'openness' in the view of the future, as plastic to the will of God, has come increasingly to give way to a more deterministic view, in which the key to understanding the future was believed to lie in unravelling the mysteries of prophecies and prophetic imagery disclosed long in advance. The entire time-scale through which prophecy was felt to be meaningful has been stretched enormously. From a message about the immediate future, prophecy has come to be understood as a mysterious disclosure of a divine mystery given centuries in advance. Such an 'apocalyptic' understanding of prophecy was evidently accepted at Qumran among the covenanters there. In consequence we can see from the distinctive form of the text of the book of Isaiah (1QIs[a]) that this was read in a highly 'apocalyptic' fashion (cf. S. Talmon, 'DSIa as a Witness to Ancient Exegesis of the Book of Isaiah', *Qumran and the History of the Biblical Text* (ed. F. M. Cross and S. Talmon), Cambridge, Mass.,

1975, pp. 116–26). There is quite evidently an important degree to which both the literary structure of the book of Isaiah and even the final formulation of the text have been affected by the way in which its contents were interpreted.

D. ANALYSIS OF ISAIAH 1–39

CHAPTER 1: INTRODUCTION TO THE PROPHECIES OF ISAIAH

1:1	The superscription
1:2–3	Rebellious sons
1:4–9	Only Zion is left
1:10–17	The way of true religion
1:18–20	If you refuse
1:21–28	The faithful city
1:29–31	The end of false worship

CHAPTERS 2–12: PROPHECIES CONCERNING JUDAH AND JERUSALEM

2:1	A further superscription
2:2–5	The glory of Zion
2:6–22	The humiliation of the proud
3:1–12	The coming anarchy
3:13–15	Further condemnation of the rulers of Jerusalem
3:16–24	Judgment upon the proud women of Jerusalem
3:25–4:1	The fate of the women
4:2–6	The remnant in Jerusalem
5:1–7	The song of the vineyard
10:1–4a; 5:8–24	Doom upon the leaders of Jerusalem
9:8–21; 5:25–30	The continuing anger of the LORD
6:1–13	The call of Isaiah
7:1–9	The sign of Shear-jashub
7:10–17	The sign of Immanuel
7:18–20	The threat from Assyria
7:21–25	Further interpretations of Isaiah's prophecies
8:1–4	The sign of Maher-shalal-hashbaz
8:5–8	The overwhelming flood
8:9–10	A message to the nations
8:11–15	The holiness of the LORD of hosts
8:16–18	The sealing of the message
8:19–22	Interpretations of the prophet's sayings
8:23–9:7	The promise of a royal Saviour
10:5–15	Assyria, the rod of the divine anger
10:16–19	The coming destruction of the Assyrians
10:20–23	The fate of the remnant of Israel
10:24–27a	A message of hope and reassurance
10:27b–32	The advance of the enemy
10:33–34	The cutting-down of the forest

Isaiah 1–39

Introduction to the Prophecies of Isaiah: chapter 1

The first chapter of the book of Isaiah has been intentionally formulated from a selection of the prophet's sayings in order to provide a general preface and guide to his preaching. This is made evident by the presence in 2:1 of a 'second' superscription which must originally have introduced a major written collection of the prophet's words. The extent of this written collection can only be roughly established and, although Fohrer would limit it to 2:1–10:6, we have already seen (Introduction, p. 7) that it is much more plausibly to be regarded as comprising 2:1–32:20. Hence the time at which the prophecies of ch. 1 were set in their present position must be exilic, or later. However, there is widespread agreement among commentators that the five main prophecies in 1:2–26 are from Isaiah, even though it is rather difficult to establish the precise period of his ministry to which they belong. 1:4–9 undoubtedly comes from the year 701 BC, or very soon thereafter. Vv. 27–28 are an addition that has been made to the last of these prophecies, providing a general conclusion to the theme of the whole chapter. A later addition, with a more admonitory tone, has then been made in vv. 29–31 condemning certain types of illicit worship. This is certainly of post-exilic origin.

The acceptance of the authenticity to Isaiah of the sayings contained in 1:2–26 prompts the question how they came to be preserved and placed where they now stand. Since it is highly improbable that they simply survived as isolated and disconnected sayings of the prophet, or that they once formed a kind of independent collection, they must have been drawn from a larger body of the prophet's sayings. Most probably, therefore, they have been extracted from their original positions among the larger collections of chs. 2–32. Thereby they have been separated from their connection with particular crises and historical events in the prophet's ministry and made into a more general introduction to the larger book. Cf. H. Barth, p. 220n., for suggestions concerning their original locations. Their purpose is relatively clear: to show that the prophet's preaching established a lasting disclosure of Israel's sin and of the need of the people to show a deep and genuine repentance. By the addition of such an introduction the book as a whole has been given a permanent and timeless relevance, extending the significance of prophecies which were originally addressed to specific historical situations into a larger context. Cf. my book *Prophecy and Tradition*, pp. 50ff.

We can recognise a deliberate structure in the chapter as follows:

1:2–3 The nature and extent of Israel's sin
1:4–9 The judgment of God upon this sin
1:10–17 The way of deliverance from sin
1:18–20 An appeal for repentance and a return to obedience
1:21–26 The hope of purifying judgment and restoration

To this vv. 27–28 add a generalised and summarising conclusion, which has then been further expanded by a later scribe in vv. 29–31 in order to make clear that the worst kind of sin is that of idolatrous worship. Upon this the most final and fearsome of judgments is threatened (v. 31).

THE SUPERSCRIPTION

1:1

1:1. The vision of Isaiah the son of Amoz: The heading provides a simple preface to the book and dates from the post-exilic period. In form it is modelled closely upon those set at the head of the books of Amos and Hosea (Am. 1:1; Hos. 1:1) except that it contains no reference to the regencies of the Northern Kingdom. Evidently the fate of that kingdom, which constituted an important theme for the prophet, was already taken for granted, and its end assumed (cf. the glossator's addition in v. 7:8b). **The vision** is an unexpected description of the prophet's message, which contains only one full vision in ch. 6, but the word has come to be used in a broad sense to cover not only visionary experiences, but prophetic revelations and messages of all kinds. It does not, therefore, express any particular emphasis upon the manner of the divine revelation. The name **Isaiah** means 'Yahweh saves', or 'Yahweh is salvation'. **the son of Amoz** does not refer to the prophet Amos, but to an unknown figure. Jewish tradition has identified him with the brother of king Amaziah of Judah (2 Kg. 14:1–2), thereby making Isaiah of royal descent. Yet it is highly improbable that Isaiah's father is to be identified with this royal personage, or with the otherwise unknown person of that name mentioned on an ancient seal, as suggested by R. T. Anderson, *JBL* 79 (1960), pp. 57–9. **Judah and Jerusalem** is in the reverse order to what is otherwise found in the book (cf. 3:1, 8; 5:3; 22:21). This change very probably reflects the period of Persian domination after the exile when the political importance of Jerusalem had been much weakened. For the book as a whole it is too restricted as a description of those whom the prophet addressed since these certainly included members of the Northern Kingdom, as well as a number of major foreign nations. **In the days of Uzziah, Jotham, etc.**, provides a general guide to the kings of Judah in whose reigns Isaiah was active. For the important questions of chronology and dating that are raised, see Introduction, pp. 8f. If the prophet were not called to his task until the year of Uzziah's death, it is improbable that we have any prophecies from this king's reign. Furthermore, on the chronology that we have followed, Jotham had already died before Uzziah, with whom he was co-regent, so that all the prophecies can be most satisfactorily explained as belonging to the reigns of either Ahaz or Hezekiah. In this, as in the case of other superscriptions, the amount of historical information contained is limited, but can be filled out by such notes as that contained in 7:1. No reference is made to the kings of the Northern

Kingdom of Israel, in line with the geographical note concerning the addresses.

REBELLIOUS SONS

I : 2–3

These two verses establish the accusation that Israel is a rebellious and wayward people who do not know the extent of their own folly and waywardness.

2. Hear, O heavens: The appeal to the sky and earth to serve as witnesses to what has taken place between God and Israel reflects a form of speech adopted from ancient Israelite legal practice. The elements of creation are regarded as impartial in their judgment, and so the prophet calls upon them, as reliable witnesses, to pass their verdict on the events which they have witnessed. Some have sought to see here a form of cultic lawsuit which reflected the tradition of the covenant made on Sinai. So G. E. Wright, *Israel's Prophetic Heritage*, ed. B. W. Anderson and W. Harrelson, London, 1962, pp. 26–67, esp. p. 44. J. Harvey, *Le plaidoyer prophétique contre Israël après la rupture de l'alliance*, Bruges/Montreal, 1967, pp. 36ff., has contrastingly related the form to letters of ultimatum delivered by a suzerain to his vassal whom he suspected of rebellion. However, a simple adaptation by the prophet himself from legal practice is sufficient to explain all the features that are present. **Sons have I reared:** The notion that Israel's relationship to God could be compared to that of sonship is an old one and belongs as a central feature to the ancient Passover tradition. Cf. Exod. 4 : 23 and Hos. 11 : 1–7.

3. The ox knows its owner: The appeal, based on a comparison with the behaviour of animals, supports the charge that what Israel had done was unnatural, and contrary to the order of creation. Israel neither recognised its divine LORD, nor realised that its behaviour towards him was reprehensible.

ONLY ZION IS LEFT

I : 4–9

The situation in which Jerusalem was left isolated, with most of the towns and countryside of Judah ravaged and destroyed, is used to demonstrate the contention that Israel-Judah had been severely punished by God for its sins. The situation must certainly be that of the year 701, when Sennacherib conquered all of Judah and Jerusalem was only spared a like fate by Hezekiah's surrender (2 Kg. 18 : 13–16). The situation is fully described in Sennacherib's Annals (*ANET*, p. 288). The only question that is at issue regarding the date of this particular prophecy is whether it pictures the city before the surrender, or after it. Here too, however, we can confidently follow most recent commentators (Fohrer, Kaiser, Wildberger) in recognising that the prophet's portrayal here derives from his viewing the scene of Judah's ruination, with Jerusalem as the only city left intact, in the immediate aftermath of the crisis of 701 BC.

Following Barth, pp. 217ff., we may regard v. 9 as a later addition made by a redactor after the further destruction of Judah, this time including Jerusalem, in 587. It now viewed the **few survivors left in** Jerusalem as the only hope for Israel's future.

In vv. 4–8 the prophet's intention is clear. After the Assyrian forces had left Jerusalem, the inhabitants of the city were tempted into celebrating their remarkable escape (cf. 22 : 1–4, 12–14), instead of lamenting the catastrophe that befallen the nation as a whole. Isaiah was concerned that the lesson of what had happened should be correctly learned and the year 701 remembered as a time of judgment, not of special divine favour for Jerusalem. That any of the people at all had survived was a mark of divine mercy, as in the survival of Abraham and Lot from Sodom and Gomorrah (Gen. 19 : 24–29).

4. Ah, sinful nation: The opening cry (Heb. *hôy*) is usually found in threats warning that disaster is coming (as in 5 : 8ff.). Here, however, it occurs in invective and serves as a meaningful expression of rebuke. Those addressed are the people of Judah, who must not forget that they are all that remains of a once great nation. At a time when the people were tempted to see themselves as divinely favoured by their escape, especially when set against the total succumbing of the Northern Kingdom to Assyria, Judah was to remember that it, too, was guilty of the same sins. **the Holy One of Israel** is a distinctive title for Yahweh in the prophet Isaiah, and appears designed to stress, not only the element of holiness (cf. Th. C. Vriezen, *Outline of O.T. Theology*, pp. 61f.) but also the fact that he was the God of both kingdoms: Ephraim (Israel) and Judah (cf. 5 : 7). It is almost certainly an ancient title, used in the temple cult, and it appears unlikely that it was uniquely coined by the prophet himself (as claimed by O. Procksch, *TDNT*, I, pp 93f.). However, the prophet has certainly vested it with a new significance in view of the sharp division between the two kingdoms which had occurred, first with the Syro-Ephraimite conflict and then with the fall of Ephraim to Assyria (733–722). Yahweh still remained the God of the entire people.

5. Why will you still be smitten views the sufferings of the people as a fate which they have voluntarily chosen for themselves. The military defeat and humiliation which had overtaken them was a direct result of their own sin and moral corruption. Already therefore the prophet implies an idea, which he later develops explicity (10 : 5), that the Assyrians have been acting as the instrument of Yahweh with which to chastise his people.

7. aliens devour your land refers to the armies of the Assyrians who had devastated Judah, but it is a commonly found convention for a prophet not to identify explicitly the enemies and oppressors who are working as the instruments of God. The clause **as overthrown by aliens** should be read as 'like the overthrow of Sodom', and must be regarded as an editor's gloss based upon v. 9.

8. the daughter of Zion is a pictorial reference to the city of Jerusalem. The name **Zion** originally referred to the south-east hill of Jerusalem, the area upon which the old Jebusite city had been situated. It came to be applied to the royal quarter of the city, and acquired a special religious significance because the temple was situated there. Cf. G. Fohrer, *TDNT*, VII, p. 295, who, however, is scarcely correct in seeing the special religious use of the term as a late development. **like a booth in a vineyard** reflects the practice of preparing a rough shelter, or **booth**, made from tree branches covered with leaves to protect a vineyard. The watchman could then shelter in it in order to guard the ripening crops.

9. If the LORD of hosts: The entire verse is taken by Barth to be a late, exilic, addition in which the condition of Jerusalem after 587 was read back into Isaiah's prophecy of 701. This is very probable since it introduces an alleviating factor in the prophet's condemnation. The title **the LORD of hosts** is certainly an ancient one which was closely associated with the Ark (cf. I Sam. 4:4; and see O. Eissfeldt, *Kleine Schriften*, III, pp. 103–23). The **hosts** originally referred to the armies of Israel which he was believed to lead into battle. Later the title came to be associated with the 'hosts' of heaven, i.e. the stars, which he had created. **like Sodom** reflects the patriarchal tradition of the overthrow of the cities Sodom and Gomorrah recounted in Gen. 19:24–29. The fate of the two cities had become a proverbial illustration of the reality and fearfulness of divine judgment.

THE WAY OF TRUE RELIGION

I : 10–17

This, the third saying in the introductory presentation of Isaiah's preaching, sets out the classical prophetic teaching on the way of repentance and of true obedience. It bears the form of a priestly instruction, or *tôrāh*; cf. J. Begrich, *Ges. Stud.*, pp. 232–60. The prophet imitated the character of this priestly style of speech, although we may deduce that he originally addressed it to an audience gathered in the temple in Jerusalem.

10. you rulers of Sodom: The ruling classes of Jerusalem are singled out as those chiefly responsible for the city's behaviour, and also as those who displayed the greatest zeal in worship. The reference again to Sodom suggests that the catchword principle has been applied in linking together the separate sayings of I:1–26. Alternatively, if v. 9 is a gloss, then its introduction could very well have been prompted by the reference here. Entirely at variance with the way in which the proud rulers of Jerusalem saw themselves, the prophet implies that they are in reality as sinful, and as deserving of judgment, as were the notorious rulers of the ancient city (cf. Gen. 19:1–14).

11. What to me is the multitude of your sacrifices? conveys the sharp rejection by the prophet of the idea that the simple formal observance of ritual and cultic duty would suffice to maintain the people in a state of blessedness under God. Not the correctness of cultic observance, but a more far-reaching demonstration of obedi-

ence in turning away from sin was called for by God. Hence the
prophet was not asserting that the cult had no place in true religion,
but rather that it could not be used to secure God's protection and
blessing in contradiction to man's sin. Cf. H. H. Rowley, *Worship in
Ancient Israel*, pp. 144ff., and cf. Am. 5:25; Jer. 7:22. **the fat of fed
beasts** designates animals specially fattened for slaughter. *NEB*'s
'buffaloes' is not necessary, and is scarcely an improvement.

12. When you come to appear before me reflects the slight modification of the Hebrew text, which occurs in several instances, where
the traditional phrase for worshipping 'to see the face (image) of God'
has been revocalised to read **to appear before God.** Cf. Exod. 23:17;
34:23 for similar instances and F. Nötscher, *Das Angesicht Gottes
Schauen*, Würzburg, 1924, pp. 85ff. The origin of the phrase is certainly
pre-Israelite and it was clearly felt to assert too crudely the belief in the
divine presence at a sanctuary.

13. Incense is an abomination to me: Incense was a common
accompaniment of worship in antiquity, and appears to have been a
particularly popular feature of Canaanite religion. As a consequence
its use was viewed with much suspicion in Israel. The word **abomination** (Heb. *tō'ēḇāh*) is a technical term for that which was unfit for use
in worship, as shown by Lev. 7:18. **New moon and sabbath:** The
conjunction of the two names shows that the sabbath was itself
originally a lunar (full moon) day. Cf. the Babylonian *šapattu*, and see
THAT, II, cols. 863ff. When it came to be linked directly with the
seventh day rest cycle (Exod. 23:12; 34:21), probably not until the
exilic age, then this rest day acquired the name sabbath. **solemn
assembly:** The basic sense of the Heb. word *'aṣārāh* points to
'restraint' (i.e. from work, and hence from normal secular activities).
The prophet appears to be making a deliberate play on the association
of the word for 'iniquity' with the belief in a special power derived
from God through the cultus.

15. your hands are full of blood: The metaphor refers to the per-
petration of crimes of violence, but the prophet no doubt also had in
mind that the worshippers would be marked with the bloodstains of
the sacrificial animals they had slaughtered for use in worship. It
thereby served to reinforce his accusation that the people were
burdened with bloodguilt because their actions had brought suffering
and misery to many.

16. Wash yourselves: The phrase presents an excellent example of
the prophet's artistry in finding a deeper significance in a common
situation. What the worshipper must do is not simply wash his blood-
stained hands, but change his whole way of life. With this the prophet
reaches the climax of his brief *tōrāh*-instruction to the people. His
hearers must turn away from evil and re-establish justice in their city.
Underlying all the prophet's warnings and threats lies this passionate
appeal for a changed way of life. Although the passage is certainly
Isaianic in its origin, the redactor who has placed ch. 1 in its present
position has seen in this admonitory instruction an appeal of permanent relevance to Israel. Not only is there need for repentance in

times of crisis and national danger, but as a continued, and oft-repeated, way of approach to God.

17. defend the fatherless: The conjunction of fatherless children and widows as classes of people in need of special charitable concern is found frequently in the Old Testament (cf. Dt. 10:18, 24:17, etc.) and was known also in ancient Canaanite society. Cf. E. Hammershaimb, *Some Aspects of Old Testament Prophecy*, pp. 69ff. It undoubtedly reflects a feature of urban life and social grouping in the ancient world, where such people had little economic means of support without the husband-father to provide this, and where there was no larger 'extended family' to protect them. The case of such people is singled out by Isaiah as an illustration of the way in which his contemporaries displayed their disregard for the deeper requirements of true religion.

IF YOU REFUSE

1:18–20

The general theme of the opening chapter is here continued with a strong appeal for true repentance and a return to Yahweh with all the promise that this brings of well-being. Kaiser regards the section as an original continuation of vv. 10–17, but we must rather see in it a separate appeal by the prophet, possibly at one time part of a larger unit, which has been set here editorially because of its appropriateness within the general theme of the chapter. It is set out in the form of a court-room appeal, and must reflect ancient Israelite legal practice. Cf. H. J. Boecker, *Redeformen des Rechtslebens im A.T.* (Neukirchen–Vluyn, 1964), pp. 68ff.

18. Come now: The starkness of the two alternatives now set before the accused people leaves indeterminate the question of whether the speech as a whole has an admonitory and threatening tone, or a reassuring one. Both features are clearly implicit, and such appeals to reason out the rights and wrongs of a case must have been commonplace in ancient legal proceedings. It is not necessary therefore to see a deliberate element of irony in the appeal: 'In view of all this, can your sins . . . ?' (so B. Duhm). If we take v. 18*b* in a clearly affirmative sense, then it asserts that, when the wrongdoer turns from his offences, he can find an accepted and happy place in society. Only if he persists in his wrongdoing does his guilt become incurable. The original date of the prophecy can scarcely be determined, since it appears that ch. 1 has been formed out of sayings uttered during different periods of Isaiah's ministry.

20. you shall be devoured: The threat referred to is evidently a military one, and the impersonal passive formulation illustrates finely the prophet's technique of saying sufficient to drive home his warning, but not too much lest it should be too easily proved false. There are, therefore, no closer details given of whose sword is referred to, or when such a threat might be realised. We must, however, reckon that

it was the threat from Assyria which the prophet envisaged, most
probably in the period of the revolt against Sennacherib by Hezekiah
(705–701).

THE FAITHFUL CITY

I:21–28

The condemnation of the political leaders and officials in Jerusalem,
the clear implication that it is they who are responsible for the un-
healthy state of the moral, social and political life of the city, and the
threat that they will be removed (vv. 24–26), makes this one of the
most far-reaching expressions of Isaiah's social criticism. Cf. W.
Dietrich, pp. 284ff. In several respects it stands somewhat apart from
the attitude adopted by the prophet elsewhere. Frequently he
expresses opposition to the policies adopted, and to the behaviour of
Judah's leaders (cf. 5:18–23), but here he points to a more radical
overthrow of the existing political order. It is the leaders of Jerusalem
themselves who have become Yahweh's enemies (v. 24), and their
removal will make way for their replacement by a more just and
responsible group of counsellors and judges (v. 26). Nowhere is there
any hint that Judah is endangered by a major threat from an external
enemy, so we must assume that the Assyrian crisis of the years 705–
701 had not yet arisen. More plausibly we are directed to a much
earlier time in the prophet's ministry, almost certainly whilst Ahaz
was still on the throne, so that the period between 733 and 727 is the
most likely occasion for its delivery. Once again, however, the
redactor has found in the saying a more lasting and repeatedly applicable denunciation of Jerusalem's sins. With the Babylonian exile
behind him, he has found in Isaiah's words some explanation of the
city's tragic history and also a pledge for its divinely promised future.
  The limit of the original Isaianic saying must be found in vv. 21–26,
which looked for some radical change in the leadership and government of Jerusalem in Isaiah's own time. To this saying a later redactor
has added in vv. 27–28 a generalised formula about the divinely set
conditions for Jerusalem's well-being. It evidently presupposes that
Jerusalem had suffered severe setbacks, and that the way forward
could be pursued only by a deep act of repentance, issuing in a new
order of justice and righteousness.
  21. the faithful city: The LXX adds 'Zion', thereby establishing the
city's identification beyond dispute in line with v. 27, but this was
certainly not necessary to the original prophecy. The expression
intends a subtle play on the adjective, hinting at an association
between the ideas of 'firmly established' and 'faithful' (in conduct and
piety). Cities were described in Hebrew as the 'mothers' of those who
lived in them (cf. the frequent use of the expression 'daughter of
Zion' for the inhabitants of Jerusalem), so that the city's unrighteous
way of life could be vividly portrayed as moral infidelity, i.e. playing
the **harlot. Righteousness lodged with her:** An ancient and strongly
felt association appears to have existed between Jerusalem and the

concept of **righteousness** (Heb. *ṣedek*). This very probably arose
through the use of the word *ṣedek* as a divine title. Cf. the personal
names Adonizedek, Zadok, etc. What particular offences the prophet
had in mind to justify his accusation that the city tolerated murderers
in its midst is not clear. Either we must think of a relatively high level
of physical violence which was current in Jerusalem, as in many
ancient cities. Alternatively it may be, if our linking the prophecy
with Ahaz's reign is correct, that there had been a number of notorious political assassinations.

23. Your princes are rebels: The reference is to rebellion against
God and against the just order of society which he demanded, rather
than to an act of political rebellion against Assyria. The **princes** were
not necessarily men of royal descent, although these were certainly
included, but men of authority who held high civil and military
administrative posts. Their corruption undermined the entire moral
fabric of Jerusalem's life, so that the only remedy for the city's ills lay
in their removal. A typical illustration of their moral obstinacy is
provided by their lack of concern for the sufferings and misery of
those in economic need (cf. v. 17 above).

24. the Mighty One of Israel was a very ancient title for Yahweh,
the God of Israel (cf. Gen. 49:24). It was pre-Mosaic in its origin,
being associated with the patriarch Israel-Jacob, and emphasising the
divine power and strength under the simile of a bull. Cf. A. Alt,
Essays on Old Testament History and Religion, Oxford, 1966, pp. 25f.
By the time of Isaiah the prominent fertility aspects connected with
this simile had almost entirely receded into its forgotten background
and pre-history. **I will vent my wrath:** In this verse the prophet turns
from invective to direct threat but is careful to avoid introducing
unnecessary details to explain how, or by whom, the threat would be
fulfilled. The offending figures would be removed by the action of
God, although clearly the prophet understood this to be through some
human agents. We must think of a major internal political change,
rather than the action of a foreign invader. Cf. Am. 7:9 for a comparable insistence on the divine origin of an act of political overthrow.

26. I will restore your judges: What this was to mean in precise
political terms is not made clear. It can hardly refer to the period of the
'Judges' as such, before David's time, since Isaiah evidently regarded
David's capture of the city as the time of its true beginning as an
Israelite fortress and religious centre (cf. 29:1). Yet his awareness of
the way in which the royal court and its officials were able to manipu-
late the social and administrative life of the city to their own advantage
(cf. 5:8; 10:1) made it plain to him that only their removal could
improve the lot of the majority of the city's inhabitants. The **judges**,
therefore, would be leaders chosen by the people themselves, rather
than officials appointed by the crown, with all its potential for corruption.

27. Zion shall be redeemed: This, and the following v. 28, form an
addition made to Isaiah's prophecy about the reform of the government of Jerusalem, and must emanate from a time after 587.

no, anticipates conclusion of judgement of 24-26

Jerusalem had already suffered judgment in the redactor's eyes, and
he is concerned to spell out clearly the conditions through which the
restoration of the city's life and well-being could take place. The name
Zion is now clearly meant to apply to the whole city, but the time of
its return to normality is felt not yet to have arrived. The time of the
first half of the fifth century, prior to the coming of Nehemiah to
Jerusalem, provides the most likely occasion for the addition.

28. But rebels and sinners shall be destroyed points to a continuing inner tension within the city, with a sense that the final
purging must still take place.

THE END OF FALSE WORSHIP

1:29-31

These three verses represent an independent addition to the preface to
the book of Isaiah which constitutes ch. 1. Their purpose is to identify
the particular sin to which the people are tempted as idolatry, by
especially singling out for punishment those who had participated in
idolatrous cult practices. They have most probably been composed
especially for inclusion here, rather than forming a fragment of some
larger threat which has simply been included at this point. The kind
of offence referred to bears some comparison with that condemned in
Isa. 65:3-5, but in reality the resort to rituals in gardens and groves
flourished through the entire Old Testament period in a variety of
forms. It is therefore scarcely possible to identify any one particular
occasion of special concern with the sin of idolatry.

29. You shall be ashamed of the oaks: Oaks may be more precisely
identified as terebinths, which were deciduous trees which enjoyed
considerable popularity in fertility cult rites, because they were held
to symbolize the death of the god and his rebirth in the spring. **the
gardens** were small cultivated sanctuaries in which the growth of the
plants was made to express the life and fertility-giving powers of the
gods. The actual plant life cultivated could be used to symbolize a
variety of functions associated with the giving of 'life' and 'blessing'.
Cf. J. Pedersen, *Israel*, I-II, pp. 314ff. Different expressions of such a
cult were to be found in ancient Egypt, Canaan, Phoenicia and Greece,
and all of them made use of types of 'sympathetic magic'. The threat
that those who worshipped in this fashion would **be ashamed** meant
far more than a loss of prestige, and rather indicated an experience of
total failure and ruination. Cf. M. A. Klopfenstein, *Scham und
Schande nach dem Alten Testament*, ATANT 62, Zürich, 1972, pp. 5off.

like droopy h/?

30. like an oak: The prophet uses the picture of the withering of
leaves of the tree in autumn and winter to express a totally different
message from that which the worshippers found in its symbolism.

31. And the strong: 1QIs[a] adds a suffix here 'and your strong one',
i.e. 'the strongest of you'. However, this looks like an attempt to
clarify a reference that was already felt to be obscure. *NEB* is probably
correct in recognising that the original reference was to 'the strongest
tree' so that the sense follows on from the preceding verse quite

smoothly. The metaphor of the vigorously growing tree being reduced to tow enables the prophet to direct his threat in relation to the idolatrous trust shown by his hearers in the life force displayed in their tree gardens.

Prophecies Concerning Judah and Jerusalem: chapters 2–12

The appearance of a further heading in 2 : 1, albeit much briefer than that given in 1 : 1, provides some clear guide to the way in which the present book was put together. Undoubtedly this superscription originally formed an opening to a collection of Isaiah's prophecies, rather than representing a deliberate repetition of the one that had been given earlier in 1 : 1. Moreover we may fairly confidently assert that the heading in 2 : 1 is older than that in 1 : 1, and that the latter was added, either along with or subsequent to, the prefacing of ch. 1 to the whole Isaianic collection (at least as far as ch. 32*). H. Barth, pp. 203ff., gives a considered case for recognising that a major redaction and collection of Isaiah's prophecies took place in Josiah's reign (640–609 BC). The contents of this redaction are to be found in chs. 2–32, although later additions are also now included in this. Signs of earlier collections of Isaianic prophecies are to be found in 6 : 1–8 : 18* (see below on 6 : 1ff.) and 5 : 1–14 : 27* (see below on 5 : 1ff.). For the complex redaction-history of Isaiah 1–39, see Introduction, pp. 3ff.

The superscription of 2 : 1 was evidently composed to introduce a specific collection of Isaiah's prophecies at a particular phase of their redactional history, and it is of singular interest on two counts. The first of these is that it interprets Isaiah's prophecies with regard to 'Judah and Jerusalem', and thereby leaves aside the undoubted wider application of many of them to the Northern Kingdom of Israel (Ephraim), to Syria, and to other non-Israelite nations. The second factor concerning 2 : 1 is that it serves to highlight the fact that 2 : 1–4 : 6* comprises a relatively self-contained collection which very directly and specially does relate to the fate of Judah and Jerusalem. In this both the opening word of hope in 2 : 2–4(5) and the concluding promise in 4 : 2–6 concerning the fate of the survivors in Jerusalem are reassuring in tone. The intervening material (2 : 6–4 : 1), however, is consistently threatening in tone and warns explicitly of the defeat and downfall of Jerusalem through the ravages of war (cf. especially 3 : 25–26). That we have an authentic nucleus of sayings from Isaiah (although 2 : 6–22 in particular is in a poorly preserved state) is assured, and so we are faced here with the prophet's warnings of the downfall of Jerusalem. A later, post-exilic, redactor has then supplemented this at the beginning and end in order to affirm that these threats had been fulfilled. These reassuring additions most probably stem from the fifth century BC. The threatening element of Isaiah's prophecies in 2 : 6–4 : 1*, even allowing that it has subsequently been added to, appears to be authentic, however. The question then arises whether it derives from the early or later period of his ministry. It is abundantly clear from the prophecies preserved in chs. 28–31 that Isaiah foretold

disaster for Hezekiah and his kingdom at the time of the revolt against
Sennacherib in the years 705–701. Yet it appears clear, too, from the
threatening element in 6 : 1–8 : 18*, that Isaiah also foretold a disastrous
consequence for Ahaz in the years 733–725, as a result of his appeal to
Assyria during the crisis surrounding the Syro-Ephraimite war. It is
in every way plausible that Isaiah had anticipated the ruin of Judah
and Jerusalem at this time, as 8 : 8 very strongly suggests. The likelihood is, therefore, that the Isaianic kernel of the threats to Judah and
Jerusalem expressed in 2 : 6–4 : 1 belongs to these years.

If this is the case, then it would also appear likely that the present
placing of these prophecies before the account of the prophet's call
has taken place at a particular redactional stage in the composition of
the book, at a time when a renewed threat to Jerusalem was felt to
have arisen. This could only have been in the period after 605 when
the Babylonian menace appeared in Judah. We find a similar linking
of the Isaianic threat to Jerusalem with the disaster of 587 BC in a
number of redactional comments which have been added *post eventum*
(cf. 2 : 18–19; 6 : 12–13; 8 : 22, etc., and see Introduction, pp. 6f.).

A SECOND SUPERSCRIPTION

2 : 1

The superscription which has been placed here is striking on account
of the fact that it is specifically addressed to **Judah and Jerusalem**.
Precisely what collection of the prophecies it was meant to introduce
must certainly be related to this. It would appear doubtful that such a
title was intended to be appropriate to the Josianic Redaction since
this is so clearly concerned with the wider fate of all Israel, including
the Northern Kingdom. In fact it would appear to be more probable
that this superscription was linked directly with the threats to Judah
and Jerusalem which follow immediately after the promise of 2 : 2–5.
This particular heading, therefore, must have been composed at the
time when this collection of prophetic threats was used to illuminate
the experience of what had taken place in 587 BC. Alternatively we
might date it later still, to the time in the fifth century, when the
promises were added in 2 : 1–4(5) and 4 : 2–6.

2 : 1. concerning Judah and Jerusalem: Such a title, but in the
reverse order, appears in Neh. 7 : 6, and is striking on account of the
separation which it assumes between the city and the country. Already
it suggests that **Judah** has become a region, to a considerable extent
economically and politically dependent on **Jerusalem**. Cf. also 3 : 1
and the concern with Jerusalem alone in 4 : 2–6.

THE GLORY OF ZION

2 : 2–5

The portrayal of the exaltation of Mount Zion to become the highest
of the mountains of the earth is found repeated in Mic. 4 : 1–4, where a
further concluding verse is added (Mic. 4 : 5). There are also a number

of relatively minor variations of text. H. Wildberger, *VT* 7 (1957), pp. 62–81, and *Comm.*, I, pp. 75ff., has presented a careful defence of the claim that the prophecy is authentic to Isaiah, but rests heavily upon the theme of 'the pilgrimage of the nations to Zion', which he regards as a part of the unique cultic tradition of Jerusalem. However, it is clear that, whatever traditions may be held to underlie the prophecy, it expresses a picture of the future exaltation of Jerusalem and Mount Zion, not one that was thought currently to exist, even in a mythological frame of reference. Quite certainly, therefore, we must ascribe the prophecy to a time after the destruction of Jerusalem in 587. Cf. especially O. H. Steck, *Friedensvorstellungen im alten Jerusalem*, TS III, Zürich, 1972, pp. 69ff., and H. Barth, pp. 222f. (also G. von Rad, *Old Testament Theology*, II, p. 294). The presentation is certainly not of a status of pre-eminent exaltation which Mount Zion was believed currently to possess, but rather a future promise of a role that it would fulfil in the days to come. It may be held to presuppose the pictures of the pilgrimage of the nations to Jerusalem found in Isa. 45:14–23; 60:1–18; 61:5–7. It draws upon traditions of great antiquity concerning the myth of the cosmic mountain which stood at the centre of the world, and from which the divine order and truth were given to the world. Cf. R. J. Clifford, *The Cosmic Mountain in Canaan and the Old Testament*, pp. 131ff. Here, however, such images furnished by ancient tradition have been made into a genuine prophecy concerning the special role that Jerusalem was to play in bringing peace and blessing to the nations through Israel. It expresses a softening and re-minting of the imperialistic notion of a world capital into the more positively religious idea of a centre to which the nations come to find truth, justice and peace.

The date of the prophecy cannot easily be determined with precision, but the early post-exilic period, probably the early fifth century, is most likely. It expresses the prophetic eschatological vision which eventually prompted the political and social rebuilding of Jerusalem under Ezra and Nehemiah. We may compare the hope proclaimed in Hag. 2:7. It has been placed here at the very beginning of the collection of Isaianic prophecies contained in 2–32* in order to provide a thematic message of hope concerning Jerusalem to show that this lies firmly and positively in the future, beyond the words of threat and judgment contained in the book, especially in chs. 2–5. The authors of the prophecy clearly regarded this judgment as having been fulfilled through the catastrophe of 587.

2. **In the latter days:** The expression is a recurrent formula for the introduction of prophetic messages of hope about the future. It is a broad, and relatively undefined, reference to the exact period of time when the change will take place, and means rather loosely 'in the future'. Later there emerged with apocalyptic a more rigid expectation that the future was divided into fixed ages, and that the final exaltation of Jerusalem (and Israel) would only take place at 'the end time', and already such an idea appears to be implied by LXX's translation. However, this is not the expectation entertained here.

the highest of the mountains: Mount Zion, the temple mountain of Jerusalem, is not especially high, but the hope foretold here has arisen in consequence of the belief that it would become the great 'world-mountain' at the centre of the earth, which joined heaven to earth. Cf. R. J. Clifford, *The Cosmic Mountain*, pp. 156ff. Hence it was the point through which the divine truth and order for the peace of the world could be brought down to man. For the traditions which underlie this prophetic promise, cf. PS. 48 : 3, Ezek. 40 : 2, and H.-J. Kraus, *Worship in Israel*, Oxford, 1966, pp. 183ff. In the author's reinterpretation the ancient mythological idea has been transformed into a more directly religious and theological one concerning the role of Jerusalem among the nations of the world.

and all the nations: Mic. 4 : 1 reads 'peoples' here and 'many nations' in the following verse, and this may well represent more correctly the older form of the text. God's rule is to extend, not only over his people Israel, but over all those nations of the world who are to become submissive to his government. The implication is clearly that a world-wide reign of peace will be inaugurated. Cf. H. Schmid, *Šalôm, 'Frieden' im alten Orient und im Alten Testament*, SBS 51, Stuttgart, 1971, pp. 62ff.

The origin of the imagery must certainly lie in the imperialistic claims of the Davidic monarchy from Jerusalem (cf. Ps. 2 : 8–9; 76 : 3–6), but this has been transformed by the prophet into a more genuinely religious notion of an age of world-wide peace, based on the righteousness and justice of the divine rule of Yahweh.

3. and many peoples shall come: The identity of the **many peoples** is not specified, and we may naturally think first of all of nations bordering upon Judah, or even those who had at one time formed a part of the kingdom of David (cf. 2 Sam. 8 : 1–14; Am. 9 : 12). However, it is clear from the overall range of the vision that the reference is to 'all nations', and that a universal era of peace is envisaged. **that he may teach us his ways:** Nothing is said about what agency, or institution, is to serve to bring a knowledge of God's ways to men. It is possible that either a priestly declaration of divine *tôrāh* from the temple was in mind, or a prophetic revelation of God's 'plan', but most probably we should think of a tradition of an administration of justice and law through the divinely appointed (Davidic) king. Cf. Ps. 101 : 8. By the time of the prophecy, however, it is probable that the expectation of restoring the Davidic monarchy had faded and a more direct, theocratic, government was anticipated. The word **law** (Heb. *tôrāh*) includes more than juridical legislation, and must here cover the belief that a divine decision, or 'plan' (Heb. *'ēṣāh*), could be given to arbitrate between disputes among nations, rendering resort to war unnecessary.

considering criticism of monarchy in 1:23

4. He shall judge: The idea is not of passing judgment upon the nations for their rebellion against God, but rather of the settlement of disputes which arose between nations. **and they shall beat their swords** is a vivid image of the abandoning of warfare as a way of settling disagreements, since the latter will have become obsolete as a method of diplomacy. Instead weapons will be adapted for peaceful purposes. The saying evidently acquired (or possibly had already acquired) a proverbial currency, since it is used to describe exactly the reverse proceeding, from peace to war, in Jl 3 : 10.

5. O house of Jacob represents a concluding appeal by the redactor to the reader to become obedient to God so that the longed-for age of world peace might be hastened in. Evidently the appeal already hints in the direction that the eschatological hope set before Israel, and all Jews scattered among the nations, could be brought in more swiftly if a genuine repentance and turning back to Yahweh were shown. A rather different conclusion is presented in Mic. 4 : 5, and the picture of each person enjoying the fruits of peace given in Mic. 4 : 4 is absent from the Isaianic version. Overall it appears that the prophecy has been composed earlier than the time of its inclusion in either the Isaiah or Micah prophetic collections and has been adapted to each because of the importance in them of the threat of Jerusalem's destruction (cf. Isa. 3 : 1ff.; Mic. 3 : 12).

THE HUMILIATION OF THE PROUD

2 : 6–22

With this prophecy we begin an important series of threats against Judah, and Jerusalem in particular, which extends from 2 : 6 to 4 : 1, and which has been rounded off by the insertion of the hopeful prophecy in 4 : 2–6. Like the introductory message of future hope in 2 : 1–5, this promise is not from Isaiah himself, but has been introduced after the exilic period to show that the threats to Jerusalem in 2 : 6–4 : 1 were regarded as fulfilled by the destruction and defeat of the city in 587. We are left then with an important series of threats, which focus especially upon the overthrow of Jerusalem and its civil and political leaders (especially 3 : 1–5). The question arises why they have been placed here and set as a kind of preface to the much larger redactional unit 5 : 1–14 : 27*, which incorporates the prophet's account of his call. Already we have noted that this must be a consequence of the belief that these threats to Jerusalem had acquired a new significance at a later time than that to which Isaiah originally addressed them. What this later time was cannot be in doubt, since it must have been when a new threat to Jerusalem had arisen from the Babylonians. The positioning of 2 : 6–4 : 1 as a preface to a collection of Isaiah's prophecies, in which the fate of Jerusalem formed a prominent subject, took place after 587 BC. We have further evidence in ch. 39 (= 2 Kg. 20 : 12–19) that the disastrous fate suffered by Jerusalem at the hands of the Babylonians (in that case after 598; see below, pp. 293f.) was felt to cast a new light on the interpretation of Isaiah's prophecies. Furthermore, it is most probable that the prophecy in 2 : 6–22 has been added to after 587, especially in vv. 18 and 19. In connection with the prophet Micah, who also delivered a threat against Jerusalem in the eighth century (Mic. 3 : 9–12), we find from Jer. 26 : 18 that this was believed to have taken on a fresh importance in the light of what happened to Jerusalem in 587.

The question remains of the situation to which Isaiah himself had originally addressed his threats of a military defeat facing Jerusalem. Only two possibilities seriously present themselves. The first relates to the time after Ahaz had spurned Isaiah's advice and had appealed to Assyria during the Syro-Ephraimite crisis. 8:8 shows that Isaiah did expect a disastrous outcome to arise as a consequence of this (cf. also 8:14f.), and would point to a belief that Judah remained threatened throughout the latter years of Ahaz's reign. We should then place these threats in the years from 733 to 725. Dietrich, pp., 133ff., 195, would prefer to locate these threatening prophecies in the time of Hezekiah's rebellion against Sennacherib in the years 705–701, to which the threatening prophecies of chs. 28–31 must be ascribed. This remains a possibility, but the earlier date appears the more probable. The present position of the threats contained in 2:6–4:1 may then be accounted for on the recognition that a new vitality and force had been given to them at the time of the threat from Babylon in 598 and 587. Old prophecies had been applied to new situations. We may then conclude that these threats, which have undergone some measure of expansion, were originally delivered by Isaiah in the wake of Ahaz's appeal to Assyria during the Syro-Ephraimite crisis. In consequence of that appeal, not only did the Northern Kingdom suffer irreparable ruination, but Judah also was severely reduced in size and Ahaz became a vassal of the Assyrian throne. The prophecy of 2:6–22 is in a rather damaged state of preservation, so far as the text is concerned, and it has undoubtedly undergone a considerable measure of expansion. Several scholars have sought, with the aid of substantial textual emendation, to find an original unity, which can be divided into strophes (cf. Kaiser, Eichrodt, and see R. Davidson, *VT* 16 (1966), pp. 1–7). However, the unevenness of the material can be better explained as a result of the progressive expansion of an original Isaianic unit of smaller compass (Barth, pp. 222f.). At most we might deduce that two separate prophecies, one against the proud and the other against idolatry, have become intertwined. Yet this is improbable, and we can find the original Isaianic unit in vv. 10, 12–17, which calls upon the people to flee from Yahweh because he has a day against all that is proud and complacent in rejecting him. This has then been enlarged by the addition of vv. 7–8*a*, 9*a*. Subsequently further additions have been made condemning idolatry in vv. 18, 20–22, and v. 19 has been developed as a rather literal understanding of the poetic image of v. 10.

6. For thou hast rejected thy people: The saying presupposes that the judgment consequent upon this divine rejection had befallen the people so that the time when this verse (and v. 8*b*) was added is hard to determine. Clearly Judah is already felt to be suffering under judgment. The opening particle **For** (Heb. *kî*) is best taken in an asseverative sense, 'Surely', rather than as a connective to a preceding description of judgment which must be supposed to have fallen out. The phrase **thy people** contrasts with the authentic Isaianic pointer to such rejection with the sharply hostile 'this people' of 6:10. The word

No! God rejects before He judges

If talking about different times phrases should differ

diviners is missing in the Hebrew text and must be restored with the aid of Targ. The polemic against the semi-magical activities of divination and soothsaying marks a new element in prophetic invective. The particular association of such practices with **the Philistines** is also novel. All such practices are sharply condemned and outlawed in Dt. 18:9ff. That they were a foreign importation into Judah need not be doubted, but they were certainly semi-religious activities which enjoyed great popularity throughout most of the ancient orient. **strike hands with foreigners** refers to the negotiation of business with foreigners, which would have involved the sealing of an oath by a ceremony of striking of the hands together by those making the deal. When such extensive involvement in foreign business deals was current in Judah is not easily determined, but we may think of Nehemiah's age and the religious problems to which this gave rise (Neh. 13:15-29).

7. **Their land is filled:** Vv. 7-8a, together with 9a may be regarded as the first of the secondary expansions which have been made to the prophecy of vv. 10, 12-17. The implication of the reference to the abundance of silver and gold is that this wealth has had an adverse effect upon the life of the people, by encouraging them into apostasy. Again the situation dealt with by Nehemiah would be appropriate for such a condemnation. **filled with horses** can scarcely point to the military use of the horse, but must rather indicate the presence of numbers of trading caravans passing through Judah, bringing foreign merchandise including items regarded as idolatrous in their nature.

8. **filled with idols:** The association of wealth with idolatry was later to lead to the interpretation that desire for possessions was itself a form of idolatry (cf. Col. 3:5). Here, however, it was an inevitable development of trade between Judah and foreign nations that it should have brought in *objets d'art* of a religious nature. **they bow down:** must represent a further addition to v. 8a, designed to stress that it was not simply the possession of such illicit images that constituted Judah's sin, but an active veneration of them. The implicit rejection of the religious use of images because they are made by human hands must presuppose the anti-idolatry polemic of Isa. 44: 9-20. *why not anticipate? either way, genuine connection of thought*

9. **So man is humbled:** The introduction of the reference here to the humbling of men is dependent upon the original Isaianic saying in v. 17, where it was not connected specifically with idolatry, but with pride in all human achievements. The redactor who has added v. 9a has drawn out the lesson that man humbles himself by his foolish resort to idolatry. The sudden appeal to God—**forgive them not!**—is a yet later editorial comment intended to stress the heinousness of the sin of idolatry.

10. **Enter into the rock** commences the original Isaianic saying which conveys a threatening message by appealing to the hearers to flee from the wrath of God by hiding in rocks and holes. It is deliberately ironic, since it fully recognises the impossibility of the notion that man can escape from God (cf. Am. 9:2-4). When he finally

chooses to act against those who have made themselves his enemies they will find that they are powerless to escape his judgment. **the terror of the LORD** designates the presence and activity of God, but, in accord with prophetic convention, takes it for granted that this manifestation of divine wrath will operate through human agents.

11. The haughty looks of man: V. 11 is certainly an addition which now breaks up the connection between vv. 10 and 12–17. It introduces the rather trivial lesson that men will lose all their proud looks when Yahweh's day of judgment comes. The idea that a proud and arrogant bearing would be justly punished by being turned to shame and humiliation is a popular and frequent feature of proverbial wisdom teaching (cf. Prov. 11 : 2; 13 : 10; 16 : 18, and J. W. Whedbee, *Isaiah and Wisdom*, pp. 105f.). **in that day** is a broad and loosely defined reference to the time of the coming day of judgment, and now rather anticipates the reference to the Day of the LORD which follows in vv. 12–17.

12. For the LORD of hosts has a day: For the divine title, see on 1 : 9. The assumption that men must expect a coming Day of the LORD, and that this will be a time of punishment upon evil, relates closely to Am. 5 : 18–20. To what extent it indicates a familiarity with the sayings of Amos on the part of Isaiah (as R. Fey, *Amos und Jesaja*, pp. 77ff.), is far from clear, since there are undoubted differences of emphasis. Certainly, however, the idea of a special Day of Yahweh took its origin in the cultus with the belief that in the great Autumn (New Year) Festival he appeared to renew the life and welfare of his people (cf. Jl 1 : 15; 2 : 11). With Isaiah the reference is not primarily to this special festival day, but to the future time when he would intervene to act in judgment against sinners. The threat here must be directed at Judah and Jerusalem, as the entire context shows, and especially at the proud leaders and rulers of the people, who must now face judgment. The association with the threat contained in 3 : 1–5, therefore, must be an intentional feature of the redaction. **all that is lifted up and high** follows the LXX, since the Heb. has 'all that is lifted up and low', which cannot be correct.

13. lofty and lifted up must certainly be removed as a mistaken repetition. It overloads the line and breaks up the parallelism of the verse. The threatening note of vv. 12–17 is enhanced by the cumulative effect of listing poetically examples of features possessing great height and grandeur. The implication is that men, especially the king and princes of Judah, who had by their actions set themselves up against God, must expect the same crushing downfall that could take effect in the natural order against all that was beautiful and exalted.

16. ships of Tarshish: These were merchant ships, the name **Tarshish**, which means 'refinery', being applied to more than one ancient location. Primarily it was used of Tartessus in Spain, which may be the intended reference here. Cf. 1 Kg. 10 : 22, and see U. Täckholm, 'Tarsis, Tartessos und die Säulen des Heracles', *Opuscula Romana* 5 (1965), pp. 143–90. However it is not necessary to suppose that any one particular location was intended here. **beautiful craft:**

The Heb. *s^ekiyyôt* is to be connected with the Egyptian *śk.tj*, 'ship' (*K–B*, p. 921). The picture envisaged in vv. 12–17 is of a storm sweeping down from Lebanon, destroying the fortresses, trees and ships along the coastal plain, and extending into the very southernmost part of Judah.

17. the haughtiness of man: The sin of pride, and especially of an arrogant disregard of God (*hybris*), became in Isaiah the fullest illustration of man's attempts to live and control his life without regard for God. In prophecy more generally it appears prominently in prophecies against foreign nations (cf. espec. Isa. 14; Ezek. 27–28).

clinging to idols + boats?

18. And the idols: The glossator has added in v. 18 a rather prosaic and obvious note respecting the idols mentioned in v. 8. When Yahweh's judgment falls, idols will be of no avail to men.

19. the terror of the LORD: This further addition points to a rather literal interpretation of the call to flee from Yahweh's wrath made in v. 10. It appears to have in mind a military situation when the citizens of Judah had been forced to hide in caves from an attacking army.

again, Isaiah knew nothing of Day of flood?

20. In that day: Vv. 20–22 are an addition to the original prophecy, almost certainly made in the post-exilic age, to describe the effects of the Day of the LORD upon the life of men. It has a pronouncedly eschatological character, and awaits this final day of divine judgment, not upon Judah and Jerusalem only, but rather upon **men** in general. All those who have resorted to idols will be punished for this, and the final appearing of God (v. 21) now seems to be taken in the sense of a great theophany in which at last the full divine reality will be disclosed to all men.

it is a logical conclusion, tho.

22. Turn away from man contains a brief appeal to the reader not to let himself be impressed by men and all their achievements, but rather to heed the warning contained in the preceding prophecy that all man's works will eventually come to judgment. Man himself is a creature, dependent upon air to breathe, who must eventually succumb to death. In contrast to the eternal God he is of no account.

THE COMING ANARCHY

3:1–12

The message contained in this section is clear and unequivocal. Jerusalem and Judah are about to face a time of great deprivation and suffering, which will result in a state of anarchy. Famine will reign over the land, and there will be a loss of all responsible leadership, so that even the poorest will be elevated to the position of counsellors and leaders. The entire pronouncement is summed up effectively in v. 8: **Jerusalem has stumbled and Judah has fallen.** The picture overall is a vivid forecast of coming confusion and dismay, leading on to anarchy and chaos. The reason is made plain in v. 8: **their speech and their deeds are against Yahweh.** The picture of the internal decay of the nation and city presupposes the pressure from some external threat, and here we must certainly think of that posed by the

but present tense until v. 7

Assyrians after Ahaz had become their vassal. The leaders of the people had led the nation astray; by their arrogant confidence in their own policies and by seeking their own advantage alone, they had sold the people into ruin. The situation would be the same as that presupposed in 8 : 5–8. The leaders of Jerusalem have embarked upon a policy which will bring them and their city to destruction. The original prophecy is to be found in vv. 1–9*a*, and vv. 9*b*, 10–11 are later *No !* additions which develop the theme that God punishes the wicked but blesses the righteous. The aim of this expansion has been to <u>use the prophecy as a more general illustration of the working of divine retribution, and especially to show that there is hope for the righteous</u> (v. 10). The concluding note of lamentation draws from the threat contained in v. 4 and sees it as already fulfilled in his own day through the unworthy and unsuitable leaders who exercise control over the people. When such people have power, what hope can there be for the people who are dependent upon them?

1. For, behold, the LORD, the LORD of hosts: The introductory **for** is superfluous and must probably be regarded here as a connective which has been introduced editorially in order to link the prophecy with what precedes. Cf. above, on 2 : 12. The **stay and staff** are metaphors of the military and political rulers of Judah, described more fully in vv. 2–3. Hence the two lines which follow and interpret them differently: **the whole stay of bread, and the whole stay of water** must be an <u>editorial gloss</u> which has <u>come in in order to link the prophecy with a situation of famine brought about by siege.</u> In this case it is probable that the words have been introduced *post eventum* to connect the saying with the siege of Jerusalem in 587.

2. the mighty man and the soldier: The two classes of soldier are referred to again in conjunction in Ezek. 39 : 10; Jl 2 : 7; 4 : 9. The former were certainly professional troops, whereas in some, if not in all cases where the latter are mentioned, these were private citizens who were called upon for military service in time of war. Cf. R. de Vaux, *Ancient Israel*, London, 1961, pp. 218f. The **diviner** receives a very unexpected mention, and this may be related to the additional references to these which have been made in 2 : 6. Undoubtedly <u>diviners were regarded as an important adjunct to military campaigns and strategy in the ancient world, although their presence in any official capacity in ancient Judah appears unlikely in view of Dt. 18 : 9–14.</u> No doubt Isaiah was simply reflecting a widespread ancient practice in referring to such in Jerusalem, but that such figures operated in the city without public interference is highly likely. For **the captain of fifty** (v. 3) we may compare 2 Kg. 1 : 9, where he appears as a relatively junior military officer. The **man of rank** (Heb. literally 'uplifted of face') was a person who had some recognised status at the royal court such as Naaman (2 Kg. 5 : 1) at the Syrian court. For the role of the counsellor, cf. P. A. H. De Boer, *VT Supp. III*, Leiden, 1955, pp. 42–71. The **skilful magician** (Heb. *ḥārāš*; cf. Aramaic *ḥarsā*, 'magical art') was a person expert in various kinds of magical techniques. Here they must undoubtedly have been thought to be connected with obtaining oracles. The **expert in charms**, was a person skilled in incantations, and who was believed thereby to be able to cast spells on people and so undermine their strength and rational faculties. It is improbable that Isaiah had any clear intention of singling out different types of magical art. Rather he was concerned to assert that all the customary sources of guidance and advice would cease to be available to the people. They would fall into total confusion because of the lack of any kind of counsel upon which they could rely. His purpose was not to comment or reflect upon the capabilities of such people, but rather to insist that they would simply cease to be available, whatever people thought about their services.

4. And I will make boys: The prophet did not have in mind any special boy prince, but was pointing to the future time when there would be a total lack of competent leadership. In the situation envisaged by Isaiah the leaders and rulers of Judah had sealed their own fate by the policy of rebellion against Assyria which they had advocated. They would therefore be the first to suffer judgment, leaving the people leaderless, and sinking into anarchy.

maybe Ahaz?

6. When a man takes hold: Because there would not be any accepted and accredited leaders for the people, even a relatively trivial symbol of wealth such as a **mantle** would be sufficient cause for a person to be regarded as a leader. The prophet gives voice to an element of irony in drawing attention to the **heap of ruins** which Judah would become in the time of retribution, and also no doubt in ridiculing the depths of poverty to which the people would sink. It would become unusual for citizens to possess anything at all!

7. I will not be a healer: The word means literally 'one who binds up (wounds)', but is applied here metaphorically to the process of attempting to revitalise the ruined nation. This is preferable to connecting it with 'binding (a turban)'.

8. For Jerusalem has stumbled: The picture is of a man falling headlong on the road, and is used to describe what had already taken place so far as Jerusalem was concerned. By their actions the city's rulers had chosen the way to ruin and destruction. Evidently it was not the flamboyant way of life of the rulers, but the disastrous policies they had advocated which the prophet condemned. **defying his glorious presence:** The Hebrew is literally 'rebelling against the eyes (presence) of his glory', but the defectively written 'eyes' is certainly wrong. Either it is to be deleted altogether (so Kaiser), or more probably it is a scribal error for $p^e n\hat{e}$ (presence). The rulers had chosen a policy which the prophet regarded as in open defiance of God (cf. 8:12).

9. Their partiality witnesses: The error of the leaders is here ascribed to their corrupt manner of showing favouritism towards particular individuals. What exactly was being referred to is not clear, since the prophet's attack is certainly directed against something more than mere court favouritism. Rather we may conclude that forms of bribery and corruption had been employed to silence any opposing voices. The fact that the leaders had been compelled to resort to such behaviour was an open condemnation of their rottenness. **like Sodom** *Why?* is certainly a gloss by a scribe, who has no doubt been influenced by the comparison of Jerusalem with Sodom in 1:10.

Woe to them!. V. 9*b*, together with vv. 10-11, form an editorial comment, couched in the style of a Wisdom saying, and drawing general conclusions from the prophet's condemnation of Judah and its rulers. It reasserts the proverbial dictum that God rewards each person according to his deeds, the righteous with prosperity and the wicked with ruination. Its purpose here is not simply to establish a general application, but more specifically to show that those who had suffered in Jerusalem had deserved their fate. Since it was not the divine will to destroy the righteous with the wicked (cf. Gen. 18:23), there must be hope for Jerusalem and its inhabitants if they pursued righteousness.

12. My people—children are their oppressors: *NEB* has 'money-lenders strip my people bare, and usurers lord it over them'; cf. G. R. Driver, *JTS* 38 (1937), p. 38. Instead of **women** (Heb. *nāšîm*), we should read 'usurers', as attested by LXX and Targ. The verse has been introduced as an expression of lament that the threat expressed in v. 5 has been realised in the oppressive leadership inflicted on the people.

FURTHER CONDEMNATION OF THE RULERS OF JERUSALEM

3:13-15

The theme of misgovernment is here taken up afresh in a further piece of invective addressed to the elders and officials of Judah. It is their misdeeds which have made necessary the punishment which will shortly come. As in the case of 1:2-3 and 18-20, the language and formal structure have been borrowed from the speech-forms of civil lawsuits. The borrowing is quite direct, and does not suggest any mediation through a cultic lawsuit, or a knowledge of the conventions of international treaties (see above on 1:18-20). The point of the prophet's attack is that the elders and princes oppress the poor, apparently by forms of extortion and abuse of the laws of debt (v. 14). Cf. W. Dietrich, pp. 44, 49f. Hence the point of the prophet's condemnation is different from that in vv. 1-11, where it is the policies adopted in international relations which appear to be uppermost in the prophet's mind. Nevertheless it is probable that the prophecy comes from a similar period in Isaiah's ministry, although this cannot be closely determined. Both in the reign of Ahaz, especially in the aftermath of the Syro-Ephraimite war, and again during the latter part of Hezekiah's reign, Isaiah had much cause to condemn the attitude and policies of the leaders of Jerusalem, and to warn them of the dire judgment that they were heaping upon themselves. No serious reason exists for doubting its origin from Isaiah.

13. The LORD has taken his place to contend: The imagery of a lawsuit (Heb. *rîb*; cf. B. Gemser, *VT Supp. III*, pp. 120-37), is consistently maintained throughout vv. 13-15. The picture is of God standing up to present his charge against the elders and officials of Judah. **to contend** could be better translated as 'to present his case (against)'. **to judge his people:** MT has 'peoples', but *RSV* is correct in following LXX and reading the singular with suffix. F. Hesse, *ZAW* 65 (1953), p. 48, defends the reading of the plural on the grounds that the prophet was assuming the role of a cult-prophet addressing non-Israelite nations, but this does not fit the context, which is explicitly directed against the rulers of Judah.

14. with the elders and princes: The ruling classes are assumed by Isaiah to bear responsibility for the behaviour of the people as a whole. More particularly, however, they are guilty because they have oppressed those for whom they should have been concerned, and to whom they should have shown charity. **devoured the vineyard:** The metaphor of Israel as a vineyard is developed more extensively in 5 : 1–7. A wild animal let loose in a vineyard could obviously wreak great havoc. The meaning of the verb translated 'devoured' (Heb. *biʿēr*; K–B, p. 140, suggest 'to burn up') is not entirely clear, but the context requires the sense approximating to 'lay waste, destroy'.

15. What do you mean: This is the rendering in accordance with the *Qᵉrē'* reading of MT. The title **the Lord GOD of hosts** appears to be unnaturally long, and many commentators would delete the name **Lord** as a secondary addition. The entire clause is lacking in LXX.

JUDGMENT UPON THE PROUD WOMEN OF JERUSALEM

3 : 16–24

The theme of coming judgment on Jerusalem, and especially upon its wealthier upper classes, is carried further here with an indictment (v. 16) and threat (vv. 17, 24) directed against the wealthy and proud women of the city. Into this a later hand has inserted in vv. 18–23 a lengthy catalogue of the clothing and adornments worn by such women. This addition is of uncertain date and origin, and has occasioned much discussion on account of the difficulty of identifying the separate items of finery. The original prophecy belongs undoubtedly to Isaiah, and fits alongside other sayings condemning the ruling classes of Jerusalem (cf. Dietrich, pp. 255f.). Its precise time of origin cannot be identified, but the period of 733 to 727 would appear to be most appropriate.

16. the daughters of Zion. The title evidently refers to the wealthier women of Jerusalem (cf. also 4 : 4; Ca. 3 : 11), and may have been chosen because Zion was the area of the city on which the royal palace stood, and where most probably other pretentious houses could be found. The opulence of these elicited the prophet's scorn, and marks a point of similarity with the preaching of Amos (Am. 4 : 1–3; cf. R. Fey, *Amos und Jesaja*, p. 79). The flamboyant behaviour of the women attracted the prophet's attention and indignation, when contrasted with the abject poverty that existed in the city (vv. 14f.). The reference to such people scarcely warrants the deduction of itself that

Isaiah himself belonged to the upper section of the Jerusalem population, although this may have been the case. **glancing wantonly**
(Heb. $m^e\acute{s}aqq^e r\^ot$) appears to imply that the women made seductive
gestures to passing men. More probably the verb means 'painted,
made up' (cf. Arab. *šaqira*). **mincing along** indicates walking with
short steps like a child (on account of their style of dress?), and the
tinkling sound was made by wearing metal bands around their ankles,
all intended further to attract masculine attention. *so why not seductive gestures?*

17. the Lord will smite with a scab reveals how the prophet
matches his threat of coming punishment to fit the particular form of
vanity and self-aggrandisement displayed by the women of Jerusalem.
When God punishes them they will lose all their finery, and will
instead suffer the humiliations of rape, dirt and disease. The cause of
this suffering is not mentioned, but the prophet was clearly implying
that the women would be taken as prisoners of war, as in the comparable threat in Am. 4:2–3. This making of the punishment fit the
offence is not to be traced to any fixed doctrine of an inner principle of
retribution at work in the world, but rather to a poetic sense of justice.
Cf. F. Horst, *Gottes Recht (TB* 12) Munich, 1961, pp. 235–59; *THAT*,
II, cols. 507–30. Instead of **will lay bare their secret parts**, G. R.
Driver, *JTS* 38 (1937), p. 38, suggests 'will shave their foreheads'
(Akk. *putu(m)* 'forehead').

18. In that day marks the typical connecting phrase of an editor,
who here elaborates on the various items of women's clothing and
adornment that will be lost. The purpose of the addition would appear
to be to mark out certain items of feminine dress and make-up as
contrary to the true divine order. Their wrongfulness would appear to
have been found in their being luxuries, and consequently symbols of
disregard for the poor. They were certainly not all worn at the same
time, and their precise identification is, in several instances, dis-
puted. For the various items, cf. *IDB*, I, p. 871. The **headbands** and
the **crescents** were very similar items of dress, the former being
plaited, or woven out of wool, and the latter beaten from metal. It is
quite probable that some of the items mentioned were associated with
magic, and so represented an element of charm-symbolism. However, this does not appear to have been the redactor's main point
of objection. This was certainly in the element of love of luxury
which they displayed. Trust in human beauty could signify a lack of
regard for God.

19. scarfs: *NEB* 'coronets'.

20. the sashes: *NEB* 'necklaces'; **the perfume boxes.** *NEB*
'lockets' (Heb. *bāttē hannepeš*, literally 'houses of the person'.)

22. and the handbags: *NEB* 'flounced skirts'.

24. Instead of perfume: This verse represents the original continuation of v. 17 and elaborates upon the theme of the coming
degradation to be experienced by the women of Jerusalem when
disaster overtakes their city. Continuing with a pattern of threat based
on a poetic sense of justice, Isaiah establishes a vivid contrast between
their present confidence and beauty and the coming shame and

wretchedness. **instead of well-set hair:** The Syriac has a slightly briefer text, but the sense is clear. **instead of beauty, shame:** The rendering of the *NEB*, 'and branding instead of beauty', is almost certainly more original. The clause is missing altogether in LXX and Vulg.

THE FATE OF THE WOMEN

3:25–4:1

The theme of the coming punishment of Jerusalem is now continued by the inclusion of a threat to Zion in the form of an elegy. The city is portrayed as a woman who is about to suffer the death of her husband, and the agony and shame of her forthcoming widowhood is vividly described. The passage must certainly be regarded as separate from what precedes it, although it has a connection through the basic similarity of subject matter. Its authentic Isaianic origin has not gone uncontested, and such a brief unit suggests that it may have been preserved in only a fragmentary way. It expresses more categorically than many comparable passages that the coming divine judgment on Jerusalem will be accomplished by the defeat of the city in battle (v. 25).

25. Your men: The transition into direct second-person address to the city is striking. It marks the beginning of a new unit, although the use of the third person, **her gates,** of Jerusalem in the following verse suggests that the use of the second-person form in v. 25 is the work of a redactor who has established a connection with the invective that precedes in vv. 16–24. The explicitness of the threat of the downfall of Jerusalem in a battle most probably belongs to the period 733–725, if the saying is authentic. More probably, however, a redactor has inserted such a dire pronouncement here in order to make clear how the punishment alluded to poetically in vv. 16–24 was to be accomplished.

26. And her gates takes up the image of 'the daughter of Jerusalem', picturing the city as a young woman, whose husband has been killed in battle.

4:1 And seven women shall take hold: The metaphorical imagery is now abandoned, and the real fate of the women of Jerusalem who will see their husbands killed is described. The slaughter in battle will be such that few men will survive, so that large numbers of women will be left childless, and without husbands. In order to remove the social stigma attaching to childlessness they will waive aside all the usual expectations and responsibilities demanded of a husband in marriage. All they will ask is that a man should be willing to father children for them. By such a portrayal of human misery the condemnation of the women of Jerusalem, which began with Isaiah's threat in vv. 16–17, 24 is brought to a close. The coming fate of Jerusalem is made unmistakably plain.

THE REMNANT IN JERUSALEM

4:2-6

The portrayal in these verses of a purged and purified remnant of the
population of Jerusalem enjoying the special protection of God stands
in marked contrast to all that has come before it in 2:6–4:1. Virtually
all modern commentators (Fohrer, Kaiser, Wildberger, Schoors,
Eichrodt) have argued that these verses do not come from Isaiah, and
this verdict must unquestionably be upheld. They are a later post-exilic
addition which has been introduced by a late redactor of the book in
order to show that the threat to Jerusalem had passed. The reason for
such an addition is scarcely to be ascribed purely to liturgical needs
(so Wildberger), but belongs to the wider process of establishing an
ongoing and lasting meaning to prophecy. The aim here has certainly
been to show that Jerusalem had been justly threatened with punishment by God, but that this punishment had befallen the city in its
tragic history from 587 and after, and that the time of this punishment
would shortly be complete. The opening phrase **in that day**, therefore, points forward to a coming dawn of salvation for Jerusalem, after
which it would be the object of a special protective providence. Such a
hope is properly eschatological and took its roots in an understanding
of Yahweh's purpose for Israel, rather than in a reading of the possibilities inherent in the contemporary political scene. God would
break into human affairs to glorify Jerusalem, and this action would
herald the dawning of the 'end-time', an age when a permanent state
of blessedness for Israel and Jerusalem could be expected (vv. 5–6).

There is a break in the rhythm after v. 2, and Wildberger (I, p. 153)
is undoubtedly right in seeing that the original addition was made in
v. 2 only, and that this has subsequently been expanded upon in vv.
3–6. The simple affirmation of a happy and blessed future for Israel
was felt to require fuller amplification. Hence v. 3 comments upon the
salvation of those who will form a remnant in Jerusalem, and v. 4 has
taken up the theme of the fate of the women of Jerusalem, by affirming that they, too, will be purged from all their guilty stains.

The date of these additions is impossible to determine with any
certainty. Wildberger thinks of the late Persian period, whilst Kaiser
comments (*Isaiah 1–12*, p. 54), 'A date even as late as the third or early
second century BC is not excluded.' It remains doubtful, however, in
spite of claims to the contrary by many scholars (especially Duhm,
Kaiser) whether any material later than the close of third century is to
be found in the book of Isaiah. The indications are that the book had
assumed very much its present form by the end of the third century.
The expression of such a firm and thoroughgoing eschatological
hope, with its picture of lasting salvation for Israel beginning in the
near future, marks an important element in the transition from
prophecy proper to apocalyptic. The effect of such additions as are to
be found here is to lift the relevance and applicability of the prophet's
message from the sphere of concrete history into a more supernatural
and supra-historical realm. It may appropriately be called 'proto-

apocalyptic', and it is in accord with this type of literature that it makes heavy use of evocative, but undefined imagery. Cf. 'spirit of burning', 'cloud by day . . . fire by night', 'a canopy and a pavilion'. Poetic metaphor has been extended to become a new kind of symbolism.

but Branch is a name later, so why discard?

2. **In that day the branch of the LORD** is a reference to the wonderful growth which Yahweh will cause to spring up in the age of salvation, as is shown by the parallel expression **fruit of the land**. We can discount the interpretation to be found in the Targum therefore that it is a reference to the Messiah, the coming 'branch of David' (cf. Jer. 23:5; 33:15; Zech. 3:8). The purpose of the addition, which must certainly have originated in the Persian period, is to pick up the theme of the fate of the survivors of Israel and Jerusalem as adumbrated by the 'remnant' passages of 10:20-23 (see below) and 1:9. There will be a rich and fertile land, yielding plentiful crops, for those who form the Remnant of Israel (cf. 37:30).

suggestion of only ten left consistent w/verses preceding

3. **And he who is left in Zion** elaborates upon the preceding promise with special reference to the survivors of Jerusalem (cf. 1:9), who formed the kernel of the struggling Jewish community which re-established a vigorous religious life in the city during the Persian period. The reference to those who have survived as those whose names were **recorded for life** in a book initiated an important theme which re-appeared in later apocalyptic literature (cf. Rev. 5:1ff.). The origin of the metaphor is not entirely clear. Either the practice of keeping a register of citizens for purposes of civil administration, which appears to have flourished under Persian rule, or a more indirect reference to the Babylonian concept of 'tablets of destiny' are possible sources of its origin. The verse fills out the picture of the future of the inhabitants of Jerusalem given in 1:26, and adds to it a more lasting sense.

continuity of thought so why a author?

4. **when the LORD shall have washed** picks up a concern with the fate of the women of Jerusalem, since the threat of 3:16ff. related to them. It follows the previous verse in giving a more enduring and ultimate sense to the imagery of purification and removal of guilt found in 1:16. Furthermore the pictures of a purging and cleansing by burning hint strongly in the direction of a further interpretation of 1:25, 31. **by a spirit of judgment**. The Heb. word translated **spirit** (*rûʿaḥ*) also connotes 'wind' and this would appear to be a better rendering here. A hot, searing, wind will purge away all that stains and continues to defile the **daughters of Zion**. The idea seems to be introduced here that, before the final era of salvation can come, there must be a final, and painful, purging.

5. **Then the LORD will create:** The LXX supports a reading 'Then he will come and stand' (Heb. *ûḇāʾ wᵉhāyāh*), which is preferable to MT. The divine protection of Jerusalem in the time when her full salvation will have been achieved is described by the use of traditions drawn from Israel's earliest history. The presence of a pillar of cloud, seen blazing with fire at night, had signified Yahweh's accompanying presence at the time when the nation's ancestors came out of Egypt

(Exod. 14:19, 24, etc.). It is here promised that this accompanying presence of God will again appear in the future, no longer to move about with the people, but to be a permanent symbol of his watch over Jerusalem. It is evident that this divine presence is regarded as an exceptional phenomenon of the past, which was expected to appear again in the coming age of salvation. **for over all the glory** reflects the language of the post-exilic age in which the glory of God has been developed into a carefully considered theological expression of the way in which the divine presence could move among men. Cf. *THAT*, I, cols. 798ff. The reference to **a canopy and a pavilion** which are to give shelter from the heat of the sun and from the rainstorm adds a very prosaic final note to this richly described picture of the coming salvation. The promise of such protection must be understood literally, rather than as an assurance of protection from more fearsome dangers. The underlying idea is that the very conditions of daily life will be changed in the Jerusalem of the New Age.

THE SONG OF THE VINEYARD

5:1–7

Before examining in detail the important Song of the Vineyard in 5:1–7, it is important to note the significant new redactional unit which begins with 5:1 and extends as far as 14:27. This has subsequently been substantially expanded by the insertion of further prophecies, especially in 11:1–14:23 (but see below, p. 139, for the possibility that 14:4b–21* once stood within the original unit). The theme of this redactional unit is clear, for it is the advent of Assyria, whose coming is foretold in 5:26–30, and whose final overthrow in the land of Israel is then promised in 14:24–27. Assyria represents a threat to both Israel and Judah (and also Syria), and the message that heralds the devastation which they were to bring upon the land is marked by the refrain 'For all this his anger is not turned away, and his hand is stretched out still' (5:25; 9:12, 17, 21; 10:4). This originally formed the refrain of one prophecy, but has been extended to cover the larger unit (see on 5:25). The centrepiece of this redactional unit of 5:1–14:27* is made up of the prophet's own memoir from the Syro-Ephraimite war in 6:1–8:18*. This fills out the picture of the circumstances which occasioned the coming of the Assyrians, and explains why their advent became a threat to Judah (8:8). We can then see the following main structure in the original redactional unit of 5:1–14:27:

1. Indictment of all Israel as Yahweh's vineyard (5:1–7), and of the leaders of Jerusalem in particular (5:8–23 + 10:1–4).
2. The Isaiah memoir (6:1–8:18*), showing why the threat from Assyria became a special threat to Jerusalem and the Davidic dynasty.
3. The possibility of new hope with the accession of a new Davidic ruler after the death of Ahaz (9:1–7).

4. The indictment of Assyria and the forewarning of its ultimate overthrow (10:5–15*).

5. The manner and certainty of the downfall of Assyria (10:16–34*;
[14:4b–21*]; 14:24–27).

There would appear to be good reasons for recognising in 5:1ff. the
original beginning of the Josianic Redaction of the collection of
Isaiah's prophecies, and for regarding the threats of 2:6–4:1 as having
been prefaced to this Josianic collection later (see above on 2:1ff.).

If the picture we have presented of the redactional setting of the
Song of the Vineyard of 5:1–7 is upheld, then its theme and significance is correspondingly increased. J. Vermeylen, I, p. 168, is almost
alone in denying its authenticity to Isaiah, seeing in it rather a
Deuteronomistic composition of the exilic age. Yet this is an unnecessary and rather radical conclusion to draw from its obvious
redactional position. Even so, its prophetic form is not entirely clear
and has occasioned considerable discussion (cf. W. Schottroff, *ZAW*
82 (1970), pp. 68–99; J. T. Willis, *JBL* 96 (1977), pp. 337–62; J. W.
Whedbee, *Isaiah and Wisdom*, pp. 43–51). The climactic disclosure in
v. 7 that the vineyard that has been described in the song represents
Israel, and its disappointed owner is Yahweh, the God of Israel,
shows that we are basically dealing with an allegory or parable (Heb.
māšāl; so Schottroff, Willis, Whedbee). Yet this overall form is not
the major difficulty, which is rather to be found in the opening speech
of v. 1, **Let me sing for my beloved** (Heb. *yādîd*), and the description
of the composition as a 'love song' (Heb. *šîrat dôdî*). Fohrer has
argued that the speaker is the bride, or young lover, who is speaking
about her husband-lover. Yet this cannot be carried through consistently in the interpretation, and in fact renders the role of the
speaker of little significance. In vv. 3f. it is the 'beloved' who speaks.
Willis argues that the characterisation as a love song is in reality an
erroneous interpretation of the phrase *šîrat dôdî* used in v. 1. The
assumption that the noun *dôd* is always used of love between the
sexes is contested by him, and he advocates rather the view that it
simply means 'friendship'. Hence there is no allusion to sexual love
in the poem at all, and the attempt to find this in the imagery of the
'vineyard' is, he argues, mistaken. It is, therefore, on Willis's reckoning, simply a parabolic 'song of friendship' by the prophet about the
experience of his 'friend', who is then revealed in v. 7 as no less a
figure than Yahweh, the God of Israel. Yet this results in a somewhat
inadequate interpretation of the allegorical features of the song which
does appear to intend a skilful *double entendre* on the application of
the metaphorical use of 'vineyard'. 'Friendly song', or 'song of friendship' would appear to be too weak an understanding of the phrase
šîrat dôdî in v. 1. When this is taken in conjunction with the most
probable allusion intended by the reference to the 'vineyard' as a
popular metaphor for a 'bride, lover', we may conclude that the introduction as a 'love song' is an intrinsic part of the prophetic form.
Essentially this is that of a parable, with a number of allegorical
features, but the aim has been to disguise the meaning of the allegory

by hinting at its application to a husband who has been deceived over his lover and bride. The singer of the song then, who appears as the 'me' of v. 1, is assuming the role of 'the friend of the bridegroom' (best man), who is pleading his friend's case (so H. Wildberger, and cf. also A. Bentzen, *AFO* 4 (1927), pp. 209f.).

We may conclude that reference to the parable (Heb. *māšāl*) as a 'love song' is an intrinsic element of its parabolic form. The closest comparable biblical example of this parable form is to be found in 2 Sam. 12:1–10, the story of the poor man with a ewe lamb, which is employed by Nathan in order to induce king David to pass sentence on himself. Here we have a skilfully constructed artistic tale which has been designed to elicit, first the 'gossipy' interest of the hearers; then their sympathy, and finally their verdict on the 'villain' of the song. In doing so they are led into condemning themselves for their behaviour. It shares much in common with other forms of skilful, or artistic, story-telling, such as the fable and riddle, popular with raconteurs and sages of many nations (cf. Jg. 14:10–18; 2 Sam. 14:1–20). Undoubtedly such types of instruction were part of the repertoire of the teachers of 'Wisdom' in Israel, but there is no need to suppose, with J. W. Whedbee, *Isaiah and Wisdom*, pp. 43–51, that this type of didactic tale was a special prerogative of a separate class of Wisdom teachers, from whence Isaiah may be assumed to have adopted it. Rather it appears to have been a sophisticated and artistic form of speech, such as might be adopted by a skilled public speaker in a number of different situations. In part it had links with types of entertaining story-telling, yet also with the far more serious concern of legal indictment. Its use here is to establish the reason why judgment was appropriate for Yahweh's people, and to show that their behaviour was tantamount to a total failure to live up to the demands of their privileged position. The song therefore is a sophisticated form of legal indictment, which both pronounces sentence upon the wrongdoers (vv. 5–6), and combines this with a parabolic 'motive', or 'reason', for such a judgment. Disaster is about to overtake those whom the prophet is addressing, and they are invited to see that this is an earned and merited punishment from God for their lack of response to him.

The question arises of identifying the situation when such a prophecy was made by Isaiah. Wildberger locates it early in Isaiah's ministry, but largely on account of its placing early in the book. Of itself this is an inadequate criterion for such a dating, since it is possible that some of the threats contained in chs. 2:6–5:30 are from a late period. He further cites Duhm's comment that Isaiah would have been too well known in his later years for such a song-form to have retained any value as a clever ruse. Yet in reality the evidence of date is hard to establish, and largely hinges on the identity of the 'vineyard' disclosed in v. 7. This sets a striking parallelism between the 'house of Israel' and the 'men of Judah'. If the name 'Israel' were to be understood as a reference to the Northern Kingdom, which Isaiah preferred to describe as 'Ephraim' (cf. 7:2), it would point to a time before the fall of the Northern Kingdom in 722. Yet clearly Isaiah uses 'Israel' primarily in a religious sense for the heirs of the old Davidic-Solomonic empire, so that it would not have been out of place for him to use it in reference to Judah. We could, therefore, be dealing here with yet another instance of Isaiah's utterance of a threat against Judah in Hezekiah's reign. It is more plausible and attractive, however, to see in the parallelism of the names 'house of Israel' and 'men of Judah' Isaiah's recognition of the oneness of Yahweh's people whom he was addressing. In this case we must refer the threat to both kingdoms and see in it his warning that the coming threat would engulf both of them. In this case the prophecy can be located very convincingly in the period between 733 and 722, when Samaria fell. Ahaz, by his appeal to Assyria for protection at the time of the Syro-Ephraimite war, had invited a power which would prove disastrous, not only for Ephraim (Israel), as Ahaz sought, but Judah also (cf. below on 8 : 5–8). The original scope of the threat contained in Isaiah's Song of the Vineyard, therefore, extended to both kingdoms of Israel, Ephraim and Judah.

The song falls clearly into three parts, after the brief introduction in v. 1a: (i) vv. 1b–2 contain the story of the vineyard; (ii) vv. 3–4 an appeal to the hearers for a verdict on what should be done; (iii) vv. 5–6 a declaration of the verdict; (iv) v. 7 the interpretation of the parable by the disclosure that the vineyard represents Israel-Judah, and that the fruit that was looked for, consisted of justice and righteousness.

5 : 1. Let me sing for my beloved: The word **beloved** could be better translated 'friend' (Heb. *yādîd*) and would imply that the singer of the song is not the young man's 'lover-bride' (as Fohrer), but rather his close friend who could be expected both to mediate for him in any lover's quarrel and to make public representation on his behalf. The description of the poem as a 'love song' must then be understood as 'a song concerning love', rather than as one from a lover addressed to her beloved. **concerning his vineyard** must intend a conscious allusion to the metaphor of the bride-lover as a **vineyard** (cf. Ca. 2 : 15; 4 : 16; 8 : 11). That the song was composed for delivery at a vintage festival, when such love songs would have been expected, is possible, but rather overpresses the significance of the poetic form. For the methods of viticulture in Israel and Canaan, cf. *BHH*, III, cols. 2150f.

2. but it yielded wild grapes: It is better to read 'bad grapes', for the implication is clearly not that the vines proved to be of the wrong species, for which the owner would have been responsible, but that the grapes, when they appeared, were of a very poor quality. *GNB* translates 'but every grape was sour'.

3. And now, O inhabitants: Those who are addressed by the poem are evidently in Jerusalem, and are called upon to provide a verdict concerning what the owner should do with the vineyard. At this point the parable reveals something of its legal character as the pressing of a charge against the 'vineyard'. A similar legal affinity is also to be found in the closely related parable of Nathan (2 Sam. 12 : 1ff.). If allegorical innuendo concerning the lover who has been betrayed by his beloved is correct, then the implication at this point is that some expression of public wrath and indignation against the young woman's betrayal is called for. Cf. Ca. 8 : 8–9. It belongs to the essence of the poetic parable form that the hearers are led to make up their minds about the verdict that the story demands before they are told about the identity of the persons involved.

4. What more was there to do: The owner of the vineyard establishes the point of culpability by re-affirming that he undertook all proper care of the vines. The fault in the quality of the grapes that were produced must therefore lie elsewhere.

5. what I will do to my vineyard: The framework of the parable begins to be stretched here by the necessity for including a declaration of the way in which the uselessness of the vineyard is to be publicly demonstrated. In doing so a number of allegorical features are woven into the parable (cf. a similar stretching of the parable (*māšāl*) form in Ezek. 16 : 1–43). The owner will himself set about laying waste the cultivated soil in which the vines are growing, and will return it to its original wild state. By such a threat Isaiah intends a hint at the physical devastation which will shortly come upon the land of his hearers. At this point the parable assumes an explicitly prophetic character by making this pronouncement of coming judgment.

6. I will make it a waste: Cf. G. R. Driver, *JTS* 38 (1937), p. 38, who relates Heb. *bātāh* to the Akk. *batū*, 'to reduce to ruins'. **and briers and thorns:** Cf. the development of the prophecy and its application to later events in 7 : 23–25, etc. **I will also command the clouds** introduces into the story a further reflection of the knowledge that the 'owner' of the vineyard who speaks in vv. 5–6 is in fact none other than God himself. The purpose of such a command is evidently to make unmistakably plain that the fate of the vineyard is a final one, and that it will not, in the future, be given a second chance to show that it could be fruitful and productive. Such a command on the part of the owner is tanatamount to a curse.

It was this note of finality in the judgment that is pronounced by the song that has made it a subject of a significant further development in the 'new song of the vineyard' in 27 : 2–6 (see below pp. 218ff.).

7. For the vineyard of the LORD of hosts: The prophet now reveals how he intends the parable to be understood. It refers to the relationship between Yahweh and Israel. There is no hint here, or elsewhere, in Isaiah's preaching that the prophet defined this relationship in terms of a covenant. Nevertheless the assumption made by the prophet is clearly that Israel-Judah had enjoyed a unique privilege under the care and protection of Yahweh, but that they have not produced a way of life commensurate with the privileges which this divine care has bestowed. In particular it is the lack of righteousness and justice in the social order which contradicts the purpose of Yahweh's providential concern. H. Wildberger argues that **house of Israel** and **men of Judah** must be understood in parallel to each other, and not in contrast. Cf. Introduction, p. 16. In this case the title 'Israel' would have to be understood in a religious-historical sense, and be a title adopted by Judah. However, we have argued above that the two titles can be best interpreted as complementary so that Isaiah was here affirming that both 'houses' of Israel and Judah had proved a failure in Yahweh's purpose. This would have been of special relevance in Ahaz's time, since his policy was directed at saving his own kingdom Judah at the expense of the Northern Kingdom Ephraim.

and he looked for justice: For the prominent element of social criticism in the preaching of Isaiah, cf. especially W. Dietrich, pp. 37ff.

DOOM UPON THE LEADERS OF JERUSALEM
10 : 1–4a; 5 : 8–24

That a connection exists between 10:1–4a and 5:8–24 has been widely recognised by scholars since the work of B. Duhm. We are presented here with a series of seven 'woes' pronounced by the prophet against the leaders and rulers in Jerusalem, which bears close comparison with similar prophetic threats in 2:6–22 and 3:1–12. The reason for the separation of vv. 1–4a of ch. 10 from the main bulk of the woes in 5:8–24 has been variously explained. We have every reason to conclude that they originally formed part of a single connected series, so that Duhm, followed by Giesebrecht, Marti, Gray and others, has argued for a measure of fragmentation, and scattering, in the way in which the separate collections of prophecies have been preserved. However, the redaction-critical approach of H. Barth, pp. 110–17, is certainly more correct in seeing that the dislocation has arisen as a result of the lifting out and relocation of 5:8–24 from their original position. The threat pronounced by Isaiah against the ruling classes in Jerusalem has been given a new prominence, and thereby a new relevance, by setting it, along with other threats to Jerusalem, before the account of the prophet's call in 6:1ff. This has then resulted in the placing of 5:25–29 in its present position, detached from its original connection with 9:8ff. (Heb. 9:7ff.). For this rearrangement of the prophecies, see further below on 5:25ff.

The form of the woe-saying was a very important one for prophecy, and already appears in Amos (Am. 5:18ff; 6:1ff.). It establishes a further possible point of connection between Amos and Isaiah (though cf. J. W. Whedbee, *Isaiah and Wisdom*, pp. 8off.); but we must reckon that such woe-sayings were already an established prophetic speech-form before the time of either prophet. It was undoubtedly used much more widely than with these prophets, and is probably to be explained as an adaptation from an ancient form of curse. However, E. Gerstenberger, *JBL* 81 (1962) pp. 249–63, has argued for its origin in forms of admonition used in early folk-wisdom, whereas W. Janzen, *Mourning-Cry and Woe Oracle*, pp. 81ff., has sought to link it more directly with cries of lamentation for the dead, through the utterances of threats for those held responsible

for causing the death. This appears very improbable, and its derivation from an ancient form of curse appears more likely. Within Old
Testament times it had undoubtedly established itself as a genuinely
prophetic form of threat. It is an affirmation that doom (woe) is
coming upon the wrongdoers, not an appeal to God that it may come.

The origin from Isaiah of the series of woes is not to be doubted,
and its threat to the rulers of Jerusalem indicate that we should link it,
either with the prophet's condemnation of Ahaz and his policy in the
period 733-727, or with the condemnation of Hezekiah in 705-701. It
would appear that the former is the more probable. However, as the
redactional repositioning indicates, the threat to Jerusalem was
clearly felt to have taken on a new relevance and vitality during a later
period, which we can confidently relate to the Babylonian threat in the
early sixth century.

There is a recognition by several scholars (cf. Barth, p. 111), that the
original order of the woes was 10:1-4a + 5:8-24. It becomes clear,
both from the subject matter and from the disturbance of the
regularity of the form, that vv. 14-17 are a later addition. When these
verses were inserted into the original series of woes is not entirely
clear. They declare that the destruction of Jerusalem, when it comes,
will be a devouring of the city by the underworld Sheol. They would
appear to emanate from soon after 587, and serve to confirm the view
expressed above that the threat to Jerusalem voiced by Isaiah was felt
to have received a terrible fulfilment in the year 587 when the city was
destroyed by the Babylonians after a prolonged siege.

10:1 Woe to those who decree iniquitous decrees: The **decrees**
(Heb. $ḥōq$) were evidently rulings passed, or determined, by a legis-
lative body formed from the upper classes of Jerusalem (cf. *THAT*, I,
cols. 626-33). Almost certainly such a body was associated with the
royal court, and probably conducted its affairs in the name of the king.
The effect of their rulings was to deprive the poor and destitute
elements of the population of their right. The indications, therefore,
are that such **decrees** were not simply legal verdicts in criminal cases,
but referred to civil disputes involving claims to land and property.
Recovery of debt also must be assumed to have fallen within their
purview. The fact that these officials issued **iniquitous decrees** shows
that what they were doing was not illegal in the proper sense, but
immoral in its effect. The rulings that they determined were wrong,
because they effectively deprived the poor and weak citizen of his
rights. The simplest explanation of this state of affairs would appear
to be that possession of property was a condition of active member-
ship of the legal assembly. The poorer, non-landowning, elements of
the population were then unable to have their cases fairly represented.
and the writers must refer to the issuing of bills dealing with trading
transactions and the transfer of property (see below on 5:8) which
worked consistently to the detriment of the poorer citizens.

2. to turn aside the needy from justice: is of interest for its relevance to the development of Israelite ethics. It frankly recognises
that the 'decrees' which were enforced were unjust, and deprived

people of justice, although they were in the strictest sense 'legal'. The
law itself could become unjust. **that widows may be their spoil**
reflects the widespread awareness in the Old Testament, and in the
ancient Near East more generally, that widows were particularly
vulnerable to exploitation. Without property and without husbands,
they had no voice to maintain their claims in the legal assembly.

3. What will you do on the day: The rhetorical question makes it
unambiguously plain that punishment will come, but the form that it
will take is not spelt out. However, **the storm which will come from
afar** must certainly be a reference to the threat of an invading army
from Assyria (as in 5 : 25–29), which is portrayed as the sudden coming
of a rainstorm (cf. 2 : 12ff.). There is little reason to doubt that, at the
time the prophecy was given, Isaiah already possessed a clear expectation of how his threats would most probably be realised. **where will
you leave your wealth** indicates that the wealthy oppressors not only
had most to lose in time of war, but were most likely to be singled out
for punishment as the responsible leaders of Judah and Jerusalem.

4. Nothing remains but to crouch: The threat abandons the metaphor of the coming storm and accepts explicitly that the punishment
will take the form of defeat in war. Hence the most that these rich
miscreants could hope for would be to lose everything, but save
their own skins, by allowing themselves to be taken as prisoners.
From this they would then undoubtedly have been transported to be
sold as slaves (cf. Am. 7–17).

For all this his anger is not turned away repeats the refrain found in
9 : 12, 17, 21, where it is properly in order at the close of each strophe
of the prophecy of 9 : 8ff. It was certainly not an original part of the
section 10 : 1–4a, but has been inserted by a redactor after the original
continuation of 10 : 4 in 5 : 8ff. had been transposed. By repeating the
refrain here an editor sought to link the four verses which had thereby
become isolated to the larger composition which preceded it. However, the subject matter makes it plain that this connection was not
original.

5 : 8 Woe to those who join house to house continues the warning
of coming judgment upon the leading citizens of Jerusalem with the
second of the 'woe'-sayings. We must take this to be an element of
invective, giving voice to a sharp expression of prophetic disapproval
of their behaviour (much stronger than *NEB*'s rendering, 'Shame on
you!', might suggest). The joining together of houses and fields
evidently refers to the formation of large cultivated estates by absorb-
ing neighbouring property. The means by which this was done can
only be guessed at, but analogies would suggest that it was achieved
by the taking over of common land and by the buying up of neighbouring properties. This process could well have been facilitated by
the manipulation of the processes of law already condemned in 10 : 1.
Cf. A. Alt, *Kleine Schriften*, III, Munich, 1959, pp. 373ff. and the
closely related passage in Mic. 2 : 1–5. As a consequence of such
activities a very powerful class of rich landowners had grown up in
Jerusalem, which not only contrasted with the abject poverty of other

citizens, but had actually been the cause of dispossessing these latter of their properties and legal rights.

9. **The LORD of hosts has sworn in my hearing:** The formula is very interesting and points to the prophet as one who has been privileged to stand in the divine council (Heb. *sôḏ*; cf. *THAT*, II, 144–8; H.-P. Müller, *ZNW* 54 (1963), pp. 254–67) and has been able to overhear the conversations and plans determined by Yahweh. Almost certainly it must be regarded as a distinctive part of the prophet's linguistic armoury for asserting his claim to be able to disclose the intentions of God, rather than as an indication of a psychological experience of an audition—the hearing of a divine voice. Unfortunately the whole area of psychological experience which underlies the prophet's claim to have received his messages directly from God lies largely hidden to us. Only rarely do we have clear distinctions made to isolate visions from other forms of receiving the word of God. The Heb. MT lacks the verb **has sworn**, but undoubtedly as a result of a deliberate ellipse. Cf. 22:14.

The content of the oath, **Surely many houses shall be desolate**, makes the punishment fit the offence. The judgment will lead to the ruination and depopulation of the land, so that the owners of the great houses and estates will lose most. There is a sense of poetic justice in this proceeding, which nonetheless enables Isaiah to spell out what form the punishment will take.

10. **For ten acreas of vineyard:** The ravaging of the land during time of war, and the inability of the population to go about their normal work will reduce the normal yield to almost ludicrously small proportions. *GNB*, rather prosaically, attempts to give an accurate modern equivalent for the ancient measures referred to: 'The grape-vines growing on ten hectares of land will yield only eight litres of wine. A hundred and eighty litres of seed will produce only eighteen litres of corn'. It is very unlikely that Isaiah ever intended his poetry to be taken quite so literally.

11. **Woe to those who rise early:** The third woe attacks the life of luxury and pleasure that the wealthier citizens of Jerusalem were able to indulge in. Isaiah appears to have been especially incensed at the heavy drinking of the upper classes (cf. 28:1, 7), and the description of their feasting shows that he regarded this as excessive, and as an affront to the justice of God. While poor men died of hunger, others spent the whole day in nothing but eating and drinking. It appears unlikely that we should follow Whedbee, *Isaiah and Wisdom*, pp. 98f., in regarding such condemnation of drunkenness as a specifically 'Wisdom' characteristic. More probably it reflects the economic shift that was taking place in Israel and Judah to the life of settled agri-culture, with viticulture as a highly prized expertise. Thus, wine may still not have been all that widely available to the population, es-pecially its poorer elements, and was treated with some suspicion as a 'Canaanite' product (cf. Gen. 9:20–27; Jer. 35:6).

12. **but they do not regard the deeds of the LORD** reflects the prophet's claim to have knowledge of the 'plan' and intended deeds of

God, which the majority of those people to whom he addresses his message have chosen to ignore (cf. 30 : 1; and see J. Fichtner, *ZAW* 63 (1951), pp. 16–33 = *Gottes Weisheit*, pp. 27–43).

13. Therefore my people go into exile shows that the prophet regarded the coming punishment as taking effect through defeat in war. Cf. v. 9 above. For *NEB*'s 'my people dwindle away', cf. G. R. Driver, *JSS* 13 (1968), pp. 37f. **for want of knowledge** indicates not so much that the people are ignorant of God's ways, but that they have chosen to ignore him. **knowledge** in this sense was not simply awareness of what constituted the will of God, but a willingness to do it. **their honoured men** points to a time of famine which would have been an inevitable consequence of war and the consequent devastation of the countryside. The reading **are dying of hunger** presupposes an emendation to *mētê* (cf. Peshitta). However, H. Wildberger suggests *mᵉzēh* (cf. Dt. 32:24) 'are weakened with hunger'.

14. Therefore Sheol has enlarged its appetite: Vv. 14–17 must be regarded as an addition to the original unit of 5 : 8–24. It recounts the horror of the judgment that came to Jerusalem when it was defeated, and of the death of its nobility. Nevertheless it was Yahweh's righteous will that brought this about (v. 16), leaving the city empty and desolate. Undoubtedly this addition was made after 587, when Jerusalem fell to the Babylonians, probably soon after, confirming that Isaiah's prophecies from more than a century previously were applied to this event. **and he who exults in her** does not make very good sense and J. A. Emerton, *VT* 17 (1967), 135–42, suggests, by a small emendation, the reading 'and the strength of her (Zion's) heart'; i.e. 'her stubbornness', or 'her courage'.

15. Man is bowed down: Cf. 2 : 9, 11, 17 for very similar assertions, which may be quite intentionally alluded to by the redactor here.

16. But the LORD of hosts: The purpose of the addition appears to have been to show that the punishment of Jerusalem, when it came, was entirely right and deserved so that it fell within his purpose for his people. The destruction of Jerusalem (in 587) did not reveal the powerlessness of Yahweh, but rather his holiness and righteousness (cf. Lam. 2 : 1–10).

17. Then shall the lambs graze refers to the depopulation of Judah and the return of the city of Jerusalem to its undeveloped state (cf. Mic. 3 : 12). The Hebrew text is difficult and certainly in need of emendation. *RSV* presupposes the reading *gᵉdāyîm*, 'goats', instead of *gārîm*, 'sojourners, aliens'. *NEB*'s rendering demands a more substantial emendation of the text. Cf. *HTOT*, p. 176 and further G. R. Driver, *JTS* 38 (1937), pp. 38f. The picture presented is certainly of a return to a primitive state, not of a pleasant pastoral scene.

18. Woe to those who draw iniquity: This third woe lacks an appended threat which has presumably been lost in transmission. However, its condemnation leaves no doubt as to its threatening nature. The wealthy rulers of Jerusalem have so attached themselves to wrongdoing that they drag it with them wherever they go. **with**

cords of falsehood: Better, 'like a sheep on a tether' (reading *śeh*, 'sheep', instead of *śāw*', 'falsehood'). **as with cart ropes:** It is preferable to follow *NEB* in rendering 'like a heifer on a rope' (*hā'ēḡel* instead of *hā'ᵃḡālāh*).

19. who say: 'Let him make haste': These ruling citizens have become so arrogant in their attitude to others that they adopt the same tone towards God. Hence they mock both him, and his prophet, by jesting about his threats that they will soon be punished. They invite God to act soon and not to delay any longer. **let him speed his work:** better 'Let the LORD . . .', following Peshitta.

20. who call evil good: By accepting bribes in reaching judicial decisions, and by disregarding all the accepted standards of public and civic conduct in their policies, the rulers of Jerusalem are accused of defying morality itself. Both this and the following two 'woes' lack any separate pronouncement of judgment, which must be assumed to have fallen out. As it has now been preserved the final declaration of coming punishment in v. 24 provides a comprehensive conclusion to the last four 'woes'.

21. those who are wise in their own eyes: The prophet now directs his condemnation to the fact that these citizens, by the policies they are pursuing for the government of their city and country, claim to be displaying their great skill and wisdom. Cf. W. McKane, *Prophets and Wise Men*, pp. 65ff. Yet the implication of the criticism expressed by the prophet is clear. This special cleverness on their part will only bring them, and the people they govern, to ruin.

22. heroes at drinking wine relates to the condemnation of excessive drinking already expressed in v. 11. Their own ebullient self-confidence, made all the more vociferous by their heavy drinking, would hasten on their doom. Their boastful and aggressive manner was based on nothing more substantial than the amount of wine they had consumed.

23. who acquit the guilty for a bribe: The existence of a special order of judicial officers in Jerusalem cannot be postulated with certainty (cf. Exod. 18 : 13–27). More usually the local citizens took a major part in the conduct of legal disputes. It appears from 1 Kg. 3 : 16ff. that some form of central court of appeal had been set up in Jerusalem under the monarchy. Since this would have drawn its officials from the upper classes, and since all judicial rights were probably related to ownership of land, the scope for corruption of the processes of law was certainly considerable. This may well have been all the more difficult to control if it were normal practice for accused litigants to offer gifts to prominent members of the court if they had been successful. Apparently the leading men in Jerusalem did not lack courage when it came to speaking up in their revelries (v. 22), but were not disposed to display moral courage when it came to defending justice.

24. Therefore, as the tongue of fire: This final pronouncement of coming doom brings to an end the series of seven woes, and introduces two vivid metaphors taken from the natural order. **their root**

will be as rottenness: Better, with *NEB* 'will moulder away' should be read, since the meaning of the Heb. word *māq* is not entirely secured. **for they have rejected the law of the LORD:** This concluding summary must certainly be a later addition by a redactor's hand. It has a strongly Deuteronomic form of words (cf. Am. 2:4), and is, in any case, otiose after the preceding woes have spelt out clearly the offences for which the judgment will be meted out. It forms a generalised conclusion to the prophet's more specialised invective, and establishes that all such wrongdoing emanates from a failure to pay heed to the law of Yahweh which he has given.

THE CONTINUING ANGER OF THE LORD
9:8–21; 5:25–30

It has been recognised by a great majority of modern scholars that some disturbance of the text has taken place, and resulted in the presence in ch. 5 of material that rightly belongs to the section 9:8–21. This is shown by the occurrence of the refrain 5:25*b* **For all this** in 9:12, 17, 21 and 10:4. In fact the occurrence in 10:4 is due to a redactor who has used it in order to fit 10:1–4*a* into its present position on the assumption that it forms the conclusion of the unit 9:8ff. *NEB* attempts to rectify the error by placing 5:24–25 after 10:4. In fact most scholars (Duhm, Marti, Fohrer, Eichrodt, et al.) regard the dislocation of the text as the result of an unintentional fragmentation of the material during the course of transmission and editing. Rather, however, we may with H. Barth, pp. 110–17, regard the placing of 5:25–30 in its present position as the consequence of a deliberate redactional decision. It belongs to the wider structure of 5:1–14:27 (for which see above on 5:1–7). The primary intention has been to set the warning of Yahweh's summoning of the Assyrians (5:26–30) at the close of the first indictment of Israel and Judah (5:1–24). The initial 'therefore' in 5:25 shows clearly that some antecedent invective is required for the pronouncement of Yahweh's intended action given by the verse. The elaboration of the form that this divine action will take with the summoning of the Assyrians given by 5:26–30 then follows quite appropriately upon this. We may infer from the content of 5:25 therefore that it belongs at the end of 9:8–21, although something has been lost in the course of the transposition since the presence of the refrain shows that we do not have a full stanza here.

The date of the prophecy and the circumstances which it presupposes can be made out with reasonable certainty. It is directed against the Northern Kingdom of Israel (cf. v. 9 'Ephraim and the inhabitants of Samaria') who have suffered a severe political reversal ('The bricks have fallen . . .', v. 10). This must be the fall of Samaria to Tiglath-pileser III in 733 BC and the subsequent cutting-off of much of its territory. Yet the lesson has not been learned and the false optimism, coupled with continuing internal strife (Cf. v. 20, 'each devours his neighbour's flesh'), betrays the steep plunge into disaster which marked the Northern Kingdom in the last days before the final revolt and the second fall of Samaria to the Assyrians in 722. By the present positioning of 9:8ff. after the royal accession oracle of 9:2–7 the redactor has sought to affirm that the path of obedience and repentance for Ephraim should have been to return to the house of David for its salvation, but this idea is not expressed in the words of the prophecy itself. The same linking of the royal accession oracle with the plight of the Northern Kingdom has been established by the historical note in 9:1 (see below *in loc.*). We may confidently place 9:8–21 + 5:25–30 in the years 733–722 BC.

9:8 The LORD has sent a word against Jacob: The prophecy is addressed directly to the Northern Kingdom of Israel in the aftermath of its defeat and the loss of much territory (cf. below on 9:1) in 733. Instead of **word** LXX reads 'death' in the first line, evidently taking the Heb. *dābār* as *deḇer*, 'pestilence'. But this is almost certainly an over-zealous interpretation, rather than a more accurate understanding of the text. The message that the prophet has to bring is Yahweh's powerful **word** which warns that the tragedy of what had happened is not the end of the misfortunes of the Northern Kingdom. For the conception of the 'word', cf. G. Gerleman, *THAT*, I, 433–43.

and it will light upon Israel: Rather, 'and now it falls . . .'. The title **Israel** here relates only to the Northern Kingdom, and the prophet affirms that, as he delivers his message, so its content is beginning to take effect.

9. and all the people will know: D. Winton Thomas, *JTS* 41 (1940), pp. 40f., would see here an instance of the Hebrew verb *yd'*, 'shall be humiliated' (cf. Arabic *wadu'a*), but such a change is scarcely necessary. Vv. 9–10 contain the main indictment of the Northern Kingdom, which consists of their 'pride' and 'arrogance of heart'. The resilience and determination not to be overwhelmed by the defeat, which might in other circumstances have appeared morally worthy and virtuous, is the very ground for their condemnation. The victims of defeat have learnt nothing from their experience, so that it will take an even worse disaster to bring home to them a knowledge of their true condition. They are unwilling to learn, and their own pride hides the truth from them. Cf. 3:10; 5:15, 21 for similar condemnations of pride in Isaiah. It is not simply the expression of an attitude towards men and circumstances, but a hardened face against God.

10. The bricks have fallen: The description of the destruction of buildings is metaphorically used for the destruction of the whole kingdom. Almost certainly it is the defeat of 733 that is referred to, although Kaiser would see here an allusion to the more extended period of the decline of Israel, which began before this. However, the prophet's point is not to dwell on the past but to affirm that the time of judgment had not yet passed. **but we will put cedars in their place:** Instead of the usual understanding 'we will put . . . in their place' (Heb. *naḥ*ᵃ*līp*), G. R. Driver, *JTS* 34 (1933), pp. 381f., would understand the verb as 'we will cut . . .' (cf. Syr. *ḥalupṯa*), but the established rendering is perfectly satisfactory.

11. So the LORD raises adversaries against them: The Heb. has 'the adversaries of Rezin' (cf. *RSV* margin), but 'of Rezin' must be deleted. It was probably a gloss identifying one such adversary, perhaps aided by the fact that some MSS read the noun as 'princes' instead of 'adversaries' (Heb. *śārê* instead of *sārê*). Many commentators (Duhm, Marti, Gray, etc.) understand the verse as a reference to the future 'will raise . . . ', in spite of the Heb. impf. + waw cons. *RSV*'s present tense is equivocal, and it is preferable to translate as a past tense and to see in the verse a reference to misfortunes that had already over-taken Israel as a result of its politically weak condition.

12. The Syrians on the east: Schoors takes this to refer to the strife before the conclusion of the Syro-Ephraimite alliance, but it could equally well refer to disagreements with Syria after the settlement imposed by Assyria in 732. With the cutting off of the coastal plain ('the way of the sea', 9 : 1) and Transjordan ('the land beyond Jordan', 9 : 1), the inhabitants of these regions were left very much more exposed to the depredations of the neighbouring provinces. **and the Philistines on the west:** No doubt the prophet's reference to the adversaries included an element of traditional suspicion and antipathy to those nations bordering Israel with whom a very prolonged, and sometimes bitter, sequence of disputes had prevailed.

13. The people did not turn to him who smote them: Behind the action of the Assyrians the prophet discerned the punitive work of Yahweh, and it was the total failure of the Northern Kingdom to share this perspective which prevented them from learning the true mean-ing of their experience. In consequence they made no effort to return (Heb. *šûḇ*; cf. *THAT*, II, cols. 884–91) to Yahweh. What this meant in moral and political terms is not clear, but the redactor who placed the whole section after 9 : 1–7 seems to be hinting at a return of the Northern Kingdom to allegiance to the Davidic monarchy.

14. So the LORD cut off from Israel: By the aid of two metaphors taken from the natural order, one concerning animals and the other vegetation, the prophet affirms the severity of the punishment that had been inflicted on Israel. The very disaster which the people no doubt regarded as a mark of Yahweh's indifference to their fate, was in reality a sign of how much he cared and how firmly he sought to recall them to himself.

15. the elder and honoured man is the head: The verse is a gloss by a redactor who has interpreted the metaphors in an attempt to show the root causes of the downfall of the Northern Kingdom. The political leaders (**the elder and honoured man**) and the prophets had misled the common people. Isaiah does not himself complain of the lies of false prophets, although his contemporary, Micah, does so (Mic. 2 : 11; 3 : 5–8).

16. for those who lead this people: The aftermath of the settle-ment of 733 led to a progressively deteriorating political situation in the Northern Kingdom, which finally sank to the level of anarchy and chaos. Cf. Hos. 5 : 1; 7 : 3; 8 : 4; 13 : 10f.

17. Therefore the Lord does not rejoice: 1QIs[a] reads the verb as 'does not spare' (Heb. *lō' yaḥmōl*), and *BHS* suggests retaining the MT but understanding the verb in the sense 'does not spare', citing the Arabic *samuḥa* 'to be merciful'. Undoubtedly this yields a better sense.

18. For wickedness burns like a fire: It is striking that the imagery of the forest fire makes use of the picture of 'briars and thorns', which originally appeared in 5 : 6 (cf. the secondary developments in 7 : 23–25). In the present context it appears authentic to Isaiah and simply to reflect the general picture of the spread of wickedness in the Northern Kingdom likened to the rapid spread of a forest fire. The overall description of the political chaos that brought Ephraim to final collapse is revealingly effective.

20. They snatch on the right: The LXX reads the singular, thereby continuing the typical instance introduced at the end of v. 19, 'no man spares . . .'. **each devours his neighbour's flesh:** The clause should almost certainly be transposed to the end of v. 18 (cf. *BHS*). Heb. reads 'the flesh of his arm' (cf. *RSV* margin), but the revised text follows Targ. (Heb. *rē'o* instead of *zᵉrō'ô*).

21. The clause **and together they are against Judah** must be understood as a redactor's addition who has sought to bring out more forcefully that the final defeat of the Northern Kingdom arose because the people there refused to reunite with Judah and accept the Davidic monarchy. Isaiah's original prophecy was concerned more directly with the turmoil within the remains of the Northern Kingdom after 733.

5:25. Therefore the anger of the LORD was kindled: The occurrence of the refrain shows that 5:25 belongs to 9:8ff., but evidently something has been lost since the verse represents only the conclusion of a stanza. What is presupposed is a summary indictment of Israel. A noteworthy feature of the pictures of judgment that has overtaken the people is the combination of images from the storm theophany—**the mountains quaked**—with more direct descriptions of the sufferings inflicted by war—**and their corpses were as refuse.** The intention is evidently to blend traditional conceptions of the divine activity with the particular misfortune which had overtaken Israel.

26–30 At one time possibly formed a quite separate prophecy announcing that it was Yahweh's intention to summon the Assyrians to execute his will upon Israel, Judah and Syria. More directly however, these verses must be understood in relation to the crisis of the Syro-Ephraimite period, and their present position is clearly determined by their appropriateness as showing how Yahweh's judgment upon his vineyard (Israel–Judah, 5 : 7) will take effect. It is scarcely likely that they formed the original conclusion to the section 9 : 8–21; 5 : 25, since this prophecy must be dated at a time when it was already clear that the major threat to both Israel and Judah was from Assyria. In fact the closest parallel to them is to be found in 7 : 18f. It is possible, therefore, that the original address of 5 : 26–30 was to Judah at the time of Ahaz's refusal to heed the message of the sequence of prophecies concerned with the names of Isaiah's children. As it now stands they present an impressive preface to the memoir of Isaiah's prophecies at the time of the Syro-Ephraimite crisis (6:1–8:18*), even though they introduce a threat—the coming of the Assyrians against both Judah and Israel—which only emerged during the course of that crisis.

26. He will raise a signal for a nation afar off: The Heb. has 'to nations from afar', but clearly one nation is intended, and only a slight emendation is required for the sense given (to *le̊ḡôy mimmerḥāq*). The reference is unmistakably to Assyria, and this would have been clear to the prophet's hearers, as would the identity of the subject at the beginning as Yahweh.

27. None is weary, none stumbles: The picture given is of the well disciplined and well trained army of the Assyrians. How direct the prophet's knowledge of this army was can only be conjectured, but already the achievements of Tiglath-pileser would have been fully and popularly reported in Judah. The prophet's aim is to show the unfailing certainty with which Yahweh's action will be carried out.

28. their arrows are sharp: The military skill and preparedness of the Assyrians left no hope for the inhabitants of Israel or Judah that they would be able to defend themselves against so powerful a force. There is an obvious element of hyperbole in describing the soldiers' bows as **bent**, i.e. ready strung and prepared for use. **seem like flint** requires a slight re-pointing of the Heb. supported in 1QIs[a].

29. like young lions they roar: The Heb. requires a slight emendation to *we̊yišʾag*. The metaphor of roaring makes allusion to the general noise and din of an army, which the prophet interprets in the most threatening way possible by the association with the lion's roaring.

30. And if one look to the land: The second half of v. 30 is a redactor's addition which has been introduced to fill out the picture of the effect that the coming of the enemy will have. Its close similarity to 8:22 almost certainly betrays the work of the same hand in both instances. The note must have been added during the exilic age, after 587, and thus to have interpreted the threat of 5:26–30 in relation to the Babylonian army. It presents an interesting example of how prophecies came to be re-applied and re-interpreted at a time long after that of their original utterance.

THE CALL OF ISAIAH

6:1–13

The position of the account of Isaiah's call in ch. 6 has occasioned much discussion and has drawn attention to the problems relating to the redactional structure of chs. 6–9. Undoubtedly we have in 6:1–8:18* a memoir written by the prophet himself, and relating to prophecies at the time of the Syro-Ephraimite war (cf. O. H. Steck, *BZ*, NF 16 (1972), pp. 188–206; H. Barth, pp. 277ff. The original suggestion goes back to K. Budde, see Introduction p. 4). Such a memoir (German *Denkschrift*) was composed in the first person narrative form and must have been set down shortly after the ending of the crisis in 733. Several scholars have noted the connectedness of 6:1–9:6 (K. Budde, G. Fohrer, J. Lindblom; A. Schoors would extend this to 12:6), but undoubtedly 8:18 forms the end of the original memoir. Certain later additions have been made in it, especially in 6:12–13; 7:1, 8*b*, 15, 18–23 and 8:9–10, as well as in some other small glosses. The scope of the original memoir was concerned with the events relating to the Syro-Ephraimite war, and the refusal of Ahaz to heed Isaiah's message of assurance that he had nothing to fear from the threat to depose him. There is no need therefore to suppose (as M. M. Kaplan, *JBL* 45 (1926), pp. 251–9; J. Milgrom, *VT* 14 (1964), pp. 164–82), that ch. 6 recalls a commissioning of the prophet which took place sometime after he had begun to prophesy. The overall theme of this memoir is how Ahaz came to refuse the message which Isaiah gave to him, and how, in consequence, the promises which this original message contained were turned into judgments upon the king of Judah. There is throughout, therefore, a marked note of ambivalence in that words which are full of promise and assurance are interpreted in a threatening fashion. It is important to bear in mind consequently that the sharply threatening words which conclude the memoir in 8:17–18 have been allowed to shed light upon the whole. There is no serious reason for doubting the origin of this memoir with the prophet himself, nor for accepting that he himself was responsible for its written form. It has been set as a unit, with the additions noted, into the larger redactional unit of 5:1–14:27 to show the circumstances surrounding the origins of the threat from Assyria.

The setting of the call can be seen to have been provided by the Jerusalem temple, and we may infer that, at the time of his startling vision of God (6:1), Isaiah found himself looking through the entranceway into the main *aula* of the temple building. By what right Isaiah was there, whether as court official or temple servant, can only be a matter of conjecture. The call is dated from the year of Uzziah's death, which A. Jepsen places in 736/5, and H. Wildberger a little earlier in 739. For the problems of chronology, see Introduction, pp. 8f. The fact that the immediate sequel to the account of the call is found in prophecies relating to the Syro-Ephraimite war suggests that no significant interval of time elapsed between the call and the outbreak of the war. In this case the date given by Jepsen would appear to be the more likely. In any event it precludes any need to postulate an earlier period of preaching by the prophet before the time of the war.

A special problem relating to the call, and the prophet's report of it, has been felt in connection with the forewarning given in vv. 9–10 that the effect of his preaching will be to harden the hearts of the people. Did this come to the prophet at the actual time of his call (cf. R. Kilian, *Bausteine biblischer Theologie*, Bonn, 1977, pp. 209ff.), or does it, as many have concluded, contain a backwards reflection by the prophet from a later period of his ministry? Many recent commen-

tators (Fohrer, Eichrodt, Wildberger, Schoors) have recognised the
latter to be the case, but this leaves open at what time such a recognition came to him. O. H. Steck, *op. cit.*, pp. 198ff., has rightly
perceived the importance of the connection with the prophecies
which follow in chs. 7–8 as a key to understanding the forward
looking element in the divine forewarning of the hardening of the
people's hearts. It refers to the response which Isaiah's prophecies,
linked with the three sign-names of his children (7:2–8:4*), were to
elicit from Ahaz and the rulers of Judah more generally. The
reference in 8:17 to Yahweh's 'hiding his face' from the house of
Jacob shows the negative response which greeted the prophet's
message with its accompanying demand. It is this forewarning of the
reception which would be accorded to his prophecies from the time of
the Syro-Ephraimite crisis, which forms the immediate point of
reference in the divine commission to 'harden' the hearts of the
people. Most probably the memoir itself was composed by the prophet
shortly after the crisis was resolved by the fall of Damascus and
Samaria to the Assyrians in 733, with the consequent breaking up of
the territory controlled by Ephraim in the North (cf. Introduction, pp.
10f.; and see below on 8:23). There is contained within the scope of
the prophet's memoir, therefore, beginning with his account of his
call and proceeding to report his prophecies and the refusal of Ahaz to
heed them, an element of theodicy showing why the disaster inflicted
on Israel by the Assyrians in 733 had come about.

The account of the call falls into three parts: (1) 6:1–3: a vision of
God. (2) vv. 4–7: an act of cleansing and prophetic preparation. (3) vv.
8–11: the giving of the divine commission. Vv. 12–13 are a later
addition to the original call account, made most probably during the
sixth century (Wildberger: cf. also Barth, pp. 195f., 248, who relates it
to other redactional additions from the period of the exile in the sixth
century) to take account of the destruction of Judah brought about by
Babylon. The final clause of v. 13 has then been added later still,
towards the latter part of the exilic age, to introduce an element of
hope into the sombre note of threat which otherwise dominates the
entire chapter.

The form of the prophetic call-narrative has occasioned a good deal
of discussion, and it is evident that the account of Isaiah's call shows
marked similarities with the vision of the heavenly court of Yahweh
to be found in 1 Kg. 22:19–23. Cf. O. H. Steck, *op. cit.*, pp. 189ff.,
who argues strongly that the Isaianic account must be interpreted as a
record of the prophet's entry into the heavenly council (Heb. *sôd*) of
Yahweh, rather than as a call proper. Yet there is no reason to
question the generally accepted view that Isa. 6 intends to show how
Isaiah came to be a prophet of God, and the special commission that
he had received. It bears comparison, therefore, with similar accounts
in Jer. 1:4–10 and Ezek. 1:3–3:15 and it is questionable whether
we can use the narrative to discover anything of the prophet's inner
experience, or even of his spiritual autobiography. Cf. my *Prophecy
and Tradition*, pp. 34ff. The narrative is concerned with the divine

origin and authority of the prophet's message, and the prophet's own personal authority is seen to be derived from this. In the case of Isaiah, it is also evident that the royal rejection of his message, recounted in 7:2ff., has reflected back heavily upon the prophet's claim to be God's spokesman. By incorporating a divine forewarning that this rejection would come, the prophet has established even more emphatically his own claim to have stood in the council of Yahweh, and to be in a position to reveal his intentions to his people.

6:1. In the year that King Uzziah died: The year is most probably 736/5, but in any case Uzziah's leprosy (2 Kg. 15:5) had precluded the king's active participation in politics for some time. Affairs had been conducted by his son Jotham, who acted as co-regent until his death, and then by Ahaz. On the chronology that we have followed, Jotham had predeceased his father, and had been succeeded by his own son Ahaz, who was co-regent at the time of Uzziah's death. We do not have any prophecies from Isaiah, therefore, dating back to Jotham's reign, nor at all before the time of the outbreak of the Syro-Ephraimite crisis. See below on 7:1ff. According to 2 Kg. 15:37 this alliance of the Northern Kingdom and Syria against Judah had already begun in the time of Jotham's co-regency, but this is almost certainly a rather extended perspective. It no doubt reflects, however, the worsening of relations between Israel and Judah before the time of Uzziah's death, which made Isaiah's concern with Yahweh's will for both kingdoms of Israel (Ephraim) and Judah all the more relevant. Uzziah's death was important as marking a change in the political intentions of Judah, since it left Ahaz free to implement his own plans concerning the two threatening kingdoms in the north, and concerning his own relationship to Assyria. This was to prove the decisive turning-point in the entire fortunes of the two sister kingdoms which had developed from the once great kingdom of Israel. It marked the beginning of Israel's confrontation with Assyria and the first stage in the decline and dissolution of both kingdoms in the following century and a half. It was, therefore, to prove 'a year of destiny' in the history of Israel. **I saw the LORD sitting upon a throne:** Although the prophet found himself in the earthly temple, what he saw was the heavenly throne of God, which the earthly building merely symbolised. Cf. my *God and Temple*, pp. 40ff. Fohrer denies that the prophet was in the temple at all, and claims that the entire scene is visionary, but this is to ignore the many elements drawn from the setting and liturgy of the Jerusalem sanctuary. There is no need to suppose that Isaiah regarded the Ark as forming the throne of God, nor even that the prophet was actually peering into the inner sanctuary, the *deḇîr*, at all. Yet it seems certain that the vision occurred during the celebration of some solemn act of worship, as the choral antiphon of v. 3 suggests. That it was the New Year's Day of the Autumn Festival, in which the divine kingship was especially celebrated, certainly goes beyond the reasonable evidence. To what extent the divine disclosure and commissioning have been stylised as a vision is now impossible to determine.

Visions are not elsewhere clearly evident in Isaiah's prophecies, but
the whole psychological basis upon which the prophet's reception of
the divine message was established cannot now be confidently reconstructed. Cf. my *Prophecy and Tradition*, p. 38.

his train filled the temple suggests that God was conceived to be
wearing a robe so large that its train occupied the whole space of the
main hall (Heb. *hêkāl*) of the temple. This may be coupled with the
notion which many commentators have discerned (cf. Steck, *op. cit.*,
p. 194n.) that God was regarded as a figure of giant proportions. However, it may simply be a more stylised convention for asserting the
'hiddenness' of God, and his incomparable splendour, by pointing to
his garments, rather than the appearance of his Person. In any case it
is possible that the smoke, mentioned in v. 4, was symbolically
associated with this **train**.

2. Above him stood the seraphim: The seraphim are described
sufficiently fully for us to make out the basic characteristics of their
appearance. See especially K. R. Joines, *JBL* 86 (1967), pp. 410-15; J.
de Savignac, *VT* 22 (1972), pp. 320-5. Their name indicates that they
were conceived to be of serpent form (cf. the 'fiery serpents' of Num.
21:6; Dt. 8:15), but possessed of three pairs of wings and hands and
feet like a man. Such creatures of mixed form were popular in
Egyptian royal symbolism, where the winged cobra (*uraeus*) was a
widely used symbol for a divine protective spirit guarding the king. It
appears prominently both on royal headdresses and as a throne adornment. The seraphim must be regarded, therefore, as guardian deities,
or servants, protecting the way to the throne of Yahweh, and comparable to the cherubim, images of which stood in the inner sanctuary
of the Jerusalem temple (1 Kg. 6:23-28). These latter certainly had
the forms of winged lions. There is no indication that any images of
seraphim were set in the *sanctum* of the Jerusalem temple, although a
bronze snake had been set there and was removed in Hezekiah's reign
(2 Kg. 18:4). More probably the *uraeus*-serpent form was familiar in
Israel in the relief-work adorning thrones (cf. *ANEP*, fig. 381ff.).

and with two he covered his feet, must be a euphemism for the
covering of the sexual parts, further heightening the portrayal of the
part-human character of the creatures.

3. Holy, holy, holy is the LORD of hosts must derive from a choral
antiphon actually sung in the Jerusalem temple. This strongly points
to the prophet's vision having taken place during some act of worship,
although it is possible that the account has simply made use of known
liturgical features of the Jerusalem temple worship. For the holiness
of God as a cultic concept of 'otherness', cf. N. H. Snaith, *Distinctive
Ideas of the Old Testament*, London, 1944, pp. 21ff. **the whole earth is
full of his glory.** There is no sharp distinction in the Hebrew between
the concepts of 'earth' and 'land' so that the praise of Yahweh as the
national God of Israel-Judah and the universal God of all the earth is
combined in the one ascription. For Yahweh's glory, cf. above on 4:5.

4. And the foundations of the thresholds shook: The most natural
understanding of the verse is that it describes the prophet's impres-

sion of what was taking place in the actual temple where he was. However, it is virtually impossible to distinguish between the psychological 'visionary' elements of the account and the actual liturgical features which have been subsumed into it. Hence it is impossible to isolate **the voice of him who called** as a heavenly rather than an earthly one. Similarly **the smoke** which filled the house must derive from the smoke of incense and offerings in the sanctuary, even though it has become linked as a part of the visionary accompaniment of a theophany (cf. the 'cloud' of glory in 4:5, and in the Priestly Writing more generally; G. von Rad, *Studies in Deuteronomy*, pp. 41ff.). For **foundations** (Heb. *'ammôṯ*) Schoors would prefer 'hinges (of the doorposts)'.

4–7 commence the second part of the call account which consists of an act of cleansing and preparation of the prophet for his task.

5. And I said: 'Woe is me! For I am lost': The prophet's utterance of woe is one of grief, not wrath, although both *hôy* and *'ôy* are used to express both grief and anger without clear distinction between them. The verb translated **I am lost** (Heb. *niḏmêṯî*) is of uncertain meaning. The ancient versions took *dmh* as a variant of *dmm*, 'to be silent'. Cf. L. Köhler, *Kleine Lichter*, pp. 32f., and O. Kaiser who translates 'I must be silent'. Yet this gives too weak a meaning in the context, which points to a more complete sense of being overwhelmed. Hence, 'I am finished, doomed' appears more likely to be correct; cf. *K–B*, p. 216, and *RSV*'s **I am lost. for I am a man of unclean lips** points to the prophet's intense awareness, not simply of guilt in general, but specifically of unfitness to use his mouth in the service of God. There is in this a very real understanding that he was being called upon to become the spokesman of God's word. The fact that he lived **in the midst of a people of unclean lips** refers to his conscious-ness of the prevalence of sins of speech among the people generally (cf. Exod. 20:7, 16; Ps. 15:3; Prov. 10:18ff.). The reference to the guilt of the people generally is used to emphasise that the prophet felt that he had hitherto been no different from the rest of his nation, but that he was now being called upon to fulfil a task which required him to be quite separate from them.

6. Then flew one of the seraphim to me: The ritual of cleansing the lips of the prophet which now takes place is otherwise unattested in the Old Testament. Its closest counterpart would appear to be in forms of 'trial by ordeal' which are more widely known in the ancient Near East. Cf. R. H. Kennett, *Ancient Hebrew Social Life and Custom* (Schweich Lectures 1931), London, 1933, pp. 95ff. It seems probable, however, that Isaiah was familiar with such a practice of touching the lips with a live coal, not as a form of trial, but as a ritual of cleansing. Whether it ever existed as a regularly repeated ritual in the Jerusalem temple (as inferred by I. Engnell, *The Call of Isaiah*, pp. 31f.) can only be conjectured.

7. your guilt is taken away: With the cleansing of the lips the whole being of the prophet is assumed to have been purged from sin, and thereby made ready for the service of Yahweh as his prophetic messenger. For the conceptions of **guilt** (Heb. *'āwôn*) and **sin** (Heb. *ḥaṭṭāṯ*), see *THAT*, I, cols. 541–9; II, cols. 243–9. Although the vocabulary still retains many of its features of a cultic 'taboo' notion of sin, the reference to sins of the lips shows a strongly moral element to have been present here. The prophet is not submitting to a cultic ceremony of ordination, but rather to the whole preparation of his being which could alone be the pre-condition of such an ordination.

8. Whom shall I send: The dialogue reflects the prophet's feeling of being allowed to overhear deliberations that were taking place in the heavenly court among the members of the divine council. Yet it is clear that Isaiah recognised that the question addressed to the other members of the heavenly assembly could only be answered by himself, and that it was, in this way, directed towards him. With this verse the commissioning of the prophet begins, although it would be artificial to make a strong distinction between the acts of calling and commissioning. What the prophet was summoned to do was inseparably bound up with the message that he was called upon to deliver. In a very real sense the call was derivative from the nature of the message which required to be delivered to the people. The prophet had no status or authority outside of the status and authority of the word which God had placed upon his lips. The question **and who will go for us?** reflects the idea that God was surrounded by the court made up of his heavenly servants. **Then I said, 'Here am I! Send me':** The prophet's response indicates his acceptance of the commission to take God's message to the people. In a sense it was viewed at this point as a single assignment, but there can be little doubt that Isaiah regarded it as only the first of a number of such assignments so that his entire life thereafter was to be at the disposal of Yahweh. Up to this point no indication has been given of the content of the message the prophet will be called upon to take. It is clear from the way that the account has been constructed, however, that the prophet's special purging from all guile and deceit has been stressed in order to prepare the way for the disclosure that the message will not prove to be a popular or readily acceptable one.

9. And he said, 'Go, and say to this people': The addressees of the message are now made known, and it becomes evident from the manner of Yahweh's describing them as **this people** that he will no longer lay claim to them as constituting 'his people' (cf. 1:2–3). Not only is there a note of divine rejection implicit in the title used, but also some awareness that the people of Judah and Jerusalem whom Isaiah will address do not constitute the whole of the people who were once Yahweh's. The political dissension between Judah and Israel (Ephraim) had already emerged before the time of Isaiah's call, and the policy that Ahaz was so soon to embark upon was calculated to make the rift wider still. Against this Isaiah still held to the belief that both houses of Israel belonged to Yahweh but had rebelled against him. Their current differences with each other were simply a reflection of this wider rebellion against God.

Hear and hear, but do not understand: The saying is in part full of irony, for the prophet undoubtedly did, very passionately and sincerely, want the people to hear and to understand. Cf. E. M. Good, *Irony in the Old Testament*, London, 1965, p. 136. At the same time we must undoubtedly accept that the prophet has written down this report of his call at some interval after the actual experience on which it was based had taken place. He has thereby incorporated into it features of the reception of the message which were only subsequently discovered by him. Yet, since he fully accepted that Yahweh was sovereign over his word, he understood the hardening that had taken place as entirely within the divine purpose. Cf. O. H. Steck, *EvTh* 33 (1973), pp. 77–90; J. M. Schmidt, *VT* 21 (1971), pp. 78–90. The forewarning of this feature, with its implication that God knew in advance that the people would not respond to his message, provides an essential basis for the understanding of it. It was a word of assurance that Ahaz had refused to heed. Therefore it had become to him and his people a word of judgment. Cf. below on 7 : 1ff.

10. Make the heart of this people fat: The heart was the seat of reasoning and intelligence in Hebrew psychology. Cf. H. W. Wolff, *Anthropology of the Old Testament*, London, 1974, pp. 40ff. To **make the heart fat**, therefore, was to dull the sense of the people so that they became incapable of making intelligent and rational decisions. Their senses had become so dulled that they failed to act responsibly to the situation in which they found themselves. By such an insistence that he had been told by God in advance to render the people incapable of reasoned judgment, Isaiah made absolutely clear to them that their refusal to listen to his words, and to act accordingly, was an action of the grossest irrationality. **lest they see with their eyes** shows that the prophet did deliver his message with a firm hope that it would enable his hearers to turn to Yahweh **and be healed**. Yet he was no conventional preacher of a message of repentance, for it was not a general willingness to obey the laws of Yahweh that he demanded, but a more specific response to a concrete political issue at a decisive moment for the existence of Judah and Israel. Once that moment had passed, and the wrong decision had been taken, it would be too late subsequently for remorse.

11. Then I said, 'How long, O LORD?'. The cry **How long?** is regularly used for the opening of laments (cf. Ps. 89:46). Although the element of questioning God is genuine, the cry was not simply a request to know how long the suffering must be endured, but a deep-rooted plea that it might be swiftly brought to an end. The picture that then follows in the verse **Until cities lie waste without inhabitant** pictures the devastation that would be caused by war. The reference intended by **the land** must primarily have been to Judah and Jerusalem, which would suffer as a result of the threatened judgment, but we must certainly accept that Isaiah also saw the Northern Kingdom as included. In this reflection on his prophetic commission and its meaning for his people, he saw it to have contained a threat of military destruction that would embrace both houses of Israel (cf. 8 : 14). To what extent Isaiah was conscious at the time of his call that a grave new military threat from Assyria faced both Judah and Israel is not clear. Certainly it must have been politically obvious to any well-informed citizen, but equally certainly here Isaiah was recalling his divine commission in the light of what had happened in the Syro-Ephraimite war of 735–733.

12. and the LORD removes men far away: Vv. 12–13 (apart from v. 13c) are an addition made later by an editor to show how the judgment had taken effect in the deportation of many from **the land**. Wildberger, I, pp. 257f., would relate this to the situation after 721 when many citizens of the Northern Kingdom were carried off by Assyria. Barth, p. 196, argues that it emanates from the exilic age and relates primarily to Judah, with the removal of many of its inhabitants to Babylon. He thus connects it with such other additions as 3 : 25–4 : 1, 5 : 14, 17, etc.

13. And though a tenth remain in it: The verse is in a difficult state of textual disrepair, and numerous suggestions for emendation have been proposed. Cf. S. Iwry, *JBL* 76 (1957), pp. 225–32; W. F. Albright, *Strasbourg Congress Volume* (*VT Supp.* 4), (1957), pp. 254f.; G. W. Ahlström, *JSS* 19 (1974), pp. 169–72. *NEB*'s rendering reflects the widely adopted view that Heb, *bām* should be restored to read *bāmāh*, 'high-place'. Hence the noun *maṣṣebeṯ*, **stump**, would then have its regular meaning of 'sacred pole'. Thus 'a sacred pole thrown out from its place in a hill-shrine' (*NEB*). Cf. further G. R. Driver, *JSS* 13 (1968), p. 38, who suggests 'like an oak or a terebinth, which is cast away from the site of a high place'. This understands *miṣṣebeṯ* as a noun meaning 'site, position, location' (Heb. *ṣebeṯ*), with the preposition *min*. In spite of the textual difficulties, and the lack of a completely satisfactory resolution of them, it is evident that the metaphor is one expressing threat. Just as the stump, or trunk, of a tree may be burned after the tree is felled, so will the survivors of Israel and Judah suffer further punishment, when they already feel that they have suffered more than enough. For the idea of the decimation of a population, cf. Am. 5 : 3.

The final words of v. 13c, **The holy seed is its stump**, which are relegated to the margin in *NEB*, are a gloss from the post-exilic age. It elicits an element of hope from the metaphor used by the earlier redactor who added vv. 12–13 that even the **stump** of a felled tree may grow again. It is probable that the **holy seed** refers to the survivors of Judah in general, rather than to the royal seed of the house of David.

THE SIGN OF SHEAR-JASHUB

7 : 1–9

With the commencement of ch. 7 we are introduced to a series of prophecies from the time of the Syro-Ephraimite war (735–733), which extends down to 8 : 18, and concludes the reporting of prophecies contained in Isaiah's memoir, as shown by the preservation of the first-person form. From considerations of the chronology of Isaiah's ministry which we have already dealt with we may conclude that this period represents the earliest of Isaiah's

activity and therefore provides a key to understanding the message
with which his work began. The threatening character of this has
already been noted through the connection which exists between chs.
6 and 7 as parts of Isaiah's memoir.

The outbreak of the Syro-Ephraimite war (see Introduction, pp.
10f.) marked the beginning of the fall of the Northern Kingdom of
Israel to Assyria. With the capture of Samaria in 733 and the fall
of Damascus in the following year, both to the armies of Tiglath
Pileser III (745–727), there occurred a major reduction in Israel's
territory. Only a rump state was left in the hill country of Ephraim
around Samaria. Judah also was forced into a position of vassalage to
Assyria, a humiliation and suffering which it appears previously to
have escaped. Yet the beginning of the crisis, according to 2 Kg.
15:37, goes back even as far as Jotham's co-regency. In the year 735
(734 according to H. Donner) Pekah, king of Israel, and Rezin
(properly Raṣyān), king of Syria, attempted to draw Ahaz into joining
an anti-Assyrian coalition. Ahaz refused, and as a result the allies in the
north planned to remove him from his throne and to replace him by a
certain ben Tabeel (cf. 7:6), who would be more agreeable to their
intentions. Who exactly this nominee was has been much discussed
(see below in loc.), but the plan to remove Ahaz was evidently directed
at the royal family and palace, rather than against the people of Judah
in general. In any case the army of Judah was felt to be of great
importance in the stand against Assyria that was projected. For whatever reason, most likely that of political common sense, Ahaz held
fast to his refusal to join the coalition and instead planned to send a
deputation to Assyria with a massive tribute in order to elicit Assyrian
protection (2 Kg. 16:7–9). In pursuance of their plan the northern
allies attacked and laid siege to Jerusalem, but failed to capture it
(7:1). The calling off of the siege was undoubtedly brought about as a
result of Ahaz's appeal to Assyria and the swiftness of their response.
Inevitably the Syro-Ephraimite armies were heavily defeated by the
Assyrians. The Aramean state of Damascus was incorporated directly
into the Assyrian provincial system, whereas the rump state of Israel
was left as a vassal kingdom. However, the northern territories of
Galilee, as well as the entire coastal plain, were severed from Israel
(cf. on 9:1 [Heb. 8:23]).

The historical note in Isa. 7:1 has been taken by an editor from 2
Kg. 16:5, with which it has a close verbal similarity, in order to
provide the setting for the prophecy of Isaiah in 7:2–9. It develops
still further the work of the editor who has added the names of Ahaz's
opponents in v. 4b. It is important, however, to recognise that this
note carries the story of the alliance into a later stage than had been
reached by the time of Isaiah's encounter with Ahaz. At this point the
siege of Jerusalem had not begun, but was already feared, and Ahaz
had not sent off his deputation to Assyria. The goal of Isaiah's
message was to persuade Ahaz to maintain a position of strict neutrality, neither submitting to the plans of Pekah and Rezin nor sending the emissaries to Assyria. By so doing Isaiah clearly hoped that the

inevitable consequences of submission to Assyria could be avoided.
At the same time, as a prophet with a concern for both the houses
of Israel and Judah, Isaiah must have hoped to avoid the deeper
poisoning of relationships between the two kingdoms which would
inevitably result from Ahaz's proposed action. In the event it is clear
that Ahaz refused to heed Isaiah's message, which was essentially that
he had nothing to fear from the alliance that was ranged against him.
Isaiah then sent two further messages of a similar character to Ahaz
after intervals of time which cannot be precisely determined (7 : 10–17
and 8 : 1–4). At what point between these three prophecies the deputation set off for Assyria is not clear. If it were after the time of the first
such message from Isaiah, then the latter two prophecies must be
held to have possessed a confirmatory nature. Since the interval presupposed between the giving of the first and third of these prophecies
extended apparently over a period of more than a year, and possibly
more than two years (see below on 7 : 10ff.) it is unlikely that Ahaz
could have delayed that long. In any event it is evident from the
conclusion of Isaiah's memoir, as well as from the sharpening note of
bitterness and anger that intrudes into the prophecies (cf. especially
7 : 13), that Ahaz refused to listen to Isaiah. It is this refusal on the part
of the king that gives to the series of three prophecies a highly distinctive character. In their formal presentation they are prophecies of
assurance and hope, but those which require to be accepted and acted
upon to be effective (cf. 7 : 9). By refusing to accept them, and by
refusing to maintain the strict neutrality which such acceptance
demanded, Ahaz had turned his back on Yahweh, who in turn would
hide his face from his people (cf. 8 : 17). The promise that had been
spurned would be turned into judgment (cf. 8 : 14–15). Thus
prophecies which in their verbal content express hope had become for
Ahaz and his people threats of doom. This alone accounts for the
strange ambivalence of the language, which has greatly perplexed
many commentators. How the threat would take effect on Ahaz
himself is not altogether clear, since its formulation in 7 : 9 is very
terse. However, Isaiah certainly warned that Ahaz's throne would not
be secure, and his meaning appears to have contained the implication
that the very continuance of the Davidic dynasty would be thrown in
jeopardy (cf. O. H. Steck, *ThZ* 29 [1973], pp. 163f.). At the very least it
would have made unthinkable any reconciliation of the Northern
Kingdom with Judah under a Davidic king.

The prophecies of Isaiah are centred upon the sign-names given to
three children, all of whom either are, or are to be, offspring of the
prophet. We can, therefore, compare the three sign-names given to
children of the prophet Hosea in Hos. 1 : 2–9. There can be no doubt
that in Isaiah the names of the three children are in a connected
sequence, and that the conclusion of the memoir in 8 : 18 provides a
summarising conclusion about their role. The names given to the
three children, Shear-jashub (7 : 3), Immanuel (7 : 14) and Maher-
shalal-hashbaz (8 : 1, 3) are themselves sign-messages from God, but
in order to make unmistakably plain what they mean interpretations

are added by the prophet himself (7:7–9; 7:16–17; 8:4). A later redactor, probably from the time of the following century, has spelt out still more clearly the prophet's meaning by making explicit the references to 'the king of Assyria' in 7:17 and 8:4 (cf. also the same procedure in 7:4). The import of the sign-names and the appended interpretations, full of enigmatic circumlocutions as they are, leave no doubt as to what the prophet's message was. The attempt to depose Ahaz and to replace him with ben Tabeel would fail and the siege of Jerusalem would have to be relinquished. Both Damascus and Samaria would be plundered by the Assyrians (8:4), so that the entire aim of the anti-Assyrian coalition would prove to be disastrous. Ahaz, therefore, should maintain his neutrality, and would have nothing to fear from the threat at which he had evidently been greatly alarmed (7:2). Only by such a resolute stand could he hope to secure his throne (7:9).

A major problem in connection with this interpretation of the names of the three children, especially in connection with the understanding of the Immanuel child as that of the prophet himself, has been felt in the time-scale it implies. The first child had already been born (7:3), whereas the second child was expected but not yet born (7:14), and the third child had not even been conceived at the time of the prophet's revealing his name (8:1, 3). Furthermore, the interpretations of the names of the second and third children point to an interval of time of upwards of a year (7:16; 8:4) before the threat from Syria and Ephraim would be finally removed. All of this has to be fitted within a period of less than three years (735–732), by which time the Syro-Ephraimite crisis had passed. However, two points may be made. In the first place, it is not certain that all three children were born to the same woman, so that the period of pregnancy between the second and third births may have overlapped. Secondly, the prophet simply declared the outer limits of time, by deliberately vague circumlocutions, before which the threat to Ahaz would have been removed. That the swiftness of Assyrian action resolved the crisis sooner in no way undermines the authenticity of how Isaiah foresaw such action developing. Thirdly, we have already noted that there is some uncertainty about the time and circumstances of the beginning of the crisis. It has undoubtedly been an effect of the inclusion of the historical note in 7:1 that it suggests that the threat to Jerusalem and Ahaz had already reached an advanced stage when Isaiah was sent to confront Ahaz. As the content of the message of 7:2–9 shows, this was certainly not the case, so that the time of this confrontation may, in reality, have been earlier than has usually been envisaged. What is clear is that it took place before Ahaz sent his deputation, bearing tribute and an appeal for help, to Assyria. Precisely when this was cannot be certainly ascertained. There is no reason at all, therefore, why all three incidents involving the giving of prophetic messages through sign-names attached to Isaiah's children should not have been completed within the space of approximately three years. It may have been significantly less.

Because of the importance of the prophecy concerning the Immanuel child in Christian tradition (cf. Matt. 1:22–23), and the complexity of the prophecy contained in 7:10–17, it has given rise to a very extensive literature, which cannot be examined in detail here (see Bibliography).

7:1. In the days of Ahaz the son of Jotham: The historical note here concerning the background and circumstances of the Syro-Ephraimite crisis which led to Isaiah's prophecies, has been taken from 2 Kg. 16:5. It was not, therefore, a part of the original Isaianic memoir. Most likely it was added during the sixth century at a time when the context of Isaiah's prophecies was already in danger of being forgotten. **Rezin the king of Syria** was *Raṣyān*, who appears to have taken the initiative in persuading Pekah of Israel to unite in forming an anti-Assyrian coalition. What other states were also involved is not certainly known, but already in 738 a large coalition of central Syrian states had united against Assyria, and their revolt quelled. Tiglath-pileser's annals also mention a move against Philistia in 734, strongly suggesting that a number of the western Syrian and Mediterranean kingdoms were likely to have been involved. If this were the case, then Ahaz's refusal to join such a coalition may have made him distinctly isolated, and a potential threat to the security of the entire anti-Assyrian plan. The reference to the fact that they **came up to Jerusalem** points to the implementing of a siege against the city, but evidently this had not begun by the time of Isaiah's meeting with Ahaz recounted in 7:2ff. Similarly the mention that **they could not conquer it** indicates the eventual outcome of the attempt, which had certainly not yet been decided at the stage marked by Isaiah's prophecy, when Ahaz was still full of alarm at the threat to him and his throne (7:2).

2. When the house of David was told is of singular interest because its reference to Ahaz is in the form of a reference to the dynasty which he represented. This strongly hints in the direction of a threat to the continuance of this dynasty through the attempt to replace Ahaz by ben Tabeel (v. 6), as well as by Isaiah's own implied admonition in 7:9. Just how far Isaiah felt himself to be deeply committed to the Davidic dynasty as an essential part of Yahweh's purpose for Israel is not entirely certain. If the prophecy in 9:2–7 is authentically from Isaiah (see below *in loc.*), then it may well be that the prophet did accept the importance of the ancient tradition which linked the rule of the Davidides in Jerusalem to a special prophetic promise (cf. 2 Sam. 7:13). In this case it is reasonable to understand Isaiah's assurance that the plan to remove Ahaz would fail as linked to such a tradition. However, it is abundantly plain that Isaiah did not accept that the Davidic dynasty could be assured of Yahweh's protection and support in all circumstances as the threat implied by the condition in v. 9b shows. The phrase **Syria is in league with Ephraim** has occasioned some difficulty because the interpretation of the verb **is in league with** (Heb. *nāh*) is not clear. Wildberger is probably correct in seeing here a form of the verb *nûah*, 'to settle down, rest', with the meaning 'has

settled on, imposed its will on', whereas the *RSV* translation postulates a denominative verb meaning 'is brother with'. Cf. O. Eissfeldt,
Kleine Schriften, III, ed. F. Maass and R. Sellheim, Tübingen, 1966,
pp. 124–8. Wildberger's view would reflect the fact that the main
initiative to deal with Judah came from Syria. The fear of the king is
fully acknowledged with the mention that **his heart and the heart of
his people shook**. The reference to the people indicates the popular
attachment to the Davidic dynasty, which may have been a factor that
the very contrary view held in Samaria had not taken adequately into
account.

3. And the LORD said to Isaiah must originally have been
recorded in the first person, 'and the LORD said to me', as a part of the
prophet's own memoir. **You and Shear-jashub your son** introduces
us to the prophet's child and his mysterious sign-name, which is
clearly intended to provide a major constituent part of the prophet's
message to the king. Presumably the name had already been conferred
prior to this time, although we cannot rule out the possibility that it
was given especially for this occasion. If the former is the case then it
undoubtedly opens the possibility that it was originally applied to a
different situation from that which now faced Ahaz. An immense
variety of possible interpretations have been canvassed for the understanding of the name (cf. Wildberger, I, pp. 277f.). Certainly the idea
of a 'remnant' of an army (Heb. *šᵉʾār* cf. H. Wildberger, *THAT*, II,
cols. 844ff.), points to the defeat and flight of that army. Yet the
interpretation of the name given in vv. 7*b*, 8*a* and 9*a* (see *in loc.*).
shows that Isaiah intended the presence of the child with his
message-bearing name to be a word of assurance to Ahaz that he had
nothing to fear from the alliance that was ranged against him.
Possibly the name originally bore a significance applicable to another
context, but so far as Isaiah's encounter with Ahaz is concerned it
must mean one thing only: the armies of the Arameans and Israelites
which were now threatening to march against Jerusalem would be
defeated and reduced to a remnant. Certainly Isaiah had no illusions
that such an overthrow of the threatened attack on Jerusalem could be
inflicted by the relatively small army of Judah, so he must have intended this message to refer to a defeat inflicted by the Assyrians. For
Ahaz the import of the message was that he should maintain his strict
neutrality by not appealing for aid to Assyria and thereby inviting
them to interfere more extensively in the affairs of both Israel and
Judah. There are no indications that the prophet cherished any
utopian notions that Jerusalem could always be assured of Yahweh's
protection, or that he failed to take seriously the strength of the
opposition that was now directed towards deposing Ahaz (see below
on 8 : 11–15). The decision that he sought from Ahaz was a perfectly
sane and well-considered one in the circumstances.

The location of the meeting-place **at the end of the conduit of the
upper pool** has not been certainly identified, but may have been that
of the ancient reservoir at the site of *Birket el Hamra* (cf. *BHH*, II,
cols. 841f.).

4. Take heed, be quiet, do not fear: The emphatic repetition of the admonitions not to be afraid shows clearly that the substance of Isaiah's message to the king was one of assurance. Yet it was an assurance that needed to be believed and acted upon if it were to become effective. **because of these two smouldering stumps of firebrands** expresses ironic contempt for the two kings which headed the alliance. It is a later redactor who has interpreted the metaphor by the addition of the words **at the fierce anger of Rezin and Syria and the son of Remaliah.** No doubt it was the same redactor who added the glosses in 7:17, 20 and 8:4 to identify the prophet's metaphorical allusion. Barth, p. 198, argues that all four glosses were made at the time when the Isaianic memoir was still an independent source.

5. Because Syria, with Ephraim effectively captures the sense of where the initiative for the attack on Judah lay.

6. Let us go up against Judah and terrify it reveals something of the circumscribed aims of the alliance against Ahaz. By terrorising the population into an acceptance of their plan, the Aramean-Israelite coalition hoped to get rid of Ahaz without impairing the strength of Judah's army for resistance against Assyria. Very probably they could also count on a faction within Judah which was sympathetic to their aims. The declaration **and set up the son of Tabeel as king in the midst of it** introduces us to the nominee which the coalition intended to use to replace Ahaz. Who he was is not entirely clear, but most probably he was a 'pliant Aramean' of non-Davidic origin. Cf. H. Donner, in J. H. Hayes and J. M. Miller (eds.), *Israelite and Judean History*, p. 426; Y. Aharoni, *The Land of the Bible*, p. 328; B. Mazar, *IEJ* 7 (1957), pp. 137–45, 229–38. The last scholar links the name Tabeel (*tāḇʾēl*) with that of Tobiah (cf. Neh. 2:10, etc.), and argues that the Tobiad family ruled in Gilead at this time. A Vanel, *Studies on Prophecy (VT Supp. 26)*, pp. 17–24, identifies him as a Phoenician prince, the son of Ittobaal, king of Tyre. This would certainly presuppose the contention that the Phoenician cities supported the anti-Assyrian pact. There is no positive evidence that ben Tabeel was of Davidic descent, either directly or through marriage, and this possibility should be discounted. Ahaz's fear, therefore, must genuinely have concerned his entire household and dynasty.

7. It shall not stand, and it shall not come to pass: The brief saying provides a definitive declaration of the prophet's message to the king, and the import of the name of Shear-jashub, the prophet's son. The reference is indubitably to the plot to depose Ahaz. Why Isaiah was so confident that the plan would not succeed is not clear, but most probably the major factor that weighed with his judgment was the conviction that the ultimate aims of the anti-Assyrian coalition were doomed to failure. Already the strength of Tiglath-pileser III had been amply demonstrated in his earlier campaign in the West. Cf. A. Alt, *Kleine Schriften*, II, pp. 150–62. Ahaz had nothing to gain from joining such an alliance, therefore, and participating in its downfall. Yet neither need he invite the Assyrians to be his unseemly protectors. Isaiah seems also to have felt sure that Ahaz's life was not in danger.

8. For the head of Syria is Damascus: We are here introduced to the striking feature of several of Isaiah's prophecies that they employ long and enigmatic sounding circumlocutions. The meaning in vv. 8*a* and 9*a*, which displays a parallel form, is reasonably clear. Behind each of the countries which were aligned against Ahaz was a city, and on the throne of that city was a mere man. Hence the countries were no stronger than the plans of the men who ruled them, and these were not the plans of God. They were destined for failure, therefore, as merely 'human' designs. Cf. 30:1.

The second half of v. 8, **Within sixty-five years Ephraim...
people,** is a glossator's addition which has come in much later. It serves to clarify, by referring to the events relating to the collapse of the Northern Kingdom of Israel, that the prophecy had been fulfilled. If the prophecy is to be dated in 735/4, this would bring the calculation of sixty-five years down to approximately 670 BC. This was a time when Esarhaddon ruled Assyria (680–669 BC), and when further extensive depopulation of the provinces into which the Israelite kingdom had been divided, took place (cf. Ezr. 4:2). This seems the most likely interpretation of the gloss, although Barth, pp. 200f., would count back from the time of the fall of Samaria to Assyria in 733, and see in this addition the glossator's reckoning of the period of the decline of the Northern Kingdom. Thereby it would establish a much more immediate relevance of the sign-name to Ahaz himself. D. L. Christensen, *Transformations of the War Oracle in Old Testament Prophecy*, Missoula, 1975, pp. 127ff., sees in Isa. 7:7–9 the form of the ancient prophetic 'war oracle'.

9. If you will not believe: There is a conscious play in Hebrew on the sound of the verbs **believe ... be established,** which are etymologically related. Just what exactly was implied by the threat that if he did not trust in Isaiah's message he would not be secure is not made plain to Ahaz. Clearly his own retention of the throne was shown to be in jeopardy, but Isaiah seems positively to hint at more than this and to be implying that the continuance of the Davidic dynasty would be threatened. Cf. O. H. Steck, *ThZ* 29 (1973), p. 163.

THE SIGN OF IMMANUEL

7:10–17

A second encounter between Isaiah and Ahaz is now recorded which took place at some interval of time after the first (cf. **Again the LORD spoke,** in v. 10). How long this was is not evident, and neither is it entirely clear whether Ahaz had yet sent the tribute and plea for help to Assyria. That he was bent on doing so is evident from the sharp note of anger and hostility that enters into this second encounter (v. 13). However, the fervour of the prophet, and the willingness on his part to offer a special **sign** to the king would certainly be best understood if Isaiah recognised that it was still not too late for the king to maintain his neutrality. Cf. H. Donner, *Israel unter den Völkern*, pp. 15ff., who argues that the king continued to delay sending the deputation to Assyria until a very late stage in the crisis. Yet he was clearly not convinced that neutrality was the right response, but rather hoped to delay taking a difficult and unwelcome decision. All the indications are that this second meeting between Isaiah and Ahaz took place before the deputation had left, and when Isaiah was still hopeful that a positive decision for neutrality on the part of the king could be reached.

The major problem regarding the interpretation of this prophecy has centred upon the identity of the **young woman** mentioned in v. 14 who is to be the mother of the child who will bear the name Immanuel. Answers have varied between three major opinions: (1) that 'any young woman' is meant (cf. O. Kaiser); (2) that the woman is the royal consort so that the child would be the king's, thereby assuring him of an heir (cf. E. Hammershaimb, S. Mowinckel); (3) that the young woman was the wife of the prophet so that the child, like Shear-jashub, was a son of the prophet's. This third view was advocated by such great mediaeval Jewish commentators as Ibn Ezra and Rashi, early English critical students of prophecy such as A. Collins, and in more recent years by J. J. Stamm. N. K. Gottwald and H. Donner. The first view must be dismissed, since it would effectively rob the birth of the character of a sign, by presupposing that the removal of the threat had occurred before the birth took place. Similarly the second view must be rejected on the grounds that it would make the king effectively the giver of the prophetic message which was contained in the name Immanuel. The prophet had no power to determine what name the king would choose. More importantly than this, it is not the birth which was to form the sign, but rather the name that was to be given to the child. This was declared by the prophet, and there is little reason to doubt that he was able to be sure of this name, since he alone had the right to confer it. The child was, therefore, evidently his own. Thus we have here the second in the series of three children, each bearing sign-names given by the prophet. It follows from this that there is no reason at all for connecting the promised birth of the Immanuel child with the royal birth announced in 9:2–7. In fact this latter event was in reality a royal accession, as the context shows (see below *in loc.*).

It remains to ask what this second prophetic message revealed through a child's sign-name adds to that of the first prophecy connected with the name Shear-jashub. This additional feature is to be found in the time-scale now declared by the prophet within which the removal of the threat from the Syro-Ephraimite alliance would come (7:16). Once again this is conveyed through a strangely enigmatic sounding circumlocution. For the way in which such a prophecy came to provide a basis for a later, and very different, Christian interpretation of the birth of the Messiah (cf. Mt. 1:22–23), see my *Old Testament Theology*, London, 1978, pp. 146f.

10. Again the LORD spoke: The prophet makes a direct and explicit identification between his further meeting with Ahaz and addressing him and the very speech of God to the king.

11. Ask a sign of the LORD: The sign (Heb. *'ôt;* cf. *THAT*, I, cols. 91-5) was not necessarily an event or object that was miraculous in itself (cf. Isa. 38 : 7-8), but could be a quite natural happening or thing which was vested with a special divine meaning and significance. This is evidently the case here, for it is to be the name which the child bears which constitutes the sign, rather than any circumstances surrounding the birth. The phrase **let it be deep as Sheol** is an obvious hyperbole, meaning 'let it be anything at all'. Sheol was the underworld to which the dead were believed to go, but there was no intention of inviting the king to traffic with mediums or departed spirits as did Saul (1 Sam. 28 : 8-25).

12. But Ahaz said, 'I will not ask . . .': The king's refusal to accept the sign from the prophet makes it plain that what was at issue was not simply listening to a message from God, but acting upon it in an appropriate way. Ahaz clearly knew from his first encounter with Isaiah that he would not be likely to find his further message acceptable. However, he could mask his refusal to listen behind a facade of piety, since there was probably a tradition that it was unseemly, if not improper, to put God to the test (cf. Dt. 6 : 16).

13. And he said, 'Hear then, O house of David!: The renewed address to the king as the **house of David** (cf. v. 2 above) serves to emphasise once again the traditions that lay behind the royal throne. Isaiah was determined to remind the king of the royal promises which should have assured him of the divine support for his throne. This is brought out still further in v. 17, where the prophet reminds the king that it is he who should have been ruling Ephraim, not Ephraim deposing him. The angry reply of the prophet, **Is it too little for you to weary men**, marks a significant turning-point in Isaiah's dealings with the king. From this moment onwards the ambivalence in the prophetic assurance to Ahaz that he has nothing to fear begins to display itself. By refusing the promise of God, Ahaz has set himself against God, and thereby made the very rock on which he should have relied for defence into a stone to stumble over (cf. 8 : 14-15). In this strange way the very promise that Isaiah has given to him will be turned into a threat. The complaint that Ahaz had begun to **weary men** would fit well in a situation where Ahaz had delayed and procrastinated in the hope of avoiding the necessity for making a difficult decision. Yet he had been given time enough, and his continued refusal to make a clear decision for neutrality had begun to **weary . . . God also.**

14. Therefore the LORD himself will give you a sign: The sign is voluntarily given by God, without the king's prior request for it, because Ahaz has made it evident that he will not pay heed to its implicit message. This sign is to be found in the name given to this second child, **Immanuel**—God with us. **Behold, a young woman shall conceive:** It is better to render the Heb. perfect tense 'has conceived and will bear a son'. The conception was in the past, but the birth was still in the future. It is the messianic interpretation of the verse which has encouraged the translation in the future tense, although the Heb. could possibly bear such a meaning. A good deal of discussion has centred on the identity of the **young woman** (Heb. *'almāh*). In Heb. the noun appears to refer to a young woman of marriageable age, who is not necessarily a virgin. Thus, although it could be used of a virgin, this sense was not necessary to the meaning of the word. Who she was has already been considered above, and she must be identified as the wife of the prophet. The use of the Heb. definite article with the noun may signify this, but does not indubitably do so. More probably the article simply singles out someone whom the prophet designated. **and shall call his name Immanuel:** The Heb. MT reads the verb with the third person feminine singular subject, 'she shall call his name . . .', firmly implying that the mother would give the child his name (at the prophet's command). A variant text tradition reads the second person singular, 'you shall call his name . . . ', thereby implying that the king would do this. IQIs^a and Symmachus read the third person masculine singular, 'one shall call his name . . .'. However, all these variants simply reflect the different interpretations of the prophecy which arose, and do not serve to resolve the question of the identity of the child's mother. The name **Immanuel** means 'God is with us', and would thereby serve as an assurance that there was nothing to fear from those who now threatened Judah. It has probably been adapted from a cultic affirmation; cf. Ps. 46:7. Evidently Isaiah still hoped to persuade Ahaz with his prophetic message, but his warning of the consequences of not accepting it have introduced a threatening element.

15. He shall eat curds and honey: The reference, which commences an interpretation of the message of the sign-name, has added to the difficulty of interpretation. Almost certainly the verse is an editor's gloss (so A. Schoors), which has been introduced at an early stage to interpret the meaning of the prophet's phrase about 'refusing the evil' and 'choosing the good' (v. 16). The parallel instances of the prophetic formulation by introducing the name's interpretation with a clause beginning 'for . . .' (cf. 7:8; 8:4) would support such a conclusion. If it is original to Isaiah, then it must be regarded and interpreted as subordinate to v. 16. The reference to **curds and honey** has added to the divergent patterns of interpretation. As natural foods, they could be regarded as the food resources at a time of siege and deprivation. More plausibly, however, they might appear as the rich foods which could be enjoyed in an age of plenty. In this instance it is unlikely that either nuance was intended (although the former view is that taken up in v. 21 by a later redactor). The **curds and honey** refer to the first solid foods that an infant child would be given when it was weaned, so that the reference here is intended to show that 'refusing the evil' and 'choosing the good' refer to the child's showing its likes and dislikes in respect of food.

16. For before the child knows how to refuse the evil: It is clear that no great interval of time could be intended, since already some time was needed to elapse before the birth of Immanuel was expected. Hence it is likely that the interpretation given by the editor who inserted v. 15 is correct, and the reference here is to the child's taking various kinds of solid food. It may otherwise have been intended to refer to the awakening of the moral senses, if this were assumed to begin at a very early age; i.e. when the child could be told what he should, or should not, do. The real content of the assurance of the Immanuel name is spelt out quite explicitly with the concluding phrase, **the land before whose two kings you are in dread will be deserted.** Those who now threatened Ahaz and his throne would be fully occupied in defending their own lands, and they would suffer a grievous defeat. There is no question but that Isaiah meant this to refer to an attack by the Assyrians to quell the revolt of the Arameans and Israelites. Ahaz need take no action, since those who threatened him had already sealed their own fate.

17. The LORD will bring upon you: The verse comes rather awkwardly after the previous pronouncement has said all that really needed to be said to interpret the Immanuel name. Furthermore it is not clear whether the reference to **the day that Ephraim departed from Judah** was intended in a good sense or a bad one; i.e. 'times will come when Israel and Judah will again be reunited', or 'evils will come as on that fateful day when the great kingdom of Solomon was divided into two' (1 Kg. 12 : 16–24). The editor who spelt out the prophet's meaning by adding the words **the king of Assyria** at the end has certainly assumed this threatening sense to be the correct one. Barth, p. 198, argues that this gloss was introduced to the prophecy at a time when the Isaianic memoir still existed as an independent composition. Most plausibly, v. 17 has then been introduced by Isaiah to make clear that Ahaz had refused to accept the promise of the Immanuel name, and had thereby turned it into a judgment upon himself. We should understand an implicit ellipse at the commencement of the verse: (Since you refuse this promise), **the LORD will bring upon you.** The threatening element with which the Immanuel prophecy concludes would then be in line with Isaiah's anger expressed in v. 13, and would serve to show how Ahaz had chosen to follow a policy which would bring Yahweh's judgment down upon himself and his people.

THE THREAT FROM ASSYRIA

7 : 18–20

The verses in 7 : 18–25 contain a sequence of four prophecies each beginning **In that day**, which is to be regarded as an indication that they have been set in their present position by a redactor. Vv. 21–25, which contain two of these prophecies, are not from Isaiah, but have been composed and added later. They are, therefore, best dealt with separately. In contrast with these secondary compositions, vv. 18–20 are generally recognised to derive from Isaiah (so Fohrer, Wildberger, Kaiser, Barth, Dietrich), but to have been extensively glossed. Hence their importance as explanations of how the threat which concludes vv. 1–17 was realised is readily seen. Furthermore, the manner in which the glosses have been made indicates that they have subsequently been applied to a later period. Dietrich, pp. 97, 121f., argues against this that they did not come from the time of the Syro-Ephraimite crisis at all, but rather from that of the Philistine rebellion against Assyria in 713–711. It is then the redactor who has related them to the situation of the earlier threat. It is much more convincing, however, to relate the verses to the threat from Assyria, which Isaiah saw would readily ensue upon the decision taken by Ahaz at the time of the crisis of 735–732. It is then a redactor who has added the reference to **the sources of the streams of Egypt**, not in the Ptolemaic age (as Kaiser), but at the time when Hezekiah was looking for aid from Upper Egypt (Ethiopia). Cf. Barth, pp. 198–200. The prophecy has thereby been adapted to a later period of Isaiah's activity.

7 : 18. **In that day the LORD will whistle for the fly:** Wildberger would reconstruct the original verse to have contained no reference to **the fly which is at the sources of the streams of Egypt**, so that the original prophecy referred only to **the bee which is in the land of Assyria** (cf. also Kaiser). This is unquestionably the source from which Isaiah recognised that the threat against Ahaz and his kingdom would come (cf. 8 : 4, 6–8a). However, it is more convincing, following Barth, pp. 199f., to see the glosses as made up of the interpretation of the metaphors of **the fly** and **the bee** by the additions of **which is at the sources of the streams of Egypt** and **which is in the land of Assyria**. The original prophecy would then simply have spoken of Yahweh's whistling for **the fly** and **the bee**, both of which metaphors were intended to apply to Assyria. It is then a redactor who has enlarged this to refer to two different potential enemies, once Hezekiah had become embroiled with negotiations with Ethiopia in the plans for rebellion against Assyria.

19. **And they will all come:** The picture contained in the verse elaborates very effectively the idea introduced in the preceding one. Ahaz thought to summon help for himself from Assyria. In reality, however, it would be Yahweh who summoned the Assyrians, who would prove to be as uncomfortable and undesirable a company of visitors as swarms of flies and bees. Everywhere would be covered with them, and Ahaz would prove quite unable to rid himself of them.

20. **In that day the LORD will shave with a razor:** The verse in its main substance repeats the same basic threat that is contained in vv. 18–19. This time, however, the metaphor used is that of a razor which will shave **the head and the hair of the feet**. The latter is a euphemistic way of referring to the private parts. There may be some allusion to the way in which prisoners could be ill-treated, but more probably the metaphor simply intends to affirm that the Assyrians would leave Ahaz with nothing, not even the hairs left on his body. Some conscious allusion to the gift which Ahaz was proposing to send, or had already sent, to Assyria (2 Kg. 16 : 8) may be intended. Certainly the words **with the king of Assyria** are an editor's gloss (cf. 7 : 17; 8 : 4). Very probably also the entire clause **which is hired beyond the River**, which stands in an awkward grammatical relationship to the noun a

razor, is made up of two separate additional glosses. These would then have been introduced subsequent to the first gloss which identified the metaphor of the razor with the king of Assyria. **which is hired** (Heb. *haśś^{e}k̲îrāh*), which must now be understood to stand in an epexegetic relationship to the noun **razor**, was a reference to 'a company of mercenary soldiers' (cf. Jer. 46 : 21) and **beyond the River** (Heb. *b^e'ḇrê nāhār*) has entered when this was taken as a reference to the 'hiring' of the razor, probably as a consequence of its connection with Ahaz's tribute money (2 Kg. 16 : 8).

FURTHER INTERPRETATIONS OF ISAIAH'S PROPHECIES

7 : 21–25

The two further prophecies commencing **In that day** (vv. 21, 23) are in fact made up of three further interpretations of Isaianic sayings, since v. 22*a* is a secondary elaboration of the interpretation which is to be found in vv. 21, 22*b* of the theme of 'curds and honey' from 7 : 15. The second prophecy, in vv. 23–25, is itself constituted of no less than three separate, but not necessarily independent, interpretations of the theme of the 'briers and thorns' from the Song of the Vineyard in 5 : 1–7. None of the material comes from the prophet Isaiah himself, but nonetheless it offers an extremely interesting series of examples of the way in which a pattern of developmental exegesis was applied to prophecies in order to elicit further meanings from them. It is evident in this case that the aim of such interpretative additions has been to relate Isaiah's prophecies to situations which had subsequently arisen, although in one instance (v. 22*a*) a truly prophetic feature is retained and the fulfilment of the prophecy was looked for in the future.

In vv. 21, 22*b* we have an interpretation of the reference to **curds and honey** which originally appeared in v. 15. We have already noted that in that context it was most probably already an interpretative addition to the Isaianic prophecy concerned with the Immanuel name. In the new interpretation, however, the reference to these particular foods is taken in a threatening sense to refer to the food resources which would be available to 'every one that is left in the land' (v. 22*b*). The meaning is that, when the judgment has fallen, which Isaiah had threatened, this is what the people would have left to live on. Barth, pp. 198f., relates it to the situation in Judah after 587. In this instance, however, we should certainly consider more fully the possibility that it is to be related to the situation which arose in the Northern Kingdom after 722. A yet later editor, from the post-exilic age, has turned this into a prophecy of hope by adding v. 22*a*, which sees in the saying a sign of the richness and prosperity of the life that will be enjoyed in the coming age of Israel's salvation.

The three sayings in vv. 23–25 form a connected trilogy of interpretations which express a message of warning and judgment regarding the fate that will be suffered by the land of Israel. Barth, pp. 198f., would date them all after 587 BC, but they appear rather to be earlier and related to the fate of the Northern Kingdom. Particularly does this appear likely since the interpretation given in v. 24 of the **briers and thorns** appears to be presupposed in 10 : 17 (see below *in loc.*). Each of the three sayings in vv. 23–25 concerns an interpretation of the 'briers and thorns' which are mentioned as replacing the vines of the vineyard in Isaiah's parable (Isa. 5 : 6). In the Isaianic prophecy the picture is entirely appropriate, but this original parabolic sense is completely abandoned in the developed exegesis. In v. 23 all the rich vineyards of the land are threatened with being reduced to briers and thorns. In v. 24 the nouns are taken as metaphors of men **with bow and arrows,** and in v. 25 all the agricultural land which was not suitable for vineyards is threatened with becoming fit for nothing except grazing land for cattle and sheep. Probably all three verses come from a single redactor who has sought to show how the threat to **the land** first mentioned in 6 : 11 was realised. We may compare the interpretation of the name Shear-jashub from 7 : 3 in 10 : 20–23 for a comparable instance of such developmental prophetic interpretation.

21. In that day a man will keep alive a young cow: The continuation of the verse is to be found in v. 22b, **for every one that is left in the land,** which shows that the picture of the pastoral way of life is to be understood as the aftermath of judgment. The portrayal of this dependence on a few cattle and sheep offers a further interpretation of why the Immanuel child will eat **curds and honey,** as foretold in v. 15. All the cities will have been destroyed and the grain crops ruined so that men will be left to eke out a livelihood from the few cattle and sheep that remain. The redactor who added this warning must certainly have done so *post eventum*, and is most likely picturing the ruination of the Northern Kingdom after 722. However, if Judah is the intended **land** that is mentioned in v. 22b, then the situation in that land after 587 must be presupposed.

22. and because of the abundance of milk which they give, he will eat curds: V. 22a has been inserted between the pronouncement of v. 21 and its explanation in v. 22b in order to turn its implication round in the opposite sense. We have earlier noted the ambivalence in the idea of man's eating curds and honey, either as a sign of living from natural foods, available at all times, or as a token of living off very rich dairy foods. Here the latter sense has been imposed on the former to take the prophecy as a promise of the eventual wealth and prosperity that would come to Judah. This addition must certainly date from the post-exilic age.

23. In that day every place where there used to be a thousand vines: The picture of Israel's future (cf. **In that day**) given here is taken from the parable of the vineyard in Isa. 5 : 1–7, with its threat that the vineyard will be covered with briers and thorns. This is here taken as a literal prophecy of the fate that will befall the vineyards of Israel when the judgment of Yahweh that Isaiah had foretold occurred. It is most likely that we should understand this elaboration of Isaiah's threat as a *post eventum* description of what had happened to the land of Israel in the period which followed the Syro-Ephraimite war. When Samaria fell to Assyria in 733, much of its land was stripped away and added to other Assyrian provinces, and after 722 the whole land was divided up between three separate provinces. Both by the ravages of war and the subsequent political division of Israel's territory ruination came upon its fertile and arable land.

24. **With bow and arrows men will come there:** This further interpretation of the **briers and thorns** of Isa. 5 : 6 understands the terms as metaphors of soldiers. By this the armies of Assyria must be meant (or the Babylonians if **the land** is understood to be Judah). The threat of the burning and destruction of the **briers and thorns** in 10 : 17, where Assyria must be the enemy alluded to, would then appear to presuppose the development of this theme from the parable of the vineyard given here. It reveals one of the techniques of verbal elaboration which could be employed to interpret prophecy in relation to specific situations and events.

25. **and as for all the hills:** This verse presents the last of the three interpretations of **the briers and thorns** and concerns itself with the fate of the fertile land of Israel which was not used for vineyards. The warning is found in Isaiah's prophecy that this too will cease to be cultivated, but will instead become a wild place covered with **briers and thorns.** Thereby all the useful agricultural land of Israel will have reverted to its natural state. It appears probable that the reference to **a place where cattle are let loose and where sheep tread** picks up and elaborates upon the reference to cattle and sheep in v. 21. If this is the case then it would suggest that a closely comparable date must be presupposed for the additions of vv. 21, 22*b* and 23–25, with all of them referring to the fate of the Northern Kingdom.

THE SIGN OF MAHER-SHALAL-HASHBAZ

8 : 1–4

The trilogy of sign-names given to the children of the prophet is now concluded with the third such name, **Maher-shalal-hashbaz**— 'The spoil speeds, the prey hastes' (so RSV margin). The account, which is in the first person, derives from Isaiah's memoir and forms the continuation of 7 : 10–17 from which it has been separated by the inclusion of the further prophecy, and interpretations of Isaianic sayings in 7 : 18–25. Precisely what interval of time separates the announcement of the name for Isaiah's third child (8 : 1) from that concerning the Immanuel child in 7 : 14 is not clear. Almost certainly less than a year is involved, since the birth of the latter was soon expected, whereas, according to 8 : 3, the third child appears not to have been conceived at the time his name was attested. The meaning of the name **Maher-shalal-hashbaz** is given in v. 4, where almost certainly the clause **before the king of Assyria** is a redactor's addition which has come in from the same hand that inserted comparable identifications in 7 : 4, 17. The additional factor that is affirmed for this third sign-name, beyond that given to the Immanuel name, is the narrowing down of the time-scale within which the threat from the

Syro-Ephraimite alliance will have been removed. This is now set at the time **before the child knows how to cry 'My father' or 'My mother'**. We must conclude that this was roughly one year, or a little more, after the child's birth, to which we must add the time of Isaiah's wife's pregnancy. Hence approximately two years was being affirmed, although this was the outer limit of time before which the threat would have been removed. Overall there is no reason why all three sign-names associated with Isaiah's children, and more importantly the time required for the pregnancies and births relating to the second and third of them, should not have fitted within the period 735–733. Especially is this so, if the actual Assyrian overthrow of Damascus and Samaria came rather sooner than the prophet had allowed for. Donner, p. 6, affirms that Tiglath-pileser was certainly in Israel in 733. Overall, therefore, the main purpose of this third sign-name was to strengthen and reaffirm the message that had been given to Isaiah by the other two. According to 2 Kg. 16:7–9, Ahaz sent to Tiglath-pileser asking for aid against the Syro-Ephraimite threat and sending a substantial tribute gift. This implies that the king of Judah did not heed Isaiah's message, although the necessity for the giving of the three prophetic messages attached to the sign-names may well in-dicate that Ahaz delayed his decision. He eventually went to Damascus to pay homage to Tiglath-pileser (2 Kg. 16:10–16), and had no doubt been summoned to do so.

8:1. Then the LORD said to me, 'Take a large tablet...': The first-person form clearly reflects the origins of the passage in Isaiah's own memoir recording his activity at the time of the Syro-Ephraimite war. The reference to the **large tablet** (Heb. *gillāyôn gāḏôl*) indicates what must have been a common form of recording a name, or other important legal attestation, which in v. 16 is called a 'testimony' (Heb. *tᵉʿûḏāh*) and a 'teaching' (Heb. *tôrāh*). It was an agreement, or pro-nouncement, to which some form of legally binding attestation had been given. The tablet was most probably of clay, less probably of wood, and may have been disc shaped. K. Galling, *ZDPV* 56 (1933), pp. 209ff., would read 'sheet of papyrus', emending the adjective **large** (Heb. *gāḏôl*) to 'reed, papyrus' (Heb. *gôrāl*). Cf. *BHS*. The phrase **in common characters** is not above suspicion. H. Gressmann, *Der Messias* (1929), p. 239, note 1, suggests 'in permanent (ineradicable) writing', reading *ḥereṭ 'ānûš* instead of *ḥereṭ 'ᵉnôš*. **Belonging to Maher-shalal-hashbaz** The significance of the preposition *lᵉ* has been variously understood. *RSV*'s acceptance that it indicates possession is followed by H. Donner, pp. 18f., although B. Duhm understood it to mean 'dedicated to'. In either case the purpose of introducing the name at this stage, for a child who had not yet even been conceived, was to show the certainty which pertained to the message contained in his name. The name means 'Spoil speeds—booty hastes'. This inter-pretation requires that *māhēr* is taken as a shortened form of *mᵉmāhēr*, the Piʿel participle form of the verb. Then both verbal parts of the name can be understood as participles. S. Morenz, *ThLZ* 74 (1949), cols. 697 ff., has argued that the first clause of the name is a soldier's cry, attested in Egypt from the time of the eighteenth dynasty, which should originally be taken as an imperative: 'Let the spoil hasten!' If so, it was presumably almost a popular military catch-phrase, which the prophet has taken up. Like the name Shear-jashub it indicates a forthcoming military defeat, although only the context can show who will experience this. In the present instance, however, v. 4 shows unmistakably that it will be the cities of Samaria and Damascus.

2. And I got reliable witnesses, Uriah the priest: There is no indication that either **Uriah** or **Zechariah** were in any special sense 'disciples' of the prophet. They were called in as witnesses because of the public trust which men in their position enjoyed. LXX and 1QIs^a read 'and take reliable witnesses', but the sense is not affected. The role of the witnesses is to affirm at what time the prophet disclosed the name so that later, when the message it bore had proved true, they would be in a position to uphold the prophet's claim to have foretold the defeat of Syria and Ephraim. In a sense the purpose of the entire Isaianic memoir must have been in line with this role played by the prophetic tablet. Since, when the rightness of its message was seen it would be too late to call back Ahaz's appeal to Assyria, the tablet would serve to show why its tragic consequences had been incurred. So in a similar fashion the entire memoir was a witness against Ahaz and his policy, showing where, in human terms, culpability lay.

3. And I went to the prophetess, and she conceived: Kaiser, following Duhm, Marti and Galling, reads the Heb. imperfect cons. in a pluperfect sense: 'And I had gone to the prophetess . . .' Whilst this offers some slight easing in the sense of delay in the birth of the child, as the first stage in the fulfilment of the prophecy which the child's name conveys, the advantage is slight. Overall it is the period of the pregnancy plus the time of the child's first beginning to speak which forms a substantial part of the prophetic sign. There is no need to follow N. K. Gottwald, *VT* 8 (1958), pp. 36ff., in regarding the third child of 8:1-4 as identical with that promised in 7:10-17. If we accept that **the prophetess** of v. 3 is the same young woman as that mentioned in 7:14, then some short interval before the new conception is required. This does not require an inordinately long time.

4. for before the child knows how to cry 'My father': We have a prophetic circumlocution very similar both in form and content to that given by Isaiah in 7:16. It affirms the length of time required for the sign to be fulfilled, but only in a rather loose and general way. It establishes the outer limit, before which the coming of Assyria will bring an end to the Syro-Ephraimite threat. By his intended appeal to Assyria Ahaz was not only surrendering himself to a foreign ruler, with possible adverse religious consequences (cf. 2 Kg. 16:10–16), but also embittering future relationships with Ephraim and plundering the temple of Yahweh (2 Kg. 16:8). The phrase **before the king of Assyria** is almost certainly a redactional clarification of what was perfectly clearly understood by the prophet's hearers. Cf. 7:4, 17 for similar explanatory comments. Then we should read '. . . the wealth of Damascus and the spoil of Samaria will be carried off.' The prophetic message contained in the sign-name is effectively identical with that given earlier in the name Shear-jashub, but now a more definable time-scale has been introduced.

THE OVERWHELMING FLOOD
8:5–8

It is evident that the original continuation of 8:1–4 is to be found in 8:16–18, where the role of the witnesses to the inscribing of the child's name, Maher-shalal-hashbaz, and the role of all three children as 'signs and portents', is affirmed. Nevertheless the two prophecies in 8:(5)6–8 and 8:11–15 must be regarded as authentic to Isaiah. Furthermore, they certainly belong to the time of the Syro-Ephraimite crisis, so that their inclusion at this point in the Isaianic memoir would appear to be the handiwork of the prophet himself. The purpose is quite clear: to show that, in making his appeal to Assyria, Ahaz had rejected Yahweh. In consequence the expected 'help' he had sought from Assyria would prove to bring ruin to Judah as well as to Israel. The editorial note in v. 5 may well derive from Isaiah himself, although F. Huber, p. 83 note, would see it as a later addition. It marks the following verses as a separate prophecy, which nevertheless serves to show how the deliverance promised in vv. 1–4 will have been turned to disaster by Ahaz's action.

8:5. The LORD spoke to me again: The formula shows that this is an additional prophecy, but one which now clearly presupposes that Ahaz had made his decision to appeal to Tiglath-pileser for help against the Syro-Ephraimite threat. What interval of time had elapsed since the public attestation of the name Maher-shalal-hashbaz is not clear, but it can scarcely have been as much as a year.

6. Because this people have refused the waters of Shiloah: The phrase **this people** must refer to Judah, and the act of refusal was contained in the sending to Assyria for help. The decision of the king, Ahaz, is taken to be an action shared by all the people, who will certainly share in its consequences. It is possible, however, to see also in the title the prophet's intention of showing that Yahweh had disowned Judah from being 'his people'. Cf. 1:3. **the waters of Shiloah that flow gently.** It is better to read 'gently and slowly', reading the Heb. word $m^e\check{s}\hat{o}\check{s}$ as 'gently', cf. 10:18, instead of as the verb 'rejoices in . . .' The textual confusion has no doubt been assisted by the inclusion of the gloss **before Rezin and the son of Remaliah.** Cf. on 7:4 and 8:4 where similar explanatory notes have been added. *RSV* reads the verb as 'melt in fear'. The **waters of Shiloah** refers to the sluggish stream that brought water from the spring Gihon along the edge of the eastern hill of the city of Jerusalem. Cf. J. Simons, *Jerusalem in the Old Testament*, Leiden, 1952, pp. 172ff. Clearly the choice of the metaphor has been dictated by the poetic contrast intended between the limited water supply of Jerusalem in comparison with the mighty Tigris which flowed through the Assyrian capital.

7. therefore, behold, the LORD is bringing up against them: The allusion is to the Tigris, the great river at the heart of Assyria, with its well-known propensity to an annual flood. The phrase **the king of Assyria and all his glory** must be regarded as a gloss which has come in in order to interpret the metaphor. Of course the whole point of Ahaz's appeal to Assyria was for the Assyrians to come to attack Syria and Ephraim, but the prophet makes plain that their coming will not stop there. Not only will this affect Judah both religiously and politically, as the narrative in 2 Kg. 16 : 10–16 shows, but it will mean invoking Assyrian forces against the sister kingdom of Israel, who also formed part of Yahweh's people. **and it will rise over all its channels** effectively uses the imagery of flooding to show the repercussions that Ahaz's action will bring to Judah.

8. And it will sweep on into Judah: The imagery of the flood metaphor leaves indeterminate exactly what the consequences will be so far as Judah was concerned. It is improbable that Isaiah simply shared a doctrinaire disapproval of all foreign alliances with little clear awareness of the more precise way in which it would affect Judah. Ahaz would have to submit his entire kingdom to the wishes of the Assyrian king. The phrase **reaching even to the neck** suggests that Judah also will all but be submerged by the flood. **and its outspread wings:** The sudden transition to the imagery of a bird with outstretched wings is awkward and unanticipated. With most modern commentators it should be regarded as a later addition. The concluding phrase **O Immanuel** must also derive from a redactor who has taken it from the sign-name in 7 : 14, but interpreted it very differently. In its original setting it was an affirmation of Yahweh's presence with Ahaz and Judah which should have led to the king's willingness to trust Yahweh for his protection. Now, since Ahaz had so decisively refused this divine protection, it has become a message of judgment. In this fashion the redactor has fully brought out the implication of the prophecy of 8 : 5–8. We may compare similar re-interpretations of sign-names given to children in Hos. 1 : 11; 2 : 22 over against Hos. 1 : 4.

A MESSAGE TO THE NATIONS

8 : 9–10

These two verses present a kind of summary application of the group of prophecies which have preceded in 7 : 1ff. They represent a warning to **peoples** and **far countries** that Judah is the people with whom Yahweh is present, so that no threat, or counsel, taken against her can prevail. They offer a markedly triumphalist assurance that Judah will receive divine protection, and there is no indication that there might be special conditions attached to this. Indeed the reason for this assurance scarcely permits such an interpretation. In spite of a defence of their Isaianic origin by M. Saebo, *ZAW* 76 (1964), pp. 132–43, this must certainly be rejected. Their whole tenor clashes with the warning of the havoc that will be wrought upon Judah by the Assyrians in the preceding verses. With H. Barth, pp. 178ff., we must see these two verses as a part of the Josianic redaction (AR) and elaboration of Isaiah's prophecies, which has built up a strong message of judgment coming upon the Assyrians. Cf. also my book *Isaiah and the Deliverance of Jerusalem*, ch. 2. They express a universalised doctrine of divine protection for Jerusalem based upon a highly distinctive interpretation of what occurred in 701. Cf. also 29:7.

9. Be broken, you peoples, and be dismayed: Some commentators would emend to 'Take knowledge', reading $d^{e'}\hat{u}$ in place of $r\bar{o}'\hat{u}$. The sudden transition to a form of address to unnamed **peoples** who are assumed, at least potentially, to pose a threat to Judah is unexpected. Yet the verses are not apocalyptic, affirming that Judah will one day find all nations ranged against it. Rather they seek to affirm that Yahweh, who is with Judah, will defend his people. The basis for this hope is to be found in the way in which Judah and Jerusalem had ultimately escaped the fate which befell the Northern Kingdom of Israel at the hands of the Assyrians. The close similarity to the theme of Yahweh's 'Conflict with the Nations', such as we find expressed in Ps. 2, suggests that the royal Davidic tradition has fostered this expectation. Cf. J. J. M. Roberts, *JBL* 92 (1973), pp. 329-44.

10. Take counsel together: Cf. Ps. 2:2, for the notion of a plot by unnamed nations against Judah. Such imagery probably arose in relation to the attempts of subject nations to break free from Israelite rule, but has evidently here been extended greatly beyond this. The concluding remark **for God is with us** interprets the Immanuel name wholly in line with the meaning given to it in 7:14, but contrasting with the different interpretation made in 8:8. Almost certainly it is the felt need to re-assert this more reassuring significance of the name which has occasioned the insertion of vv. 9-10 here.

THE HOLINESS OF THE LORD OF HOSTS

8:11-15

This section contains a prophetic reminiscence, and must derive from Isaiah's own memoir of the Syro-Ephraimite crisis. Hence its preservation in the first-person form. It expresses Isaiah's sense of betrayal by his king and people at Ahaz's refusal to heed the assurances that had been proferred him by God. Isaiah receives from God an admonition to remain firm in his stand against the king, together with a further warning that the final consequences of the royal decision will prove to be disastrous for Judah. Overall this reminiscence serves as a clarification of the fact, already implicit in the memoir, that Isaiah had failed in his aim to persuade Ahaz to desist from appealing to Assyria.

11. For the LORD spoke thus to me: The implication is that the message is for the prophet himself, rather than as something which he should pass on to the people. That Isaiah had been shaken by Ahaz's action seems evident from the emphatic way in which this word from the LORD is given, **with his strong hand upon me.** The warning **not to walk in the way of this people** reveals the sense of isolation that the prophet felt, since he had now been rejected by his people along with his message. Some ancient versions suggest reading 'and turned me aside from walking'. The word is one of assurance that, in spite of all appearances, it is the people (and Ahaz) who have chosen wrongly, and Isaiah is not to be deterred by the fact of his own rejection.

12. Do not call conspiracy: The *NEB*'s rendering, 'You shall not say "too hard" ', rests on a different understanding of the Heb. word *qešer*, **conspiracy**, out of the conviction that this does not fit. Cf. G. R. Driver, *JTS* ns. 6 (1955), pp. 82–4. Kaiser follows Lindblom and Fohrer in arguing that the idea of a **conspiracy** arose because there was a faction in Judah sympathetic to the aims of the Syro-Ephraimite coalition. This was possibly true, but the use of the term must lie in the popular accusations levelled against Isaiah. He had evidently been accused of treasonable disloyalty on account of his threats to Ahaz. Possibly too it had been suggested that he now wanted Ahaz to be deposed (cf. 7:9). **and do not fear what they fear** must refer to the threat from the coalition, and it is intended to point to the fear of physical violence and destruction which the people hoped to avoid by their reliance on help from Assyria.

13. But the LORD of hosts, him you shall regard as holy: The similarity of sound between the Heb. noun for conspiracy (*qešer*) and the verb 'to be holy' (*qāḏaš*) has led many commentators to attempt emendations to bring them into closer alignment. Hence many would read here 'him (i.e. Yahweh) you shall conspire with'. Cf. also *NEB*, which attempts a more complex change. However, the Hebrew is intelligible as it stands and should be retained. The prophet relies on a certain similiarity of sound for the effect of his message. Certainly 'holiness' contained the emotions of awe and fear, and Isaiah is warned to remain steadfast in his awe of God, even in the face of physical threats and ostracism by his people.

14. And he will become a sanctuary: The noun **sanctuary** (Heb. *miqdāš*) sounds strange in a verse which affirms the threatening aspect of Yahweh's purpose towards Judah now that Ahaz had rejected Isaiah's repeated and determined appeals. Several commentators have suggested an emendation to *maqšîr*, 'One who conspires against'. Cf. *NEB*'s 'hardship'; i.e. 'cause of difficulty' (cf. LXX). Schoors would retain the MT's **sanctuary** as in *RSV*, since it is the *lectio difficilior*. However, the emendation would appear preferable. **and a stone of offence, and a rock of stumbling:** Following the notion of **sanctuary**, the prophet here interprets two popular metaphorical images of God—as a **stone** and a **rock**—and turns them round in a negative fashion. For such images cf. Pss. 18:47; 62:3; 98:27; 95:1; and *THAT*, II, cols. 538–43. The **rock**, which should be a place of strength and security, will become a **stone** to stumble over. The phrase **to both houses of Israel** reveals how fully Isaiah thought in terms of the oneness of Israel, and sought the welfare of both kingdoms, not of Judah only. Ahaz, by his action, had rent further apart the two divided kingdoms, yet Isaiah was not prepared to regard them as in any sense forming two 'nations' or 'kingdoms'. They were simply the 'two houses' of one people of Yahweh. **a trap and a snare to the inhabitants of Jerusalem.** The Heb. reads only the singular, 'inhabitant', which could mean 'the ruler of Jerusalem', i.e. Ahaz himself. However, some Heb. MSS and most ancient versions read the plural, which has been followed by almost all modern translations.

15. And many shall stumble thereon: The prophet here draws out the inevitable conclusion of the new situation which had been brought about by Ahaz's action. God's word of salvation, implicit in the sign-names given to all three children, would still stand, but to those like Ahaz who had turned their backs on it, it would become an occasion of defeat and ruin. The heaping up of no less than five separate verbs—**stumble ... fall ... be broken ... snared ... and taken**—brings out with immense forcefulness the sense of the tragic consequences which Isaiah now foresaw emerging out of Ahaz's obstinate decision.

THE SEALING OF THE MESSAGE
8 : 16–18

These three verses must mark the original conclusion of the memoir and refer back to the incident of 8 : 1–4, the writing of the child's name Maher-shalal-hashbaz on a tablet. They must originally have formed the continuation of v. 4, and their placing here may serve to show that vv. 5–15 have been inserted in between, possibly by the prophet himself. More plausibly, however, we may see here the work of the editor who incorporated the memoir into a larger collection of prophecies and who has separated them from their original position because of their appropriateness to form the conclusion of the entire memoir. In this case the 'testimony' and 'teaching' in v. 16, which originally referred to the name Maher-shalal-hashbaz, have been extended to cover the entire contents of the prophet's memoir. The conclusion of the memoir at this point indicates very positively that the whole writing must have been completed by the prophet himself soon after the ending of the Syro-Ephraimite crisis with the fall of Samaria in 733.

16. Bind up the testimony: The **testimony** (Heb. $t^{e‘}\hat{u}\underline{d}\bar{a}h$) and the **teaching** (Heb. $t\hat{o}r\bar{a}h$) must originally have referred to the name Maher-shalal-hashbaz inscribed on the tablet in 8 : 1. The phrase **among my disciples** must then refer to the two witnesses to the inscribing of the name mentioned in 8 : 2, Uriah and Zechariah. Almost certainly, therefore, the translation of *AV* and *RSV* as **disciples** is too strong a rendering, since these were not disciples in the normally understood sense of that term. 'Those I have instructed' better captures the sense of the Hebrew and corresponds more precisely to their role as public figures who were able to attest publicly the time and significance of the writing of the name. The sealing of the testimony would then have been in order to prevent any further interference with the writing on the tablet, or even possibly the reading of it, until such time as the prophet determined that its message had been fulfilled. The entire action carried out at the prophet's command clearly anticipated that the message of the name would not be heeded by Ahaz, and was designed to secure proof that this prophecy had indeed been given at the time stated.

17. I will wait for the LORD: Isaiah would now give no further prophecies until such time as the message of the children's names, and the punishment occasioned by their rejection, had taken effect. The following words, **who is hiding his face from the house of Jacob**, bring out fully the note of divine rejection. As Ahaz had rejected God's word, so now he himself, and his people, stood rejected by Yahweh. The concluding comment, **and I will hope in him**, suggest some expectation that the time would come when a better prospect for the future of Israel would arrive, but even here the prophet's intention will have been to affirm that the only hope now lay with God and his mercy.

18. Behold, I and the children whom the LORD has given me: This verse effectively brings to a conclusion the Isaiah memoir which began at 6 : 1 (apart from the later insertions noted). All three children were to serve as **signs and portents** through the names which they bore. There was nothing strange or miraculous about the manner of their conception or birth. For the Hebrew understanding of a 'sign' (Heb. '*ôt*), see above on 7 : 3. A 'portent' (Heb. *môpēt*) was a happening of a more unusual nature which conveyed a significance beyond itself. Cf. *THAT*, I, cols. 93f. Sometimes it could be a perfectly natural event, as here, and sometimes a unique and scarcely explicable one (cf. Jl 2 : 30). The reference **in Israel** must certainly use the traditional title of the people to include both Ephraim and Judah, since both were affected by the message of the prophet. The description of God as One **who dwells on Mount Zion** reflects the great importance to Isaiah of the Jerusalem temple and its special cultic tradition. Cf. J. Schreiner, *Sion-Jerusalem. Jahwes Königsitz* (*SANT* VII), Munich, 1963, pp. 243ff.; *THAT*, II, cols. 543–51.

INTERPRETATIONS OF THE PROPHET'S SAYINGS

8 : 19–22

The section which concludes ch. 8 is beset with considerable difficulties, both of translation and interpretation. See G. R. Driver, *Festschrift W. Eilers*, Wiesbaden, 1967, pp. 43ff., who defends an interpretation based upon the assumption that the section is a unity. However we must, with most modern commentators, recognise at least two units, the first in vv. 19–20, which represents a comment on vv. 16–18 from the exilic age, and the second in vv. 21–22, almost certainly from the same period. 9 : 1a (Heb. 8 : 23a) is then a redactor's connecting comment, intended to form a bridge to the very different message of 9 : 1b–7 (Heb. 8 : 23b–9 : 6). Eichrodt, Kaiser and Fohrer have defended the Isaianic origin of vv. 19–20, but this must be rejected, and their obvious secondary allusion in v. 20 to the 'teaching' and 'testimony' of v. 16 is sufficient evidence of this.

The first redactional addition has then been made in vv. 19–20 with the aim of contrasting the true word of God which is to be found in the message of the prophet with that of those who trust in necromancy and the techniques of consultation with the spirits of the departed. The date of this addition can scarcely be reached with certainty, but the assumption of a background of crisis, and of despairing people resorting to techniques which they might in normal times have spurned, suggests that of the exile.

19. And when they say to you: It is not clear who **they** are, nor who are being addressed. The latter may be reckoned as the readers of the prophetic book, so that the indefinite **they** must mean 'anybody'. **Consult the mediums and the wizards:** For these illicit means of consulting the dead, cf. 1 Sam. 28:7–19 and the law of Dt. 18:10ff. The **mediums** (Heb. *'ōbôṯ*) refers to people through whom the spirit of a dead person was believed to make contact with the living. The **wizards** (Heb. *yiddᵉ'ōnîm*) appear to have been 'spokesmen' for the inhabitants of another world. For the etymology, cf. S. R. Driver, *Deuteronomy (ICC)*, 3rd edn. Edinburgh, 1902, p. 226. **should not a people consult their God:** Instead of reading **God** here it is preferable to see in the Heb. word *'ᵉlōhîm* a reference to a departed spirit (cf. 1 Sam. 28:13). The question is then a continuation of the impious advice which precedes it. The background of the saying lies with people who cannot understand their fate, and who are being encouraged to throw away their traditional scruples in seeking advice from the dead.

20. To the teaching and to the testimony!: J. Lindblom, *The Immanuel Prophecy*, p. 52, would take these words as a gloss, whereas *NEB* (following G. R. Driver, *W. Eilers Festschrift*, p. 45) sees them as the continuation of the preceding verse, '. . . for an oracle or a message'. This latter interpretation is preferable. Better still, however, we should understand an ellipse of an emphatic rejection of the suggestion contained in v. 19: 'No! Turn instead to the teaching and the testimony'. **Surely for this word which they speak** must allude back to the impious advice given in v. 19. The concluding phrase, however, **there is no dawn** occasions difficulty. If we retain the translation of Heb. *šaḥar* as **dawn**, then it must be understood as a metaphor meaning 'help' (cf. Ps. 46:5). F. Stolz, *Strukturen und Figuren*, p. 210, would see a reference to the old Canaanite deity Shachar. Better still, however, we should understand it as a word meaning 'spell, counter-spell' (cf. Akkadian *sāḥiru*). The sense is then that those who advocate prohibited forms of knowledge will not be able to save themselves from punishment.

21. They will pass through the land: Heb. simply has 'one (indefinite) will pass through it' (cf. *RSV* margin), leaving indeterminate what the 'it' refers to. Since vv. 21–22 must form a second redactor's addition, there is no help in looking for an antecedent in what precedes. Rather it is most probable, following H. Barth, p. 153, that we should take this as a reference to Jerusalem, rather than to the **land** in general as *RSV*. This would date the saying to a time shortly after 587, as the reference later in the verse to the **king** would suggest. A date later than this would leave such a comment without real meaning. The description **greatly distressed and hungry** shows the grievous plight of the survivors after the fall of Jerusalem, which was evidently understood as 'fulfilling' the warning that God was 'hiding his face' from the house of Jacob (v. 17). **and turn their faces upward:** It is better (as *NEB*) to regard the words **and their God** as marking the end of the sentence, and to take these words as the beginning of a new one. Then read this with v. 22, 'Then, whether they look up, or down to the earth . . .'

22. behold, distress and darkness, the gloom of anguish: The sense is generally clear, even though the translation of individual words is difficult, and in some cases uncertain. For etymological suggestions, see G. B. Gray, pp. 162f.; A. Guillaume, *JSS* 9 (1964), pp. 282–90, and G. R. Driver, *Festschrift W. Eilers*, p. 46. Wherever one looks there will be a picture of appalling distress and anguish. The allusion must be to the aftermath of the Babylonian destruction of Jerusalem, which is elsewhere pictured in Lamentations. The clause **and they will be thrust into thick darkness** (Heb. *wa'ᵃpēlāh mᵉnuddāḥ*) is taken by Guillaume, pp. 289f., to mean 'widespread darkness', but it is simpler to emend the second word to *minnōḡah*, 'with no brightness'; cf. Am. 5:20. If then the verse is divided into two hemistichs after *mᵉᶜûp̄*, we read:

> Behold, distress and deep darkness,
> anguish and gloom with no brightness

Cf. *NEB* and G. R. Driver, *Festschrift W. Eilers*, pp. 46, 49.

THE PROMISE OF A ROYAL SAVIOUR

8:23–9:7

The promise of the birth of an heir to the house of David who will bring salvation and greatness to Israel, contained in 9:2–7 (Heb. 1–6), make this one of the best known of all Isaianic prophecies. It is also one of the most difficult and contested. Opinions have varied between regarding it as a post-exilic 'messianic' promise of the coming of a Davidic ruler who will restore the kingship and international power to Israel (So Duhm, Marti, Fohrer, S. Mowinckel, *He That Cometh*, pp. 102ff., etc.) and interpreting it as an authentic Isaianic accession oracle for the crowning of Hezekiah as king (so especially A. Alt, 'Jesaja 8, 23–9, 6. Befreiungsnacht und Krönungstag', *Kleine Schriften* II, pp. 206–25; J. Lindblom, *The Immanuel Prophecy*, pp. 33ff.). More recently a yet further possibility has emerged (H. Barth; J. Vermeylen) of regarding the prophecy as an accession oracle for a Davidic ruler, but of identifying this ruler as Josiah (640–609 BC), and so of taking its inclusion as part of the Josianic redaction of the book. The basis of Alt's argument, and of the modification of it advocated by Barth and Vermeylen, is to be found in the interpretation of 9:1 (Heb. 8:23), and more precisely the second part of this verse, since the first sentence is undoubtedly a separate glossator's addition. The words **But there will be no gloom for her that was in anguish** (9:1a) have clearly been inserted by an editor in order to establish a transition from the threatening warning of 8:21f. and the reassuring promise of 9:1ff. This can only have been after the addition of 8:21f. in the exilic age.

In spite of the large number of scholars who have, since Duhm, regarded 9:2–7 as a post-exilic 'messianic' oracle, we must dismiss such an interpretation. There is no hint whatsoever in the prophecy itself that it is concerned with the restoration of the Davidic monarchy after an interval in which it had ceased, nor does the language of the royal birth (v. 6) and of the great international power to be achieved through the Davidic king (v. 7) accord with the hopes surrounding the expectation of the restoration of the Davidic kingship in the sixth and fifth centuries BC. Our interpretation, therefore, must centre upon the possibility of an original application either to the accession of Hezekiah (725 BC) or to that of Josiah (640 BC). The decision here must rest upon the understanding arrived at of the difficult verse 9:1, and of its connection with the accession oracle proper which follows. In either case this latter oracle must be understood, following Alt, *op. cit.*, pp. 208ff., to refer to a royal accession, and not to a literal birth (see below). For the many problems of interpreting 9:1 see, besides Alt's pioneering article, J. A. Emerton *JSS* 14 (1969) pp. 151–75; H. Barth, pp. 154ff., J. Vermeylen, pp. 232ff.; K. Seybold, *Das davidische Königtum*, pp. 82ff.

The geographical references in 9:1 (see Y. Aharoni, *The Land of the Bible*, London, 1966, pp. 331, 334) refer to the territory annexed by Tiglath-pileser from Israel in 733 and formed into three separate Assyrian provinces. The *RSV* translation (which follows *AV* and *RV*) contrasts the treatment **in the former time**, which proved disastrous and which must reflect the situation brought about in 733, with that **in the latter time**, which will be triumphantly glorious, but which is still in the future. It is this latter expectation for these territories which began to emerge for Israel (Judah) only with the age of Josiah, when the expectation arose that, with the demise of Assyrian power, these territories would both be restored to Israel and set once again under a Davidic king. However, it is very questionable, following J. A. Emerton, whether the translation **he will make glorious** (Heb. *hiḵbîd*) in 9:1 can be justified. The perfect tense should more naturally be translated as a past action, and the sense of the verb is better understood negatively as signifying further oppressive treatment for **the way of the sea**. (See J. A. Emerton, *op. cit.*, pp. 168ff., and below *in loc.*). In this case the entire geographical-historical information contained in the verse can be related to Tiglath-pileser's treatment of Israel in 733, and no difficulty arises on this score against an application to Hezekiah's accession in 725 BC.

The question of the connection of this verse to the following accession oracle proper can be answered fairly securely. Quite evidently the intention is to contrast the disastrous fate of Israel at the hands of

Assyria, which came as a consequence of the disunity between
Ephraim and Judah, with the salvation which could come if they were
reunited under a single Davidic ruler. However, the assumption that
9:1 was an original part of the royal oracle of vv. 2–7 must be
questioned. Rather it appears that a redactor has inserted this note (in
prose?—contra Alt, p. 208) in order to provide a historical background
for the element of hope which follows, much in the manner of the
note in 7:1. We may conclude therefore that this comment has been
inserted at an early stage in order to illuminate 9:2–7, but that it
probably was not a constituent part of the original oracle.

So far as the form of the royal prophecy of 9:2–7 is concerned, there
are clear signs of contact with the hymnic element of Songs of
Thanksgiving. The promises of the ending of warfare (v. 5) and of a
vast international rule for the house of David (v. 7) were not realised
in Hezekiah's time, nor yet, except very partially, with Josiah.
However, we must take these assurances as potential, rather than
positively and imminently expected. Their extravagant language has
been determined by the traditional 'court-style' of the Davidic
monarchy and its ambitions, and their purpose here is to show the
new hope that could emerge, particularly for the Northern Kingdom
of Israel (so 9:1), with the coming of Hezekiah to the throne of Judah.
There could now be opportunity for a reunion of Israel and Judah
under a Davidic king, since Ahaz, whose action had so bitterly divided
the two kingdoms, was now dead. If we can establish the original
application of 9:2–7 as the accession of Hezekiah, then nothing
stands in the way of ascribing it to Isaiah. The setting provided by 9:1
has then been added, either by the prophet himself, or by a redactor
working very shortly after Isaiah's time, in order to show the relevance of the oracle to the fate of the Northern Kingdom.

Whether the inclusion of a royal 'court-oracle' of this kind can
reveal anything concerning Isaiah's own position as an 'official', or
'court' prophet remains doubtful. There is always the possibility that
Isaiah was simply echoing very deliberately the official traditions of
the royal court in order to bring out the new element of hope that
emerged with Ahaz's death. The time of Yahweh's 'hiding his face
from the house of Jacob' could now be past (cf. 8:16).

9:1. But there will be no gloom: The words are an addition by a
redactor in order to establish a transition between the picture of darkness and distress given in 8:22 and the hope of 'a great light'
promised by 9:2–7. In their function they are significant since they
establish a yet future (post-exilic) application of the prophecy of the
royal saviour of 9:2–7. They show, therefore, how a continuing
process of reapplication and reinterpretation of prophecies took place,
which is revealed by the complex redaction history of the present
book.

In the former time he brought into contempt: These words provide
an introductory historical setting for the accession oracle which follows
in vv. 2–7. The contrast between **In the former time** and **but in the
latter time** should probably not be understood to refer to two separate

political actions against these northern territories (?738 and 733 BC), but (see J. A. Emerton, pp. 168f.) to mean 'from first to last'; i.e. they express a totality of harsh treatment. We may translate: 'First he (i.e. God) . . . then he . . .' **the land of Zebulun and the land of Naphtali:** For the cutting off of these territories from Judah by Tiglath-pileser in 733, see A. Alt, *Kleine Schriften* II, Munich, 1953, pp. 188–205; Y. Aharoni, *The Land of the Bible*, pp. 331f. **but in the latter time he will make glorious:** Rather read, 'Then he treated harshly . . .' The three regions mentioned, **the way of the sea, the land beyond the Jordan, Galilee of the nations,** correspond to the three provinces into which the northern region of Israel was divided by Tiglath-pileser: **the way of the sea** corresponds to Dor (*Du'ru*); **the land beyond the Jordan** to Gilead (*Gal'azu*) and **Galilee of the nations** to Megiddo (*Magidu*).

The content of the accession oracle of vv. 2ff, does not single out the Northern Kingdom of Israel for special mention, but this application is provided by the introduction here, and is further established by the fact that 9 : 8–21 (+5 : 24–25; see above) refers to the fate of the Northern Kingdom in the aftermath of 733.

2. The people who walked in darkness: The language has a conscious air of mystery, and does not identify precisely the extent of **the people,** which must be assumed to include both Judah and Ephraim. *BHS* would delete **who walked** as overloading the metre, but the sense remains unaffected. **have seen a great light:** The **light** is a metaphor for the saving action of God. See below on 10 : 17 for a later interpretation of this. The language of the accession oracle is evidently fairly stereotyped and traditional, appropriate to a special royal occasion. The application to Hezekiah's accession can only be a matter of reasoned conjecture, and the main function of the prophecy is to show that the period of God's 'hiding his face' can now end, since the king whose action occasioned this wrath, Ahaz, had now passed from the scene. For the uncertainty regarding the date of Hezekiah's accession, see Introduction, p. 9).

3. Thou hast multiplied the nation: Better, 'Thou hast multiplied gladness,' reading Heb. *haggîlāh* instead of *haggôy lō'*. The occasion of the rejoicing is the advent to the throne of a new king, always a time for celebration, but regarded as especially so in its reawakening of the hopes surrounding the Davidic monarchy, which Ahaz had done so much to jeopardise. **as men rejoice when they divide the spoil** uses the situation of sharing out the spoils of victory to describe the high excitement occasioned by the new ruler's coronation, and need not suggest that any recent battle had taken place.

4. For the yoke of his burden: The verse contains three images of oppression: **yoke . . . staff . . . rod** to signify that a period of tribulation and oppressive rule has passed. The imagery is secondarily interpreted in 10 : 24, 26, 27; 14 : 25 as referring to the oppression of Assyrian rule. If this direct historical application was intended in the original prophecy then it could only have arisen in relation to Josiah and his age. Almost certainly, however, we are faced here with the stereotyped 'court language' which regarded every new ruler as a saviour figure who would put an end to the oppression of the past. The imagery, therefore, is almost certainly typical, and in a measure idealistic. It is the secondary interpretation of the metaphors in relation to Assyria (for which see *in loc.*) which has given them a more directly historical application. **thou hast broken as on the day of Midian** refers back to the victorious battle won under Gideon's leadership against the Midianites in the plain of Jezreel (Jg. 6 : 33ff.). The battle was especially important in the history of the Northern Kingdom, the fate of which hung perilously in the balance after the Assyrian settlement imposed in 733.

5. For every boot of the tramping warrior: The language is traditional, celebrating the advent of a new king as the inauguration of a kingdom of peace and the ending of rebellion and war. Cf. Pss. 2; 76. It formed a part of the 'Conflict with the Nations' motif which belonged within the royal Davidic traditions of Jerusalem. For Isaiah it had a special significance and application in view of the deep rift which had arisen between Judah and Israel from the time of the Syro-Ephraimite war. The Heb. uses a very vigorous image for 'every boot stomping into battle'. **and every garment rolled in blood:** The development of a professional army in Israel, and even more in Assyria, had led to the wearing of specialised military uniforms, the destruction of which the prophet could use as a picture of an era of peace.

6. For to us a child is born, to us a son is given: The verse has occasioned most difficulty in the interpretation of the prophecy, since it appears to promise a royal birth, whose coming will bring peace. Yet the prophecy clearly has nothing to do with the birth of the Immanuel child of 7 : 14 (contra J. Lindblom), and, with A. Alt, 'Befreiungsnacht und Krönungstag', pp. 209ff., must be understood to be a reference to a royal accession, and not to a literal birth. This is in line with Ps. 2 : 7, a hymn celebrating a royal coronation. On his accession to the throne the king was elevated (?adopted) as the divine 'son' and 'heir'. The imagery and ideology is almost certainly Egyptian in its ultimate origin, but had evidently become a part of the royal ideology in Judah. Cf. T. N. D. Mettinger, *King and Messiah*, Lund, 1976, pp. 254ff.; K. Seybold, pp. 83f. The complex language and imagery was linked with ideas that the new king received the divine spirit and became a new 'person' with a new 'heart'. It was appropriate therefore that he should receive new throne-names, which were filled with power commensurate with his authority in administering God's kingdom. **and the government will be upon his shoulder:** The meaning of the word translated **government** (Heb. *miśrāh*) is not absolutely clear. *NEB* has 'symbol of dominion'. Possibly 'entitlement to rule' is intended.

and his name will be called: The series of four names which follow, built up in word couples, almost certainly derives from the Egyptian practice of giving throne-names to the Pharaoh. Cf. H. Frankfort, *Kingship and the Gods*, Chicago, 1948, pp. 46f. The Egyptian practice was for a series of five names to be given, suggesting that this was

originally the case here, and that one name has been lost in the transmission. Cf. H. Wildberger, *ThZ* 16 (1960), pp. 314–32 and comm. *in
loc.* See further H. Barth, pp. 141–77; E. Lipinski, *Semitica* 20 (1970),
pp. 41–57; J. Vermeylen, pp. 91–5; H.-P. Müller, *EvTh* 21 (1961), pp.
408–19; H. L. Ginsberg, *JAOS* 88 (1968), pp. 47–53. H.-P. Müller, *op.
cit.*, p. 414, and R. A. Carlson, *VT* 24 (1974), pp. 130–5, would see a
pointedly anti-Assyrian character in the title given, but this seems
less than certain. Rather the separate titles express separate functions
which belonged to the royal office of the king. **Wonderful Counsellor**
stresses the king's ability as political guide and leader; **Mighty God** is
better translated as 'Divine Warrior' and affirms the supernatural skill
and strength given to the king for leadership in battle. **Everlasting
Father** is better rendered 'Father for ever' and would reflect the
concern of the king for the welfare of his people. E. Lipinski,
Semitica 20 (1970), p. 52, would repoint as '$^a\underline{b}\hat{\imath}$ '$\underline{e}\underline{d}$, 'my father is
witness', and refers it to the Egyptian title affirming the legal
primogeniture of the prince, and his consequent right to rule. **Prince
of Peace** affirms the king's role as a source of peace, prosperity and
general well-being for his people. Probably a fifth name has been lost,
and K. D. Schunck, *VT* 23 (1973), pp. 108–10, suggests reading *šōpēṭ
'ōlām*, 'Eternal Judge'. The case advocated by H. Barth, p. 177, that
these throne-names reflect the actual throne-names given to Josiah is
a conjecture that rests upon the general argument that the entire
section of 9:1–7 was composed for Josiah. Yet it is more likely
that the names were historically determined titles which were applied
to Hezekiah. At a later time, as implied by the wider hypothesis of
a Josianic redaction of Isaiah's prophecies, it appears that Josiah was
acclaimed as the Davidic ruler through whom these ancient promises
would be fulfilled (see Introduction, pp. 5f.).

7. **Of the increase of his government and of peace:** The text is
difficult, and has almost certainly been disturbed by imperfect transmission. We may suggest reading 'Great shall be the power, and peace
without end'. In this case there is no promise of a great universal
kingdom embracing many nations, but rather of a powerful and independent kingdom of Israel under a Davidic ruler. The background
setting provided by v. 1 would apply this to the Northern Kingdom,
indicating that a reuniting of Israel and Judah under a single Davidic
king was envisaged. Such a political ambition was later entertained by Josiah, even though it was only partially realised. Isaiah
appears as the prophet of the 'oneness' of Israel, and found in the
historical traditions and claims of the Davidic monarchy a strong
expression of this oneness. **upon the throne of David, and over his
kingdom:** Isaiah's attitude to the Davidic dynasty is more than a little
ambiguous. The warning to Ahaz given in 7:9 indicates that the
prophet did not hold the Davidic right to rule as unconditionally
guaranteed in all circumstances, and he may even have envisaged that
Ahaz's action would cost him his throne, and bring down the entire
dynasty. Yet this did not happen, and, if the Isaianic origin of 9:2–7 is
sustained, the prophet regarded the death of Ahaz and accession of

Hezekiah as providing a reprieve for the dynasty. From the perspective of the Josianic era in which an important redaction and interpretation of Isaiah's prophecies was made, the presence of the Davidic dynasty came to be regarded as an all-important factor in the entire history of Judah during Isaiah's ministry (cf. esp. 2 Kg. 19:34 = Isa. 37:35). Central to this belief was the tradition of the divine promise to David through the prophet Nathan that he and his house had been given a permanent and inalienable right to rule over Israel (2 Sam. 7:13). **to establish it, and to uphold it:** Undoubtedly the intention was to affirm that the entire Davidic kingdom, divided in Isaiah's day between Ephraim and Judah, would be reunited and given political freedom and independence. Although the language is forthright and direct as a firm promise from God, it is impossible to suppose that Isaiah was convinced that this would certainly be the consequence of Hezekiah's reign. Rather he here uses the traditional language to affirm the nature of Yahweh's 'order' for his people, and thereby to call that people back to a submission to this order. It is effectively an appeal, directed primarily to the Northern Kingdom, to return to Yahweh and the Davidic house whom he had given to rule his people. For such an idea of the prophet's intention, cf. H. W. Hoffmann, pp. 105ff. **The zeal of the LORD of hosts will do this:** For the idea of the **zeal** of Yahweh, cf. B. Renaud, *Je suis un Dieu Jaloux (CahRB* 2), Paris, 1964, pp. 27ff.; *THAT*, II, cols. 647–50. The formulaic character of the affirmation is evident and marks the solemn conclusion of the 'accession' oracle. The language itself is traditional and designed to affirm that what appears to be beyond the scope of political possibility has a yet stronger basis of certainty in the divine will. The rule of the Davidic house would be upheld by God, overriding all human plans and forces.

For **9:8–21**, see above, pp. 66ff., on 5:25–30.

For **10:1–4**, see above, pp. 60ff., on 5:8–24.

ASSYRIA, THE ROD OF THE DIVINE ANGER
10:5–15

The prophecy affirming that Assyria is simply the rod in the hand of Yahweh for the punishment of his people, and that it too will, in turn, be punished by him for its blasphemous *hybris* (10:13) is amongst the most important in the entire collection of chs. 1–12. It represents the surest and most reliable evidence for accepting that Isaiah did foretell a time when the Assyrians would be punished and overthrown by Yahweh. Furthermore the way in which it has been drawn upon by a number of secondary redactional developments appears fully to bear out this conclusion. There is, however, a wide diversity of opinion about the date to which it should be ascribed. Duhm, Marti, Fohrer, Eichrodt and others would relate the prophecy to the time of the threat to Judah by Sennacherib in the period 705–701. Yet this cannot be sustained, since there is firm evidence (see Introduction, p. 11) that Isaiah condemned the alliance on which Hezekiah's revolt was based, and foretold its disastrous outcome. The reference to the Assyrian conquests in v. 9 points to events which had all taken place at the latest by 717 BC. We are directed, therefore, to a time after 717, but before 705, and the most probable resulting date is the period of the Philistine revolt against Sargon in the years 713–711. This is the period favoured by H. Wildberger, A. Schoors, O. Kaiser and W. Dietrich, and it must certainly be regarded as the most likely. However, we must bear in mind that Isaiah did not foresee a favourable outcome of this revolt against Assyria, as is shown by 14:28–32 and 20:1–6 (see below *in loc.*). His assurance that Assyria would eventually be punished for its arrogant boasts cannot have been intended as any direct encouragement to Judah to join such an anti-Assyrian revolt. This would certainly leave a greater fluidity to the question of determining the date of 10:5–15*, since it appears to relate more to the offence given by Assyrian imperialist claims than to any specific revolt which appeared likely to achieve success in throwing this off. Certainly we must think of a time after 722, but before 705 when Sargon died. If the prophecy of 14:4b–21 is Isaianic and was related to the time of Sargon's death (see below pp. 139ff.), then it is possible that 10:5–15 also belongs to this time. The scope of the original prophecy is to be found in vv. 54–9, 13–15, since two separate additions have been made in vv. 10–12, the first to bring out more forcefully the reason for Samaria's downfall and the second to show that the time of Jerusalem's punishment would soon end.

The reason given for the judgment upon Assyria is that the Assyrian king was guilty of blasphemous pride. This introduces a theological motif into the whole presentation. The overall form is that of a disputation saying, in which the analogy of the **rod** in the hand of a person provides the basis for much of the prophet's argument. Since Assyria is an instrument in the hand of God, it is absurd for this instrument to claim to be fulfilling its own plans and intentions. Such a disputation form has a certain affinity with Wisdom (cf. J. W. Whedbee, *Isaiah and Wisdom*, pp. 68ff.). However, the opening interjection (*RSV* **Ah!**) must in fact be read as a cry 'Woe . . .' (Heb. *hôy*), and the connection with other 'woe'-oracles recognised (cf. on 17:12; 18:1), even though there is no consistently carried through repetition of the 'woe'-form as in 5:8ff.

10:5. Ah, Assyria, the rod of my anger: The onomatopoeic character of the opening cry (Heb. *hôy*), expresses anger and hostility, without giving any clear indication of the manner in which the anger is to be carried over into action. The whole of 10:5–15* takes the form of invective, implying that punishment will be inflicted on the Assyrians, but without pronouncing how. **the staff of my fury!** See margin for the obscurity of the Hebrew. G. R. Driver, *JTS* 34 (1933), p. 383, offers a very convincing emendation: 'and the rod of my wrath—it is in their hand!' (Heb. *ûmaṭṭēh za'mî hû' beyādām*).

6. Against a godless nation: The kingdoms of both Israel and

Judah appear to be intended, so that the use of the singular **nation** (Heb. *gôy*) is consistent with Isaiah's insistence that the people of both 'houses' form one 'people'. The alternative would be to refer the statement to Judah only; but the fate of the Northern Kingdom at the hands of Assyria appears very much to have been in the prophet's mind. It was a significant feature of Assyrian claims for the expansion of their empire that the gods of the nations they had conquered had offended their inhabitants and the power of Assyria had been invoked to correct this. Cf. M. Cogan, *Imperialism and Religion*, pp. 15ff. **to take spoil and seize plunder** recalls the elements of the name Maher-shalal-hashbaz of 8:1, to which the prophet may have been intentionally alluding.

7. **to cut off nations not a few**: Instead of **not a few** (Heb. *lō' mᵉāt*), Targ. reads 'without sparing'. Cf. S. Speier, *ThZ* 21 (1965), pp. 312f., and Hab. 1:17. The general assertion that some reasoned intention lay behind the Assyrian imperial expansion reflects familiarity with Assyrian claims. Perhaps these had already become known in Judah through public edicts and inscriptions. By conquering peoples and territory Assyria claimed to be heaping greater glory upon its god Ashur. Cf. M. Cogan, *op. cit.*, pp. 22ff.

8. **Are not my commanders all kings**: I.e. are not the commanders of the armies of Assyria of greater power and prestige than the kings which they overthrow? By showing their superiority to the kings of the nations, the officers of Assyria show that they are in reality even greater than their conquered opponents. The phrase **all kings** gives an interesting example of the wider usage of Heb. *yaḥdāw*, meaning 'altogether', and possibly 'each one'.

9. **Is not Calno like Carchemish**: In Am. 6:2 the place Calno (Heb. *kalnô*) is written as *kalnēh* (Akkadian *kullâni*). It lay in Northern Syria and was conquered by Tiglath-pileser III in 738. The Hittite city of Carchemish fell to Sargon II in 717. Hamath lay on the Orontes, falling to Sargon in 720 and Arpad in Northern Syria was attacked and defeated twice, in 738 and 720. The presentation of a list of victories in this fashion suggests that Isaiah was already familiar with the style of Assyrian victory inscriptions, which he reflects here. The greater the Assyrian claims, so much the greater does the prophet view its sins in claiming these victories as the work of their own god Ashur. The concluding rhetorical question **Is not Samaria like Damascus?** already indicates that, although there was no distinction from the Assyrian viewpoint, one did exist in reality since Samaria stood in a special relationship to Yahweh.

10. **As my hand has reached to the kingdoms of the idols**: This verse and the following one are a later addition, probably from the exilic age, which uses the reference to Samaria as an opportunity to elaborate upon the sin of idolatry perpetrated by the inhabitants of Samaria (cf. the Deuteronomic viewpoint in 2 Kg. 17:7ff.). The intention is evidently to contrast the fate of Samaria with that of Jerusalem, so that this addition presupposes the pespective given to the deliverance of Jerusalem as recounted in chs. 36–37. Whereas the

original prophecy stressed that Israel had suffered along with other nations, the present two verses have been inserted to show that a quite different fate awaited Jerusalem, a view which Isaiah himself certainly did not share.

11. shall I not do to Jerusalem and her idols: Strikingly the re-dactional addition recognises that Jerusalem too is guilty of idolatry, like Samaria, even though it presupposes the tradition of Jerusalem's deliverance from Sennacherib in 701, as the later tradition came to view it. In vv. 10–11 we have an interesting example of the growth of tradition. The narrative of Isa. 36 : 1–37 : 38 (= 2 Kg. 18 : 17–19 : 37) has largely been developed around the prophecy of Isa. 10 : 5–15* as an interpretation of Jerusalem's deliverance in 701. In turn the elab-orated narrative tradition has been reflected back into the original prophecy by the addition of these two verses.

12. When the LORD has finished all his work on Mount Zion: This verse, which is in prose, is a yet further, but separate, addition to that of the preceding two verses. It must derive from the post-exilic age, and affirms that the time for punishing **the king of Assyria** will not arise until Yahweh has finished his plan for Jerusalem. It pre-supposes the defeat of Jerusalem in 587, and probably comes from a much later time, though scarcely as late as the Seleucid era (so Kaiser). Its interpretation requires an understanding of **the king of Assyria** as a (veiled) reference to some other foreign power, or possibly to all Gentile nations. The inclusion of the addition has necessitated the insertion of the words **For he says** at the beginning of v. 13. The Hebrew *'epqōd* ('I will punish') must be emended to read *yipqōd* (cf. *RSV* margin).

13. By the strength of my hand I have done it: In this claim, set into the mouth of the Assyrian king, Isaiah sees a supreme expression of blasphemous pride. The content of the claim accords so well with the general character and tenor of Assyrian victory inscriptions and royal annals, that it seems certain that Isaiah was already familiar with these. In any case it is very probable that the vassal status of both Ahaz and Hezekiah had brought a strong Assyrian presence in Jerusalem. Most probably, therefore, Assyrian representatives would have taken the opportunity to deliver impressive, if bombastic, speeches to the citizens of Jerusalem, much in the manner ascribed to the Rabshakeh in 36 : 4–10. It is possible that, in turn, the written tradition of the Rabshakeh's speech has been built up from the words put into the mouth of the Assyrian king here. From the prophet's perspective, Assyria was acting as the instrument of Yahweh, which implied a limited commission, whereas the Assyrian king claimed that there was no limit to his power. The phrase **and by my wisdom** reflects very clearly the close connection felt in the ancient world between wisdom as a divine endowment, and its use in the formation of military and political strategy. **I have removed the boundaries of peoples:** i.e. in instituting radical changes in the political map, as in Israel after 733, by the dividing up of kingdoms and forming them into provinces of the Assyrian empire. As a consequence of such action, and as part of the 'third phase' of Assyrian domination, wholesale movements of population were enforced in order to change traditional national alignments and associations. **like a bull I have brought down:** The text appears to be in a very disturbed state. In this and the previous line we should read the imperf. cons. Possibly we should emend to 'I have struck down to the ground the cities and their inhabitants' (H. Wildberger).

14. My hand has found like a nest: The prophet projects into the mouth of the king of Assyria the same colourful imagery to be found in his own prophecies. As a man might plunder the eggs from a bird's nest, so the great ruler had stolen the kingdoms of the earth and their treasures, and the defending peoples were as powerless to stop him as the bird would be to defend its nest.

15. Shall the axe vaunt itself: The rhetorical question clearly implies a negative answer, but, more than this, it hints that the claims of the Assyrian king are so impious that they must evoke punishment. Although the form of the prophecy is that of the disputation saying, it implies some veiled threat of coming punishment. What form this will take or when it will materialise is not set out, although the later redactional addition in vv. 16-19 helps to supply this. **As if a rod should wield him who lifts it:** A slight emendation of the Heb. (to *'eṭ mᵉrîmô*; cf. *BHS*) is required. The second line of the verse simply elaborates on the absurdity of the hypothetical question set in the first, but there is no need to regard the line as a gloss on this account (as Wildberger).

THE COMING DESTRUCTION OF THE ASSYRIANS

10:16-19

Although A. Schoors would regard these verses as the original continuation of vv. 5-15, and would therefore ascribe them to Isaiah, such a view must be rejected. They emanate from the Josianic Redaction of the collection of Isaiah's prophecies, and are designed to present a firm declaration of the overthrow of Assyria (cf. H. Barth, pp. 28-34). That this overthrow was then regarded as assured by the events of 701 BC is shown by the narrative tradition of chs. 36-37. Barth rightly recognises that the section consists of an extended elaboration of the imagery of 9:14 and 17:4-6. To this we must certainly add a dependence on the image of light, taken from 9:2. All in all we have a kind of 'midrashic' development of imagery and themes which occur in authentic Isaianic passages, a feature which is very marked in the remainder of the Josianic redaction. There is no need, therefore, to see the passage coming from as late as the Seleucid age (as O. Kaiser), nor should we interpret the verses as apocalyptic eschatology.

16. Therefore the Lord, the LORD of hosts: Some MSS omit the title **Lord**, and this is probably correct. The threat **will send wasting sickness** appears to be drawn from 17:4, which also introduces the idea of **glory** as a description for a people. Barth (p. 34) sees a conscious identification on the author's part between the 'Jacob' (i.e. the Northern Kingdom) referred to in 17:4–6 and Assyria. However, it seems more likely that the Isaianic imagery has been transferred to the enemy alluded to in 17:1–6. There is no likelihood that O. Procksch was correct in seeing in these verses a threat directed against Israel as a whole. The idea of a **sickness** has been developed from that of 'leanness' in 17:4. **and under his glory:** What exactly is meant by **glory** is not clear (army, inhabitants?), but the image has come from 17:4.

17. The light of Israel will become a fire: The image of **light** has been taken from 9:2, where it is perfectly in order, but here it has been stretched to introduce the more threatening feature of **fire. and it will burn and devour his thorns and briers in one day.** The theme of **thorns and briers** has been taken from the Song of the Vineyard in 5:6, but appears here to refer to the Assyrian soldiers, indicating a dependence upon the secondary passage 7:24. This would suggest that 7:23–25 may also have belonged to the Josianic Redaction.

18. The glory of his forest and of his fruitful land: Barth, pp. 28f., sees the origin of the **forest** imagery in 9:14 (Heb. 13), but it may also have been encouraged by the 'staff' and 'wood' imagery of 10:5, 15, as well as that of 'thorns and briers' and the 'olive trees' of 17:6. The phrase **both soul and body** reflects the 'head and tail' emphasis of 9:14, whilst the image of 'wasting away' reflects 17:4.

19. The remnant of the trees: The picture of only a few trees left seems to point to 17:6 and to establish a sense of poetic justice by showing that the attacker in 17:1–6 will himself be attacked and overthrown. The threat of the overthrow of Assyria presented here and elsewhere (cf. on 14:24–27; 17:12–14, etc.) by the Josianic Redaction of Isaiah's prophecies saw a primary measure of fulfilment in the tradition of the destruction of Sennacherib's army in 701 (especially cf. Isa. 37:36 = 2 Kg. 19:35). Very probably the stress upon the suddenness of the Assyrian overthrow (cf. 'in one day', v. 17) has contributed to the build-up of the tradition regarding the action of the angel of Yahweh.

THE FATE OF THE REMNANT OF ISRAEL

10:20–23

The section 10:20–23 reflects a further example of the 'midrashic' type of exegesis which we have seen to belong to the Josianic Redaction of the book. This time the basis for the exegesis is to be found in the name 'Shear-jashub' of 7:3, which has given rise here to three interpretations of the idea of a 'Remnant returning' in relation to the Northern Kingdom. Wildberger and Barth, pp. 40f., date this addition to the post-exilic age, on the assumption that the idea of the 'Remnant' is applied broadly to the Israel of the post-exilic age. Yet this is not so, and more plausibly the title 'Israel' and 'Jacob' must be applied to the survivors of the Northern Kingdom after 722. Nothing then hinders the ascription of these three verses also to the age of

Josiah, and to finding in them further instances of the developed exegesis that characterises this redactional work. Apart from the primary dependence on the interpretation of the name Shear-jashub from 7:3, v. 20 contains an allusion to the imagery of 9:13, whilst the 'end' decreed in v. 23 alludes back to 6:11.

20. In that day the remnant of Israel: The opening formula shows a typical mark of a redactional addition, and the theme of **the remnant of Israel** follows the application of the name Shear-jashub to the Northern Kingdom quite accurately. **will no more lean upon him that smote them:** The language echoes that of 9:13, but understands it differently. There the one who smote them is Yahweh, but here it clearly refers to Assyria, upon whom the people had become politically dependent (**lean upon**). The idea of the remnant is thereby given a positive significance as a promise that there will be survivors from Israel, whose salvation will only be achieved when they turn to Yahweh in truth; i.e. in sincerity and with a whole heart.

21. A remnant will return, the remnant of Jacob: The opening words repeat exactly the name 'Shear-jashub' from 7:3, but interpret its meaning in a positive sense; i.e. there will indeed be a remnant of Jacob, and it will return to God. Clearly this secondary interpretation has arrived at a very different understanding of the meaning of the name Shear-jashub, since the 'returning' is now a returning to God. However, it still appears to be the fate of the Northern Kingdom that is envisaged, the misfortunes of which are regarded as a consequence of apostasy. **to the mighty God** recalls the title of the Davidic king from 9:6 (Heb. *'ēl-gibbôr*).

22. For though your people Israel be as the sand of the sea: The simile of the sand of the sea to express the size of the population of Israel was no doubt a traditional one (cf. Gen. 22:17; 32:12; Jos. 11:4, etc.). Its employment here, however, is in conjunction with a further, and more restrictive, interpretation of the name Shear-jashub. There will indeed be a remnant of Israel, thus implying a positive significance for the name which means 'A Remnant Returns', but this remnant will not be a large one. **Destruction is decreed:** The recognition that Yahweh has pronounced (**decreed**) an irrevocable threat against Israel (9:8–21) precludes that more than a remnant can survive. The phrase **overflowing with righteousness** appears ambivalent, but must be understood in the sense 'fully, and justly, deserved'. The participle **overflowing** (Heb. *šôṭēp*) picks up the description of the threat from Assyria given in 8:8.

23. For the Lord, the LORD of hosts, will make a full end: If this comment belongs together with vv. 20–22, which is most likely, then the verse should be understood as a general elaboration upon the message of Isaiah given in 6:11, designed to show that there can be hope for no more than a remnant of the Northern Kingdom. Several commentators (Kaiser, Wildberger) take it as a post-exilic warning of the final eschatological judgment of the world, whilst more improbably J. Fichtner, *ZAW* 63 (1951), p. 26, regards this as an isolated saying from Isaiah.

A MESSAGE OF HOPE AND REASSURANCE

10:24–27a

These verses also, which are formulated as a comforting address to Jerusalem ('my people, who dwell in Zion', v. 24) reveal the same kind of 'midrashic' elaboration of, and comment upon, words and themes which have appeared in Isaiah's authentic prophecies. Here the theme of the **rod** and **staff** has been taken from 9:4 (v. 24); the ending of Yahweh's **indignation** and **anger** (v. 25) reflects the refrain of 9:12, 17, 21, etc., and the allusion back to Yahweh's defeat of **Midian** (v. 26) picks up the allusion from 9:4. Finally, the references to **yoke** and **burden** in v. 27a contain a further allusion back to 9:4. Overall, therefore, we have in these verses a kind of 'midrashic' commentary upon 9:4, which in itself must be taken as a strong pointer to the Isaianic authorship of the oracle of 9:2–7 from Isaiah (against Barth and Vermeylen, who would ascribe it to the Josianic period). The date of origin of this passage has been very variously inferred. Kaiser would see in it a late (second century BC) encouragement not to fear the Hellenised Seleucid rulers, who would then be the enemy referred to under the guise of **the Assyrians** (v. 24). However, there is no reason at all why the title 'the Assyrians' here should not be taken at its face value and referred to this great imperial power. In this case the assurance that Jerusalem has nothing to fear from them cannot reasonably be later than the age of Josiah, which witnessed the fading of Assyrian influence in Judah, and their loss of world power (cf. the fall of Nineveh in 612 BC). We may conclude, therefore (with A. Schoors), that these verses were composed in Josiah's reign, and they must then belong together with other similar midrashic-type expansions from this age.

24. Therefore thus says the Lord, the LORD of hosts: The form of the divine title follows precisely that given in 10:16 and 20. The formula employed is typical of prophecy, but the style of the comforting address which follows, based on an interpretation of prophetic words, is very untypical of prophecy, and betrays an obviously written, scribal, form of interpretation based on individual words, rather than general context. **when they smite with the rod** refers back to 9:4, where its imagery must be taken to apply to any potential oppressor of Israel. Here it is precisely and exclusively applied to the imperialist domination of Assyria. The address to the people **who dwell in Zion** points to a sense that Jerusalem can be assured of a very different, and better, destiny than the remainder of Israel, a theme developed in chs. 36–37, and most especially in 37:35; cf. also 37:32. The phrase **as the Egyptians did** links the whole experience of foreign imperialist oppression to the tradition of the deliverance from Egypt, as recounted in Exod. 1–15.

25. For in a very little while: If we place the time of composition of vv. 24–27a in Josiah's reign this must be taken as a reference to the hope of the ending of Assyrian rule at that time, rather than as an intended allusion back to the event of 701 as the occasion when the

Assyrian armies suffered a major reversal, as in the tradition of Isa. 36–37. **my indignation will come to an end** takes up the picture of Yahweh's continuing anger against Israel as expressed in the refrain of 5:25, 9:12, 17, 21, and affirms that shortly this anger will cease. By means of such a reference the author has incorporated an allusion to the fate of the Northern Kingdom also into his assurance. Instead of being directed continually against Israel and Judah, Yahweh's wrath will turn against the Assyrians. Instead of **will be directed to their destruction**, G. R. Driver, *JTS* 38 (1937), p. 39 would read 'will be wholly brought to an end' (Heb. *ʿal tēkel yittōm*).

26. as when he smote Midian at the rock of Oreb: The primary reference is once again back to 9:4, but the author has filled out the meaning of the allusion to 'the day of Midian' by elaborating upon its significance in connection with the historical tradition of Jg. 7:25. **and his rod will be over the sea** should be emended to 'against them' (Heb. *ʿalêhem* instead of *ʿal-hayyām*), which has probably come in as a result of the association with the Exodus story. The assurance **and he will lift it as he did in Egypt** refers back to the tradition of Aaron's rod in Exod. 7:9ff. We have therefore a very comprehensive 'midrash' around the theme of Yahweh's **rod**, which must also contain some allusion to 10:5.

27. And in that day his burden will depart contains a further reference back to 9:4, affirming that it is when the Assyrian rule is ended that the promise of that verse will be realised. This points strongly in the direction of regarding the Davidic promises contained in 9:2–7 as having been applied to Josiah, even though this was not the king for whom they were composed.

THE ADVANCE OF THE ENEMY

10:27*b*–32

The description of an approach of hostile forces against Jerusalem, and their encampment close to the city, has several difficult features. Coming as it does immediately after the Isaianic threat of judgment upon the Assyrians for their pride and arrogance (10:5–15), its position, together with the most probable understanding of appended redactional comment in vv. 33–34, suggests that the reference is to an Assyrian advance. This could then have been either that of Sargon II in 711, or that of Sennacherib in 701 BC. Yet the difficulty occasioned by this latter interpretation is that the route described (see map in Wildberger, I, p. 431) was certainly not that taken by the Assyrians at that time. The historical reality then was of an advance from the south, whereas the prophet's visionary description is of an advance from the north. H. Schmidt and, with some modifications, H. Donner, pp. 30–8 (also *ZDPV* 84 (1968), pp. 46–54), have consequently suggested that the reference is to the Syro-Ephraimite attack upon Jerusalem in 735–733. Yet this necessitates that the enemy whose advance is described is not Assyria, as the chapter

undoubtedly implies, but rather the Syro-Ephraimite alliance. It also
raises the problem that Isaiah certainly did not regard the threat from
Pekah and Rezin to be a serious threat to Ahaz (cf. on 7:1ff.). Hence
Donner is forced into a very hypothetical reconstruction of the circumstances in which the advance took place, and the timing of Ahaz's
appeal to Tiglath-pileser for help against his attackers.

Two ways out of the difficulty have been suggested. The first is to
look for some other historical occasion when a threatening army
advanced against Jerusalem. O. Procksch (as earlier, T. K. Cheyne)
referred the description to an advance of Sargon against Judah in 715,
at the time of the Philistine revolt. This is followed by H. Wildberger,
who postulates that, during the time of this uprising led by Ashdod,
Sargon marched against Jerusalem and thereby effectively dis-
couraged Hezekiah from joining the revolt. V. Herntrich and E. Jenni
(*Die politischen Voraussagen der Propheten*, p. 18, note 13) reckon
with a predominantly visionary advance by an (unnamed) world
power, for which no precise date can be given. Duhm and Marti
would deny the description to Isaiah altogether and apply the
prophecy to a final eschatological attack by Gentile powers against
Jerusalem. Certainly the visionary element of the description must be
taken fully into account so that it is not necessary to regard it as
recording an advance as it actually happened. Rather, the prophet may
be allowed to have projected into his visionary portrayal knowledge of
a typical route of advance by a Mesopotamian power. It is possible,
too, that certain traditional elements may have entered into the description given, as D. L. Christensen, *VT* 26 (1976), pp. 385–99,
argues. He would infer some knowledge of an old religious processional route. Overall we must take fully into account the context of
10:5–15, besides the additions made by a redactor in vv. 16–27a, all of
which undoubtedly refer to a threat from Assyria. Furthermore, H.
Donner, pp. 30f., would regard v. 33 as authentically Isaianic and to be
part of the unit, vv. 27b–33. He then takes v. 34 as a gloss, whereas H.
Barth, pp. 54ff., understands v. 33a as belonging to 11:1–5 (see below
in loc.) and takes vv. 33b–34 as Isaianic, but separate from 27b–32.

There is no reason for questioning the rightness of the assumption
that the unnamed attackers in v. 27b ('**He has gone up**') are the
Assyrians. Moffatt's translation actually inserts 'the Assyrian', whereas *GNB* refers to 'the invader'. If an actual historical advance is being
described, as the amount of circumstantial detail would certainly
support, then the strongest case can be made, with Wildberger, to
refer the picture to an advance by Sargon's army at the time of the
Ashdodite rebellion in 713–711. To what extent that advance did include a direct threat against Jerusalem is not clear. For a hypothesis
regarding such a development, cf. A. K. Jenkins, *VT* 26 (1976), pp.
284–98. The more widely adopted view has been to relate the advance
to the threat to Jerusalem in the year 701. There can be no strong case
for following Donner in relating the vision of the advance to the
Syro-Ephraimite crisis (735–733 BC).

Since the details of the route would best fit the situation of 713–711, we may conclude that either this was the time of the original prophecy, or possibly that the prophet himself or his redactor has applied the knowledge of what happened in 711 BC to the later Assyrian threat of a march on Jerusalem in 701. Ch. 20 points to a further linking of the two rebellions, with the implication that the failure of the rising against Sargon provided an overwhelming case against further rebellion against Sennacherib. The visionary account is intended to serve as a threat, and is designed to warn that the counteraction by the Assyrian king for rebellion against him (by joining forces with Ashdod) would be swift, sharp and disastrous. It in no way implies a happy outcome, as vv. 33-34 now give to it.

27. **He has gone up from Rimmon:** Cf. the *RSV* margin for the reading of the MT, which has no doubt suffered through assimilation to the first part of v. 27. The *RSV* translation is based on a conjecture, and it is questionable whether the reference to Rimmon (Duhm, Marti, Gray) is correct. O. Kaiser, G. Fohrer and D. Christensen would read 'Samaria', and other suggestions ('the North'; 'Bethel'?) have been proposed. Probably 'Samaria' gives the most satisfactory route. The attacker (**He**) is not identified, but there is no reason to doubt that the implication from the context that it is the Assyrian army is correct. At least it seems evident that the redactor of the chapter intended this reference to be understood.

28. **he has come to Aiath:** The town must be identified with the Ai of Jos. 7:2ff. Migron (probably modern *Makrun*) lay north of Michmash, where Jonathan achieved a notable victory over the Philistines (1 Sam. 14:2ff.). **he stores his baggage** is better understood as 'he examines his weapons' (cf. Donner, pp. 30f.; Gen. 27:3; Jg. 18:11, 16, for this use of Heb. $k^e l\hat{\imath}$, 'weapon'). The picture is intentionally that of preparing for battle.

29. **they have crossed over the pass:** Read the singular 'he has . . .', with 1QIs^a. The picture given is of an advance through Benjaminite territory, which had been made famous as the home of Saul. **at Geba they lodge for the night:** Read 'At Geba he pitches camp for the night' (Heb. *mālôn lô*). Geba was barely six miles from Jerusalem and for an attacking force to pitch camp there would indicate complete mastery of the tactical situation, together with confidence that the defenders in Jerusalem were demoralised and powerless. **Ramah** and **Gibeah** were fortified towns on the route which led from Bethel to Jerusalem.

30. **Cry aloud, O daughter of Gallim:** The towns that lay in the immediate vicinity of Jerusalem are portrayed as panic stricken and helpless, with no hope of offering any effective resistance to the advancing foe. Only Jerusalem, which was marked out as the main target for attack, could have hoped to offer any semblance of defence and opposition to the unchecked advance. It seems beyond question that the manner in which the attack has been described is intended to show that it will be completely successful, although this should not necessarily be taken to imply that such an attack was actually mounted in this fashion. The prophet must be allowed a certain visionary

license, since it was a part of his purpose to show the inevitable
suffering that such an attack would bring. A comparable picture of
siege forces moving against Jerusalem is to be found in 29:1–4,
where the attacker is identified as Yahweh himself (cf. 'I will
encamp . . .', 29:3).

31. Madmenah is in flight: Already the inhabitants of the towns
close to Jerusalem are pictured as having abandoned all hope of resistance and as having fled.

32. This very day he will halt at Nob: For the location, cf. 1 Sam.
21 : 1. The site is not certainly identified, but has been linked with
that of the present day Mount Scopus, only two miles from Jerusalem.
he will shake his fist at the mount of the daughter of Zion: The
threatening posture of the attacker is clear, but it is noteworthy that it
does not proceed into a description of ensuing siege or battle. If the
connection with the period 713–711 is correct, then, as Wildberger
conjectures, the advance against Jerusalem was sufficient to dissuade
Hezekiah from taking any action to support the rebels of Ashdod. On
the other hand, if the prophet intended to portray the situation
leading up to the siege of 701 by a visionary anticipation of how it
would be, then this too did not lead to an ultimate siege and conquest
of Jerusalem. Instead, Hezekiah surrendered before the city suffered
serious damage. In understanding the prophet's description of the
attack in relation to either action, it is perfectly reasonable to understand the threat as having concluded at this point. There is no need,
consequently (as Procksch, Fohrer, Donner, pp. 30ff.). to link vv.
33–34 with the original Isaianic prophecy.

THE CUTTING DOWN OF THE FOREST

10:33–34

These two verses have occasioned a good deal of discussion, and have
been interpreted in two quite sharply contrasting ways. J. G. Herder
was among the earliest to connect them with the prophecy that
follows in 11 : 1–5(9), and this has most recently been followed by O.
Kaiser. The picture is that of the cutting down of a forest, but it is not
made clear to what this image of the forest and of 'Lebanon' (v. 34)
refers. In Kaiser's view it is a picture of the sufferings of Israel which
have been described in order to provide a background to that of the age
of salvation which was to begin with the coming of 'a shoot from the
stump of Jesse' (11 : 1). Both Auvray, pp. 138ff., and Wildberger, I, pp.
427ff., take the verses as Isaianic and expressive of a threat against
Judah and Jerusalem, possibly in the time of the Ashdodite rebellion
(so Wildberger), although Auvray links the verses with the ravaging
of the countryside in 701. F. Huber, pp. 32f., suggests tentatively that
it is a threat against the Assyrian forces attacking Judah, but regards
such an interpretation as so uncertain as to provide no conclusive
evidence that Isaiah voiced such a message.

The context is not entirely a decisive guide, but the generally close
similarity to other passages affirming that Yahweh would act **with**

terrifying power against the Assyrians (cf. 29:5–8; 31:8) suggests that the Assyrians are intended as the enemy here (the 'invader' of v. 27b). In this case the most convincing explanation for vv. 33–34 is that they are a further part of the Josianic Redaction of Isaiah's prophecies, made in development of the prophet's threat against Assyria (10:5–15). The imagery of the **forest** and of **Lebanon** are a further extension of the metaphor of the 'forest' from 10:18, and of the idea that Assyria is Yahweh's 'rod' (10:5). We may therefore see here a further part of the Josianic Redactor's elaboration of Isaiah's themes and imagery. The time would come when the Assyrians would be **cut down**. Cf. further, on 14:24–27; 17:12–14.

33. Behold, the Lord, the LORD of hosts will lop the boughs. For the divine title, cf. above on 10:16, 20, 23. The metaphor of **the boughs** of trees clearly presupposes the 'forest' image used of Assyria in v. 18, which has itself been developed out of the combination of the images of 5:6; 9:13; 10:5. Instead of **with terrifying power** (Heb. $b^e ma^{ca} r\bar{a}s\bar{a}h$) we should possibly emend, with Targum, to 'with an axe' (Heb. $b^e ma^{ca} s\bar{a}\underline{d}\bar{a}h$).

34. He will cut down the thickets of the forest: For the sake of emphasis the imagery of the cutting down of the forest is given a very full, and repetitious, development. The word **with an axe** (literally 'iron') is not the same as that employed in the emendation of v. 33. **and Lebanon with its majestic trees:** The imagery of the most majestic of forests has been occasioned by 'the glory of his forest' in v. 18. Cf. *RSV* margin, although we can better understand an ellipse: 'and Lebanon in (all its) majesty . . .'.

THE SHOOT FROM THE STUMP OF JESSE

11:1–9

The theme of the prophecy which now follows upon the threat of the destruction of Assyria in 10:33–34 is that of hope centred upon the coming of a new Davidic king who will restore the fortunes of the house of David. A large number of modern critical commentators have regarded the prophecy as authentic to Isaiah and as a genuine expression of the hope which he cherished and encouraged in connection with the Davidic monarchy (so Duhm, Gressmann, *Der Messias*, p. 247, Procksch, Eichrodt, Kaiser, Seybold, pp. 92ff., S. Herrmann, pp. 137ff., H. Wildberger). The picture is understood to be that of the future ideal ruler of the Davidic house who will come, bringing salvation and an end to the faithless politics of such kings as Ahaz (and Hezekiah?). A close comparison can be made with Mic. 5:2–4. Yet this conclusion regarding an Isaianic origin for the prophecy must be seriously questioned, both on the grounds of content and also those concerning its redactional placing at this point. In content the prophecy clearly presupposes that the Davidic dynasty had been severely judged and reduced to a mere 'stump' (11:1). The most natural understanding of this is that it presupposes a time when the Davidic dynasty had been deposed from the throne of Judah altogether (587 onwards), and that it is a promise of its restoration. As regards its position, it has evidently been set to show how the promise given by Isaiah to Hezekiah at the time of his accession (9:2–7) will ultimately be realised. It is therefore a redactional addition from the post-exilic age, which has endeavoured to elicit from the prophecies of Isaiah a further word of assurance about the future and in particular about the restoration of the Davidic monarchy. It develops into a more extended future expectation the hopes surrounding the Davidic monarchy which are to be found in the accession oracle of 9:2–7, and thus belongs along with Jer. 33:19–26; Ezek. 37:24–28. Such redactional developments in the great prophetic collections extended the hopes which had originally been attached to the Davidic monarchy as an institution into a more remote, and ultimately eschatological, direction.

The unity of the prophecy has been seriously questioned by a number of scholars, since vv. I–5 alone deal with the question of the future king, and vv. 6–9 with the return to the conditions of paradise which will be enjoyed in the idyllic future age. More than most other comparable passages it seems to presuppose a mythological tradition concerning a paradisal 'Golden Age' which had once been enjoyed by mankind and which was expected to return at the time of the close of the present age. Cf. H. Gressmann, *Der Messias*, pp. 246ff. We cannot, therefore, rule out the possibility that we are faced here with two separate promises concerning the conditions of the future, the first (vv. I–5) concerned with the future of Israel and the peace and righteousness it will enjoy through its divinely given ruler. The second promise then extended this more broadly to involve all mankind in a new age of peace and happiness. Yet, with Wildberger, we must recognise the possibility that the two passages are two parts of what was intended to be one comprehensive picture of the new age. Against Wildberger, however, who ascribes the whole prophecy to Isaiah, we must see it rather as a later, post-exilic, expression of hope. Probably it belongs to the late 6th, or early 5th, centuries BC.

II:I. There shall come forth a shoot: The portrayal of **Jesse**, the father of David (I Sam. 16:I), as a **stump** presupposes the hard times which had befallen the Davidic dynasty. Although this might, with some plausibility, be referred to the major territorial losses during Isaiah's lifetime by Israel and Judah, which had at one time together formed the Davidic kingdom, it is more probable that the taking of the throne from the Davidic family in 587 is meant. The purpose of referring to the dynastic ancestor is scarcely likely to have intended that a 'new David' would arise, still less a 'David *redivivus*'. Rather the power and blessing of the ancestor would manifest itself afresh through a new descendant who would recover the throne of Israel. **and a branch shall grow out of his roots:** This is preferable to 'and a branch shall become fruitful' (reading Heb. *yiprāḥ* instead of *yipreh*).

2. And the Spirit of the LORD: The new king would be endowed in full measure with all the *charismata* appropriate to his office, in politics, the conduct of war and the administration of justice. For the latter, cf. especially 1 Kg. 3:16–28. The belief that the king was endowed with special gifts, similar in kind but richer in quality, than those enjoyed by other notable people was a prominent feature of Israelite and other ancient Near Eastern views of kingship. See T. N. D. Mettinger, *King and Messiah*, pp. 233ff. There is no justification, therefore, for regarding such a notion as a distinctively post-exilic development, even though the stigma of failure that attached to the monarchy in the period of its holding office may have strengthened such an emphasis. There is in consequence a rather 'idealised' character vested in the future king which is described here, even though the ideals concerning his character have been drawn from ancient royal traditions. **the spirit of counsel and might:** For **counsel** (Heb. *'ēṣāh*), see especially P. A. H. de Boer, *H. H. Rowley Festschrift* (SVT III), Leiden, 155, pp. 42–71. It refers particularly to skill in political diplomacy so that **might** must point to strength and firmness in negotiation, rather than physical virility. **the spirit of knowledge** indicates 'insight, discernment'; **and the fear of the LORD** points to reverent humility, i.e. taking God's purposes into account (contrast Isa. 29:13; 30:1), and a concern to maintain the due order of religious cultic life.

3. And his delight shall be in the fear of the LORD: The clause should be omitted as a variant reading of the last part of v. 2 which has come into the text. It is omitted by *NEB* accordingly (see *NEB* margin). **He shall not judge by what his eyes see:** The ability to discern the inner motives and reasonings of people, and especially to detect when a person was lying was a supreme asset for the administration of justice. Cf. Prov. 16:10. It becomes very evident in examining the ancient Israelite legal system that particular difficulty was encountered in combating perjury and the risk of deliberately malicious accusations. Cf. Exod. 20:7, 16; Ps. 15:2–3.

4. and decide with equity for the meek of the earth: It is better to emend to 'for the oppressed ones (Heb. *'ăniyyê*) of the earth', since the point is that the true king will right the genuine grievances which people have, and not that he will favour those who are unable, or unwilling, to defend themselves. The royal virtue was that the king sought justice, without favour for either the rich or the poor (cf. Exod. 23:3). **and he shall smite the earth with the rod of his mouth** must clearly be wrong, since **earth** is irrelevant and out of place in the context of jurisprudence. We should emend to 'he shall smite the violent' (reading *'āriṣ* instead of *'ereṣ*). The phrase **he shall slay the wicked** presents a rather stern conception of justice, but the hyperbolic emphasis is designed to show that the true king will not hesitate to inflict the most severe penalties when this is necessary.

5. Righteousness shall be the girdle: Heb. reads the definite article with **faithfulness**, but not with **righteousness**. We should, with Wildberger, delete it with the former, although *BHS* prefers to achieve conformity by adding it to the latter. The repetition of **girdle** is inelegant, and we should, with *BHS*, change the first one to 'belt' (Heb. *'ēsûr* instead of *'ēzôr*). The use of the metaphors of royal vestments is not drawn from any special symbolism attached to them, but is designed to show that the entire royal office will be directed towards the maintenance of justice and good order.

6. The wolf shall dwell with the lamb: The verse begins a new section which describes the paradisal conditions which will pertain in the natural order, and which accompany the just social order described in vv. 3–5. It is possible that vv. 6–9 represent a further addition to the presentation of the age of the 'messianic' ruler, but more probably the two pictures have been intended in their origin to complement each other. The person of the king in the ancient Near East was, as v. 2 affirms, more than an official functionary. Through him the divine power and blessing were made available to his people and affected the entire order of life. Cf. H. Gressmann, *Der Messias*, pp. 247f., who describes the conception of the Messiah as that of a 'demi-god'. It is appropriate, therefore, that the king who shared many aspects of an ideal nature and existence (cf. Ps. 45:2), should introduce a new peaceful world order. Wild animals would become tame and harmless, so that they would live tranquilly with domesticated creatures. The imagery is very possibly traditional, deriving from a mythological picture of the primal age of the world. **and a little child shall lead them:** The reference is to any child who will be able to lead animals in this fashion, and not to a special royal child.

7. The cow and the bear shall feed: Read 'shall become friends' (**Heb.** *tiṯrāʿeynāh* instead of *tirʿeynāh*). The removal of all violence from the animal order will be a mark of the extent to which peace will reign throughout all creation.

8. and the weaned child shall put his hand: With this image, together with that of 'the little child' in v. 6, the author's anthropocentricity becomes evident. By the cessation of all violence in the natural order man himself, and even the weakest and most vulnerable of his species will have nothing to fear. The word describing **the adder's den** (Heb. *meʾûraṯ*) is scarcely correct, and we should emend either to *meʿāraṯ*, 'cave', or *meʿônaṯ*, 'den, dwelling'.

9. They shall not hurt or destroy: H. Barth, p. 60, (cf. also Duhm, Marti, Gray) regards v. 9 as an addition to vv. 6–8 (which are themselves taken to be independent of the preceding). Certainly the verse provides a summarising assessment of the pictures given in vv. 6–8, and are, for this reason, unnecessary. Yet in a poetic composition of this kind it is not at all surprising that a degree of repetition should intrude in order to achieve a heightened emphasis. The fact that the verse has connections with other parts of the Old Testament does not in itself prove that it is a secondary insertion. The first part of the verse echoes 65:25*b*, whilst the second half, which sounds like a liturgical refrain, occurs in Hab. 2:14. The phrase **in all my holy mountain** must be a reference to the entire land of Israel, and not simply to Mount Zion. Cf. Exod. 15:17. The language is traditional, so that an early narrow (and mythological?) connotation has apparently been extended to regard the whole world as the sacred 'mountain' of God.

THE PROMISE OF ISRAEL'S RESTORATION
11:10-16

V. 10 is a later addition by a redactor of the post-exilic age who has introduced a new and different interpretation of 'the shoot of Jesse' from 11:1. Since it also links this with the 'ensign', or 'flag' from 11:12, it clearly presupposes the presence of vv. 11–16 and attempts to provide a transition from the one promise to the other. The list of countries in v. 11b from which the remnant of Israel will be recovered is also the result of a later editorial expansion, perhaps from as late as the third century. The primary basis of the promise is to be found, therefore, in vv. 11a, 12–16 and is concerned with the theme of the 'remnant' of Israel, which is identified with the Jewish Diaspora. Cf. H. Wildberger in *THAT*, II, cols. 853f. The section presupposes, not only the original 'remnant' prophecy of 7:3, but the later development of the Shear-jashub name in 10:20–23. It also presupposes that the Diaspora of the post-exilic age had become sufficiently conscious of itself as a 'dispersion' for the hope of a restoration to the land of Israel to have become a central feature of eschatological hope. The section, therefore, must belong to the fourth century BC. That the return will take place at the giving of a signal from Yahweh himself presents a highly theological picture of the circumstances, aims and occasion of such a return. Already the interpretation of prophecy has come to border very closely upon apocalyptic with the idea of a remarkable divine intervention in the world by a special manifestation of Yahweh himself.

10. In that day the root of Jesse shall stand: See above for the dependence of this verse upon 11:1 and v. 12. It represents an attempt to link the two promises together, but achieves this in a very clumsy fashion, as is shown by the confusing of the 'shoot' of Jesse (v. 1) with a 'root'. This **root of Jesse** is usually taken to stand for the (messianic) Davidic ruler (so Duhm, Gray, etc.). However, H. Barth, p. 59, interprets it collectively in v. 10 as a figurative representation of the post-exilic community in Judah. This is a very attractive suggestion, since it provides a convincing example of the gradual fading of hope regarding the restoration of a Davidic monarch in the 6th-5th centuries BC (cf. Hag. 2:23, and see P. R. Ackroyd, *Exile and Restoration*, London, 1968, pp. 164ff.). **shall stand as an ensign to the peoples:** The idea of a flag, or **ensign** (Heb. *nēs*) occurs in Isa. 30:17 in an authentic Isaianic saying. From there it has been taken up in v. 12, in a figurative sense, to affirm that, when God gives the signal, all the scattered Jews of the Diaspora will return to their homeland. What form this 'signal' would take is not specified. The redactor who has added v. 10 has found the key to the nature of this signal in **the root of Jesse**. If this is taken in a collective sense it refers to the community in Judah who will have established a central basis in the land to which the other, Diaspora, Jews can then return. The absence of a Davidic king is then no objection to the hope of the ending of the age of dispersion and of the return of all scattered Jews to their homeland as promised in 45:20ff.

him shall the nations seek: as in the promises of 45:14ff., 49:22ff. **and his dwellings shall be glorious:** Literally 'and his resting-place (Heb. $m^e n\hat{u}h\bar{a}h$) shall be a glory'. The 'resting-place' must be a reference to the land of Israel.

11. In that day the Lord will extend his hand: The formula **in that day** is a very characteristic mark for a redactional addition and cannot be taken as more than a vaguely specified reference to the future age of salvation. The word translated **a second time** (Heb. $\check{s}\bar{e}n\hat{i}t$) is superfluous and *BHS* rightly conjectures that a verb should be read here. Read 'will raise his hand' (cf. Arabic *saniya*, 'to be high'. Wildberger would read $\check{s}^{e}\!{}^{,}\bar{e}t\ y\bar{a}d\hat{o}$, with similar meaning. **to recover the remnant which is left of his people:** The idea of the remnant goes back to the secondary passage 10:20–23, which is itself built up from the name Shear-jashub of 7:3. Here the post-exilic redactor has given it a positive 'saving' connotation as a reference to all Jews scattered among the nations of the world. **from Assyria, from Egypt:** Heb. reads 'from Assyria and from Egypt', which undoubtedly marked the original end of the geographical references. It is a later editor who has expanded this by the addition of **from Pathros, from Ethiopia:** in order to accommodate other countries to which Jews were known or were believed to have gone. It is likely that such a gloss marks one of the latest additions to the entire book.

12. He will raise an ensign: The image of the flag, or flagstaff (**ensign**), comes from 30:17, where it is used as a simile for the isolation of the few survivors of Judah. Here it is given a positive significance as the basis for a word-picture of the raising of a flag as a sign to which people may rally. The reference to **the outcasts of Israel** and **the dispersed of Judah** regards **Israel** and **Judah** as virtually synonymous and evidently makes no distinction between the two kingdoms or the circumstances by which their inhabitants were brought into exile.

13. The jealousy of Ephraim: The reference is to the hope that there will no longer be any bitterness between the two 'houses' (cf. 8:14) of Israel, as mentioned in 9:21. Cf. Ezek. 37:15–23. **and those who harass Judah:** The context shows that the adversaries (Heb. $\d{s}\hat{o}r^{e}r\hat{e}$) of Judah are from Ephraim. P. Joüon, *Biblica* 10 (1929), p. 195, proposes reading the participle as an abstract plural noun $\d{s}^{e}r\hat{u}r\hat{e}$, 'hostility', which improves the sense. The second half of the verse, **Ephraim shall not be jealous,** is regarded by Duhm, Cheyne, Fohrer, Wildberger as a secondary expansion, and this view must be upheld. It is a needless repetition. The 6th–5th century date proposed for vv. 11–16 would accord very well with the sense of a continuing tension between Ephraim and Judah, with the new provincial government of Samaria coming into conflict with the community in Jerusalem. Such tension was undoubtedly a significant part of the background to the Samaritan conflict and schism.

14. But they shall swoop down: The **shoulder of the Philistines** refers to the coastal plain occupied by the Philistines. The expansion of the territory of Judah at the expense of the Philistines, Edomites,

Moabites and Ammonites reflects the experience in which these neighbouring peoples had greatly enlarged their own territories during the period of Judah's weakness after 587. Probably too the tradition regarding the extent of the old Davidic kingdom has exercised some influence and established a sense of a historic claim to regions which Judah had lost by the 5th century BC. The verb **swoop down** (Heb. $w^{e'}\bar{a}\hat{p}\hat{u}$, literally 'fly') is strange, but no convincing emendation has been found and the sense is tolerable as translated in *RSV* and *NEB*. Read 'Edom and Moab shall be their plunder' (Heb. *mišlōaḥ yāḏām*).

15. And the LORD will utterly destroy: The Heb. verb ($w^eheḥ^erîm$) is literally 'put to the ban', but it is preferable to emend to $w^eheḥ^erîḇ$, 'will dry up' (so Wildberger). Cf. LXX. G. R. Driver, *JTS* 32 (1931), p. 251, would retain the MT but understand it as 'will cut off', cf. Akk. *ḥarāmu*, 'to cut through'. **with his scorching wind** (Heb. *ba 'yām rūḥô*) is difficult, and has received no entirely satisfactory emendation. *BHS* suggests $b^{e'}\bar{o}ṣem$, 'with the strength of his wind'. Targ. took as 'through the word of his prophets', but is clearly interpreting. The picture of Yahweh's action against the Sinai peninsula for the sake of his people is evidently heavily indebted to the tradition of the exodus from Egypt. However, the heavy (and clumsy) pictorial imagery shows the progressive departure from historical realism that marked the post-exilic eschatology.

16. And there will be a highway from Assyria: The image is drawn from Isa. 40:3–5; 42:14–17, suggesting, although not altogether necessitating, that chs. 40ff. had been added to the Isaianic collection by the time that the present prophecy was introduced (cf. Introduction, p. 8). Instead of **from the land of Egypt**, Wildberger would read simply 'from Egypt' (Heb. *mimmiṣrayim* instead of *mē'ereṣ miṣrayim*). It is clear that vv. 15–16 are concerned only with the return of scattered Jews from Egypt and Assyria, confirming that it is these two regions alone that were originally mentioned in v. 11.

It is attractive to link the inclusion of 11:1–16 with the process of redaction which formed chs. 1–12 into a self-contained section of the book of Isaiah (cf. Introduction, p. 3). If so, this would suggest that such a dividing up of the material took place in the 5th century BCE, which is the most likely date for these verses. Whether ch. 12 was added at the same time, or later, would not then significantly affect the issue. What is clear is that chs. 1–12 did not originally form a separate 'book' of Isaiah's prophecies, which must rather be found in 2–32*, but has been established as a separate unit within the larger collection at a relatively late stage in the redaction. This must have been related to the formation of a separate collection of 'foreign nation' prophecies in 13–23.

THE SONG OF THE REDEEMED

12:1–6

These verses are a prophecy only in a rather extended sense, and form a Song of Thanksgiving which has its closest counterparts in Psalmody.

The reference in v. 1, **You will say in that day**, gives to it an eschatological application, which thereby links it to the preceding and to the time of the return of Jews from the diaspora. The form is not consistently maintained, since v. 1 indicates that of an Individual Song of Thanksgiving (cf. S. Mowinckel, *The Psalms in Israel's Worship*, Oxford, 1962, I, pp. 91ff.; F. Crüsemann, *Studien zur Formgeschichte von Hymnus und Danklied in Israel* (*WMANT* 32), Neukirchen, 1969, pp. 227ff.), whereas v. 3 already introduces a second person plural form of address. V. 4 then appears as a new beginning (**And you will say in that day**). The vocabulary shows many links with the language of the Psalter, so that we may conclude that the author has assembled together a number of psalm themes and images in order to compose a Song of Thanksgiving appropriate to the situation which he envisages. The composition is not a true psalm, therefore, but a specific redactional piece composed as a conclusion to the overall message of judgment followed by hope which is to be found in chs. 1–11 of the book. If it is to be called an 'eschatological Song of Thanksgiving' then clearly this did not form a special *genre* of psalm compositions, but is rather to be seen as an adaptation of psalmic language and idioms to fulfil a particular literary redactional purpose. There can be no question of its origin from Isaiah, nor is there any special link with cult-prophecy. Rather, the origin of the verses lies within the editorial history of the book of Isaiah and the attempt to establish an appropriate division of the book between chs. 11 and 13, with its series of 'foreign nation' oracles. It may be that this section was added at the same time as 11:11–16, or some time after it. In any case it presupposes the strong message of hope which those verses contain and which it interprets as a kind of end point to the period of history covered by chs. 1–11.

12:1. You will say in that day: F. Crüsemann, *op. cit.*, pp. 50f., sees in this an instruction to a herald (*Heroldinstruktion*) formula. It is employed here to relate the joyous thankfulness expressed in the Song to the time of the return from the diaspora expressed in the preceding verses. **I will give thanks to thee:** The formula is commonplace in individual Songs of Thanksgiving, but here presupposes that a time of judgment has been inflicted, but is now passed. There is, therefore, a similarity, but no more, with the 'doxology of judgment', through which a convicted person was urged to affirm the justice of the sentence passed on him. Cf. Jos. 7:19 and G. von Rad, *O. T. Theology*, I, p. 358.

thy anger turned away: The Heb. MT reads the jussive, 'may thy anger', both here and in the following verb. However, we should emend to read the impf. consecutive in both instances. The author looks forward to a time when the judgment will have passed, even though he accepts that this is not yet true.

2. Behold, God is my salvation: 1QIs[a] introduces the preposition *'el*, 'Behold, in the God of my salvation I trust, and I . . .'. **for the LORD GOD is my strength and my song:** The language is echoed in Exod. 15:2 and Ps. 118:14, and **song** requires the addition of the suffix, with two Heb. MSS. However, instead of **song** it is better to

read the noun as 'energy, vitality' (cf. Arabic *ḏamara*. 'to drive on').
See *K–B* under *zmr*, III, and G. R. Driver, *JTS* ns. 2 (1951), p. 25,
who notes that the title **LORD** (Heb. *yhwh*) must be deleted as otiose
after *yah*.

3. With joy you will draw water: The imagery is designed to stress
the limitless possibilities which Israel will enjoy when the time of
its salvation has arrived.

4. And you will say in that day: It is possible that vv. 4–6 have
been added later than 1–3, as the new beginning would suggest. More
probably, however, the formula has been introduced in order to
accommodate the renewed summons to thanksgiving after the
affirmation of v. 3. The language then follows closely that of Ps.
105 : 1. **proclaim that his name is exalted:** The language and ideas
follow closely those of Ps. 148 : 13. The **name** of God in such a context
is clearly simply a surrogate for God himself.

5. Sing praises to the LORD: Those who have experienced the
greatness of God's salvation are pictured as summoning all their
fellow Israelites to give the maximum of praise to him. **let this be
known in all the earth:** Better, we should read the $Q^e re'$ text 'this is
known . . .'. LXX reads 'proclaim this . . .'

6. Shout, and sing for joy, O inhabitant of Zion: The address
collectively to the inhabitants of Jerusalem (Zion) reflects the unique
political and religious significance of this city in the post-exilic
period. Undoubtedly the historical fortunes of Jerusalem, and the
unique religious traditions with which it had become associated have
been reflected very prominently in the formation and development of
the book of Isaiah. Cf. 62 : 1–12. **for great in your midst is the Holy
One of Israel:** The divine title reflects a continuing theme in the
growth of the Isaianic literature. Cf. 1 : 4, 24; 5 : 24, etc. The emphasis
here upon the presence of God in the midst of his people marks a goal
of the post-exilic Jewish hope. Cf. Ezek. 48 : 35; Jer. 3 : 17, etc.

Prophecies against Foreign Nations: chapters 13–23

There now begins a collection of prophecies addressed to foreign
nations and peoples which are predominantly threatening in their
tone. Interspersed within this we find prophecies concerning Judah
and Jerusalem in 22 : 1–14 and a unique series of prophecies concerning a high official in 22 : 15–25. Evidence of an earlier redactional
structure is to be seen in the presence of 14 : 24–27, which once
formed the conclusion of the 'Assyrian' redactional unit which
commenced in 5 : 1ff. (See above, Introduction, pp. 3f.) There is no
complete uniformity in this collection of prophecies, therefore, and
G. Fohrer's attempt (*Introduction to the Old Testament*, pp. 367f.;
Jesaja, I, pp. 177ff.) to trace a weaving together of two separate collections—an Isaianic collection dealing with Assyria (14 : 24–27),
Philistia (14 : 28–32), Damascus and Ephraim (17 : 1–6), Egypt (18 : 20)
and Jerusalem (22 : 1–14, 15–19), and an anonymous collection of

prophecies introduced by the title **oracle** (Heb. *maśśā'*)—presupposes a more systematic structure than is properly to be found. Certainly 14:24–27 is a redactor's conclusion, and is not from Isaiah himself. Nevertheless we may discern an original and authentic Isaianic nucleus of prophecies in 14:28–32, against Philistia; 17:1–6 against Damascus; 18:1–7, against Ethiopia (Cush); and 20:1–6, against Ethiopia and Egypt. The Judean prophecies of ch. 22 must have formed part of a separate series, and the prophecies against Babylon in 13:1–14:23 have also evidently been formed into a distinct unit. It is nevertheless possible that authentic sayings from Isaiah are to be found between 13:1–14:23, but, if so, they have been much developed at the hands of redactors. All the signs are therefore that the special character of the prophecies of chs. 13–23 marks an attempt to bring together a special sequence of 'foreign nation' prophecies on the part of the later editors of the book. Traces of earlier editorial units are still to be seen within this, firmly establishing a link with prophecies that are to be found in chs. 1–12. It is certain, therefore, that there was never an entirely independent collection of Isaianic 'foreign nation' prophecies.

Comparable collections of prophetic sayings against foreign nations are to be found in Jer. 46–51 and Ezek. 25–32. Furthermore, the series of threats in Am. 1:3–2:6, as well as the book of Nahum, which proclaims the downfall of Nineveh, and Obadiah, which proclaims a threat against Edom, contain closely related material. We can discern, therefore, a clear category of prophecy concerning foreign (non-Israelite) nations and cities. There is no doubt, therefore, that the office of prophet to which Isaiah was called made him a spokesman to the nations, and that such a wide commission already had a long tradition behind it in the history of Israelite prophecy. We may also compare the role of the Moabite seer Balaam, who was called upon to prophesy on behalf of Moab against Israel (Num. 22–24). For the discussion regarding the traditions and assumptions implicit in such prophecy, see my *Prophecy and Tradition*, pp. 58–72. A number of features emerge with regard to them which have resulted in their becoming amongst the most obscure and difficult passages of the entire prophetic corpus of the Old Testament to understand. We may note the following major points:

(1). The word of God through the prophet was regarded as a powerful and effective weapon, so that it was not necessary for those primarily threatened by it to be physically present as hearers when it was uttered. There is, therefore, a certain kinship with magical practices in which symbolic acts and gestures of destruction were enacted against real and potential enemies. Cf. G. Fohrer, 'Prophetie und Magie', pp. 257ff. Widespread use has been made of the comparison with certain Egyptian 'execration texts', in which the name of an enemy was mentioned, accompanied by the symbolic smashing of a pot. Cf. especially A. Bentzen, 'The Ritual Background of Amos i.2–ii.16', *Oudtestamentische Studien VIII*, Leiden, 1950, pp. 85–99.

(2). It is not necessary to assume that Israel was at war with the nation, or people, concerned in the prophecy at the time that it was uttered. There is no reason for assuming, therefore, that such prophecies were uttered only in time of war or holy war. Cf. J. H. Hayes, *JBL* 87 (1968), pp. 81–92. Nevertheless, the connection of such prophecies with situations arising in war, or related to it, is clear. It is reasonable, therefore, to discern a special form of 'war-oracle'. Cf. D. L. Christensen, *Transformations of the War Oracle in Old Testament Prophecy. Studies in the Oracles Against the Nations (Harvard Dissertations in Religion* 3), Missoula, 1975. In some instances, therefore, we may conclude that such threats were a round-about way of bringing assurance to Israel by uttering threats against its enemies.

(3). In several instances, as we can see especially in the prophecy against Ethiopia (Cush) in 18:1–7 and Ethiopia and Egypt in 20:1–6 (cf. also against those who trusted in Egypt in 30:1–5; 31:1–3), the foreign power that is mentioned as threatened can be seen to have been considered a potential ally of Judah, whose help was thereby affirmed to be vain and useless. In such instances a clear relevance of the message to the prophet's hearers is evident. However, prominent as this motive is in several of the prophecies of Isaiah, it cannot always be assumed to have been the case that such reliance on an ally is necessarily presupposed.

(4). Because Judah found itself constantly involved politically with its neighbours, such collections of foreign nation prophecies appear to have been subjected to a considerable process of expansion and addition. As a result the nucleus of Isaianic prophecies here has been greatly augmented by others to form a quite comprehensive range of expression concerning God's plan for the nations which were politically influential upon Israel as enemies, or potential enemies, or allies.

(5). Such prophecies, once given, appear in some instances to have been reapplied when later circumstances occasioned the need and opportunity for doing so. It is often difficult, to the point of becoming impossible, therefore, for us to identify the original setting and date for many such prophecies. In one instance, that of Isa. 14:4*b*–21, a number of scholars have discerned an original Isaianic prophecy ironically lamenting the death of a world ruler, which has subsequently been applied to the death of a king of Babylon, most probably Nebuchadnezzar (see below, *in loc.*).

From all of these considerations we must rule out the attempt of S. Erlandsson, *The Burden of Babylon*, Lund, 1970, to claim almost the entire collection of prophecies against foreign nations in Isa. 13–23 as authentic to the prophet whose name they now bear. Rather, as we have already noted, there is a central core of Isaianic material which has subsequently been much enlarged. Whether any of this additional material does itself originally stem from Isaiah must be considered in connection with the separate units. In some respects the question of authorship cannot be allowed to become an overriding pursuit since the available evidence within the smaller units is necessarily limited.

PROPHECIES CONCERNING BABYLON

13 : 1-22

A further superscription has been inserted in 13 : 1 to identify Isaiah as the author of the prophecies concerning Babylon which follow in 13 :2–14 :23. This superscription must be seen as the work of an editor, very probably the same one who has been responsible for placing the Babylonian prophecies at this juncture. He has thereby marked off the prophecies which follow from those that have preceded, even though this has resulted in a certain breaking-up of the connections which are still discernible (especially between 14 :24– 27 and 10 :33–34). There then follows in vv. 2–22 of ch. 13 a series of prophetic utterances directed toward Babylon. The first two of these, in vv. 2–3 and 4–5 respectively, have a positive and affirmative sense, seeing in Babylon a divinely given destiny to conquer and to achieve greatness. Then in the next two such prophecies, in vv. 6–8 and 9–16, the theme of the Day of the LORD is taken up, with the very clear implication that it is the armies of Babylon which will bring such a day of divine punishment upon Judah and Jerusalem. Unquestionably the threat to, and destruction of, Jerusalem in 587 forms the background of these latter two prophecies, and the theme of the earlier prophecies that Babylon's power has been conferred by Yahweh is carried into a new situation of direct relevance to Judah. The fifth such prophecy in vv. 17–22 then foretells the destruction of Babylon, and so is closely comparable to such threats as are to be found in Isa. 46 : 1–4 and 47 : 1–15. Since Babylon had apparently not yet fallen when this prophecy was given, we may presuppose a date for it c.540 BC. This prophecy carries yet further, therefore, the history of Judah's encounter with Babylon, but this has now led to an explicit threat against Babylon itself.

Most commentators have reckoned that none of the material comes from Isaiah himself, or from the eighth-century situation which his ministry presupposed. However, this has largely been based on the assumption that vv. 2–22 form a single connected prophecy. Such a view must now be rejected, and we should see rather in this section a series of no less than five prophecies concerning Judah's relationships with Babylon. In this case it is possible that the first of them relates to the period of the rise of Babylonian power in the late eighth century, when a new era of greatness could be foreseen for this. At this time Babylon may well have appeared as a potential ally of Judah. It is not impossible, therefore, although by no means a necessary corollary of this, that the first such prophecy is from Isaiah.

13 : 1. The oracle concerning Babylon: The word **oracle** (Heb. *maśśā'*) otherwise means 'load, burden', hence *AV*'s 'burden'. It derives from the 'lifting up' of the voice (Heb. *nāśā'*). The ascription to **Isaiah the son of Amoz** must derive from a relatively late editor.

THE FIRST PROPHECY: THE CONSECRATED ONES

13 : 2–3

2. On a bare hill raise a signal: The situation presupposed can only be guessed at. Since the armies—**the nobles**—of Babylon are designated as Yahweh's **consecrated ones** in v. 3 that conquest must be viewed as a part of his plan. But what plan is meant and who are the enemy? If we assume this latter to be Assyria, then we should think of the Babylonian revolt against Assyria led by Merodach-baladan in the years 722–720. A further revolt took place after Sargon's death in the years 705–702. Cf. S. Erlandsson, pp. 89f. Either of these actions may have given rise to the hope that a measure of divine retribution was to be exacted of Assyria. The phrase **the gates of the nobles** in v. 2 is difficult and *NEB* renders 'draw your swords, you nobles'. This is based on LXX and yields a better sense, reading 'gates' (Heb. $pi\underline{t}^e h\bar{e}$) as a verbal imperative 'open, unsheathe' (Heb. $pi\underline{t}^e h\hat{u}$). The **nobles** must then be the Babylonian soldiers who are about to achieve a victory which will further Yahweh's purpose.

3. I myself have commanded: The Heb. text is disturbed. We should transpose to read: 'I have given command to my consecrated ones to execute my wrath; I have summoned my warriors—my proud and exultant ones.'

Who the enemy is, is not stated, although the designation of the Babylonian soldiers as **consecrated ones** makes it clear that they have been commissioned by Yahweh to fulfil his purpose. It is possible that both vv. 2–3 and 4–5 now represent only fragments of longer prophecies in which the historical context was originally made clear. As it now is, the redactor has linked these prophetic sayings with Yahweh's judgment of Judah by the hand of the Babylonians.

THE SECOND PROPHECY: DESTINED TO CONQUER

13 : 4–5

Like the first, the second prophecy regarding the divine role accorded to Babylon, assumes that it is Yahweh's will which is guiding and controlling the armies of Babylon. Whereas in the first prophecy it is a single act of conquest that is envisaged, here it is now a much larger purpose which can be summed up as **to destroy the whole earth** (v. 5). It would appear to be most likely, therefore, that we are no longer concerned with the relatively isolated victory of Babylon against Assyria in the eighth century, but with the long march of Babylonian victories which began towards the end of the seventh. The rise of the neo-Babylonian empire in the last quarter of the seventh century marked both the eclipse of Assyrian power and its replacement by a new world-ruler. The purpose of the prophecy, therefore, appears to be to herald the Babylonian power as the new world-ruler which was destined to replace that of Assyria. Although the language has affinities with that of the much later apocalyptic eschatology, it is not in such terms that it is to be understood. As it is now placed it marks a necessary 'bridge' between the acclaim given to the Babylonian achievements of the eighth century (vv. 2–3) and their role as the bearers of Yahweh's judgment upon Judah and Jerusalem in the sixth (vv. 6–8).

4. Hark, a tumult on the mountains: The opening appeal to listen (Heb. literally 'a voice!') reappears again in 40:3. The tumult referred to is that of the assembling together of a great army ready for a campaign, or even for a specific battle. The references to **kingdoms** and **nations** should not be taken as an indication that the prophet was envisaging a world-wide eschatological battle between the nations of the world. Rather, the terms reflect the different ethnic elements which made up the armies of the ancient imperial powers, and the large scale of the conquests which Babylon achieved. Then the threat that they pose **to destroy the whole earth** can be seen as in line with this. Those who, in vv. 2–3, have been greeted as dedicated instruments of Yahweh's purpose are here seen to pose a threat to the nations of the world by their lust for power. For the idea that **the whole earth** was divinely destined to be subdued by Babylon, cf. Jer. 27:6–7.

5. They come from a distant land: As in the case of Assyria, Babylon appeared remote from Judah, and many of the ethnic groups that were conscripted into its army seemed to originate at the very end of the world. The reference to **the LORD and the weapons of his indignation** follows out the theme that the Babylonians were fulfilling Yahweh's purpose, which is now understood in a negative and threatening sense. The translation **destroy** (Heb. *ḥabbēl*) is probably rather strong for a verb meaning fundamentally 'to bind, twist' (*BDB ḥbl*, I; a second stem, *ḥbl*, II, meaning 'to ruin, destroy', is also listed). The sense 'to subdue all the earth' would be perfectly adequate to describe the notion of Babylonian domination which is referred to. It is 'world dominion', rather than 'world destruction' which Yahweh had committed into the hands of the Babylonians.

THIRD PROPHECY: THE DAY OF THE LORD IS NEAR

13:6–8

The third of the prophecies concerning Babylon takes up the theme of the Day of the LORD, which first appears in written prophecy with Am. 5:18–20, and re-appears earlier in the book of Isaiah in Isa. 2:12ff. The historical reference here is undoubtedly to the destruction of Jerusalem by the Babylonian armies in 587 BC. This was interpreted as 'the Day of the LORD' in Ezek. 7:10–13, which must itself contain a conscious allusion to the earlier prophecy of Amos. By means of this connection a new dimension is introduced into the history of Judah's dealings with Babylon. With this it is made unmistakably plain that Yahweh's 'consecration' and use of Babylon is in connection with a purpose which he has to fulfil concerning his own people.

6. Wail, for the day of the LORD is near: It is not incontrovertibly clear from the prophecy whether the fall of Jerusalem to the Babylonians was imminently expected, or had actually taken place. It is likely that the latter is the case so that the prophecy is *post eventum*, and aimed at showing that the disaster that had happened to Judah in 587 was, in spite of all appearance, a part of Yahweh's purpose (cf. Lam. 2 : 7ff.). **as destruction from the Almighty:** There is a poetic assonance in the Hebrew between the words for **destruction** (Heb. *šôḏ*) and **Almighty** (Heb. *šadday*).

7. Therefore all hands will be feeble: Cf. Ezek. 7 : 17 for the general picture of shock and fear which the people of Judah were to experience as they faced the horrors of capitulation to a foreign army.

8. and they will be dismayed: Either the first part of this line has been lost (so Kaiser), or we should omit it as a gloss (so Wildberger). G. R. Driver, *JSS* 13 (1968), p. 43, connects it with the following noun (Heb. *ṣîrîm*) and interprets this as 'inside, stomach' (from the Arabic *maṣṣārun*). Hence *NEB*'s 'his stomach hollow with fear'. *RSV*'s **their faces will be aflame** scarcely provides a good description of being horror-stricken. *NEB*'s 'burn with shame' is better.

13:9–16

The fourth prophecy elaborates and expands on the third, but appears to go beyond a reference to the events of 587 BC, when Babylonian armies laid siege to Jerusalem. Instead the judgments inflicted at the time of the Day of the LORD will be world-wide. It is only the final verse which bears a distinctively historical character, since the preceding imagery relates much more to a catastrophe of cosmic proportions. It is probable therefore that we should see in vv. 9–16 an eschatological reinterpretation of the prophetic theme of the Day of the LORD which had first been applied in vv. 6–8 to the events of 587. The concluding prophecy which follows in vv. 17–22 then once again picks up the sequence of historical events concerning Judah's dealings with Babylon. This fourth prophecy must then be seen as a late insertion providing a further, eschatological, interpretation of the Day of the LORD as a coming catastrophe which will embrace all nations. The whole earth will become a desolation, all sinners will be destroyed, and the sun, moon and stars will cease to give light (cf. Jl 2 : 30–31). We may compare Isa. 24 : 1–13 for a similar eschatological re-interpretation of an earlier prophetic theme. The message of this prophecy is then to be found in the assertion that all sinners, throughout the entire world, will be judged by Yahweh, and none shall escape. Such an eschatological expectation must certainly be ascribed to a late date, no earlier than the fourth century BC.

9. Behold, the day of the LORD comes: The emphasis throughout in this section is upon the revelation of the divine wrath which this day will bring. Whereas earlier prophecy had focused upon its significance as a day when Israel and Judah would be punished for their sins, it has now been enlarged to become a day when all sinners will be judged. Hence its primary purpose is made clear with the affirmation that it will be a day **to destroy its sinners** from the earth.

10. For the stars of the heavens: The darkening of the world at the advent of the Day of the LORD (the close parallel in Jl 2 : 31 discloses the same imagery), appears to have developed out of the earlier imagery of a theophany in a storm-cloud. Cf. Pss. 29 : 3ff; 97 : 2. The heavy black storm-clouds which obscured the heavens marked the presence of God, so that here, in the picture of Yahweh's coming to judge the world, the darkening of the sky is a token of his presence. Out of this there emerges further the idea that the Day of the LORD will witness a complete transformation of the ordered life of the universe (cf. 24 : 17–21).

11. I will punish the world: Once again the theme of punishment reappears. Instead of being applied to the specific situation of a military defeat of Jerusalem, as in vv. 6–8, the whole world, with all its sinners, is now seen to be involved. Just as in 587 Judah had to bear the consequences of its sins, so when the final Day of the LORD comes will all nations and peoples have to suffer the just punishment of their sins. **I will put an end to the pride of the arrogant:** Cf. 2 : 12ff. for the emphasis upon the divine condemnation and punishment of human pride.

12. I will make men more rare: Because no one will escape on the day of Yahweh's punishment, and because all men are sinners, there will be a fearful slaughter when the final reckoning comes.

13. I will make the heavens tremble: The LXX renders 'the heavens will tremble', which provides a closer parallelism for the following line. Once again the ancient language concerning the theophany of Yahweh in a storm provides the imagery for a picture of his coming to judge the world. Cf. Ps. 97 : 4.

14. every man will turn to his own people: The author is conscious of the many upheavals which have led to the great movements of peoples across the face of the earth. When each man flees to his own country and people in order to find security there, he will be disappointed. He will find that there is no place of safety, for Yahweh's judgment will be world-wide.

15. Whoever is found will be thrust through: It is this and the following verse alone of this section which appear to have some specific historical defeat in mind. If so, it must be that of 587 which the author has used to provide a picture of the punishment which will one day be meted out to all sinners. Just as in a military defeat no mercy is shown to the vanquished, so Yahweh will not pity those whom he must punish. In this case the imagery of the defeat of 587 has been made into the basis of a description for the final judgment of the world.

FIFTH PROPHECY: THE DESTRUCTION OF BABYLON

13 : 17–22

In this, the fifth of the series of prophecies in vv. 2–22, the dealings of Judah with Babylon are reverted to. There is no serious reason for questioning the conclusion of a large number of scholars (Fohrer,

Wildberger, Schoors) that this final prophecy relates to the same period which is presupposed by the prophecies of chs. 40–55. This is the time immediately preceding the fall of Babylon to the armies of the Persians and Medes in 538. Since the overthrow of Babylon is still in the future, and did not in historical fact take the form of a dramatic military overthrow, we may place this prophecy in the period 545–538 BC. So clear in fact does this setting appear to be that those scholars who have sought to interpret vv. 2–22 as a unity have regarded the circumstantial evidence provided by this section as a sufficient basis for dating the whole unit. However, it is preferable to see in the unit a series of prophecies, or fragments of prophecies, from different ages, which have been woven into a sequence to relate the story of Judah's ill-fated relationships with Babylon. Only vv. 9–16 fall outside this sequence, since they apply the notion of the Day of the LORD to a still future eschatological day.

17. Behold, I am stirring up the Medes against them: Cf. 41:25 for the same basic understanding of Yahweh's control of the Medo-Persian armies. The Medes were an Indo-Iranian people who first began to make their impact on the Near East in the ninth century BC. They assisted the Babylonians in the overthrow of Nineveh in 612, but subsequently, under Cyrus, gained control of the eastern provinces of the Babylonian empire. After the defeat of Croesus, king of Lydia, in 547 BC, they posed a major threat to Babylon itself. Cf. further, G. Widengren, *Peoples of Old Testament Times*, pp. 315ff. Since Babylon appears not to have fallen at the time that this prophecy was made, we may ascribe it to a date *c.* 540 BC. **Who have no regard for silver:** The meaning is that their pity cannot be bought for money, so there will be no escape for the Babylonian oppressors when their turn for judgment comes. They will not be able to buy their way out of danger.

18. Their bows will slaughter: The meaning literally is 'will dash in pieces', which scarcely makes sense. Serious disturbance of the text appears to have taken place and *NEB* simply omits the first three words of the verse, rather than hazard a very uncertain reconstruction (cf. *HTOT*, p. 179). **the fruit of the womb** most likely refers to infant children, although Kaiser suggests that the unborn foetus may be meant.

19. And Babylon ... will be like Sodom and Gomorrah: The destruction of the cities of the plain (Gen. 19:24–28) serves as a suitable basis for comparison because of the permanent ruin which resulted from their overthrow. Cf. Isa. 1:10, which may have encouraged the use of the simile here.

20. It will never be inhabited: The completeness of God's judgment upon Babylon will be shown by the fact that no reconstruction of the ruins will be undertaken. In fact the capture of Babylon by the Medo-Persian armies in 538 BC took place without any significant destruction of the city, further strengthening the conclusion that this prophecy was made before that event took place. No reason is given by this prophecy to explain why a divine judgment of Babylon was necessary, but the oppression of Babylonian rule is assumed to be so well known as to call for no further description. When the overthrow of Babylon comes it will be a well merited act of retribution for the ills that it has brought to Judah, as the prophecy of ch. 47 shows. **no Arab will pitch his tent there:** With poetic hyperbole the utter uselessness of the ruins that are to be left is described by the fact that not even a nomadic tent-dweller would wish to pitch his tent there.

21. But wild beasts will lie down there: *NEB* identifies the **wild beasts** (Heb. *ṣiyyîm*) as 'marmots' and the **howling creatures** (Heb. *ʾōḥîm*) as 'porcupines', although certainty is not possible. The **ostriches** of *RSV* (Heb. *bᵉnôṯ yaʿanāh*) are identified as 'desert owls' (*NEB*) and the **satyrs** (Heb. *śᵉʿîrîm*; literally 'hairy ones') as 'he goats'. The sense is clear, and is not really dependent upon the precise identity of the species of wild animal that are referred to.

22. Hyenas will cry: Once again there is some problem of identifying the animal species. Instead of **hyenas** and **jackals** *NEB* suggest 'jackals' and 'wolves'. The presence of the wild creatures is to demonstrate that the site of a once great city will be reduced to nothing, and will revert to an entirely wild, undeveloped condition.

A NOTE CONCERNING THE RESTORATION OF ISRAEL

14:1-2

A redactor has introduced at this point a concluding assurance regarding the restoration of Israel after the overthrow of Babylon. It summarises in a very concise fashion the main lines of Jewish hope which emerged late in the sixth century with the prophecies now preserved in chs. 40–55. It seems in every way probable that the author has had the contents of these prophecies before him, and, writing either late in the sixth or early in the fifth century, has set out a hope of Israel's restoration. Three points stand out as of marked significance: the hope is based on a return from exile in foreign lands; the return will be assisted by foreigners (cf. Isa. 49:22–23), and these aliens will then become the slaves of Israel (cf. 61:5–7). The redactor's purpose appears to have been to present a fitting conclusion for the sequence of prophecies regarding Judah and Babylon by showing that in the end it will all result in a happy and blessed future for Israel. The presence of such a brief note at this point strongly supports the contention (see Introduction, p. 8) that some attempt has been made to weave together the book of Isaiah into a unity. Its overall message concerning the fate of Judah and Jerusalem has taken full account of the episode of the Babylonian exile, indicating that the joining of chs. 40ff. on to 1–39* is the result of a conscious thematic connection.

14:1. The LORD will have compassion on Jacob: The very titles **Jacob** and **Israel** re-appear frequently in chs. 40–55 as a description of those who were deported to Babylon. To what extent the author also had a consciousness of the fate of those elements of the Northern Kingdom which had earlier been transplanted by Assyria is not evident (cf. Jer. 31:7–22). The reference to the promise that Yahweh **will again choose Israel** points to the idea that the entire history surrounding the former election of Israel had been brought to an end with the Babylonian exile. A whole new beginning would have to be made, which would amount to a new act of divine election. For the great importance of such a theological concept, see *THAT*, I, cols. 275–300; *TWAT*, I, pp. 592–608. In many respects the notion expressed here is tantamount to the Jeremianic promise of 'a new covenant' (Jer. 31:31ff.). The promise **and aliens will join them** appears to be drawn from such passages as 45:14–17; 49:7.

2. And the peoples will take them: 1QIsᵃ reads 'many peoples'. The identity of these servant peoples is not made plain, probably because already when the redactor was writing the Babylonian exile was beginning to spread into a more scattered 'Diaspora'. Thus, although it appears to be primarily Israel's captors who are to perform this task of bringing them back, more than one nation was recognised to be involved. Whether there is any conscious allusion to the role of Persia, and to the Edict of Cyrus in particular (cf. Ezr. 1:2–4), cannot be discerned. The phrase **and the house of Israel will possess them in the LORD's land** is of interest because it recognises that, in its scattered existence, Israel was a 'house', but no longer a nation. Furthermore the belief that the territory of Israel-Judah was 'Yahweh's land' reflects the pre-exilic understanding which provided a major stimulus towards the restoration of Judah in the sixth century. Cf. W. Brueggemann, *The Land*, Philadelphia, 1977, pp. 151ff.

THE DOWNFALL OF THE WORLD-RULER

14:3–23

The prophecy which follows in 14:4b–20a (vv. 5 and 20b–21 are additions) is a magnificent mocking-song set out in the form of a lament for the death of a great world-ruler. His descent into the underworld is described with incomparable irony. It has been provided with an introduction in vv. 3–4a identifying the ruler as the king of Babylon, and this identification has been further strengthened by a brief appended note at the end in vv. 22–23, mentioning the permanent ruination that is to befall Babylon. On the assumption that the poem is from Isaiah and that a Babylonian ruler is being referred to, S. Erlandsson, pp. 161ff., argues for an eighth-century background and a connection with the situation of 701. Yet it is hard to see how this Babylonian rebel ruler could be described as one who **smote the peoples** and **ruled the nations** (v. 6), since his greatest achievement was a partially successful revolt against his Assyrian suzerain. A whole list of candidates has been suggested as the subject of the song (see Kaiser, II, p. 30, note b). Since the identity of the ruler is not made explicit in the poem itself, but appears in the introductory v. 4a, it is possible that the original composition was for an Assyrian, rather than a Babylonian, king. In this case it is attractive to follow Barth, pp. 136ff., in regarding the poem as composed for the death of Sargon

(721–705) in 705 BC. In this case Isaianic authorship would certainly be possible, and could even be regarded as probable. Cf. further H. L. Ginsburg, *JAOS* 88 (1968), pp. 47–53. Another possibility would be to identify the world-ruler as Sennacherib, whose death took place in 681 BC. (Cf. W. Staerk, *Das assyrische Weltreich im Urteil der Propheten*, p. 144). In this case Isaianic authorship would be less probable at so late a date in the early seventh century. If the view that the original poem was composed for the death of Sargon, which best fits the portrait of an awe-inspiring world-conqueror that is given, then a redactor has adapted this to the situation of a later age by making a reference in v. 4*a* to **the king of Babylon**. Which king of Babylon was intended by this is not explicitly clear. The most plausible candidate would be Nebuchadnezzar (605–562 BC), whose conquests affected Judah most adversely. However, since the king's death in some degree is intended to reflect the waning of the power he represents, it might be thought even more probable that one of the last kings of Babylon, such as Nabonidus (555–539 BC), was intended to be referred to. Coming as it does after a series a prophecies regarding Judah's experiences at the hands of Babylon (13:2–14:2), it is evident that the placing of so powerful and expressive a prophecy at this point has been aimed at celebrating the passing of a hostile and hated world-dominion. It is pointless speculating about possible allusions in the mocking lament to other world rulers after the downfall of Babylon in 538. Nevertheless it is apparent that, in the later apocalyptic literature, **Babylon** took on a revived significance as a symbolic cover-name for oppressive world government, so that its final downfall became a part of Jewish apocalyptic eschatology (cf. Rev. 18:2ff.).

The poem is in the form of a lament for the dead, such as would be sung at a funeral (cf. H. Jahnow, *Das hebräische Leichenlied im Rahmen der Völkerdichtung* (*BZAW* 36), 1923, pp. 239–53). However, it is heavily ironic and satirical in its expression, and is designed to express rejoicing that, with the death of a tyrant, an age of oppressive tyranny has been removed from the world. V. 5, which breaks up the flow of the song, must certainly be regarded as an addition. It makes direct citation of the theme of the **staff** and **sceptre** from 9:4 (Heb. 3), and appears to be the work of a redactor who has endeavoured to show that, with the death of the tyrant, this Isaianic prophecy had been fulfilled.

14:3. When the LORD has given you rest: Vv. 3–4*a* provide an introduction which links the following funeral lament with the general subject of Babylon which has preceded it. The reference to Israel's obtaining **rest** from **pain and turmoil** shows that it is the situation brought about by the ending of Babylonian world dominion that is uppermost in the redactor's mind, rather than the specific occasion of any one Babylonian monarch's death. Certainly, if a particular king's death is intended to be referred to, we might most readily think of Nabonidus, whose death occurred in 539 BC. **and the hard service with which you were made to serve:** must be a reference to the period of the Babylonian exile in which the circumstances of those in Babylon appears to have been tantamount to a harsh form of slavery.

4. you will take up this taunt: The word **taunt** (Heb. *māšāl*), properly means 'likeness', and is used for proverbs, allegories and parables. It is apparently used in this instance for a composition which is in the form of a lament because it is in fact an ironical, or satirical, lament. **against the king of Babylon:** See above for the possibility that this was intended to be Nabonidus, the last king of Babylon. However, it is evidently not simply one ruler, but the whole tyrannical rule which he represented, which formed the subject for this celebration of its passing.

How the oppressor has ceased: This line marks the original beginning of the lament proper, which does not name the tyrant over whose passing it so rejoices. That it was originally an Assyrian ruler, such as Sargon, would make possible an origin from Isaiah. The phrase **the insolent fury** is difficult, and scarcely intelligible in the original Hebrew (*madhēbāh*). *NEB* reads 'frenzy'. and, like *RSV*, presupposes an emendation to *marhēbāh*, which is supported by IQIsᵃ, and goes back to J. D. Michaelis. Cf. H. M. Orlinsky, *VT* 7 (1957), pp. 202f., and S. Erlandsson, pp. 29–32, for further discussion of the *hapax legomenon*.

5. the staff of the wicked: The verse is an insertion in the original lament, and the references to the **staff** and the **sceptre** appear to hark back quite consciously to the promise of the breaking of the 'rod' and 'staff' in 9:4 (Heb. 3). A redactor has sought to show that, with the passing of the tyrant, this Isaianic prophecy had been fulfilled.

6. that smote the peoples: Evidently it is not simply the oppression perpetrated against one nation, but against many, that forms the basis of the grievance against the tyrant. It is the picture of such a world conqueror which suggests that the original subject of satirical lament was Sargon or Sennacherib, or even Nebuchadnezzar, if a Babylonian candidate is sought, who did achieve great conquests. However, it is possible that the particular ruler has been given credit for victories actually achieved by his predecessors. The phrase **with unrelenting persecution** requires a small emendation in Hebrew to the pi'el ptc. *mᵉraddēp* (cf. *BHS*). Other commentators have suggested a noun *mirdāt*, 'dominion', hence 'with unremitting dominion' (so Duhm, Marti, Procksch, Fohrer). S. Erlandsson, p. 32, following H. S. Nyberg, suggests that we should read the Hoph'al participle with the meaning 'persecution'.

7. The whole earth is at rest: There is an evident element of poetic hyperbole in regarding **the whole earth** as subject to the ruler. Yet both Assyria and Babylon achieved conquests which embraced a large part of the effective world which surrounded Judah, making them truly world powers. Hence it was legitimate to picture a period of world peace arriving with the death of the tyrant.

8. The cypresses rejoice at you: For cypresses *NEB* reads 'pines'. The reference is to the extensive felling of trees to provide timber for military construction, as well as the taking of it from the forested regions of Syria for other building projects. By felling the tallest and mightiest trees, the tyrant had displayed his own disregard for the divine order, and a measure of arrogant pride which had now come to an end.

9. Sheol beneath is stirred up: The poem now moves into its most triumphant satirical theme by picturing the abject humiliation of the tyrannical king. The ruler who had once felled the cedars of Lebanon had now been brought to the lowest depths of Sheol, the underworld abode where the shades of the departed went. For Sheol, cf. *THAT*, II, cols. 837–41. **it rouses the shades to greet you:** The customary picture of Sheol was one in which all human distinctions disappeared (cf. Job 14:12, 12f.). Here, however, the **shades** (Heb. $r^e\bar{p}\bar{a}'\hat{i}m$), or shadowy remains, of the dead rulers of earth are pictured as getting up from their thrones in astonishment to greet this great world-ruler who has come to share their fate. The use of the past tense (cf. *NEB*'s rendering) indicates that the ruler was thought of as already dead, although this could be simply a poetic device. Probably the death had already taken place, so that this is not truly a prophetic pronouncement, but rather an indication that a downfall foretold in other prophecy had now occurred.

11. the sound of your harps: The implication is that the time when the ruler could indulge in rejoicing and musical festivities is now finished for ever. The good times were over. He is portrayed as coming to a place where there would be no further opportunity for any merrymaking. **maggots are the bed**. Heb. has 'are spread', but a slight change of pointing produces the noun **bed** (Heb. $y^e\dot{s}\hat{u}a'$), which yields a better sense.

12. How you are fallen from heaven: Vv. 12–15 appear to contain either a fragment of, or at least an allusion to, an ancient myth of the banishment of a divine being from heaven (cf. Ezek. 28:12–19; Ps. 82:6f.). M. H. Pope, *El in the Ugaritic Texts*, (*VT Supp*. 3), pp. 61ff. has suggested that the original subject of this myth was the Canaanite deity El. Cf. also F. Stolz, *Strukturen und Figuren*, pp. 149ff. For the notion of the 'mount of assembly' of the gods, cf. also R. J. Clifford, *The Cosmic Mountain in Canaan and the Old Testament*, pp. 160ff. The title **Day Star, son of Dawn** must certainly be a reference to the morning star, the planet Venus, and the deity consistently associated in Canaanite mytholoy with this planet is Attar. Cf. J. Gray, *JNES* 8 (1949), pp. 27–34; F. Stolz, *Strukturen und Figuren*, pp. 182ff. The rising up of this planet in the early morning sky, followed by its sudden descent without the completion of a true arc, have found echoes in mythology at more than one point. Whether there was a coherent myth of the 'fall' of a high-god from the heavens to the underworld is not yet firmly established, although it appears plausible enough from various fragmentary echoes in the Old Testament and elsewhere. The phrase **who laid the nations low** applies the theme of the myth to the historical achievements of the tyrannical world-ruler.

13. You said in your heart: The allusion appears to be to a scene in the myth in which the god represented by the Day Star (Attar) has attempted to assume the role of the king of the gods by taking over the highest throne.

above the stars of God: The picture is that, in heaven itself, some stars were set higher than others to mark the position of the various divine thrones. The throne of God, properly El, rested in the highest place, until this attempt to usurp its pre-eminence.

I will sit on the mount of assembly is a reference to the Canaanite mythological tradition in which the throne of the god Baal was situated on Mount Zaphon, which was the ancient title of Mount Casius in Syria. Cf. R. J. Clifford, *The Cosmic Mountain*, pp. 160ff.; *God and Temple*, pp. 6f. It appears unlikely that we can reconstruct any completely coherent and uniform pattern of mythology regarding all the various Canaanite deities and their divine dwelling-places. However, it certainly appears that the prophet has reflected a significant and popular theme from such mythology in vv. 12–14, and has used it as an appropriate comparison for the world-shattering significance of the great tyrant's death.

14. I will make myself like the Most High: The divine title **Most High**, or 'Elyon (more fully El 'Elyon; cf. Gen. 14:19–20), appears as that of an ancient Canaanite deity, whose name indicates his position of exaltation over the other gods, and so as fitted to occupy the 'mount of assembly' where the gods could meet to sit in council. It appears very probable that it was the title popularly used in Jerusalem, before David's conquest of the city, for the major deity worshipped there. Cf. my *God and Temple*, pp. 42ff., and now, F. Stolz, *Strukturen und Figuren im Kult von Jerusalem (BZAW* 118), 1970, pp. 149ff. It would be appropriate that, as the 'highest' god, El 'Elyon should preside over the divine council, and that the Day Star (Attar) should have endeavoured to take over this position of eminence. Possibly the myth also contained some explanation of why El 'Elyon's throne was vacant, perhaps as a result of his descent into the underworld after defeat by Death (the god Mot). For a rather different reconstruction, cf. M. H. Pope, *El in the Ugaritic Texts*, pp. 61ff.

15. But you are brought down to Sheol: At this point the narrative element of the myth is dropped and the prophet resumes the imagery set out in v. 11 of the descent of the tyrant into Sheol. For **the Pit** as the place of the dead, cf. v. 16.

16. Those who see you: It is a delicate touch of dramatic irony which leads the poet to picture the astonishment of the inhabitants of the world of the dead at discovering that they are joined by one who had, until so recently, been such a powerful ruler. On his arrival he came with nothing but the memory of his former glory. **Is this the man who made the earth to tremble:** The beliefs about Sheol reflected in the Old Testament emphasise its drab and colourless character, as a place where all earthly distinctions and pleasures are past. It offered an existence that was so attenuated and weak as to be totally undesirable to all but those who had become weary of life itself (cf. Job 7:7ff.; 14:13ff.). Cf. R. Martin-Achard, *From Death to Life*, Edinburgh/London, 1960, pp. 36ff.

17. **and overthrew its cities:** The suffix in **its cities** (Heb. *'āraw*) is masculine, yet it must refer back to the feminine noun **world** (Heb. *ṭēḇēl*). For such a *genus potens*, cf. *G–K*. p. 135*o*.

18. **All the kings of the nations lie in glory:** It is preferable, with *NEB*, to take the phrase **All the kings of the nations** with v. 17, thereby identifying these kings as being among the prisoners taken by the tyrant. Then read 'All of them lie in glory'. The point is then that all the rulers captured by the tyrant had been given a decent and honoured burial, but such was not to be the fate of so hated an oppressor, whose corpse would be desecrated and humiliated. Cf. Am. 2:1; Jer. 22:19. **each in his own tomb:** For **tomb**, Heb. has literally 'his house' (*bêṯô*), hence *NEB*'s 'in his last home'.

19. **but you are cast out, away from your sepulchre:** It is better to take the preposition as *min privativum* and read 'without a proper burial chamber'. **like a loathed untimely birth:** Heb. has 'like a loathed branch' (*nēṣer*), which *RSV* has emended to *nēp̄el* 'untimely birth', following Symm. 1QIs* follows MT, and *NEB* 'mere loathsome carrion' presupposes an emendation to *nēṣel*, 'carrion', lit. 'what is stripped off'. **who go down to the stones of the Pit:** The reference is to Sheol (cf. v. 15), indicating that the place of the dead was thought to share a very earthy and stony character, appropriate to its subterranean location. V. 19*c* clearly begins a separate verse unit, suggesting that **who go down** should be read as singular referring to the tyrannical ruler. This then matches the singular **dead body** of v. 19*d*. The plural has arisen by a false assimilation to the plural subject of v. 19*b*.

20. **You will not be joined with them in burial:** The **with them** must refer to 'the kings of the nations' of v. 18. The king himself is held to be entirely responsible for the fate of his people. It is his decisions and excesses which have brought ruin upon them. **because you have destroyed your land:** LXX reads as 'my land'; i.e. 'Yahweh's land', which would make it a more precise reference to the Babylonian destruction of Judah in 587. However, this is clearly a secondary interpretation that has come in with LXX's translation.

May the descendants of evildoers nevermore be named: V. 20*b* and the following v. 21 are to be seen as additions to the original lament (cf. Barth, pp. 124, 128f.). The use of the plural **evildoers** here, and again in the reference to 'fathers' in the following verse, points to a collective interpretation of the tyrant power whose passing is celebrated. In this case what we have is an indication of the application of the lament to mark the passing of Babylonian world-domination. The cause for rejoicing is no longer the specific instance of a monarch's death, but the belief that it is the 'death' of Babylonian world-rule that has taken place.

21. **Prepare slaughter for his sons:** As so often in the ancient world the deposition of a ruler was to be followed by the putting to death of his sons who might have succeeded to this throne. Here, however, the reference to the plural **fathers** in the phrase **because of the guilt of their fathers** shows that it is the ending of a series of oppressive rulers that is in mind. Collectively they represent Babylon

itself, and the assassination of the sons is made into a picture of the permanent ending of this source of foreign domination. There is no need, therefore, to emend to the singular 'father', as has sometimes been advocated. The phrase **and fill the face of the world with cities** is a reference to the power of the imperial ruler to assert his greatness through the building and naming of cities. LXX and Syr. read 'war' instead of **cities**, but this is probably the result of an inner Greek confusion (*polemōn* instead of *poleōn*).

22. I will rise up against them: Vv. 22–23 have been introduced by a redactor to round off the mocking lament for the death of the tyrant, and to affirm its application to Babylon (as v. 4*a*). These verses serve to reaffirm the identity of the tyrant as a Babylonian ruler, and also to show that his passing represents the ending of the period of Babylonian world-rule. Nevermore will it pose a threat to Judah. It thus fittingly concludes the entire sequence of prophecies concerning Babylon which began with 13:1. Although it is set in the form of a future pronouncement **I will rise up**, we must conclude that it has been added *post eventum*, after 538, and is designed to affirm the finality of the fate that had overtaken Babylon.

THE LORD'S PLAN CONCERNING THE ASSYRIANS

14:24–27

This short section marks a break in the sequence of foreign nation prophecies proper, although it has an affinity with them on account of its assertion that it is Yahweh's plan to defeat the Assyrians on the soil (**mountains**) of Judah. It has played a large part in modern discussion of Isaiah's prophecies in regard to his attitude to, and expectations concerning, Assyria. Its authenticity, or otherwise, to Isaiah provides a major issue in determining the prophet's expectation concerning the outcome of the threat to Jerusalem by Sennacherib in 701 (see Introduction, p. 11, and below, on chs. 36–37). H. Barth has rightly argued that it once formed the conclusion of the larger redactional unit relating to the conflict between Assyria and Judah, Ephraim and Syria which began with ch. 5. (see Barth, pp. 103–19). The summoning of the nation that is far off in 5:26–29 marks Yahweh's calling of the Assyrians to threaten these three nations, and 10:5–15* indicates the turning point when Yahweh's threat to Assyria is first pronounced. 14:24–27 then provides a fitting conclusion to the plan regarding Yahweh's dealings with Assyria by announcing that it is Yahweh's intention to 'break' the Assyrian in Judah. Several scholars (Duhm, Marti, Fohrer, Wildberger, and now also H. Barth, p. 46) have regarded v. 25*b*, which is dependent on 10:27*a*, as a later addition. However, in view of the fact that the entire section is 'a passage pasted together from Isaianic phrases' (B. Stade, *ZAW* 3 (1883), p. 16, cited by Kaiser, II, p. 48n.), this must be considered further. In any case, there is a dependence both here and in 10:27*a* on 9:4 (Heb. 3).

Those scholars (S. R. Driver, G. von Rad, B. S. Childs, J. Schreiner) who have regarded the passage as authentic to Isaiah, have found in it a strong indication of his dependence on the supposed 'Zion tradition' and also a firm pointer to his message to Hezekiah at the time of the Assyrian crisis of 701. See further, my *Isaiah and the Deliverance of Jerusalem*, Ch. 2. We may note the following points:

(1). The passage must be considered along with those other passages in the book of Isaiah (especially 10:33f.; 17:12–14; 29:5–8; 31:5–9), which express a similar message concerning the coming dramatic overthrow of the Assyrians by the hand of Yahweh. There is, therefore, a similarity of content between these passages, but no reason to accept that 14:24–27 was at one time joined with 10:5–15 (as Procksch, F. Huber, pp. 47ff.; J. Schreiner, pp. 263ff.)

(2). These verses are certainly not from the prophet Isaiah, but have been built up by a form of developmental exegesis into a threat of the overthrow of Assyria from Isaiah's prophecies (chiefly 9:2–7; 10:5–15).

(3). This developmental elaboration of Isaiah's message concerning the fate of the Assyrians was the central theme of the Josianic Redaction of his prophecies (see Introduction, pp. 5ff.).

(4). From the perspective of this redactional development the overthrow of the Assyrian forces was still in the future, although its realisation was felt to be imminent.

(5). The connection of these prophecies with the events of the year 701, and to the sparing of Jerusalem by Sennacherib, was a late extension of them, which has come particularly to give rise to the tradition now recorded in 37:36 that the 'angel of the LORD' slew the Assyrians outside the gates of Jerusalem.

(6). The placing of the prophecy at this juncture is intended to mark the conclusion of the sequence of prophecies which began with 5:1–7 (cf. Barth, pp. 103–19).

B. S. Childs, pp. 128–36, has discerned the form of the prophecy as that of the 'summary appraisal', which has close affinities with the didactic form of Wisdom (cf. also J. W. Whedbee, *Isaiah and Wisdom*, pp. 75–9; H. Barth, p. 106).

The prophecy can therefore be seen to mark a significant step in the message that was discerned in Isaiah's preaching concerning the ultimate fate of the Assyrians, and the way in which this came to be connected with the tradition regarding Jerusalem's deliverance in 701 BC.

14:24. The LORD of hosts has sworn: Cf. 5:9 for the formula of a divine oath as a means of God's communicating a message to his prophet. Yahweh's 'plan' (Heb. *'ēṣāh*) is referred to in 5:19, and is here regarded as concerned with his intention of using the Assyrians to punish Judah, Ephraim and Syria. Then in turn he would inflict his punishment upon the Assyrians (10:5ff.). For the idea of Yahweh's 'plan' in Isaiah, cf. J. Fichtner, *ZAW* 63 (1951), pp. 16–33. Although the conception of such a plan arose authentically out of Isaiah's prophecies, the full nature and content of it has been constructed during the redactional stage of the collection of them. For **planned**

(Heb. *dimmāh*, cf. Ps. 48:9). The formula **so shall it stand** asserts the certainty of the completion of the plan, which in turn entailed the fulfilment of Isaiah's prophecies disclosing the plan. So far as the point of view of the Josianic Redactors was concerned the fulfilment of this plan was believed to be imminent in their day. Cf. further on 10:24–27a.

25. that I will break the Assyrian in my land: It is evident that this expectation of the overthrow of the Assyrians was believed to have been anticipated by the frustration of Sennacherib's attempt to take Jerusalem in 701. Cf. further 31:8. Whether the intention here is to point to the events of that year, or to a more distant overthrow of the Assyrians, no longer remains clear.

and his yoke shall depart from them: The citation is directly from 9:4 (Heb. 3), and this has led those who would regard 14:24–27 as authentic to Isaiah to remove v. 25b at a gloss (so Wildberger). Cf. also 10:27a. Yet in fact the whole of the section comprised of vv. 24–27 is made up from an extension of Isaianic words and themes, especially that of the **yoke** and **burden** theme from 9:4, as a reference to vassaldom to Assyria. **from their shoulder:** The Heb. has 'his shoulder', but *RSV* rightly follows the ancient versions in reading the plural suffix.

26. This is the purpose that is purposed: V. 26 is of great interest in extending the scope of Yahweh's purpose to include **the whole earth.** This universalising of the idea of the divine plan is found further in 29:7. What Yahweh was believed to have purposed concerning the Assyrians was a demonstration of his power over all nations and peoples, and his intention to protect Jerusalem. Just as the rule of Assyria extended over many nations, so was Yahweh's power greater still, and entailed a world-wide plan in which Judah and Jerusalem had a special place. The phrase **and this is the hand that is stretched out** is drawn from the refrain of 5:25; 9:12, etc. and attests further the thematic connections between these verses and the section that begins with 5:1ff. The phrase **over all the nations** adds a new dimension to the symbolism of the metaphor of Yahweh's outstretched hand.

27. For the LORD of hosts has purposed: For the basic idea that God's plan is incomparably greater and more sure of realisation than that of men, cf. 7:7–9; 29:14; 31:3. It is evident from this verse that it is the certainty of the divine purpose regarding Assyria which forms the main subject of vv. 24–27. From the perspective of the time of their composition in Josiah's reign, this purpose had already been set in motion in the year 701, when Sennacherib failed to take Jerusalem. Its final consequence lay still in the future with the ending of the last remnants of Assyrian control over Judah.

A PROPHECY AGAINST PHILISTIA

14:28-32

The prophecy which follows is a peculiarly interesting one on account of the chronological features inherent in the text and the uncertainties regarding the precise historical circumstances to which it relates.

In spite of doubts expressed by Duhm, Marti, and now W. Dietrich, pp. 208f., about its authenticity, and their attempts to date it in the post-exilic period, most recent scholars (Wildberger, Schoors, Erlandsson, Donner) have defended its authenticity to Isaiah. This is surely correct, although O. Kaiser would regard only vv. 29–31 as belonging to Isaiah's age (cf. also K. Fullerton, *AJSL* 42 (1925–6) pp. 99ff.). This Isaianic nucleus has been expanded at a later time by the addition of vv. 30a + 32b by a redactor who drew upon the tradition of Zion as the place where Yahweh protects his people. However, v. 32b does express very effectively the message of Isaiah to Hezekiah at a time when he was clearly under some pressure to join a Philistine revolt against Assyria.

The time reference given in v. 28, **the year that king Ahaz died**, is of only limited assistance in dating the prophecy since the year of this king's death is itself a matter of debate. J. Begrich would place this event in 725, which accords with the chronology that we have followed, whereas W. F. Albright would place it later, in 715/4 BC. In any case, however, we should follow Kaiser and Schoors in recognising that the locating of the prophecy in the year of Ahaz's death is the work of a redactor and may not be correct. The occasion of the prophecy is the death of a ruler (the **rod** of v. 29) who has inflicted defeat on the Philistines, but who is to be replaced by a stronger power. This must certainly refer to an Assyrian ruler, either Tiglath-pileser III, whose death took place in 727/6, or Shalmaneser V, whose death occurred in 722. J. Begrich, *ZDMG* 86 (1933), pp. 66–79 (= *Ges. Stud. zum A.T.*, pp. 121–31) argues for the former view, which has the attraction that it does correlate with the most probable year of Ahaz's demise. Furthermore, Tiglath-pileser III had certainly brought defeat to Philistia. However, H. Donner, pp. 112f., argues strongly that the political context of the prophecy relates to Shalmaneser V's passing, when a period of unrest occurred in Assyria before the usurper, Sargon, secured the throne. Isaiah counselled Hezekiah to maintain a position of neutrality, since like Philistia, Judah was in the first stage of vassaldom to Assyria. This he did, and, in the outcome, the Philistine revolt was put down at the battle of Rapiḫu (Donner, p. 113). This view of the circumstances of the prophecy is the most likely, and is preferable to attempting to relate it to the period of 705–701 (S. R. Driver, J. A. Bewer) by linking it with the death of Sargon in 705. Still less is it likely that we should regard the **rod** of v. 29 as a Judean ruler (cf. K. A. Kitchen, *POTT*, p. 65), either Uzziah (cf. 2 Chr. 26:6–7), or Hezekiah (2 Kg. 18:8).

14:28. In the year that King Ahaz died: This would be 725, as noted above, and would correspond roughly with the time of Tiglath-pileser's death. However, the chronological reference is from a redactor,.and there are good reasons, as noted above, for locating the prophecy at the time of Shalmaneser V's passing in 722. **came this oracle:** The suggestion (cf. *BHS*) to read 'then I saw' in preference to this is unnecessary, although some influence upon the reference from Isa. 6:1 appears probable.

29. Rejoice not, O Philistia: The occasion of the prophecy is the death of the Assyrian ruler, which had aroused Philistine ambitions and plans to break free from the burden of vassaldom. In this hope they clearly had sought the support and complicity of Hezekiah, and the main purpose of Isaiah's prophecy was to dissuade the Judean king from joining such a revolt. There was no cause for Philistine rejoicing, therefore, because the death of the king did not mean the weakening of Assyrian rule. The Philistines were a people who originated from Caphtor (Crete) according to Am. 9:7. Thus they were an Aegean people, who had settled in the land of Canaan-Israel about the same time as the Israelites, and who were destined eventually to give their name to the land—Palestine. For their history, cf. K. A. Kitchen, *POTT*, pp. 53–78; Ph. Reymond, *BHH*, III, cols. 1455–8. **that the rod which smote you:** The reference to a defeat inflicted on the Philistine cities by Assyria would better fit either the reign of Tiglath-pileser III, or that of Sargon, who subdued a revolt from that quarter in 711. Cf. H. Donner, p. 112. However, it is quite plausible that the occasion of Shalmaneser V's death has occasioned a rejoicing because he had maintained the control which his predecessor (Tiglath-pileser) had established. **for from the serpent's root will come forth:** The imagery is somewhat strained, and relates to a sequence concerning the generation of three different types of snake (**serpent—adder—flying serpent**), combined with the metaphor of a plant cut down to its roots. The meaning is nonetheless quite clear and probably reflects popular tales about the procreation of snakes. The **flying serpent** was not a native of the Near East, and the description has almost certainly been influenced by fantasy and popular mythology. Mesopotamian iconography shows several winged snakes, and we may compare the winged seraphim of 6:2.

30. And the first-born of the poor will feed: V. 30*a* is out of place, and introduces an alien idea after the threatening aspect of the preceding verse. Its comforting message belongs after v. 32. Fohrer removes it as inauthentic, and Kaiser places it after v. 31 and before v. 32*b*. A transposition after v. 32*b* is preferable. Its authenticity cannot be beyond question, and it may have arisen from such hopes concerning Mount Zion such as we find expressed in 37:30–32. The phrase **firstborn of the poor** must mean 'very poorest', but we may follow the suggestion of *NEB* which reads 'in my meadows' (Heb. *bᵉḵārāy* instead of *bᵉḵôrê*). **but I will kill your root with famine:** It is better to read the third person, 'he will kill', following 1QIsᵃ, and 'your seed, offspring' (Heb. *zarᵉᶜēḵ*), instead of the Heb. *šorᵉšēḵ*, 'your root', following LXX with Duhm, Marti, Begrich, Donner. **and your remnant I will slay:** We should read 'he will slay', with MT.

31. Wail, O gate; cry, O city: The rejoicing of the Philistines over the death of their oppressor was premature and misguided, since an even stronger ruler would replace him. Their rejoicing should therefore be turned into mourning, and, with that, their plans to break free from Assyrian rule should be abandoned. Undoubtedly the prophecy was aimed in the direction of Hezekiah who was under some pressure to join the revolt. **O Philistia, all of you:** The repeated drawing of attention to all the Philistines (cf. v. 29) may have arisen because this people consisted of five independently governed cities: Gath, Ekron, Ashdod, Ashkelon and Gaza. H. Donner, p. 111, would, however, delete **all of you** here as a gloss from v. 29. **For smoke comes out of the north:** The **north** almost certainly points to Assyria as the source of the attack, and the **smoke** refers to the smoke of battle, with the burning of villages and towns, rather than to the sending of smoke signals. **and there is no straggler in his ranks:** This follows an emendation to *môdēd* instead of *bôdēd*, with 1QIs[a]. Nevertheless the last line of the verse still remains difficult and uncertain and Begrich attempts a much bolder reconstruction to 'and its pillars do not waver'.

32. What will one answer the messengers: The ancient versions read the plural 'nations'; but this is not a necessary improvement. The reference must be to messengers from Philistia who have come to elicit Hezekiah's support for their plan. See above for the view of Kaiser and others that the verse is not original to the prophecy. Such a conclusion is not necessary, however, since at this point Isaiah affirms his demand upon the king of Judah to retain his position of neutrality. The dangers of joining the revolt were obvious, once Assyrian power reasserted itself. **The LORD has founded Zion** reflects the importance of the area of the temple mount as the place where Yahweh's presence was to be found. By trusting in Yahweh and his ultimate purpose for his people, Hezekiah should have nothing to do with any attempt to break free from Assyria, and thereby risk the safety and security of himself and his people. The phrase **and in her the afflicted of his people find refuge** has frequently been taken to reflect the post-exilic understanding of the 'poor, afflicted' as the 'pious, godly'. Yet this is not necessary in this reference, which rather affirms that all the people, even the poorest, will be secure if they trust in Yahweh, whereas if they join the revolt the poorest will have least to gain and most to lose.

PROPHECIES CONCERNING MOAB

15:1–16:14

As in the case of prophecies against Babylon we have here a series of prophecies connected together by brief comments and notes. Hence the first such prophecy is found in 15:1–9, the second in 16:1–5 and the third, in lament form, in 16:6–11. To these three prophecies two further notes have been added in 16:12 and 16:13–14. Throughout the interpretation of the material is rendered difficult on account of problems of translation, many of which have so far defied satisfactory resolution. To this must be added the general obscurity regarding the historical background and circumstances which affects so many of the prophecies regarding foreign nations. W. Rudolph, *G. R. Driver Festschrift*, Oxford, 1963, pp. 130–43, suggests that the first prophecy in 15:1–9 is from the age of Jeroboam II (786–746), and is thus earlier

than Isaiah's time. Yet in reality no clear or certain identification of
the historical background of the prophecies can be made, as Kaiser
readily acknowledges, on the basis of a resume of the history of Moab
and its relationships with Judah. In consequence there is little basis
for either asserting or denying an Isaianic origin to any of the
prophecies, although the opening word **oracle** (Heb. *maśśā'*) in 15:1
would suggest that it has been drawn from the separate collection
which began each of its prophecies with this title. A. H. van Zyl, *The
Moabites*, Leiden, 1960, pp. 20ff., regards 15:1–9*a* and 16:6–11 as a
taunt-song in lament form, derived from bedouin circles. However,
there is little to support the case for regarding the two sayings as
belonging together. Parts of 16:6–11 re-appear in a modified form in
Jer. 48:29–38.

For the history of the Moabites in Old Testament times, see,
besides the work of A. H. van Zyl, J. R. Bartlett, 'The Moabites and
Edomites', *POTT*, pp. 229–58; G. Molin, *BHH*, II, cols. 1229–32.

THE DESOLATION OF MOAB

15:1–9

The poem consists of a lament for Moab which has suffered a disastrous defeat at the hands of enemies who are not named. The attack
has taken place at night (v. 1) and has left Moab desolate and mourning. The threatening prophetic element has been introduced into the
prophecy in v. 9 which affirms that there is further suffering for Moab
yet to come. With H. Wildberger, we should, however, regard this
verse as the work of a later editor who has extended the original
lament into a future threat. W. Rudolph revives the view originally
proposed by F. Hitzig, that the defeat referred to was at the hands of
Judah under Jeroboam II. This would connect it with the Judean
conquests referred to in 2 Kg. 14:25. This view cannot, however, be
more than one among several possibilities. B. Duhm ascribed the
composition to the time of John Hyrcanus (135–104 BC), although a
date as late as this must certainly be ruled out. The fact is we simply
cannot now determine what particular defeat of the Moabites lies
behind the prophetic lament. Throughout there is expressed a deep
sensitivity to the sufferings of the Moabites, to whom the Israelites
were closely related, which appears to be more than the consequence
of poetic artistry, as O. Kaiser claims (cf. especially v. 5). There is no
gloating over the defeat of the Moabites, and these considerations
suggest that the enemy was not Judah, but some other people,
possibly the bedouin suggested by A. H. van Zyl.

15:1. An oracle concerning Moab: The title **oracle** (Heb. *maśśā'*)
points to this lament having been taken from the '*maśśā'*' collection'.
Because Ar is laid waste in a night. The initial **Because** (Heb. *kî*) can
better be taken in an asseverative sense, 'Surely', and this removes any
necessity to presuppose that a preceding clause has been omitted. The
battle had evidently taken place during a night attack, in which the
Moabites had been caught entirely unawares and defeated. **in a night**

is read with 1QIsᵃ and the ancient versions. **Ar** and **Kir** were the principal cities of Moab (Num. 21:15; 2 Kg. 3:25). The name **Kir** means simply 'city' and is to be identified with the Kir-hareseth of 16:7 (Kir-heres in 16:11).

2. **The daughter of Dibon** The Hebrew is difficult and the *RSV* translation rests on the emendation of *bayit*, 'house', to *bat*, **daughter**, understood as a metaphor for a city. Heb. has literally 'the house has gone up—and Dibon', so that 'house' could be taken to refer to the royal house (of Moab) (cf. Pharoah = 'Great House'), or the noun be regarded as a metaphor for the inhabitants of a town. Cf. *NEB*, 'The people of Dibon go up.' However, in view of the other references to places, we should expect one here, and we may follow Schoors, therefore, in reading *bēt* and taking it as a reference to the *bēt gāmûl* of Jer. 48:23. This was a town in the region of **Dibon** (modern *Hirbet Gumeil*), this latter being the northern capital of Moab. **over Nebo**: Nebo was the mountain region where Moses was believed to have died (Dt. 34) and **Medeba** lay close by this. **On every head is baldness**: baldness was a sign of mourning in which the mourner disfigured his normal appearance as a mark of grief.

3. **on the housetops**: Read 'and on the housetops they lament'. Cf. Jer. 48:38.

4. **Heshbon and Elealeh cry out**: **Heshbon** is modern *Hesban*, seven and a half miles north of Madeba. **Elealeh** (modern *el-ʿAl*) is two miles further north. **Jahaz** was close to the Moabite border and had once been an Israelite town (cf. Jos. 21:36) which was later taken by Moab (cf. the Mesha Inscription, *ANET*, p. 320).

the armed men of Moab cry aloud: M. Dahood, *Proverbs and North-west Semitic Philology*, Rome, 1953, pp. 29–30, would see here the stem *rʿʿ* 'broken'; hence 'Moab's loins are broken'. Cf. LXX which reads 'loins tremble' (cf. *BHS*), but *NEB* retains the Heb. and takes *hᵃluṣê* as 'men prepared for war'. **his soul trembles**: better 'his courage deserts him'. The **soul** (Heb. *nepeš*) was the seat of resolution and desire. Cf. H. W. Wolff, *Anthropology of the Old Testament*, pp. 15ff.

5. **My heart cries out for Moab**: As the poet pictures the sufferings of Moab he shares in their grief, thereby suggesting very strongly that Judah was not the attacker. **his fugitives flee**: The Heb. reads the singular, perhaps portraying a particular typical instance. **Zoar** was at the southern tip of the Dead Sea (Gen. 19:22). The phrase **to Eglath-shelishiyah** rather overloads the text and has come from a marginal cross-reference to Jer. 48:34. The location of **Luhith** is unknown. **they raise a cry of destruction**: This requires an emendation of the verb to *yāʾōrû* with 1QISᵃ. Cf. *HTOT*, p. 180.

6. **the waters of Nimrim**: **Nimrim** was on the south edge of the Dead Sea. Its desolate location may have been regarded as appropriately illustrative of the sufferings of Moab; otherwise it must be presumed to have been among the places sacked and burnt in the battle.

7. **Therefore the abundance they have gained**: *NEB* conveys the sense better with 'their hard-earned wealth'. **they carry away**: Heb.

treats the subject Moab as a masc. sing. word. Hence 'he shall carry away . . .' (cf. G. R. Driver, *JTS* 38 (1937), p. 40). **the Brook of the Willows** (modern *Wadi el-Hesa*) marked the border with Edom.

8. For a cry has gone round: The places mentioned, **Eglaim** and **Beerelim**, cannot be identified with certainty, but they were most probably located in the north-west of the country. The overall effect is to stress the countrywide mourning that had overtaken Moab.

9. For the waters of Dibon are full of blood: Possibly this first clause of v. 9 was a part of the original poem, but the remainder of the verse has been added later by an editor who has sought to turn the lament for Moab into a threat. **Dibon,** the chief northern Moabite city, has already been mentioned in v. 2, but here the Heb. reads 'Dimon', and it is the Vulg. which identifies it as Dibon. More probably a different location was intended and Kaiser suggests modern *Khirbet Dimne*. F. M. Abel identifies with *'Ain el-Megheisil*. **a lion for those of Moab who escape** is extremely obscure as to its meaning and the text is almost certainly corrupt. However, only conjectures are possible, and these arouse little confidence. **for the remnant of the land.** Perhaps we should read 'the remnant of Admah' (*NEB*), although most commentators emend more substantially. Rudolph and Eichrodt read 'remnant of fear' (Heb. *ʾēmāh*).

A REPLY TO THE LAMENT OVER MOAB

16:1–5

These verses are not from the same hand as the preceding lament and cannot originally have belonged to it. They are an addition, but one which appears most likely to have been composed intentionally as a reply to the preceding lament. 16:2 is awkward, however, and can hardly have been the original continuation of v. 1. It cannot be taken as a gloss, and several commentators have regarded it as originally a part of the lament of 15:1–9, describing the distress of the women of Moab at the fords of the Arnon. The aim of the unit is given in v. 5 with its description of the re-establishing of the **tent of David**. This must be a reference to the Davidic monarchy and kingdom, of which Moab had been a part (cf. 2 Sam. 8:2). It indicates that vv. 1–5 stem from the early post-exilic period, probably in the fifth century. O. Kaiser, however, would regard vv. 4*b*–5 as a secondary addition to vv. 1, 3–4*a*, intended to provide an answer to the question when Jerusalem will have a ruler strong enough to supply the assistance asked for in v. 1. There is much to support such a view, leaving us with vv. 1, 3–4*a* as the original unit.

16:1. They have sent lambs: The Heb. text is difficult, and the reconstruction is partly based on the Targum. It is preferable to take **ruler of the land** as the subject, in which case it is to be construed as a plural, and to refer to the rulers of Moab who have sent a gift to Jerusalem in order to elicit help. The phrase **to the mount of the daughter of Zion** must be taken as a poetic synonym for Jerusalem, although in this instance, since the gift was brought to the Judean king, it is no doubt the palace rather than the temple area that is signified by **Zion**.

2. Like fluttering birds: The picture of the distress of the Moabite women at the crossing of the River Arnon resumes the lamentation from 15:1–8, and there can be little doubt that this verse originally belonged there. It has been misplaced, and we should, therefore, transpose it to come after 15:8.

3. Give counsel, grant justice: This is the plea which the emissaries to Jerusalem mentioned in v. 1 carry with them. The request is for protection and asylum for the Moabite fugitives who manage to escape across the River Arnon and gain entry into the territory of Judah. We are left to assume that traditional enmity between Moab and Judah was such as to make it necessary to secure such a special guarantee of protection.

4. let the outcasts of Moab: RSV here presupposes reading **outcasts** (Heb. *nidd^{e}hê*), with LXX and Syr., instead of the Heb. 'my outcasts'. **from the destroyer:** Still the identity of Moab's enemy is not disclosed, but evidently it was one with whom Judah was not also at war.

When the oppressor is no more: It is better to read 'oppression, plundering' (Heb. *hāmûṣ*) with 1QIs^a. The reference is to the harassing and despoiling of the Moabite population. The phrase **and he who tramples under foot** must refer to the victors in the battle with Moab who are able to make spoil of their defeated enemy.

5. when a throne will be established: This verse must be regarded as an addition, made probably in the late sixth, or early fifth, century to answer the question when this assistance for Moabite help would be forthcoming from Judah. The reply that is given is that it will come when a descendant of David reigns once again on his throne in Jerusalem. The verse thus presupposes the fall of the Davidic dynasty in 587 BC. The promise **will sit in faithfulness in the tent of David** points to the hope of stability, peace and prosperity with the restoration of the Davidic monarchy. The idea of **faithfulness** contained that of 'firmness, stability'. Cf. H. Wildberger, *ZThK* 65 (1968), pp. 129–59. **the tent of David** refers to the 'household' of David, which by extension covered his entire kingdom, including Moab.

THE PRIDE OF MOAB

16:6–14

A further prophecy against Moab in 16:6–11 presents a sharp threat against that nation, continuing the threatening element which is now to be found in 15:1–9. Some scholars (Kaiser, Schoors) have argued that this second prophetic threat is in fact the original continuation of 15:8, showing that the tones of lament voiced in the former prophecy were only the result of poetic simulation. 16:6–11 is then taken to pronounce that a well merited judgment from Yahweh is to befall Moab. Whilst such a view cannot be altogether ruled out, it seems preferable to regard the composition of 15:1–8 as a genuine lamentation for Moab in defeat, which probably derives from before the time of the Babylonian exile. The threatening element which has subsequently been added in 15:9, together with this markedly threatening prophecy in 16:6–11, may then be taken to derive from the post-exilic period. Wildberger regards the present composition as a later reflection upon Moab's fate. Two further editorial notes have then been added, the first in 16:12 linking the prophecy of vv. 6–11 with 15:2 and its reference to Moab's prayers in the sanctuaries. A still later addition has then been made in vv. 13–14, endeavouring to bring out with some precision the timescale within which the judgment pronounced in vv. 6–11 was expected to take effect. The particular area of Moab threatened is shown to be that close to the borders of Judah, rich in vineyards, but still no indication is given as to the identity of Moab's enemy. There is no clear reason for supposing this to have been Judah, although a deeper feeling of animosity against Moab is evidently present, suggesting that a period of worsening relationships has intervened between the time of the composition of 15:1–8 and 16:6–11.

16:6. We have heard of the pride of Moab: The accusation refers to a widely reputed **pride** on the part of the Moabites, which is here further interpreted as arrogance towards God for which they will suffer a divinely ordained punishment. Evidently the author's intention was to provide a reason for disaster which the following verses then go on to declare. It is very distinctive of the prophecies against foreign nations that they frequently denounce the sin of pride as the fundamental motivation for prophecies of doom. Cf. my *Prophecy and Tradition*, pp. 60f. **his boasts are false:** Better, 'his strength is not sound'. Cf. C. Rabin, *JSS* 18 (1973), pp. 57f., for the rendering of Heb. *baddāw* as 'his strength'.

7. Therefore let Moab wail: The language echoes very closely that of 15:2, and provides one of the strongest reasons for regarding the two prophecies as in some fashion connected. This need not be entirely ruled out; but equally it may be argued that, whereas in 15:2–8 a defeat had overtaken Moab, in 16:6ff. the disaster is still to come in the future. It looks as if the language of the earlier prophecy has provided a basis for the later one. The words **for Moab** may possibly be an addition in the second line. **Mourn, utterly stricken:** The Heb. requires a slight emendation to *yehgû* = 'let them mourn'. **Kir-hareseth** is the Kir of 15:1.

8. For the fields of Heshbon languish: The Heb. is awkward, having a plural subject **fields** with a singular verb **languish**. *G–K.* 145*u* would take the subject as a collective, but rather we must assume that a verb, probably 'are destroyed' (Heb. *šudd^edû*) has fallen out, and that 'languishes' (*'umlāl*) belongs with the subject **vine. the lords of the nations** are not more closely identified, and, whilst such vagueness is often typical of true prophecy, it is strange if the allusion is to a defeat that had already taken place. The **vine** is made the symbol of all the population of Moab, the rich product of the soil symbolising its inhabitants. **Sibmah, Heshbon** and **Jazer** were all rich vine-growing areas.

9. Therefore I weep with the weeping of Jazer: Whereas in 15:1–8 the tears, grief and lamentation appear to have been genuine and heartfelt, here the mention of such signs of mourning is intended as a warning of the judgment which still lies in the future. **I drench you with my tears:** The Heb. verb must be emended to *'ᵃrawwāyēḵ* (cf. IQIsᵃ *'rzyk*).

10. And joy and gladness are taken away: The normal happiness of harvest-time will be turned into mourning, a familiar enough theme, drawing its imagery by the use of sharp contrasts. The shouts of festivity will be replaced by the shouts and screams of battle. **the vintage shout is hushed:** This requires reading the verb as *hošbaṯ* ('is silenced'), instead of the MT 'I have silenced'.

11. and my heart for Kir-heres: The location is the same as that mentioned in v. 7. A verb appears to have fallen out at the end, and Wildberger suggests that we read 'my heart groans for' (Heb. *yehgeh*). *BHS* suggests a reading 'wails like a pipe'.

12. And when Moab presents himself: This saying has been added by a redactor who has endeavoured to link the threat of 16:6–11 more closely to that of 15:1–9 by making a reference back to a theme from 15:2. All attempts at prayer on the part of Moab are affirmed to be doomed to failure. The two verbs **presents himself** and **wearies himself** should most probably be taken as duplicates of the same expression occasioned by a misreading of one letter (*nir'āh/nil'āh*). We may, therefore, omit one of them. **he will not prevail:** Better, 'he will be unable to do so'.

13. This is the word which the LORD spoke concerning Moab: This and the following verse are a further addition made after that of v. 12. The verses, however, still regard the fulfilment of the prophetic threat against Moab as reserved for the future. A fixed time scale of 'in three years' (v. 14) is given for the awaited fulfilment, but it is unfortunately, impossible to know the situation when this further interpretation of the ancient prophetic threat was made.

14. In three years, like the years of a hireling: The phrase **years of a hireling** must refer either to the period for which a labourer contracted his hire to work for a fixed period (cf. Gen. 29:18) or to the period of enlistment for a mercenary soldier. In either case the time of service would be very carefully reckoned, which is the point of making the comparison here. After a very long history of the ancient prophecy regarding the punishment of Moab, the time of its fulfilment was at last felt to be drawing near. **and those who survive:** The Heb. reads 'and a remnant', but a verb is wanted. Read *wᵉniš'ār*, (will be left).

A PROPHECY CONCERNING DAMASCUS AND ISRAEL

17:1–11

The section which follows contains a prophecy directed against Damascus (vv. 1–3) followed by a threat against the Northern Kingdom of Israel—**the glory of Jacob**—in vv. 4–6. Since v. 3 already couples Israel with Syria we may take it as certain that the prophecies form part of a single unit and belong to the time of the Syro-Ephraimite war (735–732). In this case there is no reason to doubt its origin from Isaiah as a prophetic threat delivered against the two kingdoms which threatened Judah at this time (so Wildberger, Donner, Schoors, and earlier Duhm, Marti and Procksch). Among recent commentators Kaiser denies this authenticity and would place the prophecy in a much later date in the Hellenistic Seleucid era. Yet this would raise more difficulties than it solves. More difficulty concerns the scope of the original prophecy. Donner would see the entire section of vv. 1–11 as a single prophecy in three strophes (vv. 1–3, 4–6, 7–11). Yet the appearance of the formula **in that day** in vv. 7 and 9 show these passages to be almost certain additions, and we may conclude that we have in fact to deal with two major additions to the original prophecy in vv. 7–8 and 10–11, with v. 9 being added as a secondary comment upon vv. 7–8. All of these additions are concerned to assert the heinousness of the sin of idolatry which Israel has committed, and v. 9 seeks to explain that it is on account of such sin that the land will revert to the condition of desolation which it possessed when Israel conquered it. Donner, p. 42, argues that this accusation of idolatry reflects Isaiah's contemporary information regarding the Canaanite-Phoenician influences that were current in the Northern Kingdom. Much rather, however, we must see here the effort of the scribes of a later age to fill out the threatening message of vv. 1–6 by showing that it was for the sin of idolatry that Israel had been punished and its land brought to ruination. The date at which these additions were made cannot be determined with any precision, but most probably the early post-exilic age is to be assumed.

The original prophecy of vv. 1–6 belongs to the time of the Syro-Ephraimite war, but the exact point in the progress of that war remains to be considered. Since Israel had clearly not felt the weight of Assyrian power in vv. 4–6, and the reduction of Ephraim to a rump state had still not taken place, we must locate this at a time before 732. We must then regard v. 2 as misplaced from ch. 15 (see below, against Donner), and v. 1 as a genuine prophecy which was not literally fulfilled in the way expected since, as Donner points out, 732 did not bring any massive destruction to Damascus and Syria, which became a flourishing Assyrian province (H. Donner, p. 41). We may, therefore, locate the prophecy of vv. 1–6 against Damascus and Ephraim to the period between 735 and 733.

If we take the original unit to have consisted of vv. 1–6 only, with vv. 7–11 being added later, then the original prophecy contains no invective, or motivation, to show why judgment is to be inflicted on Syria and Israel. This must undoubtedly be correct, since the historical situation of the Syro-Ephraimite war provided all the justification that was needed. We may in any case couple the threat with the prophecy of Isa. 7 : 2–9 concerning the Shear-jashub name.

17 : 1. An oracle concerning Damascus: The prophecy in fact concerns both Israel and Damascus and it is likely that the title here has been added by a redactor in conformity with the sequence of prophecies headed **oracle** (Heb. *maśśā'*). The kingdom of Syria, or Aram, with its capital in **Damascus**, was a neighbouring kingdom to Israel with which it had close cultural, linguistic and religious ties. Cf. M. F. Unger, *Israel and the Arameans of Damascus*, 1957, esp. pp. 95ff.; A. Malamat, *POTT*, pp. 134–55. The occasion of the Syro-Ephraimite war reflects these longstanding ties between Israel and the Arameans, and the importance of political solidarity between them in the face of the threat from Assyria. **Behold Damascus will cease to be a city:** The Heb. for **will cease to be** (*mûsār*) is awkward. The feminine *mûsārāh* is required. H. Donner, p. 39, takes it as the *hoph'al* of *ysr*, 'to chastise', hence 'is punished so as not to be'; but it is preferable with Wildberger and most commentators to see a form of the verb *sûr*, 'to turn aside, deport', with the sense 'is removed from being'. In the event the physical destruction of Damascus in 732 at the hands of the Assyrians was not great, and strengthens the contention that we are dealing here with a genuine prophecy from before the arrival of the Assyrians in that city.

2. Her cities will be deserted for ever: The Heb. has literally 'the cities of Aroer are deserted' (cf. *RSV* margin), and the *RSV* rendering is based on a conjectural emendation from P. de Lagarde which most modern commentators have followed. However, Aroer was a city of the Moabites, which is not mentioned in the lament over Moab in 15 : 1–8 (9). Wildberger, therefore, very convincingly suggests that the saying is correct as it stands, but is misplaced and belongs to the lament over Moab, perhaps at 15 : 9. In this case it is the whole of v. 2 which is out of place, and needs to be transposed to the lament over Moab.

3. The fortress will disappear from Ephraim: In spite of the superscription it is evident that **Syria** and **Ephraim** are linked, which points unmistakably to the time of the Syro-Ephraimite war. Donner, p. 39, would emend **Ephraim** to 'Syria' (Heb. *mē'ªrām*). **And the kingdom from Damascus:** It is better to read 'kingship' (Heb. *mamlākāh*), implying the complete loss of sovereign political authority from the nation. In this respect the prophecy proved right, since Syria was brought under the second stage of vassaldom to Assyria in 732.

And the remnant of Syria will be: The idea of the **remnant** here clearly understands it as an indication of judgment, with its implied defeat of the Syrian army by Assyria. It is thus entirely in line with the interpretation given above (p. 83) for the name Shear-jashub of 7 : 3, so that it is possible that Isaiah has consciously intended to make such an allusion here. The clause **like the glory of the children of Israel**, scarcely makes good sense, and must be the result of some corruption. Read with LXX 'and the remnant of Syria will perish' (Heb. *yō'bēḏ*) (Duhm, Marti, Donner). Then insert the copula and delete the verb *yihyû*, to read 'together with the children of Israel'. There is then no need to emend **Ephraim** in the first hemistich since the two lines balance smoothly.

4. And in that day the glory of Jacob: The concluding formula at the end of v. 3 marks the end of the first strophe and the second, which begins with v. 4. is concerned solely with the fate of Ephraim, the Northern Kingdom. Very vividly it portrays the grim consequences that will befall Israel when the Assyrians come and ruin their land. The two images used in vv. 5 and 6, of the reaper leaving ears of grain at harvest time and of some olives left on the trees, in both cases for the gleaners, interpret very effectively the notion of a remnant. It is very likely, therefore, that the imagery used here should be seen as the prophet's own interpretation of what the name Shear-jashub means in 7 : 3. In any case it is undoubtedly a further development of the same idea.

5. And it shall be as when the reaper: The Heb. MT actually reads 'harvest' (*kāṣîr*) instead of **reaper** (Heb. *ḳôṣēr*), but the emendation is certainly correct. The law of Dt. 24 : 19f. demands the leaving of some grain for the poor of the community to glean, but it certainly rests on a very ancient custom. The prophet recognises that the harvesters do not leave much, and this provides a fitting image of what will be left to Ephraim after the Assyrians have finished with them. **And as when one gleans the ears of grain:** The pointed emphasis upon gleaning the **ears of grain** stresses the pitiable nature of what will be left.

6. Gleanings will be left in it: This time the picture of only **gleanings** left is taken from the olive harvest. Donner regards the concluding line **four or five on the branches of a fruit tree** as an elaborate gloss, but this is scarcely necessary. The reading **branches** follows 1QIs[a], and requires a slight emendation of MT.

7. In that day men will regard their Maker: In spite of Donner's defence of vv. 7–11 as a part of the original prophecy supplying the motivation for the coming judgment, these verses must be regarded as additions. The situation of the original prophecy made such further explanation unnecessary, and it is a later, post-exilic, redactor who has added vv. 7–8. They seek to show that the punishment of Israel was rendered necessary on account of the illicit cultus—the **altars**—which they had set up and the idols—the **Asherim**—which they had venerated. Such an addition was clearly made *post eventum* in 'the sense that it sought to explain a judgment that had taken place, not one that was still expected.

8. They will not have regard for the altars, the work of their hands: From the later, post-Josianic, point of view the presence of any **altars** in the Northern Kingdom at all was illicit, since Jerusalem alone was claimed as the sole authorised place for sacrificial worship. The phrase **the work of their hands** applies to such altars the polemical objection which more appropriately applied to idols. **Asherim** describes the standing posts, or trees, set up at the many rural shrines at one time popular in ancient Israel (cf. Jer. 2 : 27).

9. In that day their strong cities will be: The conventional formula **in that day** shows this to be a yet later addition, which comments upon that of vv. 7–8. The references to incense altars and Asherim had highlighted the point that these formed part of the cultic equipment of the **Hivites** and **Amorites** who had occupied the land before Israel.

As they had been dispossessed because of their idolatry, so subsequently had Yahweh inflicted the same punishment on those who replaced them when they reverted to the same idolatrous practices. There is no hint of any outstanding hope for Israel, and Wildberger sees here the mark of a Judean scribe looking upon Samaria as still ripe for judgment. The first line of the verse is unintelligible in the Heb. (cf. *RSV* margin), and the emendation given follows the reading of LXX (with Duhm, Gray, Fohrer, Donner, etc.). **the Hivites and the Amorites** formed part of the pre-Israelite occupants of the land of Israel. Cf. Gen. 15 : 16, 21 for the **Amorites,** and Gen. 34 : 2; Jos. 9 : 1ff., for the **Hivites.** Evidently many of the ruined sites for towns that were found in the land were identified as belonging to these peoples.

10. **For you have forgotten the God of your salvation:** Wildberger does not rule out a derivation of this and the following verse from Isaiah. However, this appears so unlikely as best to be discounted altogether (so Kaiser). They derive from a scribe of a much later age who has sought to elaborate further upon the theme of idolatry mentioned in vv. 7–8. In particular the glossator here has endeavoured to condemn the 'Gardens of Adonis', in which, by a kind of sympathetic magic, small slips of plants were induced to grow rapidly. By this means the life and fertility of the god were thought to be made available to the worshipper. Such a practice, in varied forms, appears to have retained a great popularity from the earliest to the latest Old Testament times, even though it was consistently condemned as a pagan undertaking. Cf. Isa. 65 : 3f. Its prevalence into Hellenistic times may have served to awaken the glossator's inclusion of a reference to it here. There is a veiled hint of threat at the end of v. 11, even though it lacks some of the more forthright characteristics of prophetic pronouncements of judgment.

Therefore, though you plant pleasant plants: Refers to the planting of cuttings of plants in specially prepared gardens in order to induce them to grow rapidly. In Hellenistic times such a practice was associated with the god Adonis, but the origin goes much further back both in Canaan and Mesopotamia. It was a form of private ritual which was believed to bring life and fertility to the participants. **And set out slips of an alien god:** By making **slips**—cuttings—take root the life giving power inherent in such a process was thought to become accessible to the worshipper. The identity of the **alien god** ('alien' = Heb. *zār*; cf. L. A. Snijders, *OTS* 10 (1954), pp. 1–21; R. Martin-Achard, *THAT*, I, cols. 520–2) is not entirely clear, but some form of the Adonis cult must be meant. Earlier the Tammuz cult (cf. Ezek. 8 : 14) had appeared in Judah, but aspects of the Baal cult were no doubt also involved since the ritual could be applied to more than one deity whose resuscitation to life from death could be sought.

11. **Though you make them grow:** The rapid growth of the plant slips was an important part of the ritual. By forcing the shoots under artificial conditions the special 'fertility' power of the ritual was demonstrated and made accessible to the worshipper for other aspects of his life. **in a day of grief and incurable pain:** Better 'on a day of

grief when (epexegetic *waw*) the pain is unrelieved'. The reference is to a coming day of judgment when all idolaters will be punished for their sins. Such a view would appear to presuppose the late Jewish eschatological outlook.

DIVINE JUDGMENT ON THE ASSYRIANS
17:12–14

The threat that has preceded in 17:1–6 uttered against Syria and Ephraim clearly presupposed that the judgment of these peoples would be inflicted by the Assyrians, even though this power is not explicitly mentioned. The 'Assyrian Redactor' (Barth's phrase) who has been responsible for 8:9–10; 10:33–4 and 14:24–27 has now inserted a further announcement of the judgment that Yahweh will inflict upon Assyria. In spite of the claims of many recent scholars for its origin from Isaiah (G. von Rad, J. Schreiner, B. S. Childs, J. Bright) and its relevance to the situation of 701, such claims must be discounted. It is a piece of editorial composition, once again like 14:24–27 set out in the 'summary-appraisal' form (so B. S. Childs, pp. 50ff.), which develops an authentic Isaianic theme by a process of 'midrash'-like exegesis.

In this case the basic theme has been taken from 8:7 which compared the arrival of Assyria in Judah and Israel to a mighty river in flood. This theme of the **mighty waters** is then developed in 17:12–14 by the simple assertion that Yahweh will rebuke the waters, and they will flee away. By this means some allusion to the ancient myth of creation is made (cf. Ps. 104:7). By combining this imagery the 'Assyrian Redactor' has expressed the warning that it is part of Yahweh's plan to defeat Assyria in the land of Judah. The reference was originally intended to refer to a future overthrow of the Assyrians, and only indirectly has this come to be read back into the account of what took place in 701 (see above on 14:24–27 and below on chs. 36–37). The time of this composition must be located during Josiah's reign. That the summary-appraisal form has close affinities with Wisdom speech and didactic forms is noted by J. W. Whedbee, p. 78; Barth, p. 182. The introductory cry **Ah!** (Heb. *hôy*) has been taken by many commentators to be a broad interjection, and not a true woe oracle (Duhm, Procksch, Childs). Barth, however, following W. Janzen, *Mourning Cry*, pp. 6of., regards it as a true woe threat.

12. Ah, the thunder of many peoples: Barth would read as 'Woe to the thunder . . .', since undoubtedly a threat to the advance of the **many peoples** is meant. The plurality of the number of advancing nations causes some difficulty, since in the original threat to Judah posed by the coming of the Assyrian (5:26–29) only one nation (Assyria) is referred to (5:26). The assertion concerns a future overthrow of the power of Assyria, which v. 14 has developed in the direction of a more universally valid assurance of protection for Judah and Jerusalem. Cf. below on 29:7. The sparing of Jerusalem in the reign of Hezekiah in 701 came to be regarded as a demonstration of this intention of Yahweh to defend his people against the **nations** more generally. Probably there has been some influence upon the language from the Davidic royal ideology which promised defeat for rebellious nations (Ps. 2:9). Cf. H.-M. Lutz, *Jahwe, Jerusalem und die Völker*, pp. 175f.; J. J. M. Roberts, *JBL* 92 (1973) pp. 329–44. An emphasis upon the great sound of the advancing army had earlier appeared in the Isaianic passages 5:29 and 9:5 (Heb. 4). Hence the phrase, **Ah, the roar of nations** appears intentionally to allude back to 9:5 through an alliteration (Heb. *še'ôn/se'ôn*). The idea of the roaring of **mighty waters** which threatened to engulf the world at creation and in recurrent storms was an ancient mythological motif (cf. Ps. 104:5–9). The **thunder** could be understood as Yahweh rebuking the waters.

13. The nations roar like the roaring of many waters: The stress upon the threat from several nations is explicit, but the primary reference must be to the threat from Sennacherib and Assyria. The universalising of the imagery of the threat has certainly been assisted by the language of the Jerusalem cultus (Pss. 2:9; 48:4–8), and by the desire to use the interpretation of what had taken place in 701 as the basis for a larger and more universal hope. The first line of v. 13 is missing from some MSS, and it must be regarded as a variant of v. 12*b* (*rabbîm* for *kabbîrîm*). **But he will rebuke them, and they will flee far away:** The reference may be to the defeat which, in retrospect, the author believed to have been inflicted upon the Assyrians in 701, although the final overthrow of the Assyrians and their departure from Judah was still in the future so far as he was concerned. To this extent the application of the 'prophecy' to Jerusalem's deliverance in 701 must be seen as only a partial and incomplete fulfilment of it. The phrase **chased like chaff on the mountains before the wind** elaborates by the use of a popular metaphor. Cf. Isa. 29:5ff.; Ps. 83:13 (Heb. 14).

14. At evening time, behold, terror: The emphasis upon the suddenness and swiftness of the overthrow of the attacking forces is very marked. It may be related to the claim in 37:36 (= 2 Kg. 19:35) that the Assyrian forces of Sennacherib were slaughtered by the 'angel of the LORD' in a single night. Since the introduction of the action of this mysterious angel comes entirely unexpectedly and strangely in 37:36 it is probable that we should see the mention of his action there as influenced from such passages as this.

The language here is to be regarded as poetic and hyperbolic in tone, arising from an emphasis upon the overthrow of the attackers as the work of God. No doubt also the ancient cultic language involving the 'Conflict with the Nations' motif has affected it. Cf. Ps. 46:5 (Heb. 6) for Yahweh's help coming **before morning**. **This is the portion of those who despoil us:** We could take the meaning to be 'of those who would despoil us', but it is better to regard the reference here as directly conscious of the long period of Judah's vassaldom to Assyria, in which the country had been greatly despoiled and plundered. **and the lot of those who plunder us:** This requires a small emendation to *gôrāl bôzezēnû* (*lamed* is a dittography).

The placing of vv. 12–14 after 17:1–11 must reflect a conscious redactional choice. As vv. 1–6 had forewarned of the overthrow of Syria and Ephraim by the coming of the Assyrians, so it was appropriate to record afterwards how Yahweh would, in turn, himself defeat and scatter the Assyrian invaders from his land. More particularly, since the redactor must have had the events of 701 in mind as at least a partial fulfilment of this overthrow, he has sought to use this as the basis for a more universal assertion of Yahweh's power to repel all invaders from his land (cf. 29:7).

A PROPHECY AGAINST ETHIOPIA

18:1–7

This prophecy is directed against the ancient land of Cush, which was a large territorial region to the south of Egypt, embracing modern Ethiopia, Sudan and Somaliland. This territory was closely linked with Egypt, and for a period in the eighth century provided the ruling dynasty (the twenty-fifth) in Egypt. Hence the prophecy here may be compared with that of ch. 20 which is directed against both Egypt and Ethiopia and, like this further prophecy, was intended to serve as a warning to Judah against trust in Egyptian support for an alliance against Assyria. In the case of the present prophecy it becomes plain that it was occasioned by the arrival in Jerusalem, probably by means of a sea passage to the coast near the capital (see on v. 1), of ambassadors from Ethiopia to Hezekiah. Their purpose is not openly referred to, but it can readily be inferred that it was to enlist Judah's support for a coalition of western states to resist Assyrian domination. This could have been on either of two occasions: the first in the period relating to the Ashdodite rebellion 713–711 BC, or a little before this, and the second in 705–701 BC, when Egypt appears to have led the plans for revolt. On the first occasion Hezekiah appears not to have been drawn fully into the revolt, although some Judean involvement seems likely. On the later occasion, as becomes fully reflected in chs. 28–31, Hezekiah became an early and prominent member of the revolt. Donner, p. 124, would link the visit of the Ethiopian emissaries reported in 18:1–7 with the rebellion of 705, whereas Wildberger (II, pp. 683ff.), after careful re-examination of the issue favours the earlier period. Such a view is followed here, although almost any year in the period between 720 and 713 would seem possible for such a mission to have taken place from Ethiopia to Judah. Life under Assyrian domination was evidently of such a nature as to promote rebellious plans.

The original prophecy extends through vv. 1–6, although Wildberger would regard v. 3 as a later addition. Certainly v. 7 has been added later by a post-exilic redactor who appears to have been influenced from 45:14. In any case it regards the relationship of Judah to Ethiopia from a very different perspective from that of the original prophecy. Kaiser takes the entire prophecy to be a late, post-exilic, pronouncement regarding the final overthrow of Ethiopia. Yet there are no adequate grounds for supposing such a late date, and if we assign it to the period before 713 BC, when Hezekiah was being tempted into joining a revolt against Assyria, then Isaiah's beautifully expressed insistence upon Yahweh's neutrality (vv. 4–5) provides a strong and decisive counsel to the king of Judah not to allow himself to be drawn into the Ethiopian-Egyptian plan.

18:1. Ah, land of whirring wings: The opening cry (Heb. *hôy*), which *RSV* takes as a simple interjection, should rather, with W. Janzen, *Mourning Cry*, pp. 49f., be seen as a 'woe'-formula expressing a stern rebuke to the subject addressed (so also Wildberger). Hence 'Woe to . . .'. *RSV*'s **whirring wings** (Heb. *ṣilṣal kᵉnāpayim*) would then be a reference to the great notoriety enjoyed by Ethiopia as a place of insects of all kinds. However, G. R. Driver, *JSS* 13 (1968), p. 45, would translate the Heb. *ṣilṣal* as 'boat', comparing the Arabic *ẓulẓul*. Then 'winged boats' would be a reference to 'sailing ships'. Cf. *NEB*'s rendering. This is attractive in view of the reference to **the rivers of Ethiopia**, and the mention made in v. 2 of the journeying of the ambassadors from Ethiopia by sea (v. 2. *RSV* 'Nile'). The arrival off the coast of Judah of such ships, especially of a type designed for river traffic, would have been bound to cause a great stir in Jerusalem, so that their place of origin, and obvious purpose, would quickly have become a major subject of discussion. **the rivers of Ethiopia:** The ancient kingdom of Cush extended further south than modern Ethiopia, so that the upper, rather than the lower, Nile region is probably meant.

2. which sends ambassadors by the Nile: There is no improvement in reading 'ships' (Heb. *ṣiyyîm*), instead of **ambassadors** (Heb. *ṣîrîm*). The **ambassadors** must be emissaries from Ethiopia to Hezekiah who had been sent to Jerusalem to enlist his support in the planned revolt of Egypt-Ethiopia against Assyria. If we place this event *c.* 716 BC then it must have been obvious to Isaiah and other citizens of Jerusalem what the purpose of their unusual journey was. For **by the Nile** Heb. has literally 'by the sea' (Heb. *bayyām*), and, in spite of the preference of almost all modern versions in rendering as **Nile** (cf. 19:5; Neh. 3:8), it is not impossible that 'sea' is correct. The ambassadors had come to Jerusalem by ship as far as the Mediterranean coast, where they would have been diplomatically received. **in vessels of papyrus upon the waters:** The boats were river-going craft, designed and built for use on the Nile, but this does not preclude that their skilful crews had navigated them along a sufficient part of the Mediterranean coast to bring them to Judah.

Go, you swift messengers: If we assume that the **messengers** (Heb. *mal'ākîm*) mentioned here are the same as those referred to in the first line of the verse, then the prophet is adjuring them to return to their homeland. W. Janzen, *Mourning Cry*, pp. 60f. (cf. also Barth, p. 13), suggests that the prophet was rhetorically summoning other (divine) messengers to go to Assyria to tell the ruler there what was happening. This is attractive as a clarification of a difficulty, and is preferable to the assumption that ambassadors from Hezekiah to Ethiopia are referred to. **To a people feared near and far:** It is better to omit **to a people** with LXX.

A nation mighty and conquering: The Heb. phrase translated **mighty** (*qaw-qaw*) is obscure and Donner, p. 122, takes it as most probably an onomatopoeic expression for 'foreign', unintelligible language. Certainly the meaning of the verse is clearest if the prophet is ironically inviting the messengers to go to Assyria, against whom their plans are directed.

3. All you inhabitants of the world: The prophet now directs his message to an audience of the entire world. Wildberger takes the verse as a gloss, possibly made by the same scribal circle who inserted such sayings as 8:9-10. Yet Donner, pp. 124f., would defend its authenticity on the grounds that the planned revolt of Egypt against Assyria would have world-wide significance. He therefore sees Isaiah, with some touch of irony, preparing for his announcement of what God will do (vv. 4-5), by declaring that it is for all the world to hear. Unlike the ambassadors, who were trying to keep their negotiations secret, presumably even from the inhabitants of Jerusalem, Isaiah declares that what Yahweh intends is to be known by everyone. Then the mention of the **signal** and **trumpet** in v. 3*b* are not the signs of an impending battle, but an emphatic assertion that Yahweh is announcing his plans to all the world. There is nothing secret about them. Such an interpretation is plausible, but, even so, Wildberger's understanding of the verse as a gloss seems more likely.

4. For thus the LORD said to me: Isaiah now announces in vv. 4-5 the serene calm and indifference which Yahweh will observe during the impending confrontation between Egypt, Ethiopia and Assyria. He will be neutral, and **will quietly look** (Heb. *'esq°ṭāh*; cf. 7:4 and 30:15 for *šqṭ* in the sense of 'remain neutral') from his heavenly dwelling. Yahweh will neither support Egypt-Ethiopia, nor yet uphold Assyria, so that Hezekiah could in no way rely on Yahweh's support if he joined the revolt. The message must be understood as a clear warning to the king not to listen to, or join with, the plans of the Ethiopian ambassadors. The imagery of a calm and pleasant summer evening sums up the serene indifference of Yahweh to the Ethiopian plan.

5. For before the harvest, when the blossom is over: The prophet's message now becomes more threatening, by showing that, because Yahweh will not support the planned rebellion, it will lead to disaster. Cf. 30:5; 31:3 for a similar forewarning of the consequences of relying upon Egyptian help. **He will cut off the shoots with pruning hooks:** The word for **shoots** (Heb. *zalzallîm*) introduces an intentional homophony upon the word for 'whirring insects/ships' (Heb. *ṣilṣal*) in v. 1.

6. They shall all of them be left to the birds of prey: Because Yahweh will not take sides to uphold the rebellion against Assyria it will lead to ruination for Ethiopia and Egypt. The ultimate end of the plans for which the Ethiopian ambassadors had come to Jerusalem, therefore, would, be disastrous. The message for Hezekiah, for whose ears this prophecy was clearly intended, was clear. He should not join himself to allies who were heading for disaster, lest he be dragged down with them. Although we have a prophecy about a 'foreign nation' here, it is very evident that it concerned one which had the most immediate relevance to Judah's own destiny.

7. **At that time gifts will be brought to the LORD of hosts:** This verse is certainly the work of a post-exilic redactor who has introduced an entirely different perspective to the original prophecy by mentioning that gifts will be brought to Yahweh in Jerusalem by the Ethiopians. Evidently **the people tall and smooth,** who had been referred to in v. 2, are taken to be the Ethiopians themselves. It is then asserted that they will come to Jerusalem for an entirely different purpose from that which had occasioned the visit of the ambassadors in Isaiah's time. It appears that the redactor had in mind the prophecy of Isa. 45 : 14, providing further evidence that chs. 40ff., had been added to 1–39* before the final edition of these latter chapters was reached. This increases interest in the question of when this verse was added, but little firm indication is present to determine this.

THE CONFOUNDING OF THE EGYPTIANS

19 : 1–15

With ch. 19 there begins a series of prophecies concerning Egypt which extends as far as 20 : 6. The last of these, in 20 : 1–6, has been widely accepted by virtually all commentators as authentic to Isaiah, and this consensus must be upheld. Before this there are two other prophecies concerning Egypt, in 19 : 1–15, beginning with the title **oracle** (Heb. *maśśā'*), and in 19 : 16–25. This latter prophecy is not from Isaiah, but more uncertainty exists concerning that of vv. 1–15. This falls into three separate parts: vv. 1–4 foretelling political division and turmoil in Egypt; vv. 5–10 foretelling the failure of the Nile floods, essential for the irrigation of the land, and vv. 11–14 (15), denouncing the folly of the princes of Zoan. The concluding v. 15 is undoubtedly to be regarded as a redactor's summarising comment, dependent on the text of 9 : 14 (Heb. 13). The question of the genuineness of the prophecy from Isaiah has been much contested—Schoors and Erlandsson taking its authenticity as virtually certain, whilst Duhm, Fohrer and Kaiser equally regard this as precluded. Wildberger notes the marked lack of connection between vv. 5–10 and the rest, and provides detailed arguments from the vocabulary of these verses to show that they are unlikely to stem from Isaiah. Since v. 15 is also certainly an addition, he regards the original prophecy as consisting of vv. 1–4, 11–14. That these verses derive from Isaiah would then have little against it, and they could stem from the period in the prophet's ministry before 713 BC when Judah's political interest in the affairs of Egypt was very strong. Such must undoubtedly be borne in mind as a possibility, but it must be said, against Wildberger's conclusion, that there is little that is positively Isaianic about these verses. Their repudiation of Egypt and its political strength differs

considerably from that found in undoubtedly Isaianic passages such as
20 : 1–6; 30 : 1–5 and 31 : 1–3. On balance, therefore, it seems uncertain
that any of vv. 1–15 derive from Isaiah, but rather from the separate
collection of foreign nation oracles, beginning with *maśśā'*. If we
accept that the prophecy is not from Isaiah, it does not rule out a
pre-exilic date for it, although in reality there is almost no circumstantial indication to show its age. Wildberger would locate it in the
period 720–716 BC, before the accession of the Ethiopian (Cushite)
dynasty to the Pharaonic throne, which is presupposed by the preceding prophecy in 18 : 1–6.

The theme of the prophecy is threatening, warning that civil strife
is to befall Egypt, and that the policies advocated by **the princes of
Zoan** (vv. 11, 13), will lead to disaster. What these policies were, and
how they may have had relevance to Judah, can only be guessed at,
since no clear word of motivation for the coming judgment, nor of
explanation for the foolishness of the policies, are given. If they
concerned Egyptian attempts to resist Assyria, then they can be associated with the situation of Isaiah's day, but there is no strong reason to
suppose that this was so.

19.1. Behold, the LORD is riding on a swift cloud: The portrayal
of a deity riding on a cloud was a familiar one to the ancient world. Cf.
Ps. 18 : 10–12 for a particular connection with the storm clouds and the
idea of a storm theophany. No such storm, or theophanic, significance
is intended here, and the phrase appears to have been reduced to the
level of a poetic metaphor asserting that Yahweh, the God of Israel, is
about to take action which will influence affairs in Egypt. The participle **riding** (Heb. *rôkēḇ*) simply means 'travelling, journeying',
rather than 'mounting up'. Cf. S. Mowinckel, *VT* 12 (1962), pp. 287–99.
and the idols of Egypt will tremble at his presence: The cultural and
religious life of Egypt would have been fairly well known to Judah
through the interaction of trade as well as politics. In consequence the
extensive use of very elaborate iconographic symbolism in Egypt,
which contrasted markedly with the imageless worship of Judah, was
a point of interested comparison. It is a somewhat ambiguous picture
of the idols, however, to describe them as 'trembling'.

2. And I will stir up Egyptians against Egyptians: There was a
period of internal strife in Egypt in the period 720–716, under the
Pharaoh Osorkon IV, but such dissension was so common at so many
different periods that, in itself, it does not provide an adequate basis
for dating the prophecy. The phrases **city against city** and **kingdom
against kingdom** refer to the various provinces within Egypt (cf. the
LXX's *nomos*).

3. and the spirit of the Egyptians: The reference is to the complete
failure of the Egyptian moral will to resist aggression from outside as
a result of internal confusion and suspicion. The phrase **will be
emptied out** uses the Heb. verb *bāqaq*, to be pointed in the niph 'al
form *nᵉḇaqqāh*. Because their plans are of purely human origin, and
lack divine approval, the Egyptians will, in their frustration, resort to
all the technical means available to them of necromancy and divi-

nation. The effect of this will simply be to highlight their own folly and their forsakenness by God.

4. and I will give over the Egyptians: The threat to Egypt now reaches its climax with a direct foretelling of the political disaster which will befall the country. It will be set under the power of a **hard master**, which must refer to a foreign power which threatens them. However, the identity of this **hard master** is not disclosed.

5. And the waters of the Nile will be dried up: The threat of a drought, caused by a failure of the Nile floods introduces a very different theme from that of the preceding verses and points to a 'natural' disaster. It is very likely then that vv. 5–10, which describe this failure of the Nile, comes from a different hand. The dependence of Egypt upon the Nile must have been well known in ancient Judah, as a part of a traveller's knowledge of Egypt. Hence any indication of divine displeasure towards that country was naturally felt to manifest itself by the failure of the Nile to perform in the normal way. It is very unlikely that any specific flood is in the author's mind, but rather a general inference regarding the way in which Egypt would be punished for all its political and cultic sins.

6. and its canals will become foul: Reading with 1QIs^a, $w^e hiz$-$n\hat{\imath}h\hat{u}$.

7. There will be bare places by the Nile: The phrase **by the Nile** should be deleted here as a dittography from the following line. Then, instead of **bare places** read 'the lotus, and all that is sown by the Nile'. Cf. T. W. Thacker, *JTS* 34 (1933), pp. 163–5.

8. The fishermen will mourn and lament: The writer shows a good familiarity with the manner of life of ancient Egypt and the extensive fishing of the Nile. In contrast to Judah, which had no large natural river, Egypt appeared to have been unusually, and in Israelite eyes, undeservedly, blessed by the Nile. Instead of **fishermen**, 1QIs^a reads 'fish'. This is unlikely to be correct, but may have been influenced from Exod. 7:21.

9. and the weavers of white cotton: The second line of the verse lacks a verb, and we should follow the reading of 1QIs^a in emending the noun for **white cotton** (Heb. $h\hat{o}r\bar{a}y$) to the verb $h\bar{a}w\bar{e}r\hat{u}$, 'shall become white, pale'. Cf. *NEB*.

10. Those who are the pillars of the land will be crushed: *RSV* follows the traditional derivation of the Hebrew $\check{s}\bar{a}t\bar{o}teyh\bar{a}$ from $\check{s}\bar{e}t$, 'support, foundation'. However, this yields a sense which scarcely fits with the context. The rendering 'weaver' spinner' (cf. *NEB*) is to be preferred, derived from a verb $\check{s}\bar{a}t\bar{a}h$, 'to weave'. Cf. Akk. $\check{s}at\hat{u}$; Coptic $\check{s}tit$. So *BHS*. The verb **crushed** is then to be taken in a metaphorical sense as 'downcast, despondent'.

11. The princes of Zoan are utterly foolish: There is a measure of connection, both in character and content, between vv. 11–15 and 1–4. It may well be, therefore, as Wildberger contends, that they once formed part of the same prophecy. Yet this possibility is of only limited assistance in ascertaining the political background and date of vv. 11–15. There is an almost timeless quality in the denunciation

which these verses offer concerning the folly of the political advisers of
Pharaoh, who are described as **the princes of Zoan**. Zoan lay in the
north-eastern delta region of Egypt, and, along with Memphis, is
frequently mentioned in the Old Testament as an Egyptian city. The
role of **the princes of Zoan** in Egyptian politics had clearly become
common knowledge in Judah, although it is entirely unclear whether
a specific Egyptian policy is in mind. **The wise counsellors of
Pharaoh:** Egypt was famed for its wisdom, and there is no doubt that
Israel's own traditions of Wisdom were deeply influenced from this
quarter.

Very evident in the present context is the close connection between
such 'wisdom' and political counsel. The present prophecy appears
more concerned to deride and discount such Egyptian claims to an
exceptional political sagacity, than to challenge its advocacy at a
particular time. It denounces all Egyptian counsel as folly, rather than
the counsels of a single epoch.

12. Where then are your wise men: If the **wise men** of Egypt were
truly as wise as they claimed to be they would know the purpose of
Yahweh, the God of Israel. The author of the prophecy, appears to be
familiar with the Isaianic teaching to be found in 18:1–6 and 20:1–6
that Egypt had embarked on a political path which would lead to its
ruination. The verb **and make known** is pointed as Qal ('know') in MT
and is here, rightly, corrected to the Hiph'il.

13. The cornerstones of her tribes: Heb. has the singular 'corner'
(*pinnat*), which may be taken collectively, but more probably the
plural *pinnôt* should be read. The noun **tribes** must clearly be taken
loosely as 'regional communities, ethnic groups'.

14. The LORD has mingled within her a spirit of confusion: The
Heb. verb here translated **mingled** means 'mixed, poured in' (*māsak*).
Hence *NEB* reads 'infused'. LXX reads 'within them', i.e. the
Egyptians, which is to be preferred. With subtle irony the prophet
contends that what the Egyptian princes are advising is sheer folly and
will lead to disaster. At the same time he argues that this folly has
been implanted in them by Yahweh who is doing it in order to punish
the Egyptians. Even the folly of man, therefore, may serve the purposes of God. From the point of view of the author's readers in Judah,
however, the verses are designed to discourage any looking to Egypt
for political support. The situation would appear to be that of an age
much later than Isaiah's. The phrase **in all her doings** has the singular
noun in Heb., and the *RSV* text follows LXX.

15. And there will be nothing for Egypt: The verse has evidently
been added by a late redactor by means of a quotation from Isa. 9:14.
The stimulus for the addition seems to have been provided by the
association of **palm branch** and **reed** with Egypt.

SALVATION FOR EGYPT

19:16-25

In this section there follow five short sayings, each introduced by the

familiar connecting formula **in that day** (vv. 16, 18, 19, 23, 24), which
deal with the future fate of Egypt. They have been added as a series of
supplements to the primary prophecy concerning Egypt in 19:1–15,
and cannot derive from the prophet Isaiah himself. Their outlook is
universalist in tone, and they consist largely of reflections upon the
role of Egypt in its future relationship to Judah, rather than in
connection with any readily definable historical events. It is extremely unlikely that they all come from the same hand, although the
dependence of vv. 24–25 on v. 23 suggests the possibility that these
two sayings belong together. However, even this is not a necessary
deduction to be drawn. How such redactional additions came to be
made is not entirely clear, since they each appear to centre on a single
theme. However, what occasioned the interest in this theme is
generally obscure. Unlike earlier prophecy it appears unnecessary to
suppose that some specific political crisis has aroused a renewed
interest in Yahweh's purpose for Egypt. Altogether they point to a
generally positive and saving picture of the part that Egypt will play in
the future, and this is especially marked in the final saying (vv. 24–
25).

As to the date of the sayings, little in the way of clear-cut criteria
present themselves so that opinions have differed widely. The
attempt of Erlandsson, pp. 76ff. (cf. also Mauchline), to defend an
eighth century date and Isaianic authorship is wrong. Yet so also are
the attempts of Duhm and Marti to place them as late as *c.* 150 BC.
Probably Schoors comes closest to being right in suggesting a date
towards the close of the Persian period in the fourth century. We
should regard a post-exilic origin as assured, and it is unlikely that
there is much in the present book of Isaiah that originates from as late
as the Hellenistic age.

16. In that day the Egyptians will be like women: The connective
formula **in that day** relates the saying loosely to the future, and does
not of itself presuppose any notion of an *eschaton*, although it
subsequently came to be understood in such a fashion. The present
addition adopts a threatening tone towards Egypt and evidently
regards the admonitions and warnings of vv. 1–15 as still unfulfilled.
That this is so allows the further elaboration that Judah will itself be
the source of the folly and confusion which will exist in Egypt,
because this land will strike fear into the heart of every Egyptian. It is
this linking of Yahweh's purpose for Judah with his threatening plan
regarding Egypt which provides the basis for the redactor's inclusion
of this comment. It appears that the citation of 9:14 in 19:15 has
suggested to the redactor the idea that the stretched-out **hand** of
Yahweh referred to in 9:12 will be extended over Egypt.

17. And the land of Judah: The title **land of Judah** is significant,
since such a territorial definition for the Jewish community after the
exile is not frequently found. Under Persian rule the Jewish
community in the land is often referred to as 'Judah and Jerusalem'
(Ezr. 4:6), or 'Judah and Benjamin' (Ezr. 4:1). No doubt in the
present usage a strong traditional element from the past is present,

but here too it is noteworthy that the more familiar 'land of Israel' is
not used (Ezek. 40:2, etc.). No clear indication is given why it is **the
land** which strikes terror in the hearts of the Egyptians, but the
implication is that it is because Yahweh has a 'plan' which concerns
this land. Wildberger suggests the possibility, but no more, that the
saying may have been connected with the campaign of the Persian
ruler Cambyses (battle of Pelusium, 525 BC).

18. In that day there will be five cities in the land of Egypt: This
verse forms the second saying illustrating how salvation will come to
Egypt. The circumstantial detail, and in particular the mention of **five
cities** which appear to be known to the author, point in the direction
of features which have already been realised, and which the author
regards as important pointers for the future. The 'swearing allegiance'
to Yahweh must indicate the presence in Egypt of proselytes who had
joined themselves to Jews already living in Egypt, most probably in
cities close to the borders of Judah. Jer. 44:1, 15 mention four
localities to which Jews had fled in the sixth century, but there were
certainly other Jewish migrant communities in Egypt, as the fifth
century Jewish letters from Elephantine (modern Aswan) show.
Under Persian oversight it is probable that such Jews enjoyed considerable religious freedom, which is presupposed by this verse.
Loyal Jews in Egypt had attracted to themselves native Egyptian
proselytes who made use of 'the language of Canaan' (Hebrew, or, less
plausibly, Aramaic. Cf. the Elephantine letters in Aramaic) in their
worship. The identity of **the City of the Sun** (Heb. *'îr haheres*; 1QIs^a,
Targ. *haheres*) is most probably Heliopolis; cf. Jer. 43:13.

19. In that day there will be an altar to the LORD: The presence of
an **altar** in Egypt, devoted to the worship of Yahweh, has occasioned
much discussion in connection with the date of this prophecy. There
can be little doubt that the author's intention here is to provide legit-
imation for something that had already come into existence in his day.
A popular connection has been found by many commentators with the
temple of Leontopolis in Egypt which, according to Josephus (*Jewish
War*, VII:10:2) was founded by Onias, the son of the high priest Simon
the Just, i.e. Onias III. In this case a second-century date for the
prophecy would have to be inferred. But this is probably too late a
time, and in any case what is referred to here is an altar, not a full
temple, together with a standing pillar (Heb. *maṣṣēḇāh*). This latter
should have been prohibited to Yahweh worship according to Dt. 7:5;
12:3, so that this law was apparently being discounted. It can scarcely
have been unknown, and presumably was not thought to apply beyond the borders of Judah. The Jewish military colony at Elephantine
had had a temple at Yeb in the fifth century, but its location in Upper
Egypt precludes the view that it is that which is being referred to here.
Most probably the present verse derives from the fourth century,
before the end of the Persian period, when Jewish settlers in Egypt
had established some form of cultus there, which is here seen to mark
the beginning of Yahweh's blessing of the Egyptians. The location **in
the midst of the land of Egypt** is not to be taken literally, but the fact

that it was not at the same location as the pillar is clear. The **pillar** was a standing pillar of stone, set up usually at a 'high-place' (Heb. *bāmāh*; cf. P. Vaughan, *The Meaning of 'bāmâ' in the Old Testament*, pp. 9ff.) as a mark, or symbol, of the deity's presence (cf. Jer. 2:27; Dt. 7:5) commands the destruction of such pillars at erstwhile Canaanite shrines. See L. Delekat, *BHH*, II, col. 1169.

20. It will be a sign and a witness to the LORD of hosts: The prophetic element enters into this redactor's comment with the assurance that the pillar will be a **sign** (Heb. *'ōṯ*; cf. on 7:11) and **witness** (Heb. *'ēḏ*) that Yahweh has promised to help the Egyptians. As a result, when they are threatened by oppressors (the Persians?), he will act to deliver them. For **and will defend,** 1QIs^a reads 'and will come down', but MT can stand.

21. And the LORD will make himself known to the Egyptians: The author appears intentionally to recall the earlier time when Yahweh had made himself known to the Egyptians by sending plagues upon them (Exod. 7–12). At that time, however, the effect had been simply to elicit the awe and respect of the Egyptians, but not their turning to Yahweh as the true God. Now the promise is made that the Egyptians will participate fully in all the cultic rites of Yahweh, signifying their full allegiance to the God of Israel.

22. And the LORD will smite Egypt: How this 'smiting' will take place is not made clear. Either through plagues, as in the earlier time (cf. Exod. 12:23, 27, where the same verb *nāgap̄* is used), or by means of 'the oppressors' (Heb. *lōhᵃṣîm*) referred to in v. 20. This mention of further punishment, after the conversion of the Egyptians, comes belatedly, and seems to represent the work of an expansive editor who felt that the Egyptians should not be let off without punishment.

23. there will be a highway from Egypt to Assyria: The prophecy of the eventual salvation of the Egyptians is now enlarged further to include Assyria, suggesting to many commentators that it was added in the third century, with the division of the land of Israel between the Ptolemaic (Egyptian) and Seleucid (Syrian—Assyrian?) empires. This is by no means a necessary deduction, since the political situation which emerged then offered little encouragement to the kind of visionary hope expressed here. Nevertheless, the expectation of a great **highway from Egypt to Assyria** may well reflect the international trade and commerce of the Hellenistic age.

24. In that day Israel will be the third with Egypt and Assyria: The meaning is that Israel will take an equal share with Egypt and Assyria in supporting the prosperity and welfare of the earth. The 'third part' is not a question of ranking (i.e. 'third place'), but rather implies that Israel will be as great as Egypt and Assyria. The title **Israel** must certainly include a territorial aspect here, and its use appears to point to the hope of the restoration of a national-political entity of Israel. However, its scope is not clearly defined.

25. whom the LORD of hosts has blessed, saying: It is better to read 'which (i.e. the 'earth' of v. 24, reading the verb as *bērᵉḵāh*, with third fem. suffix) the LORD of hosts . . .'. The full incorporation of

Egypt and Assyria into the blessing of Yahweh will be demonstrated
by his gift to them of the land and his confirmation of their right to it.

A PROPHETIC SIGN CONCERNING EGYPT AND ETHIOPIA

20:1–6

The present prophecy has a number of connections with, and similarities to, those of 14:28–32 and 18:1–6. In each instance Isaiah's
prophecy takes the form of a declaration concerning the impending
fate of a foreign power, but with a very real consciousness that Judah
was potentially looking to this foreign power as an ally. The present
prophecy is presented as **a sign and a portent against Egypt and
Ethiopia** (v. 3), but it is clear from the initial reference to its date (v. 1)
that its immediate setting was the fate of the Philistines. This locates
the prophecy in the time of the revolt, led by Ashdod, against Assyria
in 713–711, and this period must cover the **three years** of Isaiah's
walking **naked and barefoot** (v. 3). Isaiah's action is then interpreted
in v. 6 as representing the fate of Egypt and Ethiopia in whom **the
inhabitants of this coastland** had trusted. By this latter title the
people of Philistia, especially of Ashdod, must be meant (so H.
Donner, p. 115, against Marti, Duhm, Hoffmann, Huber).

There are, however, a number of peculiarities about the prophecy
which call for closer investigation. The chronological note in v. 1
would presuppose the collapse of the Philistine revolt with the fall of
Ashdod in 711. It is natural then to assume that this event had
occurred when the prophecy was given, since its fall is made into
something of an object lesson of the fate of those who trust in Egypt
and Ethiopia (v. 6). So Duhm, Marti, Gray, Procksch, Fohrer. Yet it
loses much of its character as a true prophecy if this event is already
presupposed, and Isaiah's action as a **sign** of the fall of Egypt and
Ethiopia is more than a little confusing as v. 6 interprets it. Donner
counters this objection (pp. 114f.) by seeing v. 2. as a parenthesis, and
placing the prophet's interpretation of his action in 711, before
Ashdod had fallen. Yet this is to assume that this sign-action was
originally intended as a warning of the fate that awaited Ashdod. We
may draw the following conclusions:

(1). The prophecy, in its present form, presupposes the fall of
Ashdod in 711, after its abortive attempt at rebellion against Assyria.
The failure of the revolt is also presupposed by v. 6, which, in spite of
the future tense **will say in that day** regards the fall of Ashdod as proof
of the worthlessness of relying upon Egypt and Ethiopia for military
assistance against Assyria.

(2). A sign-action by Isaiah in which he walked naked and barefoot
for the space of three years (713–711), was intended by the prophet
originally to foretell the fate of the Philistines, especially those of
Ashdod. There is no reason to suppose that Isaiah waited for two years
in order to explain his action, but evidently, as vv. 1–2 show, this
behaviour had lasted for some time when the present interpretation
was made.

(3). The prophecy, as it is now formulated, is directed against Egypt and Ethiopia to warn of their fate (vv. 3–4), although this was not the prophet's initial purpose in adopting his strange mode of behaviour. It has become the aim of the prophecy at a time, after 711, when Judah was still inclined to look to Egypt and Ethiopia for support against Assyria, probably after Sargon's death in 705. If so, then the present form of the prophecy must be related to the revolt of 705–701, rather than to that of 713–711 to which Isaiah's original sign-action was related. Fohrer and Huber, p. 107, regard v. 5 as a later addition, and this may well be the case. Whether, as Barth, p. 9 note, following Duhm and Eichrodt, argues, the account was originally formulated by the prophet in the first person and has been recast in a third person narrative form cannot be certainly determined. We may then date the prophecy as it now stands to the period c. 705 when Judah was being encouraged to join a coalition led by Egypt against Assyria. Cf. also 18 : 1–6.

20 : 1. In the year that the commander in chief: The year would be 711, when **Sargon** defeated and captured **Ashdod**. Judah's involvement in the rebellion was evidently not sufficient to entail any serious consequences for Hezekiah. The note must derive from a redactor who has focused on the action of Isaiah at this time as the basis upon which the prophecy is built. It may be that the whole unit belongs to this period. More probably, however, the interpretation of vv. 4–6 (Dietrich, pp. 130–2, would see only vv. 4 and 5 as preserved in an Isaianic form) belongs to the period closer to 705 when a renewed plan for the withdrawal of allegiance to Assyria was in the air, this time with the initiative coming from Egypt and Ethiopia. The title of the Assyrian **commander in chief** (Heb. *tartān*) means literally 'the second' (i.e. after the king). **Ashdod** was one of the five main Philistine cities.

2. at that time the LORD had spoken by Isaiah: Wildberger regards the account of Isaiah's performance of the sign-action as forming part of a separate collection of narratives about the prophet. In this case the precise significance of the reference **at that time** would have been clearer. As it is a measure of tension is created by the fact that the comment in v. 3 indicates that it was only after three years that the meaning of the prophet's action was given. Yet this can scarcely have been the case without depriving it of much of its character of a sign. Isaiah can hardly have waited until the meaning was plain to everyone before publicly declaring its purpose. We have suggested above that the purpose of the prophet's action was to foretell the downfall of Ashdod and the revolt which it sought to lead.

Go, and loose the sackcloth from your loins: Usually **sackcloth** was worn as a sign of mourning (cf. 2 Sam. 21 : 10), and no clear reason is offered to suggest that this had been the case with Isaiah. Such cloth was woven out of a rough material, usually goat's hair, and it may have been worn more generally by the poorer classes. Here it is not clear whether it refers to a tunic-like coat, or to a simple waistcoat. **and take off your shoes:** The Heb. MT has the singular 'shoe', but the plural is supported by 1QIs[a] and the ancient versions. The prophet's behaviour was evidently to simulate the condition of prisoners of war, and its character as a 'sign' is most readily explicable as a forewarning of the fate that would befall Ashdod in its revolt against Assyria. Whether the prophet went about entirely naked, or whether he retained a brief loincloth has been discussed by commentators, but makes no difference to the prophetic character of the action.

3. the LORD said, 'As my servant Isaiah has walked naked . . .': If the narrative is based upon a first person report from the prophet himself, as Duhm suggested, then evidently some recasting has taken place here for the sake of the narrative form. (But cf. Hoffmann, p. 74 note, who regards the prophet as referring to himself in the third person for the sake of the divine speech form). **for three years as a sign and portent:** For the action of the prophet as a **sign** (Heb. *'ôṯ*) and a **portent** (Heb. *môpēṯ*) see on 8 : 18. The period of **three years** reflects the time from the beginning of the Philistine revolt until the fall of Ashdod to Sargon, which effectively ended it (713–711). Almost certainly Isaiah must have indicated the purpose of his sign-action from its inception, so that the fall of Ashdod and the failure of the revolt would establish its rightness. We cannot follow Donner, p. 115, therefore, in regarding the present prophecy as deriving from a time in 711 before Ashdod had fallen. Rather, it represents a later reapplication of the prophet's action, when his pronouncement about the failure of the Philistine revolt had been shown to be right. The reference of the prophet's action **against Egypt and Ethiopia** reveals this new application. The promise of Egyptian aid had proved useless to Philistia when they had rebelled against Sargon, yet it was not Egypt that had suffered the consequences of their seductive promises. When later (?705) these promises were still held out to Judah, they would prove no more reliable then than they had previously. The present third-person form would appear to be constitutive of the prophecy in its extant form as a warning against Egypt and its proferred aid.

4. So shall the king of Assyria: The indefiniteness of the royal title may be deliberate (cf. Sargon in v. 1), since Sargon had died in 705, awakening new hopes of rebellion in the western coastal states, this time led by Egypt. The prophetic element arises from the sense that Egypt remained unpunished for its blandishments. The proper fulfilment of this threat must be seen in the defeat of the Egyptians by Sennacherib at Eltekeh in 701. The phrase **to the shame of Egypt** must certainly be regarded as a gloss (so Duhm, Marti, Gray, Fohrer, Donner, etc.).

5. Then they shall be dismayed and confounded: The verse is clearly dependent on the following and must be regarded as a later addition, directed against the people of Judah who had trusted in Egypt and Ethiopia to their own political ruin (so Fohrer, Huber). When Egypt is punished it will not be its people alone who suffer, but those who were foolish enough to trust in its support. **because of Ethiopia their hope:** The reading **their hope** (Heb. *miḇṭāḥām*) is supported by 1QIs[a], where the MT has 'the one to whom they looked' (Heb. *mabbāṭām*, from the verb *nbṭ* 'to look'). However, *mabbāṭēnû* is used in v. 6, so MT may very well be correct in v. 5.

6. And the inhabitants of this coastland will say in that day: The phrase **in that day** is not in LXX and may be a later addition. The question of the identity of those referred to as 'the inhabitants of this coastland' is contested. Procksch, Fohrer and Donner, p. 115, relate it to the Philistines, whereas Duhm, Marti, Huber, p. 111, Hoffmann, p. 74, would include the other rebellious states, especially Judah. The title naturally points to Philistia, but this renders the meaning strange, since Ashdod had been punished first in 711, whilst Egypt fared better then. The verse clearly intends the lesson of Philistia's misplaced trust in Egypt to provide an example to Judah, if it also maintains such a trust. To this extent, although the primary reference must be to Philistia, the obvious relevance to Judah is clear. The difficulty arises in part because Isaiah's quite precise sign-action and prophecy regarding Ashdod and its fate has been extended to relate to the later situation of 705.

A PROPHECY OF THE FALL OF BABYLON

21 : 1–10

The subject of the prophecy in 21 : 1–10 is the coming fall of Babylon (cf. v. 9), which is shown to be an event which is still in the future from the perspective of the prophet. The attackers who are to accomplish this overthrow are the Elamites and Medes mentioned in v. 2. Much discussion has consequently centred upon the question of the historical situation that is presupposed, and the possibility, consequent upon the answer to this, of whether the prophecy derives from Isaiah himself. We may consider three major possibilities for the background, each of which has found its supporters. First, if we are to consider the possibility of Isaianic origin, we must note that Babylon was attacked and captured by Sargon II in 710 BC. It was then subsequently attacked and overthrown again by Sennacherib in 700 and 689. Several scholars have been attracted to locating this prophecy at the time of Sargon's attack in 710. So W. E. Barnes, *JTS* (1900), pp. 583–92; E. Dhorme, *RB* 31 (1922), pp. 403–6. More recently S. Erlandsson, *The Burden of Babylon*, pp. 81–92, has linked the prophecy with one of the battles of either Sargon II or Sennacherib against Merodach-baladan, favouring most of all that of the year 700. There are, however, enough serious difficulties in the way of such a conclusion for us to discount this possibility, and with it also that of Isaianic authorship. It is clear from v. 2 that it is the Elamites and Medes who are the enemy of Babylon, not Assyria. Median participation in an attack led by Assyria is scarcely sufficient to account for the failure to mention Assyria at all in the prophecy. Furthermore, in Hezekiah's time Babylon was a potential ally of Judah (cf. ch. 39), which would scarcely agree with the exultant note expressed in the prophecy over Babylon's fall (vv. 9–10). Thirdly, this hostile attitude towards Babylon centres upon a knowledge of her many religious images (v. 9), which can most readily be explained as a consequence of Jewish experience of exile in Babylon.

A second possibility is to link the prophecy with the period of the Babylonian exile and of chs. 40–55 of the book. Cf. Isa. 47. In this case the prophecy, which still awaits the fall of Babylon, would have to be placed *c*. 540 BC. This date is advocated by G. Fohrer, A. Schoors, P. R. Ackroyd, *Exile and Restoration*, p. 223. In this case it may be regarded as parallel with 13 : 17–22. More recently, however, J. Vermeylen, pp. 327f., has advocated a date for this prophecy between 485 and 476 BC, ascribing a similar date both to 13 : 17–22 and 24 : 1–13, 18*b*–20. In this year the Persian ruler Xerxes II suppressed a revolt of Babylon. Whilst there are certain attractive features about Vermeylen's suggested date, we may conclude that the time *c*. 540 is most likely as the period of most direct consequence for Judah concerning the fate of Babylon. However the later date cannot be entirely ruled out.

It is striking that a prophecy directed against Babylon should be introduced as **concerning the wilderness of the sea** (but see below), when the content so clearly marks out the subject as Babylon.

21 : 1. The oracle concerning the wilderness of the sea: Since the subject of the prophecy is a threat to Babylon the meaning of **wilderness of the sea** is very obscure and various proposals for emendation have been made. *NEB* takes the word for **sea** (Heb. *yām*) to be an error for 'day' (Heb. *yôm*). Cf. G. R. Driver, *JSS* 13 (1968), pp. 46f.; *HTOT*, p. 182. Gesenius suggested that we should read 'deserts' (Heb. *miḏbārîm*), thereby eliminating any word for **sea**, although this does not really appear convincing. Other scholars have suggested understanding *yām* to mean 'west', i.e. 'western desert', which would require that we locate the author still further east in Media or Persia. Equally improbable is the attempt to explain **sea** as a reference to the Euphrates. *BHS* would read the verb *yehmeh*, 'one is sighing, groaning'. More attractive than such emendation is the suggestion of J. Vermeylen, p. 326 note, that we should see here a counterpart to the Akkadian *māt tamtim*, 'land of the sea'. No entirely convincing explanation has been forthcoming, but possibly the title has arisen from v. 13 ('oracle concerning Arabia'), with its implication of a desert region. *yām* would then be understood as a secondary insertion needed to dissociate the two prophecies. **As whirlwinds in the Negeb:** The attack of Babylon would be as fierce and sudden as the hot windstorms of the southern desert (of Judah).

2. A stern vision is told to me: The noun **vision** came to be used quite freely for the content of a prophetic revelation so that its combination with the formula **is told to me** discloses nothing specific about the manner of the prophet's reception of his message. The use of the passive verb **is told** serves further to maintain a discreet reserve about the way in which the message was perceived by the prophet. Cf. above on 5 : 9. **the plunderer plunders:** The Heb. gives a strong alliterative sound to the words (Heb. *habbôḡēḏ bôḡēḏ*). It is preferable, however, to follow the Syriac in reading the participle as passive: 'the traitor (Heb. *bgd*, 'betray' rather than 'plunder') is betrayed' (cf. *NEB*). Similarly we should follow with 'the spoiler is despoiled' (Heb. *šdd*, 'to ruin, despoil'). The meaning evidently is that retribution is about to be exacted from Babylon, the despoiler of nations. **all the sighing:** better 'groaning' (Heb. *'anḥāṯāh* is best taken as a lengthened feminine form of *'ᵃnāḥāh*). **I bring to an end:** Heb. *hišbattî* can better be pointed as an imperative *hašbîtî*, 'stop groaning', i.e. stop complaining. Hence *NEB*'s 'no time for weariness'.

3. Therefore my loins are filled with anguish: The prophet describes the emotions that seize him as he recognises the awesome content of his message. The note of terror is aroused by the frightful slaughter which he saw was about to take place, even though inwardly he perceived that Babylon would only be suffering herself the same fate that she had inflicted on others (v. 2).

4. My mind reels, horror has appalled me: The shock and **horror** of what was to overtake Babylon overwhelms the prophet. The imagery is no doubt intentionally poetic, designed to intensify the portrayal of the severity of the coming catastrophe, but we may nevertheless infer that the prophet sensed emotionally a sympathy for all who suffered in war, however deserved their fate. **the twilight I longed for:** The image is entirely poetic and hyperbolic, meaning that the strong emotions the author has experienced will not quickly pass away. By such vivid empathy with the victims of the conflict which he describes, the poet creates the verisimilitude of being an onlooker of the battle.

5. They prepare the table: K. Galling, *Festschrift Weiser*, p. 57, reads 'spear' (Heb. *šelaḥ*) instead of **table** (Heb. *šulḥān*), but this is improbable since the prophet wishes to describe the princes preparing to enjoy a feast, when suddenly they are called to arms because the enemy is at the gate. The tradition that the night when Babylon fell to the Medo-Persian armies in 538 was one of intended festivities is echoed in Dan. 5. If such a tradition were known to the author here, then his composition would require a date some time after that event. The phrase **they spread the rugs** is omitted by LXX, but this was probably because the noun *ṣāpît*, rugs, was not understood. Kimchi took it to mean 'lamps'. **Arise, O princes:** i.e. the **princes** of Babylon who will have to lead the defence of their city. **oil the shield:** Such oiling was not only a preparation for battle, but also a form of religious dedication of the weapons before their use in battle.

6. Go, set a watchman: The **watchman** is the prophet himself, and the portrayal of the prophet's function as that of a watchman was evidently a firmly established tradition in Israel. Cf. Ezek. 33 : 1–9. Yahweh appointed a prophet to proclaim publicly a knowledge of the events which were about to take place, which could be compared with the task of the city watchman who was responsible for keeping guard in order to give immediate knowledge of impending danger.

7. When he sees riders, horsemen in pairs: The **riders** are the cavalry of the Elamites and Medes attacking Babylon, and the prophet now gives warning that their attack is about to begin by imaginatively describing the instructions given to the Babylonian watchman. The phrase **horsemen in pairs** must refer to chariots drawn by pairs of horses (cf. *NEB*). **riders on asses, riders on camels**: This emends the Heb. MT, and reads *re<u>k</u>e<u>b</u>*, 'lines of,' as the participle *rô<u>k</u>ē<u>b</u>*, 'riders'. Cf. IQIs^a. However, the Heb. text makes adequate sense without such alteration.

8. Then he who saw cried: The Heb. MT reads 'the lion', but this is obviously a textual corruption of 'the lookout' (Heb. *hārô'eh*), which is supported by IQIs^a. The apparent distinction made between the speaker (the prophet) and the watchman is a result of the poetic idiomatic construction, rather than any psychological dissociation within the prophet's own mind. By portraying the experience of the watchman the prophet intimates the nearness and certainty of the event of Babylon's fall which he perceives as about to happen.

9. And, behold, here come riders: The attack is launched against Babylon, exactly as the watchman had been forewarned to anticipate, and immediately his message passes over to describe the outcome of the battle. **Fallen, fallen is Babylon**: The repetition of the verb, which is not followed by the LXX, heightens the dramatic effect. The tyrant nation which has overthrown so many others is now itself swiftly and dramatically overthrown.

10. O my threshed and winnowed one: The prophet now turns to address his audience of fellow Judeans, and is immediately conscious of the sufferings 'threshing and winnowing'—which they have received at the hands of the Babylonians. This could indicate that the prophet was himself among the Judean exiles in Babylon, but this is not a necessary conclusion. Those who had remained in Judah after 587 had much to remember the Babylonians for with anguish and bitterness. R. B. Y. Scott, *VT* 2 (1952), pp. 278–82, would apply the epithets to Babylon, but this appears improbable. In his concluding comment the prophet reveals the full depth of his personal interest in the judgment coming upon the people of Babylon.

PROPHECIES CONCERNING ARABIA

21 : 11–17

The three prophecies which are contained in these six verses are all addressed to regions of Arabia. The first is addressed to **Dumah** (v. 11), the second to **Tema** (v. 14) and the third to **Kedar** (v. 16). It is evident from its form, and the markedly hostile attitude expressed towards the people of Kedar, that the third of these prophecies is rather different from the preceding two. Moreover, the content of this third prophecy, combined with the tradition which associated Kedar with Dumah and Tema as sons of Ishmael (Gen. 25 : 13ff.), indicates that it has been composed and added to the previous two as a further interpretation of them. It is, in fact, a reapplication of the threat contained in these earlier prophecies to a new situation which had arisen. That this brings its most probable time of origin down to a relatively late date appears certain. The nature of the new enemy is not specified, but it may possibly be inferred that it is one of the Hellenistic rulers of the Ptolemaic, or perhaps even the Seleucid, era. The quite specific affirmation that this threat will certainly be fulfilled **within a year** (v. 16), points to a military and political situation in which action was expected almost immediately.

Much less clarity exists regarding the two earlier oracles in vv. 11–12 and 13–15 respectively. **Dumah** was an oasis in the Arabian desert (Gen. 25 : 14; present day *El-Jof*), although the LXX translates the name as 'Idumea' (Edom), which would be in agreement with the reference to **Seir**, a region of Edom, in v. 11. A yet further possibility of understanding is presented by the fact that the Heb. word *dûmāh* means silence. It has been suggested that this was an intentional reference in view of the obscurity of the watchman's answer in v. 12. However, we must accept the originality of the reference to the oasis of Dumah as the most probable, and the LXX's understanding as derivative and secondary. This is all the more probable in view of the linking of the very obscure oracle of vv. 11–12 with that concerning **Tema** in vv. 13–15. The question then arises of the date that is to be attached to both prophecies. Clearly anything like certainty on this question is impossible to come by, but the fact that 21 : 1–10 has been concerned with Babylon suggests that this may be the unnamed enemy of Arabia of both oracles in vv. 11–15. In this case we are directed to the military attack upon Arabia by Nabonidus (555–539 BC), and the severe repression of the region in 550–545 BC. In particular this could help to clarify the strange ambivalence of the first oracle, promising deliverance to be followed by further darkness. Such a background has been suggested by Schoors, Wildberger and Fohrer as the most likely, and clearly excludes authorship by Isaiah.

21:11. The oracle concerning Dumah: For the variant understanding of **Dumah**, see above; but almost certainly the desert oasis of Gen. 25 : 14 is meant. **One is calling to me from Seir:** The construction is poetic and imaginative, since the prophet is the **watchman** (Heb. *šômēr*), who senses someone calling to him from the mountainous southern region of Seir. Possibly the intention was to suggest that this was the voice of a fugitive from Arabia, or simply an informed observer on the southern fringes of the sown land who wanted to know what was happening in the desert. **what of the night:** The question is used metaphorically to ask when the period of misfortune, which we can best associate with that of Babylonian rule and oppression, will have passed. We are no doubt also meant to assume that a significant political or military event had recently occurred which indicated that the night might soon be over. Hence *NEB*'s 'what is left of the night?' (the Heb. uses the preposition *min* which can be partitive). In general there appears to be an attitude of sympathetic understanding of the suffering of Arabia which would be most intelligible if Judah were suffering as a result of the same oppressor (Babylon).

12. Morning comes, and also the night: The conjunction of **morn-**

ing and **night** creates an apparent contradiction which seems to be tantamount to no answer at all. However, once the metaphors are interpreted the contradiction is greatly eased. Morning is coming, i.e. the period of Babylonian oppression will soon be over; but it will in turn be followed by another period of night when another oppressor will appear.

13. The oracle concerning Arabia: It is evident that a separate **oracle** begins here and extends as far as v. 15. It directly concerns the two oases of Dedan (v. 13) and Tema (v. 14), addressing the caravan traders of **Arabia** about a military attack and defeat which the two oases have suffered. No clear indication of the identity of the attacker is made, but a broad impression of sympathy for those who have been attacked is expressed. This suggests that the enemies of the Arabians were also the enemies of Judah to whom the prophecy was delivered. Only a general connection of position and context can suffice to point to Babylon as the enemy, since otherwise a whole range of possi- bilities present themselves. It is the association with Babylon which suggests the time of Nabonidus' attack in 550 BC. **In the thickets of Arabia:** The LXX omits the summarising sub-title, but the concern with Arabia is secured by the references to Dedan and Tema, which lay in the north-west of that country. The address is to the **caravans of Dedanites** who are exhorted to bring help and relief to fugitives from a battle. Probably Israelite familiarity with the caravan traders of Arabia, and possibly also the flight of Judeans into Arabia, made this mode of address particularly appropriate.

14. To the thirsty bring water: The concern for the welfare of the fugitives indicates the prophet's own sympathy with the defeated Arabians, which serves to support the belief that the prophecy concerns an attack by Babylonian forces.

15. they have fled from the swords: The battle had already taken place according to this portrayal, although it is possible that a truly prophetic aspect is present and the prophet's intention was to declare that it would result in the defeat of the Arabian inhabitants. More probably, however, the purpose was to express some element of sympathy with those who had already become the victims of battle.

16. For thus the LORD said to me: This third saying is from a much later writer than the preceding two, and introduces a third Arabian region, **Kedar** (Gen. 25 : 13). However, it appears from its con- tent that its purpose is to assert that the time of judgment upon Arabia is now close at hand, **within a year.** Thereby it takes the threat of the preceding verses in a more eschatological sense, but insists that this punishment will soon come. A date in the third century BC would appear quite possible. The tone of vv. 16–17 is consistently hostile. **Within a year, according to the years of a hireling:** The purpose of the comparison with the years of a hired worker is to introduce the element of careful and exact counting that such a contracted worker would be expected to display. **all the glory of Kedar will come to an end:** The fame of **Kedar** concerned its considerable wealth, amassed through its caravan trading, and this had been promised to Israel according to Isa. 60:7. In this comment such wealth (Heb. *kāḇôḏ*) was quickly threatened with destruction, apparently because its existence symbolised a threat to Judah. What the Kedarites had striven so hard to gain would quickly be taken from them. In such a punishment the author evidently saw a measure of righteous retribution for what he regarded as Arabian greed.

THE UNFORGIVABLE DAY OF JERUSALEM'S COMPLACENCY

22 : 1–14

The prophecy of 22 : 1–14 is given a heading **concerning the valley of vision**, which serves to bring it into conformity with the general pattern exhibited in the previous prophecies against foreign nations and cities. It has been taken by a redactor from v. 5, and gives to the overall prophecy a slightly different significance from what its original context implied. The **valley of vision** would appear to be an allusion to Jerusalem, as shown by the reference to Judah in v. 8, perhaps because Jerusalem and its destiny were seen as the primary subject of Isaiah's preaching (= **vision**). We may compare 21 : 2 where 'vision' is used of the prophecy. The rest of the prophecy (vv. 1–4; 8b–14) clearly concerns Jerusalem, as vv. 8b–11 further substantiate. Yet vv. 8b–11 are undoubtedly an addition to the original prophecy and imply a defeat and downfall of the **tumultuous city** referred to in v. 2. Vv. 8b–11, therefore, are to be regarded as a later addition, and do not derive from Isaiah himself (so G. B. Gray, G. Fohrer, H. Donner, p. 128, B. S. Childs, *Isaiah and the Assyrian Crisis*, p. 23 note). They clearly look to a situation when Jerusalem was threatened with siege, and imply a disastrous outcome to this because the people had failed to consider the purpose of Yahweh (v. 11). There is much to indicate, therefore, that the **day** referred to in v. 8b was not that of 701 when Jerusalem was threatened by Sennacherib, but that of 587 when the city fell to Nebuchadnezzar. These verses presuppose the downfall of Jerusalem, not its deliverance. Similarly, v. 4 refers to **the destruction of the daughter of my people**, and implies the destruction of Jerusalem which did not take place until 587. This verse too, therefore, must be a post-587 addition. However, vv. 5–8a, which concern **the valley of vision**, would also appear to point to a threat in which Jerusalem was actually attacked and overthrown (cf. the **battering down of walls**, v. 5). This too, therefore, fits the situation of 587 much better than it does that of 701. Furthermore the references to soldiers from Elam and Kir (v. 6) corroborates this Babylonian setting, and J. Vermeylen, p. 338, would see the reference to **the valley of vision** as an allusion to Babylon, comparing Ezek. 3 : 22; 8 : 4; 37 : 1. However, v. 8, with its reference to **the covering of Judah**, shows that Judah-Jerusalem is the subject of the picture of warfare and once again the 'taking away' of this covering must imply that God has withdrawn his intention of protecting Jerusalem so that it has been overthrown. This also points us to what happened in 587. The original prophecy from Isaiah is then to be seen in vv. 1–3, 12–14 (O. Kaiser makes this vv. 1b–4, 12–14; J. Vermeylen, p. 339, would see it as vv. 1b–3, 7, 12–14).

The circumstances of Isaiah's prophecy can be deduced with reasonable clarity, and have been the subject of relatively strong agreement among scholars. Jerusalem had been delivered from a major threat of a military nature, and the people were filled with rejoicing at their escape. Against such celebrations Isaiah inveighs, because the people have shown no sense of grief and lamentation over the sufferings that had been brought upon Judah more generally. The occasion is that of 701 when Hezekiah's surrender to Sennacherib (2 Kg. 18:13–16) spared Jerusalem the ruination that befell the rest of Judah (cf. 1:1–8). Later scribes and editors of Isaiah's prophecies have then seen in this sharp condemnation by the prophet of the exultation at the sparing of Jerusalem in 701, which became the subject of a very elaborated tradition (cf. chs. 36–37), a reason for its subsequent downfall. Probably v. 4, which Vermeylen, p. 337, ascribes to a Deuteronomistic hand, is the earliest of these, intimating that the destruction of Jerusalem, which had been avoided in 701 was now inevitable. A further post-587 addition has then been made in vv. 8b–11 developing the theme that the inhabitants of the city had trusted in their defences of a military nature instead of turning to God. Vv. 5–8a have finally been added to fill out the picture of how this judgment befell Jerusalem at the hands of the Babylonians, apparently under the impact of the allusions to Babylon in 21:2. The structure of the prophecy overall, therefore, shows a marked consciousness of the tension between the fate of Jerusalem in 701 and that which overtook it in 587. Isaiah's prophecy appeared to offer some resolution of this tension by indicating that the behaviour of the citizens of Jerusalem after their escape had offended Yahweh. We may compare the similar resort to belief in a flaw in Hezekiah's conduct regarding the Babylonians as an explanation of the subsequent defeat of the city described in ch. 39.

22:1. The oracle concerning the valley of vision: The heading has been taken from v. 5, where **valley of vision** must mean 'valley seen in a prophetic vision'. The location must be Jerusalem, but none of the valleys on the approach to Jerusalem bore this title. It is pointless to suppose that it means the valley where the prophet's home was; rather we should see it as a redactor's way of achieving harmony with the other prophecies introduced by the heading **The oracle concerning . . .**
What do you mean that you have gone up: The meaning is 'What right have you to go up . . . ?' The inhabitants of Jerusalem were alive with excitement in celebrating their deliverance from the threat of siege and destruction by Sennacherib. Hezekiah's timely surrender had spared them the anguish and suffering of battle. Yet Judah had been ruined (cf. Sennacherib's boast of having destroyed forty-six of its towns; *ANET*, p. 288), and no thought had been given to those who had not been as fortunate as the inhabitants of Jerusalem. Isaiah saw the occasion, not as a time for rejoicing but as a call to penitence and remorse for the ruin of the country. Fields and towns had been ravaged and destroyed and only Jerusalem had been spared. **to the housetops:** The implication is that the roofs of houses were places

where festivities of eating and drinking were celebrated, although it is possible that the allusion is to rites of (illicit) worship performed in honour of various household or personal gods. This seems unlikely, however, since it is not made the explicit point of the prophet's rebuke.

2. you who are full of shoutings: The very noise and din of the celebrations is contrasted sharply with the anticipated din of battle which had so unexpectedly been averted. Hence **your slain are not slain with the sword** alludes to the people lying in drunken stupor where, only a short time before, it was feared that they would be killed in battle.

3. All your rulers have fled together: This must refer to the army commanders who had all abandoned their posts (cf. *ANET*, p. 288). Hezekiah had consequently been left with a much depleted army with which to resist Sennacherib, and this fact may have contributed to his decision to surrender. **without the bow they were captured:** the phrase is meaningless as translated and it is preferable to emend with 1QIs^a to 'without a bow being bound (Heb. '^{a}sûrāh)'; i.e. they did not even wait for the battle to begin but fled before any attempt to resist was made. *NEB* retains the MT but understands it differently as 'huddled together out of bowshot'. The Heb. 'ussārû is understood as 'bound together, huddled together'. **All of you who were found** makes little sense, and it is better to emend with *NEB* to 'all your stoutest warriors' (Heb. 'ammiṣayik̠ instead of nimṣā'ayik̠). We can then omit the following 'uss^{e}rû, **were captured**, as a dittography from the preceding line; the reading is then perfectly intelligible as 'all your best warriors have together fled far away'.

4. Therefore I said: 'Look away from me ...': See above for the view that this verse is not from Isaiah, but represents the work of a later redactor who has found in the behaviour of the inhabitants of Jerusalem after their deliverance in 701 a reason why they had subsequently to be punished. This makes best sense of the reference to **the destruction of the daughter of my people** which is a reference to the destruction of Jerusalem by Nebuchadnezzar in 587. It is mentioned as an event that lay still in the future from the perspective of Isaiah's time, but which had in reality already taken place when the redactor added this cry of lament. Very poignantly it recognises that the horror which had overtaken the people was too terrible for any comfort to soften the grief; cf. Lam. 2 : 13. The construct relationship may be used epexegetically, 'the daughter which is my people', or the reference is quite specifically to Jerusalem pictured metaphorically as the **daughter** of Judah.

5. For the Lord GOD of hosts has a day: Vv. 5–8a now fill out the picture of the destruction of Jerusalem with armies of chariots and horsemen at the city's gates. The reference must be to the attack of Nebuchadnezzar in 587 BC, and this is borne out by the allusion to 'Elam' and 'Kir' in v. 4. These nations formed a part of the forces attacking Jerusalem. The imagery of Yahweh's **day** against Jerusalem is found in 2 : 12–22 which has no doubt influenced the language of the redactor here. **in the valley of vision:** The title has been chosen by the redactor to describe the approaches to Jerusalem as the city which formed a primary subject of Isaiah's prophecy = **vision**. There is no need to follow G. R. Driver, *JSS* 13 (1968), p. 47 in reading 'valley of disaster'.

A battering down of walls is very obscure. Cf. *NEB*'s 'rousing cries for help'. For such a rendering (connecting Heb. *qir*, 'wall', with a verb *qîr/qûr*, 'to shout, raise an alarm'), see M. Weippert, *ZAW* 73 (1961), pp. 97–9.

6. And Elam bore the quiver: The reference to the presence of warriors from **Elam** and **Kir** is occasioned by the fact that these must have constituted a part of the forces of Nebuchadnezzar's army in 587. Very plausibly, however, the redactor has felt that it is specially appropriate to mention these peoples because of the reference in 21:2 to the 'stern vision' in which they appeared.

With chariots and horsemen: Heb. has 'chariots of a man' (*'ādām*) which can best be emended to *'arām*, 'Syria', indicating another region from which the attackers have come. The region of **Kir** has not been properly identified. The verse spells out the circumstances in which the punishment of the citizens threatened in v. 4 was brought to realisation.

7. Your choicest valleys: The language shows that an event that had already taken place was in mind, picturing the great military army that had gathered in the valleys of Judah. The presence of the **horsemen** completely prevented any escape from the doomed city.

8. He has taken away the covering of Judah: The reference is to God who had withdrawn his protection from Jerusalem so that no adequate defence existed to prevent the Babylonian forces from working their will of destruction. The purpose of the verse is to explain why the divine protection which was believed to have prevented the destruction of Jerusalem in 701 (cf. chs. 36–37) would not avail against the Babylonians. The same problem is clearly at the back of the interpretation of the tradition of the coming of the Babylonian emissaries to Jerusalem (Isa. 39).

In that day you looked to the weapons: It is evident that v. 8*b* begins a new section, and it becomes clear from the contents of these verses that 8*b*–11 were introduced before 5–8*a*. The fact that the citizens of Jerusalem had **looked to the weapons of the House of the Forest**, which was the armoury of the royal palace complex (1 Kg. 7:2–5), instead of to God, shows that they had misplaced their trust. The redactor who has added these verses has been very conscious of the rebuke which Isaiah gave to his people for their trust in military alliances and strength instead of in God (cf. 31:1). In searching for reasons why Yahweh had not protected Jerusalem from the Babylonians (in 598 and 587), he sought to find this in the wrong attitude displayed by the people then. Even when Yahweh had delivered them the people had falsely ascribed this to their own defensive preparedness, instead of to the power and faithfulness of God. Hence he had been compelled to leave them to the mercy of the

Babylonians in order to show up the falseness of their faith. The opening phrase **In that day** is slightly ambiguous. It is taken here to refer to the day of Jerusalem's fall to the Babylonians in 587, since this was when the city was actually destroyed. It could, however, be referred to the 'day' of 701, finding in the false trust of the people at that time a reason for their later defeat. The **House of the Forest** was the royal armoury, which is called 'the House of the Forest of Lebanon' in 1 Kg. 7:2–5; 10:17. Possibly also a garrison was stationed there, although Kaiser would regard it simply as representative of the larger palace area. The point is that Jerusalem trusted in weapons instead of in God.

9. and you saw that the breaches of the city of David were many: The reading should certainly be emended to 'you filled with water the many pools', reading *rē'îtem* (from *rā'āh*, Pi 'el, 'to fill') instead of *re'îtem*. The noun *beqîa'*, literally 'breach, cleft', is then taken to refer to a pool. Cf. *NEB*'s rendering. The special interest of the redactor in the trust of the water supply of Jerusalem during a time of siege has quite clearly been taken from 7:3, where the mention is largely circumstantial. The details of the building up of the siege defences of Jerusalem during the period of Isaiah's ministry have become a feature which the later redactor has assumed to illustrate a want of true faith in God.

11. But you did not look to him who did it: The phrase **him who did it** is better expressed by *NEB*'s 'the Maker of it all'. The phrase **him who planned it long ago** has evidently been drawn from 5:12, with its rebuke from Isaiah for those who had failed to take God's plans into account in their thinking. The phrase **long ago** appears to recognise the interval of time which separated Isaiah's prophecies from their (later) fulfilment in the fate which overtook Jerusalem at the hands of the armies of Babylon.

12. In that day ... the Lord ... called to weeping and mourning: With this verse we return to the original continuation of vv. 1–3 in which the prophet elaborates further upon his invective against the joyous citizens of Jerusalem. The Heb. places the phrase **in that day** at the end of the line so that it does not obtain the same emphasis which the *RSV* translation suggests. The use is adverbial and no specific 'Day of the LORD' is referred to, but simply 'at that time . . .'. When the inhabitants of Jerusalem were busy celebrating they should have shown concern for the appalling suffering which their country had endured and have expressed this through the customary signs of mourning.

13. Let us eat and drink, for tomorrow we die: This was evidently a proverbial saying expressing a resigned indifference to life and its problems coupled with a determination to enjoy as much of life as one could.

14. The LORD of hosts has revealed himself in my ears: This verse contains the final pronouncement of the divine punishment after the invective of vv. 1–3, 12–13. For the formula for the coming of the message to the prophet, see 5:9, where a comparable expression describing the revelation of God's plans to the prophet is used. Very probably the elaboration of the divine name **The LORD of hosts** as the source of the prophetic revelation has been added by an editor, the original passive formulation leaving this to be inferred. The divine oath which then follows provides the element of future pronouncement declaring the punishment that would come for Jerusalem's insensitive (but understandable) behaviour. Precisely how it would take effect is not specified, but quite evidently the inclusion of vv. 5–8a has served to show how the exilic redactor understood this to have occurred. For Isaiah it was sufficient to affirm that the iniquity (Heb. *'āwôn*; cf. *THAT*, II, cols. 243–9) would not be 'atoned for' (Heb. *kipper*, cf. *THAT*, I, cols. 842–57). The *RSV* interprets this by its rendering **will not be forgiven you**. The concluding **says the Lord GOD of hosts** is omitted by LXX and is the work of a later editor.

A PROPHECY CONCERNING THE STEWARD

22:15-25

These verses contain prophecies concerning important officials of the kingdom of Judah, the first of whom is named in v. 15 as **Shebna** and the second, in v. 20, as **Eliakim**. However, before we can consider the identity and significance of these names we must look at the overall structure of the prophecies. The first of these is to be found in vv. 15–18 and concerns one who is both **steward** and **who is over the household** (i.e. palace). It is self-contained and rebukes him for the pretensions implicit in his preparation of a prominent tomb for himself. The threatened punishment is that he will die in a foreign land (i.e. as a prisoner of war), v. 18. This is poetic in form and no reason exists for doubting its Isaianic origin. The second prophecy is to be found in vv. 20–23, also poetic in form, and concerns **Eliakim, the son of Hilkiah**, as the officer who will replace the **Shebna** of v. 15, and under whom the kingdom will come to honour and greatness, v. 23. A final prophecy in prose in vv. 24–25 then adds that Eliakim and the office he holds will come to grief. The language and imagery of this final prophecy is markedly dependent on that of vv. 20–23. V. 19, which falls outside these separate prophecies, has evidently been inserted by a redactor to assist the transition from the threatened fate of Shebna to his replacement by Eliakim, by mentioning the former's removal from office.

In order to understand this unique sequence of prophecies concerning royal officials we must note that Shebna, who is described as **steward** (Heb. *sôkēn*) and as 'palace governor' (Heb. *'al-habbayit*) in v. 15 appears in Isa. 36:3 (= 2 Kg. 18:18) and 37:2 (= 2 Kg. 19:2) as 'secretary' (Heb. *sôpēr*). For these offices, see especially T. N. D. Mettinger, *Solomonic State Officials*, Lund, 1971, pp. 70ff. Close examination of v. 15 shows that Shebna's name has been introduced secondarily from these narrative passages and that originally the officer who was the subject of the prophecy was unnamed and was described solely as **steward**. This then points us to note that Eliakim is mentioned in 36:3, 11, 22; 37:2 as the official who was **over the household** at the time of Hezekiah's confrontation with Sennacherib. Even more strikingly the role of Eliakim as **a father to the inhabitants of Jerusalem and to the house of Judah** and his receiving of **the key of the house of David** (vv. 21–22) points to a royal office, rather than to that of a palace governor. Vermeylen (p. 341) therefore suggests that the subject of the prophecy of vv. 20–23 is really the royal office and that it refers to Josiah. This is to go too far, but it is evident that the main centre of interest is that of the kingship, and that the palace governorship is quite incidental to this. Furthermore, the 'prophecy' of vv. 20–23 is not from Isaiah (so Duhm, Marti, Fohrer, Kaiser, etc.), but has been composed in Josiah's time. It is a part of the 'Josianic Redaction' of the collection of Isaiah's prophecies, designed in this instance to magnify the importance of the Davidic monarchy for Judah and Jerusalem. By referring to Eliakim the author intends to exalt the royal office of Hezekiah whom Eliakim served. The entire prophetic elaboration, therefore, is a part of the later perspective on Hezekiah's reign which saw him as a great deliverer-king (cf. Isa. 36–37, and especially the tradition concerning the royal sickness, Isa. 38, for which see below). The final two verses, 24–25, have then been added at a later time of disappointment and disillusionment with the Davidic monarchy, almost certainly after Josiah's death, and most probably after 587 BC. The fall of the house of Eliakim has become identified with the fall of the Davidic monarchy.

22:15. Come, go to this steward, to Shebna: The prophet Isaiah was bidden by God to go to meet the man who forms the subject of the prophecy, and the following verse makes it clear that the encounter took place at the scene of the man's offence—the place where he had dug out a tomb for himself. The name **Shebna** and the title **who is over the house** (i.e. palace) has been introduced secondarily from 36:3 and 37:2 in order to link this prophecy with persons who took a prominent part in the activities of Hezekiah at the time of the confrontation with Sennacherib. The original prophecy, however, either gave no name at all, or the name has been subsequently deleted in order to be replaced by that of Shebna. This insertion of the name probably belongs along with the addition of vv. 20–23, as well as the transition v. 19. We cannot, therefore, deduce from Shebna's name in v. 15 anything about the date of the original prophecy, nor are we entitled to speculate regarding any more political motivation which may help to explain further Isaiah's hostility towards him. The exact duties of a steward (Heb. *sōkēn*) are not known, but he was apparently a relatively junior court official who, in this instance, appears not to have come from a family of any political eminence. His folly lay in wanting for himself a prominent tomb, apparently on one of the rocky hills overlooking the city of Jerusalem. Isaiah saw in this a sign of unwarranted pride, and threatened him with an unhappy end in which his tomb would be of no use to him, but would instead remain only as a monument to his vanity. It is tempting to speculate concerning

other ways in which the steward's actions had offended Isaiah, but of
these we know nothing.

16. What have you to do here: The question means 'By what right
have you chosen such an eminent place for your tomb?' The following
whom have you here point to the steward's lack of high-born
parentage. He could normally only have expected a common grave in
the Kidron valley and his special personal concern for a prominent
burial place among the notables of the kingdom indicated his in-
ordinate personal ambition.

**17. Behold, the LORD will hurl you away violently, O you strong
man:** The Heb. is difficult and the address **O you strong man** can only
be interpreted as ironically contemptuous. We may, however, follow
G. R. Driver, *JSS* 23 (1968), p. 481, in reading *beged*, 'garment',
instead of *geber*, 'strong one, warrior', and then in adding the preposition *k* ('as'). We then obtain the rendering 'as a man shakes out a
garment'; cf. *NEB*. **He will seize firm hold on you:** (Heb. *ʿāṭāh*, 'to
grasp') is taken by G. R. Driver in the sense 'to shake out (lice)'.

18. and whirl you round and round: We may better render 'and
wrap you up tightly' (Heb. *ṣānap*, 'to wind up, wrap'; cf. *miṣnepet*,
'turban'). **and throw you like a ball into a wide land:** better 'rolling
you as tight as a ball'. There is here a grim play upon the imagery of
binding up a corpse with a long cloth wrap. The identity of the **wide
land** is not of essential import, since the primary point is that it would
effectively deprive the official of burial in his self-appointed tomb. Yet
the allusion must be to the carrying off of such a government official
as a prisoner of war, and in this case it seems certain that by **wide land**
Assyria is intended with its wide plains, so different from the rocky
hills of Judah. In this case it is possible to suggest that the official had
become identified with policies which Isaiah saw would lead to the
political overthrow of Judah by the Assyrians. The most likely
connection would then be with the advocacy of joining the anti-
Assyrian revolt, either in company with Ashdod in 713–711, or with
Egypt in 705–701. **and there shall be your splendid chariots:** This
very strongly suggests that a major part of his role as steward entailed
looking after the royal chariotry, rather than that he himself possessed
any. The address **you shame of your master's house** must certainly
refer to the king.

19. I will thrust you from your office: This verse has been introduced by a redactor, possibly the same person who introduced the
name 'Shebna' in v. 15, in order to facilitate the transition to the
introduction of Eliakim as though he were appointed to succeed the
steward of vv. 15–18. The sentence threatened in v. 18 is death in a
foreign land, not removal from office, which has been made necessary
in order to introduce the idea of a successor. The phrase **and you will
be cast down** (Heb. *yeherʿsekā*) should be emended to the first
person, 'I will cast you down' (*'eherʿsekā*).

20. In that day I will call my servant Eliakim: Eliakim is mentioned in 36 : 3; 37 : 2 as the official who was 'over the household' (i.e.
palace) in Hezekiah's government, where Shebna is noted as the

'secretary' (Heb. *sôp̄er*). The 'prophecy' of vv. 20–23 has been introduced by a redactor and provides a comment upon the role of both
Shebna and Eliakim in Hezekiah's court. Yet vv. 21–22 make plain
that the interest of these verses with their message of divine support
for Eliakim was not with the palace governor, but rather with the
person of the king himself. Thus it serves as a word of divine promise
and reassurance for the Davidic dynasty, and its representative,
Hezekiah. From this we may deduce the reason for its composition.
Jerusalem had not fallen to the Assyrians in 701, and probably the
steward of v. 15 had not been carried off to Assyria to die there. The
Josianic redactor, conscious of the tradition of Jerusalem's deliverance as expressed in chs. 36–37, has then endeavoured to explain this
by introducing the belief that the 'steward' (now identified with
Shebna) had instead been removed from office, so that Yahweh's
support for the house of David could consequently remain un-
impaired. In these verses, therefore, we are not presented with an
Isaianic saying, nor even with a prophecy in the normal sense of that
term, but with an interpretation of Isaiah's saying in vv. 15–18 to
show that it was not to be construed as in any way impugning the
royal house of David.

21. and will bind your girdle on him: The **girdle**, or 'sash' (*NEB*;
Heb. *'ab̄nēṭ*) was a distinctive mark of dignity and office. **and he shall
be a father to the inhabitants of Jerusalem:** The assurance carries
over to a royal official the imagery of the role of the king towards his
people. Cf. the title 'Everlasting Father' in 9:6. It is unlikely that the
author intended directly to refer to the king here, but rather to associate the official with his master (cf. v. 18).

22. And I will place on his shoulder the key: Eliakim was to
exercise a decisive role in supporting the house of David, and in
pursuance of this was to have the **key** of the palace. This must be
taken as a metaphorical reference to control over all officials who were
appointed to work there. He would supervise the king's affairs including those of royal appointments. The verse is cited in Rev. 3:7, and is
related to 'the power of the keys' ascribed to Peter in Mt. 16:19.

23. And I will fasten him like a peg in a sure place: The simile is
that of a tent-peg securely fastened in firm ground, and is intended to
show the saving benefit that would come to Judah under his leadership. The point of such an allusion must be seen in the tradition that
came to be associated with the year 701 concerning Jerusalem's
deliverance from Sennacherib (chs. 36–37; cf. my book *Isaiah and the
Deliverance of Jerusalem*, ch. 3). As this tradition developed a central
point of its significance was the belief that God had acted in that year
'for the sake of his servant David' (Isa. 37:35; 38:5).

**24. And they will hang on him the whole weight of his father's
house:** This and the following verse are the work of a later editorial
hand who has elaborated further upon the imagery used about
Eliakim. Their intention is clear: to affirm that the prosperity and
safety promised to Eliakim would not last, and, by implication,
neither would that of the Davidic dynasty. The addition, therefore, is

from after the time of Josiah's death in 609, and almost certainly from
after 587 when the last king of the Davidic dynasty, Zedekiah, had
been removed from the throne of Judah. The downfall of Eliakim has
become synonymous with the downfall of the royal Davidic family of
which he was a servant. In this context it is not clear whether the
elaboration of the imagery of the 'peg', now interpreted as of a peg
fixed in a wall, can be pressed in all its details. The accusation that the
whole weight of his father's house would be suspended from him
could be taken as a charge of nepotism. Possibly this was felt to be a
genuine indictment of certain royal officials generally, or perhaps it is
to be understood metaphorically to mean that too much was made
dependent upon the king and the court for the good of the nation (cf.
the 'father' of the inhabitants of Jerusalem in v. 21). In any case it is
evident that the metaphor of the peg (Heb. $y\bar{a}\underline{t}\bar{e}\underline{d}$) in v. 23 is understood differently in v. 24, so that the tent-peg has become a peg on a
wall. It is very improbable that any connection at all is to be seen with
the 'Eliakim, servant of Jehoiakim' mentioned on a seal from Beth-
shemesh. Cf. W. F. Albright, *JBL* 51 (1932), pp. 77–106.

A PROPHECY AGAINST PHOENICIA

23:1–18

The prophecy against Phoenicia which brings to a conclusion the
whole series of prophecies against foreign nations in 13–23 is a
difficult one, both on account of the relatively poor state of preservation of the text and also because of the uncertainty concerning its
historical background. There is even some question whether the
prophecy was originally addressed to Sidon only, as Duhm, Marti,
Kaiser, Vermeylen (pp. 342ff.) argue, or whether it concerns both
Tyre and Sidon as the representative cities of Phoenicia.

We may note four major epochs to which the prophecy has been
ascribed, before attempting to define further its most probable time of
origin. Very attractive, because it would point in the direction of
Isaianic authorship, is the period of Assyrian attack upon Phoenicia in
705–701, under Sennacherib. In this case an association with the
affairs of Judah, which was involved in the same rebellion against
Assyria, would be evident. Sidon was attacked and overthrown, and
Luli its king was forced to flee to Cyprus. Supporting such a background for the prophecy are S. Erlandsson, *The Burden of Babylon*,
pp. 97–101; W. Rudolph, 'Jesaja 23, 1–14', *Festschrift F. Baumgärtel*,
Erlangen, 1959, pp. 166–74, and A. Schoors.

There is little, however, to support the claim for Isaianic authorship, since, as H. Wildberger notes (pp. 863f.), neither the language
nor the ideas are Isaiah's. Once we abandon this position, but stay
within the period of Assyrian imperial power which the gloss in v. 13
points to, then we may consider the time of Esarhaddon (681–669),
who conducted two campaigns against Phoenicia. H. Wildberger
favours this background, as does J. Vermeylen, who would locate the
prophecy in the time of Sidon's destruction in 678.

A third possibility is to relate the poem to the Persian period and to link it with the siege and capture of Sidon by the Persian ruler Artaxerxes III Ochus in 343. This is the period favoured by Duhm, Marti and Kaiser. Yet a fourth possibility emerges, preferred by O. Procksch, G. Fohrer and J. Lindblom, *ASTI*, IV, 1965, pp. 56–73, which is to relate the poem to the defeat and capture of Tyre by Alexander the Great in 332 BC. Among these possibilities some clear preference has to be established, and we may take the presence of the glossator's additions in v. 13 as a sure sign that the original composition belongs to the Assyrian era. There is no need, with Duhm, Marti, Kaiser to emend **Tyre** to read 'Sidon' in v. 8, and to conclude that the poem originally only concerned Sidon, since this one city has apparently been singled out as the major representative of all Phoenicia. Besides the glosses in v. 13 it is possible that v. 5 is also an insertion. Vermeylen would also remove vv. 9 and 11 as later additions. This conclusion is probably not necessary, however, and Rudolph and Wildberger, would defend the essential unity of vv. 1–14. If we rule out Isaianic authorship, then the most likely setting for the poem is that of Esarhaddon's attack upon Phoenicia in the years 679–671, the precise year of Sidon's fall being uncertain.

The form of the poem is that of a lament for an event that has already taken place, and we may then follow most recent commentators (with the exception of Rudolph) in regarding this as actually the case. It is not then a true prophecy, although it has been turned into a future pronouncement by the addition of vv. 15–18. This in fact consists of two additions, vv. 15–16 and 17–18, which treat of Tyre under the image of a harlot plying for trade. Wildberger would ascribe these additions to the immediate post-exilic period, linking the **seventy years** mentioned with the period of the Babylonian exile, whereas Vermeylen and Schoors would bring their time down into the Hellenistic age. It is the inclusion of these additions, especially the second of them, which turns the original lament into a future pronouncement and introduces a positive, hopeful note.

The additions in v. 13 must be placed earlier than the time of the additions in vv. 15–18, and associate the threat against Phoenicia with the Babylonians. This must be an allusion, made by a later editor, to Nebuchadnezzar's unsuccessful siege of Tyre (585–573), which is the background to the prophecies of Ezek. 26–28; Jer. 27:3; 47:4.

23:1. The oracle concerning Tyre: The title is an editorial addition, made in conformity with that for other foreign nation oracles, and the mention of Tyre has been drawn from v. 8. For the history of Phoenicia, cf. D. M. Harden, *The Phoenicians*, London, 1962; D. R. Ap-Thomas, *POTT*, pp. 259–86.

Wail, O ships of Tarshish: The name **Tarshish** is taken by W. F. Albright, *BASOR* 83 (1941), pp. 14ff., to mean 'refinery' and is usually located at Tartessos on the southern coast of Spain, probably close to present day Huelva. It was destroyed by the Carthaginians towards the end of the sixth century BC, but the name continued in use after that time to describe the region where the settlement had stood. I Kg. 22 : 49 shows that **ships of Tarshish** was freely used to describe merchant ships of several ports of origin. **For Tyre is laid waste.** The name **Tyre** is not in the Heb. and v. 2 shows that Sidon was being referred to. We should follow *NEB* (cf. *HTOT*, p. 183) in reading *māb̄ît*, 'harbour', instead of the unintelligible **without house** (Heb. *mibbayit*). The following words **or haven** should then be read as *māb̄ô*, 'port of entry' (so *NEB*), referring to Sidon as the place of landfall for sailors journeying from Cyprus (Heb. *kittîm*).

2. **Be still, O inhabitants of the coast:** The Heb. reads strangely with such a command and it is preferable to emend to The inhabitants . . . 'are ruined' (*niḍmû* instead of *dōmmû*). Then **merchant,** singular in the MT, needs to be emended to the plural, with the ancient versions. The contrast is made between the bustle and wealth of the world-renowned sailors of Sidon and the deathly silence that lay over their city after its sack and overthrow. **your messengers passed over the sea** follows the reading of IQIs[a].

3. **your revenue was the grain of Shihor: Shihor** was in the Nile valley, and **the harvest of the Nile** should either be emended to 'its harvest' (*NEB*) or omitted altogether as an explanatory gloss (so Kaiser).

4. **Be ashamed, O Sidon:** The city is likened to a woman who had remained unmarried and childless. *NEB* very plausibly emends **be ashamed** to 'cries in her shame' (reading *bᵉb̄ôšet*) and omitting **sea** (Heb. *yām*) from the phrase **for the sea has spoken,** which gives no proper sense.
I have neither travailed: Sidon had become deprived of her young men and women so as to become like a woman who had never borne children.

5. **When the report comes to Egypt:** The sense of the text as translated in *RSV* is very obscure and Kaiser and Wildberger omit a gloss. The reference to **Tyre** is unexpected, especially as Kaiser and Vermeylen regard the original lament as concerned only with Sidon. However, we may take the apparent reference to **Tyre** (Heb. *ṣōr*) as a misunderstanding arising from its original sense here as 'distress, siege' (from *ṣûr*, II, 'to bind, besiege'). We can then read 'as news of distress', which makes better sense of the preposition *k*. The assumption is that the Egyptians, who had enjoyed long trading connections with Sidon, would share in the anguish over the city's downfall.

6. **Pass over to Tarshish:** Vv. 6–9 develop an interpretation of the fall of the city, which v. 8 clearly identifies as Tyre, by affirming that it has suffered its fate as a punishment from Yahweh, made necessary on account of the city's great pride (cf. Ezek. 26–28). For **Tarshish,** see comment above on v. 1. The settlement was in Spain and had evidently attained an almost legendary reputation as a source of wealth.

7. **whose origin is from days of old:** The great antiquity of Tyre and Sidon made their downfall all the more humiliating and painful to consider. **whose feet carried her to settle afar:** The metaphor

provides a splendid picture of the remarkable mercantile enterprise of the Phoenician people who had founded Carthage and developed the ancient Mediterranean trade routes.

8. Who has purposed this against Tyre: The reference to **Tyre** is rather unexpected after the exclusive concern with Sidon in vv. 1–4 and has led Duhm, Marti and Kaiser to emend to 'Sidon' here (reading *sîdôn* instead of *ṣōr*). Cf. also v. 12. This may be correct, but it is more probable that the author not only associated the two cities closely with each other, but intended his reference to the fate of Sidon to be expressive of the fate of all Phoenicia. The phrase **the bestower of crowns** is difficult and *NEB* would prefer to read as 'the city of battlements', taking the Heb. verb as internal hiph'il and regarding the phrase as metaphorical: 'which (displays) crowns', i.e. battlements.'

9. to defile the pride of all glory: Read the IQIs[a] 'to humble every proud one, to bring greatness into contempt—all the earth's most honoured ones'. Cf. *BHS*.

10. Overflow your land like the Nile: Instead of **overflow** (Heb. *'iḇ'rî*) we should read 'till' (literally 'work', Heb. *'iḇ'ḏû*) with LXX and IQIs[a]. Then omit **like the Nile** as a gloss. The citizens of Tarshish are commanded to forget their trade which was dependent on the mercantile enterprise of Sidon and to return to work their land. **there is no restraint any more:** The word **restraint** (Heb. *mēzaḥ*; literally 'girdle') is odd, and should be emended to *māḥōz*, 'market, harbour'.

11. He has stretched out his hand: The subject is Yahweh, the God of Israel; but it is better to transpose the two halves of the verse and to read 'The LORD has given command . . .' at the beginning. **strongholds** (Heb. *mā'uz'neyhā*) should probably be emended to 'markets' (*ma'z'neyhā*). Cf. *HTOT*, p. 183.

12. arise, pass over to Cyprus: The trading links between Phoenicia and Cyprus had been long established and well known. The flight of Luli to Cyrpus in 701 was also a widely known fact, so that the command to flee there must be understood as a reflection of the knowledge that the island provided a suitable refuge for the oppressed rulers of Sidon.

13. Behold the land of the Chaldeans: The phrase is undoubtedly a later addition made after the period of Assyrian domination had passed and re-applying the lament to Tyre in the Babylonian era. Its setting must be that of Nebuchadnezzar's prolonged and unsuccessful siege of **Tyre** in 585–573, which forms the background of Ezek. 26–28. Some commentators have consequently regarded the entire verse as a later addition, and this may well be correct. However, the Heb. is very obscure (cf. *RSV* margin) and does not mention **Tyre** specifically. If we omit **the land of the Chaldeans** and **this is the people** as two separate glosses, then it is possible to understand the remainder of the verse as a poetic elaboration of the military attack on Sidon and its destruction. To apply the entire verse to the assault by Nebuchadnezzar upon Tyre runs into the difficulty that the island fortress did not in the end succumb to the Babylonian attack.

14. Wail, O ships of Tarshish: The original lament over the fall of

Sidon is concluded with a repetition of the refrain from the opening verse.

15. In that day Tyre will be forgotten for seventy years: The first half of the verse has been interpolated so that the verse originally ran 'In that day . . . it will happen to Tyre as in the song of the harlot'. The reference to **seventy years** is then a part of this later addition. However, it is clear (see above) that vv. 15–16 are an addition made to the lament over the fall of Sidon in vv. 1–14. The addition compares Tyre, which is taken to have been the subject of the lament, to a harlot. Cf. Nah. 3 : 4, where a similar metaphor is used of Nineveh. Presumably a scribe felt the lack of any clear denunciation of Phoenicia in the lament and has added the simile about the ageing and forgotten harlot in order to provide one. Tyre's great reputation in trade is likened to the profession of a harlot on account of its promiscuity and emphasis upon outward show. There is a marked tone of irony and contempt for Tyre, the opulence of which is evidently resented. The date of the addition is hardly capable of being determined. A yet later scribe has then added a reference to **seventy years** as the period during which Tyre will be forgotten. The significance of this period is evidently that of a normal human life span—**like the days of one king.** O. Kaiser would relate the addition of vv. 15–16 to the siege and capture of Tyre by Alexander the Great in 332. Tyre had fallen, and the Jewish scribe saw in this fall both a fresh fulfilment of the lament of vv. 1–14 and a sign that all her merchant enterprise had been judged by Yahweh. In this case it is attractive to follow Kaiser further in linking the **seventy years** with the restoration of autonomy to Tyre by Ptolemy II Philadelphus in 274 BC. However, it is probable that the addition in v. 15, **will be forgotten . . . At the end of seventy years . . .** , has been added before vv. 17–18, which picks up the reference and elaborates upon it. This first reference to **seventy years** would then have been intended as a sign of how completely the city will have been forgotten for a whole generation (cf. Jer. 25 : 12; 29 : 10).

16. Take a harp: The comparison of merchant trading with 'harlotry' was a popular one (cf. Rev. 18 : 1ff.), and contained its own element of disapprobation. The city of Tyre is then compared to an ageing prostitute whom nobody any longer wanted. There may have been a deliberate intention of associating the city with the kind of bawdy song which would have been sung in the seaports of the ancient orient. The implication of the comparison is that Tyre, like the prostitute in the song, would have to try very hard in order to be remembered at all, so devastating would be her judgment.

17. At the end of seventy years: The mention of **seventy years** in the addition to v. 15 has prompted a further elaboration which has given to the lament a more hopeful and reassuring prospect. Tyre will eventually become prosperous again. It is attractive to follow Kaiser in linking this addition with the time of Tyre's rehabilitation by Ptolemy II in 274. The purpose of the addition is to recognise the right of Tyre and its people to return to their former trade and prosperity, but to assert that it would, henceforth, be dedicated to the service of Yahweh. Possibly the people of Judah were already conscious of the benefits to themselves of Tyre's enterprise, but no doubt also such prophecies as those of Isa. 60:5, 9 have influenced the addition here. The period of **seventy years** has then been loosely calculated from the time of the city's fall to Alexander (332) to that of its rehabilitation (274).

and will play the harlot with all the kingdoms: The verse picks up the imagery used in vv. 15–16, but this time in a more neutral sense.

18. Her merchandise and her hire: The verse provides a fitting conclusion for the entire series of foreign nation prophecies in chs. 13–23 by returning to the theme that ultimately the wealth of all foreign nations will be brought to Judah as a tribute to Yahweh as the true God. There is, therefore, a broad framework of eschatological expectation which has been given to the whole collection of such prophecies. After a long period of turmoil and suffering among the nations of the world, with that brought by Babylon forming a pivotal point, the remnant of Israel, scattered among the nations will return, bringing the wealth of the nations with them (cf. 18:7; 19:24–5). **her merchandise will supply abundant food and fine clothing:** The author was evidently familiar with the effects that Phoenician prosperity could have upon Judah, and almost certainly close political and trading ties had been established between the two peoples under the Ptolemies. However, the major point is to insist that ultimately the riches of the nations would redound to the glory of Yahweh and his people.

The Apocalypse of Isaiah: chapters 24–27

The four chapters which now follow (24–27) are clearly of a very different character from the remainder of the book, and have elicited an extraordinary variety of views from scholars as to their date and probable background. They may be referred to for convenience as 'the Isaiah Apocalypse', although it is improbable that they ever formed an independent literary unity, and several of the features which are to be found in later apocalyptic are lacking in them. They are certainly not, therefore, to be reckoned a true apocalypse, and it must be regarded as certain that they have been set in their present position, at the end of the series of 'foreign nation' prophecies of Isaiah (13–23), for a specific redactional purpose. They are designed to show how the fate of the nations, and especially of Israel among them, will ultimately be determined. They are concerned, therefore, with the eschatological turning point of human history, and it is this thoroughgoing eschatological character that has allowed several interpreters to describe the contents of chs. 24–27 as apocalyptic. They represent an important stage of hermeneutical development between prophecy and apocalyptic and thus form a bridge between the prophetic books of the Old Testament and the later apocalypses of the intertestamental period. In this respect they are to be compared with chs. 56–66 of the book of Isaiah and Zech. 9–14. Cf. especially P. D. Hanson, *The Dawn of Apocalyptic*, Philadelphia, 1975; O. Plöger, *Theocracy and Eschatology*, Oxford, 1968 (particularly pp. 53–78).

From a literary point of view the question of the date of the contents of these chapters has proved to be very difficult to establish on account of the lack of concrete historical allusions within the various sayings. In any case a number of prior questions concerning the structure and character of the material require to be dealt with, before more general conclusions can be drawn. However, certain preliminary observations may be made which affect the general framework into which such conclusions need to be fitted. The first of these is that the position of the material shows that it has been consciously placed at the conclusion of the foreign nation prophecies because the overall theme of the new material is the role that Israel is to enjoy among the nations in the eschatological age. A second point would appear to follow from this, which is that chs. 24–27 are not to be understood solely for themselves but as a guide to the way in which the preceding foreign nation prophecies are also to be understood. For this point, cf. especially J. Vermeylen, I, p. 352. It is in line with this general observation that we find in chs. 24–27 a number of citations and allusions to earlier prophecies, both in Isaiah and in other prophetic books (cf. the list of some of these in H. Wildberger, II, p. 910).

A third point has received a relatively strong degree of consensus among scholars, and this is that these four chapters must be among the very latest to have been inserted into the developing book of Isaiah. Whether this took place as a single redactional act, or whether a more extended process of growth and addition occurred, must be regarded as entirely secondary to this. A number of scholars in fact have ascribed chs. 24–27 to a very late date (second century BC, according to O. Kaiser), although such extreme views raise questions about the broader issue of when the book of Isaiah reached its present canonical form.

As to the form of the prophetic sayings in the chapters, it is evident that they are not all of one kind. Broad assertions concerning what God is about to do to the earth, and to the nations that dwell upon it, are interspersed with hymnic elements and thanksgivings. This has given rise to the theory argued by J. Lindblom. *Die Jesaja-Apokalypse. Jes. 24–27*, Lund, 1938, that we are presented here with a cantata. The idea of such a prophetic liturgy is also defended by G. Fohrer, II, pp. 1–41; cf. *Introduction to the Old Testament*, London, 1970, pp. 369f. Such an interpretation rests upon the assumption that we are dealing here with a basic unity of composition in which some overall plan can be discerned to account for the very different units which appear within it. Such a view inevitably runs counter to the conclusions, now expressed by H. Wildberger (pp. 885–911) and J. Vermeylen (I, pp. 349–81) that this so-called apocalypse is not a literary unity at all but has reached its present form by a process of additions and expansions of an original nucleus.

We may classify the main attempts at reaching a satisfactory inter-pretation of the material into two categories: the historical and the thematic. The former of these paths of interpretation has focussed on either of two main features within the chapters. 25:1–5 describes with evident relish and exultation the overthrow of an unnamed city. B. Duhm related this to the destruction of Samaria by John Hyrcanus in 107 BC, and thus saw a generally anti-Samaritan character in the prophecies. Kaiser, too, would date the whole apocalypse to the Seleucid era, placing it between 167 and 164. Other, much earlier, dates have been proposed and connections seen with major political events of the post-exilic age. M.-L. Henry, *Glaubenskrise und Glaubensbewährung in den Dichtungen der Jesajaapokalypse* (*BWANT* 86), Stuttgart, 1966, relates the fall of the unnamed city with the fall of Babylon to Cyrus in 538. Recognising a rather later date for the prophecy of the fall of the city, J. Lindblom argued that it was to be connected with the conquest of Babylon by Xerxes I in 485 BC. W. Rudolph, *Jesaja 24–27* (*BWANT* 62), Stuttgart, 1933, would connect the central core of the chapters with the capture of Babylon by Alexander the Great in 332 BC. Obviously the central assumption of such historical interpretations is that the unnamed city of 25:1–5 is Babylon, or some other city which embodied a major degree of hostility against Judah. However none of these views satisfactorily explains why the author failed to name the hostile city, when to do so was evidently so decisively important. An alternative historical approach has been attempted by looking, not at a city which is not identified, but rather at the national group which is. This points to the reference to Moab (25:10) and the foretelling of its overthrow in 25:10–12. Cf. E. S. Mulder, *Die teologie van die Jesaja-apokalipse*, Groningen/Djakarta, 1954, and O. Eissfeldt, *The Old Testament. An Introduction*, Oxford, 1965, pp. 323ff. However, this attempt at an overall interpretation of the chapters runs into the difficulty that it seizes upon one very peripheral passage in which an enemy power is named and makes this determinative for the whole. Much more plausibly we must regard the sayings about Moab as additions to the surrounding sayings and prophecies. It is these Moab-sayings which are out of character with their context by their inclusion of a specific name, rather than the context which must be adjudged defective by its failure to identify the enemy. Overall, therefore, we must regard the attempts at a historical explanation as inconclusive and unsatisfactory. The lack of identification of the hostile city which is to be destroyed, and the failure to identify the inhabitants of the earth who are to face divine judgment must be regarded as deliberate. The author is con-cerned with all nations and with the entire earth, rather than with one specific hostile neighbour of the Jewish community.

This points us to the thematic approach as more credible and satis-factory as a way of understanding the eschatological ideas and images presented in the chapters. All the more is this shown to be correct when we follow the suggestion that the authors of the material have been endeavouring to interpret, by means of imagery and ideas drawn from prophecy, the eschatological age which they believed was about to dawn for Judah. There could be no point, therefore, in seeking to identify the city whose destruction is forefold in 25:1–5. Rather, it stands as a thematic representation of the forces of evil arrayed against God's faithful people. Whatever may have been drawn, therefore, from the portrayal of the city of Babylon as the centre of such forces of evil, it must be understood as a symbol or representation of the larger reality of world evil and darkness. Such a view is advocated by H. Wildberger, who follows a number of earlier writers on these chapters (B. Duhm, W. Rudolph, O. Kaiser; cf. now also J. Vermeylen) in recognising that the chapters have acquired their present form as the result of a long process of growth. Undoubtedly much uncertainty must remain about the order in which the various component parts came to be incorporated into the whole. Wildberger defines the following major sections, or phases, in the compilation of the whole:

I. The Groundwork
    1. 24:1–6 (with three separate additions in vv. 7–9, 10–12, 13)
    2. 24:14–20
    3. 26:7–21
II. Eschatological images
    1. 24:21–23 The end of the world kingdom
    2. 25:6–8 The great communion meal on Mount Zion
    3. 25:9–10a The eschatological song of thanksgiving (two additions regarding Moab have been made in 25:10b–11, 12)
III. The song of the city
    1. 25:1–5 Hymn—the destruction of the strong city
    2. 26:1–6 Hymn—the LORD God is the protector of Jerusalem
IV. Additions—eschatological impressions
    1. 27:1 The defeat of the chaos monster
    2. 27:2–5 The new song of the vineyard
    3. 27:6–11 Israel's blossoming
    4. 27:12 The assembly of the faithful
    5. 27:13 Return to Zion

Wildberger concludes that it is impossible to determine for certain whether the material in section II or III was first inserted into the Groundwork. This latter he dates to the first half of the fifth century BC. As already pointed out, other scholars have proposed very much later dates than this, even when we allow some latitude for the process by which the additions into the Groundwork have been made. Certainly it becomes somewhat arbitrary and doctrinaire to insist on precise and firm dates, since these must inevitably remain slightly tentative. However, the fifth century origin of the Groundwork places the material firmly in the Persian period, and this seems in every way the most plausible setting for the elaborate eschatological ideas and imagery that are present in the chapters. In the growing feeling of frustration and disappointment that greeted the exiles who returned from Babylon, and in the struggles of the Judean community during the fifth century, the prophecies of the book of Isaiah, in the form in which they then existed, were reviewed and re-interpreted in the belief that they disclosed the key to understanding God's future purpose for his people. Vermeylen (pp. 379ff.) believes that these chapters were re-read in an anti-Samaritan sense during the third century BC, but it is doubtful if any, other than very minor additions, were made to the text at this late stage.

THE DESOLATION OF THE EARTH

24:1–13

The basic composition is to be found in 24:1–6, to which three separate additions have been made in vv. 7–9; 10–12 and v. 13. The original poem provides a prophetic picture of a coming world-wide catastrophe, which is interpreted as a judgment from God because of the sinfulness of its inhabitants. Great stress is placed upon the universality of this punishment, which is portrayed as still in the future, and how imminent it was felt to be is not brought out. Exactly what form it will take is also not made clear, but the imagery suggests a natural disaster of drought, and possibly also an earthquake. The important feature is that it will be an act of God, and no reference is made to the activities of hostile armies. The poet's concentration is upon the all-embracing nature of the catastrophe, its contrast with present pleasures, and its necessity as punishment for the sinful behaviour of the inhabitants of the world.

The basic poem of vv. 1–6 belongs to the Groundwork of chs. 24–27, and additions have been made to this in three stages in vv. 7–13. The first of these, in vv. 7–9, fills out the pictorial content of the coming disaster by describing the ending of all festivities. In this respect it indicates a somewhat mundane feature in view of the scale of the catastrophe envisaged. Whether particularly cultic festivities are intended cannot be made out. The second addition in vv. 10–12 describes the desolation of the city of chaos. No one particular city can be identified, and the imagery appears to be typical of any city in the time when the final, eschatological, ruination comes. The final addition in v. 13 then makes allusion back to the Isaianic prophecy of 17:16, but interprets this as applicable to all the earth and no longer to Israel only. Overall the material brings out the fundamental theme of a coming eschatological day of judgment and doom which will be inficted on the whole world. Evidently earlier prophecy was being read and reinterpreted as foretelling this day of world-judgment, and in this individual composition and its additions nothing is said about a separate destiny for Israel.

24:1. Behold, the LORD will lay waste the earth: There is an obvious element of ambiguity between 'land' and **earth**, suggesting that the eschatological prophecy here may have been developed out of such earlier passages as 6 : 11 foretelling the destruction of the land of Israel. There is no doubt, however, that the whole world is intended to be the subject of the threat expressed here. **and he will twist its surface:** The language appears to imply an earthquake, although it is possible that the disfigured contours of the land in time of drought may be meant. Cf. *NEB* 'split it open'. For the problems of the vocabulary, see G. R. Driver, *JTS 38* (1937), pp. 41f.

2. And it shall be, as with the people, so with the priest: No class of people will be exempt from the judgment when it comes, so that its universality and indifference to all human and religious distinctions will be made plain. There is no special implication of disrespect for the priesthood intended, but simply an affirmation that religious orders will not serve to protect those who hold them. God's judgment, when it comes, will be a truly world-wide event.

3. The earth shall be utterly laid waste: The content of the verse closely follows that of v. 1, and achieves a comparable alliterative effect by the use of two similar sounding expressions, *hibbôq tibbôq . . . wᵉhibbôz tibbôz.* In v. 1 the verbs are *bôqēq* (*bqq*, 'to empty out'?) and *ûbôlᵉqāh* (*blq*, 'to make desolate'?). The verb *bqq* is used in Nah. 2 : 3, 11 (cf. also v. 10 for *blq*), which suggests that this older prophecy has been influential here. If this is so, then it has lost any special reference to the destruction of Nineveh, as in Nahum, and has been extended to describe a universal catastrophe. A similar alliterative effect is striven for also in the next verse, evidently with the intention of using sound repetition to create a specially imposing effect of impending doom.

4. The earth mourns and withers: Instead of **mourns** it is preferable to read 'lies desolate' (*NEB* 'shrivels'). The description would fit that of a severe drought, but certainly a more far-reaching and cataclysmic misfortune than this is in the author's mind. **the heavens languish together with the earth.** The word here translated **heavens** (Heb. *mārôm*) means 'height, high point', and by a small emendation (cf. *HTOT*, p. 184), a better sense 'high-places of the earth languish' can be attained. It cannot have been the original author's intention to suggest that heaven was also caught up in the disaster, but rather that everywhere on earth would come to ruin.

5. The earth lies polluted: The cause of this world-wide catastrophe is the sinfulness of its inhabitants. The ancient belief that sin is a kind of uncleanness which pollutes and defiles the earth is reflected (Cf. Dt. 21 : 1-9). **for they have transgressed the laws, violated the statutes:** The Heb. reads the singular 'statute' (*ḥōq*), but it is probable that the phrase **transgressed the laws, violated the statutes** is a marginal gloss which has been introduced to fill out the clause **broken the everlasting covenant.** Exactly what **covenant** of Old Testament tradition is referred to by this latter phrase is not made explicit. Since it is a covenant with all mankind, Kaiser concludes that the covenant with Noah (Gen. 9 : 1ff.) must be intended (cf. especially Gen. 9 : 16 for the phrase **everlasting covenant**). However, it is not impossible that the Mosaic covenant with Israel is meant, as the glossator at least seems to have understood by his reference to **laws**. In this case such laws are evidently held to be applicable to all mankind (cf. Rom. 1:18-23).

6. Therefore a curse devours the earth: The curse is understood to be against those who transgress God's laws (cf. Dt. 27:1ff.), but is here thought of as having a permanent power to effect the harm it threatens. In this way **curse** comes to be nearly synonymous with the power of divine anger against human sin. **and its inhabitants suffer for their guilt: Guilt** here is regarded as a universal condition, so that there is no necessity to specify what particular sins have occasioned such guilt. If the allusion to the Noachic covenant is intended, then the shedding of blood must be especially in mind (cf. Gen. 9:6).

7. The wine mourns, the vine languishes: Vv. 7-9 contain an addition to the picture of world-judgment given in vv. 1-6. They fill out the picture of the suffering that will be endured then by stressing that there will be no time or opportunity for festivities. The imagery appears rather stilted, and the general thought rather trivialising in view of the awesomeness of the subject matter. However, once again it is likely that earlier prophecy has suggested much of the imagery. Cf. especially Jl 1:10, where the picture of the destruction of the vintage by a natural disaster is described. In a severe drought, the new wine (Heb. *tîrôš*), still in the grape, will be ruined. All of this will come about as a consequence of the judgment described in the preceding verses. Possibly Isaiah's references to drunkenness have suggested the basic idea (cf. Isa. 5:22; 28:7).

8. The mirth of the timbrels is stilled. Cf. Jl 1:12. No festivities, normally celebrated at the completion of the vintage, will be held. That these also had a cultic side to them does not directly affect the basic understanding.

9. No more do they drink wine with singing: The world-wide disaster will ensure that there is no room or occasion for rejoicing at all on the part of those few who are left (v. 6).

10. The city of chaos is broken down: This is the first mention of **the city** (Heb. *qiryāh*) in chs. 24-27, and the problem of its identity has aroused considerable speculation. Vv. 10-12 form a further addition to the picture of coming world-judgment given in the Groundwork in 24:1-6. The **city of chaos** (Heb. *qiryat tōhû*), therefore, must either be taken here as typical of the situation that will befall any city at that time, or, more probably, possesses some kind of typical or representative function. There is a complete lack of any specific national reference, and none of the activities which are pursued within the city differentiate it in any special way. It can best be understood, therefore, as a pictorial description of the body of organized human society, a type of 'Vanity Fair', which is to be subjected to the divine judgment. When God asserts his will in judgment he will bring to an end the existing human order, so that in a sense every city will be brought to chaos. The word translated **chaos** (Heb. *tōhû*), has a distinctively mythological connotation in Gen. 1:2 as a description of the primeval, unformed, state of the world, but it does not necessarily convey such a specific meaning. It refers to the arid and barren desert in Dt. 32 : 10; Ps. 107 : 40, so that it would be the portrayal of its desolation that is uppermost in the description here. It is the city destined for ruination. Cf. v. 12.

11. **There is an outcry**: The reference has been determined by vv. 7–9, and introduces a rather trivial idea. **all joy has reached its eventide**: Better, read 'is dimmed', since the Heb. *ʿārᵉḇāh* means 'has become darkened'. Some commentators would emend to 'has gone away' (Heb. *ʿāḇᵉrāh*).

12. **Desolation is left in the city**: The picture is certainly evocative of the condition of a city after a military defeat, but without any specific mention of a battle.

13. **For thus it shall be**: This verse makes a final addition to the picture of the coming universal disaster, and has been strongly influenced by 17 : 6, with its picture of a remnant that will be left. There, in its original Isaianic context, the image was applied to the Northern Kingdom of Israel, whereas here it applies to the whole earth. This is certainly preferable to referring it to the 'city' only, since the idea is that only a remnant will be left from among the nations. W. Rudolph would transpose the verse to follow upon v. 6, but this is not necessary. It is the last in the series of additions which endeavour to fill out the picture of world-judgment, before the Groundwork resumes in vv. 14ff.

THE TERROR OF GOD'S JUDGMENT

24 : 14–20

The section falls clearly into two parts, vv. 14–16*a* forming a 'doxology of judgment' describing how the inhabitants of the earth will praise God for his righteousness, and vv. 16*b*–20 picturing the terror and violence of the judgment of God. Several commentators regard the two sections as quite separate, and Kaiser would take vv. 16*b*–20 as the original continuation of vv. 1–13. However, we follow the division of Wildberger and understand vv. 14–20 as part of the original groundwork, the praise of God, and awesome nature of his judgment, being two contrasting sides of his divine righteousness. M.-L. Henry and W. Rudolph, who seek to connect vv. 1–13 with the overthrow of Babylon, interpret the theme of praise in vv. 14–16*a* with Jewish jubilation at the news of this. However, the sentiment expressed is not a national one, but is more truly theological as an affirmation of the glory of the divine righteousness. Its hymnic form must not be allowed to mask its truly prophetic character as a foretelling of the song of submissive praise that will be sung by all nations (cf. the indefinite **They lift up their voices**, v. 14) over the final triumphant act of God. Wildberger would prefer rather to regard the hymn of praise in vv. 14–16*a* as sung by Jews in the Diaspora (cf. **from the ends of the earth**, v. 16*a*), in expectation that they will escape the final judgment. Then the picture of the awesome nature of the final judgment in vv. 16*b*–20 has been introduced in order to repudiate such a premature and complacent expectation. However, it is more natural to understand the hymnic element as genuinely universal, designed to show that, in spite of its awesome character, the day of divine judgment will establish justice, and will therefore be an occasion for praise.

14. They lift up their voices: The subject is indefinite, and can hardly be the inhabitants of the city of vv. 10, 12. The language is no doubt traditional, so that the hymnic element of vv. 14–16*a* may have been adopted from an earlier composition. The joy is occasioned by the final overthrow of evil, and the establishing of a kingdom of righteousness. Certainly there is no antecedent expectation given which would limit the voices of praise to those of Diaspora Jews. However, since only the righteous would be left after the judgment, there may be some implication of this sort. **over the majesty of the LORD.** The **majesty** (Heb. *gā'ôn*) appears in man as a form of pride, but is an exaltedness which is entirely appropriate as a description of the majesty of God.

15. Therefore in the east give glory to the LORD: The Heb. is very uncertain and reads, literally, 'in the lights' (*bā'urîm*). Kaiser suggests 'in the lands of light'. **in the coastlands of the sea:** Better 'islands of the west'. *NEB* reads 'coasts and islands'.

16. From the ends of the earth we hear songs of praise: Just as the judgment of God will be universal, so also will the acclamation of praise which affirms that it is righteous will also be world-wide. There is an element of conflict between this idea of universality and the emphasis upon the comprehensiveness of the judgment which will leave only a few (cf. v. 6). The phrase **glory to the Righteous One** is obscure, but probably refers to gifts of tribute to God.
But I say, I pine away: The prophet-author now introduces his own contrasting reaction to the note of praise by re-emphasising that it will be no occasion of joy which elicits this, but a terrifying act of judgment. The Heb. for **I pine away** (*rāzî-lî*) is very uncertain and *NEB* would read instead 'villainy' (*r^ezîlay*). Kaiser would see a form of the word *rāz*, 'secret'. In this case it would be the mysterious and terrifying prophetic message which is interpreted as a secret mystery disclosed to the prophet by God. **For the treacherous deal treacherously:** The language is clearly directly dependent on that of 21:2, which seems to have been utilised because of its mysterious alliterative effect. Here is must refer to the wicked of all nations, and not to any one specific nation. Possibly the repetitious **the treacherous deal very treacherously** should be deleted as a dittography. It is omitted by LXX.

17. Terror, and the pit, and the snare are upon you: The alliterative effect is carried still further by these expressions of a very similar sound (Heb. *paḥadwāpaḥatwāpāḥ*). They are all simply metaphors of the coming judgment, and Wildberger rightly comments that they fit better in the context of Jer. 48, which may have been influential here.

18. He who flees at the sound of the terror: Exactly how God will bring his judgment to bear on the earth is conveyed by this heavy use of metaphor. The theme of its inescapability appears to have been taken up from Am. 5:19, indicating still further the use made by the author of earlier prophecy in order to convey a sense of the final act of God's judgment. **For the windows of heaven are opened:** The imagery is taken directly from Gen. 7:11; 8:2, and is intended to show that at the end-time there will be a return to the fearful conditions such as pertained in the time of the great Flood. So similarly the fact that **the foundations of the earth tremble** marks a return to a primeval condition of chaos.

19. The earth is utterly broken: The imagery suggest an earthquake, but quite evidently something more than a natural event within the order of the universe is intended. The very basis upon which the whole cosmic order rests will be changed and threatened. So the event that the prophet describes takes on a truly eschatological and apocalyptic dimension.

20. The earth staggers: The imagery is more than a little forced, but the impression that is created is sufficiently intelligible. **it sways like a hut:** The word **hut** (Heb. $m^e lûnāh$) refers to a temporary shelter made of leaves and branches. Cf. 1:8, which may well have suggested this particular simile to the author.

THE REIGN OF GOD

24:21–23

This short section comes from an editor who has expanded upon the Groundwork. It presents a gripping and dramatic affirmation of the cosmic nature of the Kingdom of God which he will inaugurate with his act of judgment. Not only will the wrongdoers on earth suffer judgment, but so also will the powers in heaven, which either have, or might conceivably have, rebelled against God. One phase of history will have come to a close, and a totally new era will then begin. Several scholars (Duhm, Marti, Procksch) regard these verses as continuous with 25:6–8, from which they have been separated by the intervening hymn of praise (25:1–5). Possibly the two sections did have a common author, since they each give expression to different images of the triumphant character of the end-time. They represent a further filling-out of the picture of the eschatological judgment of God, affirming the fact that it will be a full and inescapable victory for him. There is no hint at any specific historical context, nor any indication precisely when this eschatological event will take place. The notion introduced here, that there are powers in heaven which may resist the will of God, provides an important theme taken up in later Jewish apocalyptic writings, which pictured the final confrontation between God and evil as a heavenly battle, in which men had only a subordinate role to play.

21. On that day the LORD will punish the host of heaven: The LXX translation abbreviates this verse considerably, but this scarcely attests a different Heb. original. The question of the identity of the **host of heaven** is not made incontestably clear. Most probably we should think of a divine army in heaven, who are thought to have disobeyed God. Thus the **host** (Heb. *ṣābā'*) would be the angelic beings who control the destiny of the non-Jewish nations (cf. Dt. 32:8). In many earlier contexts the **host of heaven** refers simply to the stars, but, if that is the case here (cf. Jer. 19:13; Ps. 33:6, etc.), it points to the belief that these stars were believed to control the destinies of nations, as the parallel with **kings of the earth** shows. More probably, however, we should think of angelic beings (cf. Dan. 10:13; Enoch 90:22f.). Several commentators have discerned Persian (Zoroastrian) influence in this idea, which may well be justified.

22. **They will be gathered together:** The imagery becomes rather strained and grotesque, in portraying all earth's kings as imprisoned in this fashion. The intention, however, is to stress the universality of judgment. Worldly rulers are assumed to have acted in disobedience to God. There is no suggestion here that the **pit** (Heb. *bôr*) is the underworld of Sheol. Cf. Isa. 14:15.

23. **Then the moon will be confounded:** The intention is evidently to show that even the most splendid and brilliant of the luminaries seen from earth—the **sun** and **moon**—will pale in splendour before the magnificence of God when he appears. The idea appears to be that, when Yahweh rules from Mount Zion, he will be seen by the elders of Israel. Cf. Exod. 24:9-11, which has undoubtedly influenced the picture here. As Yahweh had once before revealed his glory to the elders of Israel at the time when he had founded the nation, so in the end-time he will disclose it again.

THE REFUGE OF THE RIGHTEOUS

25:1-5

This section has been introduced here by a redactor in order to bring out the fact that, in the face of the awesomeness of the universal judgment, Yahweh will not cease to be a refuge for those who trust in him. The section has undoubtedly been added to still further by later glossators, but throughout the theme is consistent and is presented with a striking single-mindedness. Whatever catastrophe threatens the universe will hold no terrors for the man who puts his trust in God. The 'I' who introduces his theme of praise in v. 1, therefore, must be not the specific prophet-author but rather any righteous Jew. The language is heavily stereotyped, but evidently the effect of breaking-up the continuing picture of doom and disaster by pointing to the One who is a Refuge, achieves a certain balancing effect. It is this that has given rise to the impression that a specific compositional form as a 'cantata' (Lindblom, Fohrer, etc.) has been sought. Much of this structural form disappears, however, once the process of the building up of the sections has been noted. The precise date at which this section was introduced into the larger composition cannot be determined.

Wildberger discerns a planned structure in this individual unit as follows:

v. 1*a* Reason for praising God.
v. 1*b* The wonderful activity of God.
v. 2. The destruction of the city.
v. 3. A summons to the people to praise Yahweh.
v. 4. The grounds of thanksgiving. Yahweh is a refuge for the poor.
v. 5. Hope for the future arising from present help.

There are a number of pointers to indicate that the language has been made applicable to its specific setting and function here, so that, although stereotyped formulae appear, the composition is unlikely ever to have formed an independent unit.

25:1. O LORD, thou art my God: The opening invocation immediately establishes a relationship to God on behalf of the reader (or hearer), in the face of the threat of the final judgment which precedes it. Thereby the concern with the message of doom becomes more than a question of unveiling future mysteries, and establishes a basis for loyalty and commitment in the present. The language is traditional, and has emanated from hymns of praise used in worship, but scarcely from an independent hymn. **for thou hast done wonderful things:** Better, 'thou hast accomplished wonderful plans' (Heb. *pele' 'ēṣôt*). This echoes earlier Isaianic language (cf. 9 : 5; 28 : 29), and here must refer to Yahweh's purposes which were being accomplished and brought to fruition through the eschatological vision of the prophet. **plans formed of old:** The word translated **plans** belongs with the preceding; then read 'from far off (or 'from of old', Heb. *mērāḥôq*) in steadfast certainty' (Heb. *'ᵉmûnāh 'ōmen*; cf. H. Wildberger, *THAT*, I, cols. 177ff.).

2. For thou hast made the city a heap: The Heb. is difficult and has given rise to many suggested emendations. Cf. J. A. Emerton, *ZAW* 89 (1977), pp. 64–73. Read here *'îr*, instead of *mēʿîr*. NEB prefers to read as a plural, 'cities'. For *NEB*'s rendering of the verse, see especially G. R. Driver, *Von Ugarit nach Qumran (BZAW 77)*, 1958, p. 44. The phrase **the palace of aliens** reads strangely, and several commentators emend to 'violent men' (Heb. *zēḏîm* for *zārîm*). G. R. Driver prefers to read as a verb, 'is swept away' (cf. *HTOT*, p. 184). J. A. Emerton suggests 'the palace of foreigners is destroyed' (reading *mûʿār*, Hoph 'al ptc. of *'rr*).

3. Therefore strong peoples will glorify thee: The **peoples** are not precisely identified (Heb. reads singular both for **peoples** and **cities**). However, the intention is to affirm that, when the final judgment comes, foreign nations will turn to Yahweh the God of Israel in awe at his achievement. **cities of ruthless nations: Cities** is singular in Heb. (to conform with 24 : 10ff.?), although the plural is read in LXX. In any case it is preferable to omit the word for 'city' (Heb. *qiryaṯ*) as a gloss. The basic idea is that when Yahweh finally manifests his glory other nations will turn to reverence him.

4. For thou hast been a stronghold to the poor: The language is traditional of God's protection of the weak and defenceless, but the context here would suggest that the **poor** are to be identified with pious and downtrodden Jews. **For the blast of the ruthless:** The entire phrase, commencing **For the blast . . . to like heat in a dry place** in v. 5*a*, is a marginal comment which has been added by a glossator. It gives a rather wooden and clumsy interpretation of the metaphors used in v. 4. *NEB* takes the phrase **storm against a wall** (Heb. *zerem qîr*) as 'icy storm'.

  5. Thou dost subdue the noise of the aliens: Cf. above on v. 4 for the recognition that the opening clause of v. 5 is a gloss. It is preferable with Targum to emend **aliens** (Heb. *zārîm*) to 'arrogant' (Heb. *zēḏîm*; cf. v. 2). The clause **as heat by the shade of a cloud** should be deleted as a further development of the imagery to be found in the gloss of vv. 4*b*–5*a*. It is not in LXX.

THE GREAT BANQUET OF THE NATIONS

25 : 6–8

The picture given here of a great festival banquet celebrated by all nations in honour of Yahweh, the God of Israel, and to be held **on this mountain** forms the original continuation of 24 : 21–23 (cf. Wildberger, II, pp. 899f., 960). It must derive from the same author, and did not form part of the Groundwork. It develops in a universalist direction the picture of the elders who had assembled before Yahweh on Mount Zion given in 24 : 23. Thus the mountain must be Mount Zion, even though the presence of the elders eating and drinking before God contains echoes of what happened on Mount Sinai (Exod. 24 : 9–11). The other traditional 'image' which has exercised a powerful effect is that of the pilgrimage to Mount Zion, celebrated by the representatives of all nations (Isa. 2 : 1–4; cf. Pss. 96 : 7f.; 72 : 10; Zeph. 3 : 9f., and especially Isa. 45 : 14 and 60 : 3ff.). Whether the idea of a royal banquet or of a cultic meal is uppermost makes no difference to the essential understanding. Finally, the nations are to join in the praise of Yahweh and to honour him, since they too will share in the blessedness which Yahweh will bring through the salvation of Israel. The great feast on the mountain, therefore, provides a picture of the joy of the nations at the salvation of Israel and a fitting climax to the pilgrimage which has taken them to Zion. It also describes a triumphant ending of the years of grief and sorrow which have afflicted all nations and peoples (vv. 7–8). Many commentators would delete the opening clause of v. 8 **He will swallow up death for ever** as a later addition. The idea of the resurrection of the dead occurs in the Old Testament only as a very late idea (cf. Dan. 12 : 2; see below on 26 : 19, and especially R. Martin-Achard, *From Death to Life*, pp. 130ff.). Wildberger (II, pp. 963f.) would defend the authenticity of the clause in its context, which is in any case an addition to the Groundwork of chs. 24–27. However, on balance the probability appears to be that it has been added by a later redactor (cf. *in loc.*).

  6. On this mountain the LORD of hosts: There can be no doubt that Mount Zion is intended, since the prophecy resumes the picture of the future broken off in 24 : 23. The description of the feast then simply reaffirms by the use of repetition its extreme richness and bountiful provision. The basic imagery is drawn from the tradition of a royal banquet, in this case with God as King, but ideas of a sacrificial meal, interpreted as a communion meal in the presence of God, and of the 'eating and drinking' of the elders of Israel on Mount Sinai (Exod. 24:9–11) have played a part. The meal provides the climax to the pilgrimage of the nations to Mount Zion.

7. **And he will destroy on this mountain the covering:** This is not the veil of ignorance, as in 2 C. 3 : 15–16, but the veil worn as a sign of mourning. The implication is that the sorrow and suffering which have led to the need for such tokens of grief and misery will be taken away. The phrase **the covering that is cast** requires a slight emendation of the Heb. text (pointing the second *hallôt*, 'Covering', as a participle *halût*).

8. **He will swallow up death for ever:** In spite of the defence of its originality here by H. Wildberger, this clause would appear to be a gloss. The text spoke originally of the removal of all suffering, bearing especially in mind the unique sufferings experienced by Israel since the time of the conquest of Judah by Babylon in 587 BC. The glossator has discerned a wider and more individual cause of sorrow and suffering in the fact of death itself. He has therefore understood the removal of the veil (v. 7) to mean the removal of death which occasions the wearing of veils as a sign of mourning. **and the reproach of his people he will take away** refers to the special suffering experienced by the Jews in their exile and dispersion, which has made them an object of contempt and ridicule (*ḥerpāh*) in the eyes of the nations of the world. When the final vindication comes all nations will perceive how mistaken has been their estimate of these people. The picture seems to imply, although it does not explicitly state that there will be a return of the Jews in Diaspora to Mount Zion (cf. 11 : 12–16; 27 : 12–13). The concluding formula **for the LORD has spoken** gives added emphasis to the triumphant picture of the future that has been given. The fact that the circumstances of the author's time seemed not to warrant such a triumph and expectation gave added cause to stress that its certainty lay in the purposes of God. On the verse, cf. further, R. Martin-Achard, *From Death to Life*, pp. 125ff.

ISRAEL'S FINAL SONG OF THANKSGIVING

25:9–12

This section consists of no less than three short units which have been added in expansion of the picture of the great feast on Mount Zion given in vv. 6–8. The first of these in vv. 9–10a consists of a short song of thanksgiving to be sung by Israel in celebration of the salvation God has brought to them. It belongs closely with vv. 6–8, although it must be ascribed to an editor who has expanded the original unit. A further addition has then been made in vv. 10b–11, by an editor who felt it necessary to make clear that Moab would be excluded from the final triumphant banquet and would, by implication, have no share in the ultimate salvation. Instead it would suffer a shameful and inescapable end. The overall effect is very much that of spoiling the otherwise grand portrayal of the final age in which earth's wrongs would be righted. That a great intensity of feeling against Moab came to exist in Judah after the Babylonian Exile is shown elsewhere in Isaiah (cf. 16:6-14). The origin of this piece is certainly late in the post-exilic period, but the precise political circumstances which occasioned it cannot now be unearthed. It would be quite wrong (with O. Eissfeldt, E. S. Mulder) to allow this short note regarding the fate of Moab to be used as a basis for reconstructing the context of the main body of chs. 24-27. For the exclusion of the Moabites from the Jewish cultic assembly, cf. Neh. 13:1. A final addition has then been made in v. 12 asserting that all the military fortifications and defences of Moab will be destroyed.

9. It will be said on that day: The stereotyped formula shows this to mark the beginning of an addition. The MT reads the indefinite third masc. sing. form of the verb, which 1QIs[a] varies to read the second person sing., 'you will sing', thereby stressing still more the involvement of the hearers in the jubilation. If this was intended literally, and is more original, it shows how imminent the coming of the 'End' was at one time felt to be. The phrase **that he might save us** and the following clause are omitted by LXX, which is probably an abbreviation of the original.

10. For the hand of the LORD will rest on this mountain: The clause marks the conclusion of the original addition, stressing the important role that Mount Zion was expected to play in the future salvation of Israel—a theme that constantly recurs in the book of Isaiah, and which has its roots in the sayings of the original prophet. **and Moab shall be trodden down in his place:** This represents the beginning of a short addition that has been made to show that Moab will be excluded from the coming final salvation. Instead it will be defeated and humiliated, a fate which the author of this addition feels to be richly deserved. The intensity of feeling against Moab is evident, and represents an attitude that grew in strength during the post-exilic age. The precise occasion for the outburst here, however, is not clearly shown. **as straw is trodden down in a dung-pit:** NEB 'in a midden'. The reference is to a cesspit, which the author regards as a suitable place of humiliation for the Moabites.

11. And he will spread out his hands in the midst of it: No effort on the part of Moab to save himself will be of any avail. **but the LORD will lay low his pride.** The Heb. is difficult and obscure. Cf. G. R. Driver, *JTS* 38 (1937), pp. 42f., who interprets as 'but he (i.e. Moab) will make his pride to subside in spite of the struggles of his hand'. *RSV* takes the indefinite subject as God and consequently inserts **the LORD**; but it is simpler to regard Moab as the subject. Cf. *NEB* 'but he shall sink his pride with every stroke of his hands'; i.e. in spite of the skill (or strokes—the Heb. meaning is uncertain; G. R. Driver compares Arabic *'irbatun*, 'skill', understood as 'movements, strokes') of his hands.

12. And the high fortifications of his walls he will bring down:
The mention of the bringing down of the pride of Moab has suggested
to a later redactor the idea that this will also mean the bringing down
of **the high fortifications** for which the Moabites were highly reputed.
The verse is an additon, prompted by the preceding verse, and
designed to emphasise still further that Moab will be unable to save
himself. The verb *lay low* is better omitted as a gloss on the preceding
verb **he will bring down**; cf. *BHS*. The subject of the action must be
Yahweh himself, who is expected to act against Moab.

A FURTHER SONG OF TRIUMPH

26 : 1–6

This short section consists of a hymn of triumph and rejoicing to be
sung by loyal Jews at the time when God's final victory has been
granted to them. It is secondary, and did not form a part of the
Groundwork of these apocalyptic chapters. In a great many respects it
is closely parallel to 25 : 1–5 and appears most probably to have been
composed for its present context, although making use of traditional
hymnic themes and language. It speaks in v. 4 of the overthrow of a
lofty city, which must be associated with the 'city of chaos' of 24 : 10.
This symbolises the organised power of human evil and godlessness.
On the other hand the **strong city** mentioned in v. 1 must be identified with Jerusalem, which becomes the fortress and centre for all
loyal and godly Jews. The use of the liturgical form of a hymn is
carefully planned, and serves to bridge the gap between the fears and
tensions of the present, in which the final triumph appears remote
and improbable, and the certainty of ultimate victory and joy. The use
of the hymnic form may then assist in drawing the reader more
directly into the confidence of this ultimate victory by drawing forth
his own confession of its certainty. Cf. **We have . . .** in v. 1.; the
beautiful affirmation of assurance in v. 3, and the exhortation to trust
in v. 4. G. Fohrer suggests that this hymn has been modelled upon
the form of ancient victory songs, and holds out the possibility that an
older authentic victory song has been used as its basis. This may be
so, but more probably it is the language which is traditional, and
which has here quite deliberately been transferred into the context of
an eschatological hope. Hence, even though in vv. 5–6 the overthrow
of the **lofty city** is spoken of as a past event, this must be taken as a
future, visionary, expectation of the ultimate overthrow of evil and
oppression. In spite of a certain repetitiveness in the liturgical
structure the overall effect is to create a sense of the nearness and
certainty of the victory which will one day come to the Jewish
community. In this instance the outlook is no wider, or more universal, than that.

1. In that day this song will be sung: The familiar joining formula
is used, indicating that this hymnic section has been inserted
secondarily into its context. The **day** here must be the day of final
victory for all Jews, who will then be able to return to their homeland

so that the song, quite appropriately, is to be sung **in the land of Judah**. **We have a strong city** undoubtedly refers to Jerusalem, which increasingly in the post-exilic period became a central symbol of hope and faith for all Jews. Cf. N. W. Porteous, *Living the Mystery*, Oxford, 1967, pp. 93–111. This ultimately led in the development of apocalyptic imagery to the belief in a new 'heavenly' Jerusalem. Cf. Rev. 21 : 2. **he sets up salvation** implies that God is the subject, although Targ. and Vulg. among the ancient versions achieve this sense by reading as passive.

2. Open the gates: The language points to a processional entry into Jerusalem, but whether of soldiers in a victory march, or of pilgrims on a religious festival occasion, cannot be determined. There are strong echoes of Ps. 24 : 7, 9, which may directly have influenced the composition here. The clause **that the righteous nation which keeps faith may enter in** points back to the older form of a liturgical entrance-*tôrāh* (cf. Pss. 15 : 1ff.; 24 : 3ff., and below on 33 : 13–16), by which the worshipper seeking entrance into the temple was questioned as to his righteousness. Here it is the entire nation which must be righteous (Heb. *ṣaddîq*), and this demand seems intended to re-assert the need for loyalty and faith on the part of Jews who were wavering in the hope of a final vindication.

3. Thou dost keep him in perfect peace: This beautifully expressed word of assurance gives confidence that God will guard those who remain loyal to him so that they may be assured of a place in the final triumph. The Heb. lacks any pronoun for **him** and the sense is 'Thou dost keep in peace (adverbial acc.) the man of steadfast purpose' (*NEB* 'of constant mind'). The word translated 'mind, purpose' (Heb. *yēṣer*) was widely used in rabbinic writings to express the whole attitude and direction of life of a person. In this eschatological hymn the author affirms the note of confidence which will characterise the faithful in the time of their triumph, but also recognises that God preserves those who look forward to this time so that they may be assured of reaching it.

4. Trust in the LORD for ever: The exhortation brings out the practical implication of the assurance given in the preceding verse. **for the LORD God:** The Heb. has 'in Yah, Yahweh', using an abbreviated form of the divine name which has no counterpart in LXX. The metaphor of God as **an everlasting rock** is a familiar one in the Psalter (Ps. 18 : 31, etc.).

5. For he has brought low: God's power is especially manifest in that he shows himself able to overthrow those who are in positions of power and greatness. Possibly the author has been influenced by 25 : 12, although equally the influence could have been in the reverse direction. **the lofty city** must be the symbolic 'city of chaos' of 24 : 10, although in the tradition-history of ancient victory hymns it could refer to any city. However well-defended the situation, and however strong the appearance of impregnability, this is no defence against the power of God. For this reason the ultimate victory is assured to 'the righteous nation' (v. 2). The traditional language of victory hymns has

given rise to the description of the overthrow of the city as in the past,
but in the perspective of the author it is an eschatological victory that
is still to come.

6. The foot tramples it: The ancient versions and 1QIs^a omit **the
foot** giving a much smoother sense: 'the feet of the poor trample
it—the footsteps of the weak.'

THE LIFE OF THE FINAL AGE

26:7-21

The precise delineation of the unit which is found here has been
much contested. J. Lindblom considers vv. 7-14 as continuous with
the preceding vv. 1-6, whereas Rudolph sees vv. 7-19 as constituting
a self-contained piece, but with expansion in vv. 14, 18 and 19.
Schoors also would see in vv. 7-19 a separate unit consisting of a
psalm concerning the life of the end-time, followed by a short section
in 26:20-27:1 giving a prophetic answer, or answers (cf. 27:1) to the
cries of lamentation and distress voiced in the psalm. Wildberger,
however, (II, pp. 901ff., 981ff.), would regard vv. 7-21 as forming a
kerygmatic unit belonging to the Groundwork of the apocalypse.
Certainly there appears to be some tension between the assurance
voiced in vv. 19, 20f. and the cries of lamentation and distress expressed in vv. 7-18. This may be the result of a deliberate structure,
mirroring the pattern of a number of lament psalms in which the
prophetic oracle of assurance (*Heilsorakel*) comes as the divine
response to the worshipper's complaints and questions. If so, this
oracular element is to be found primarily in v. 19. It then becomes
questionable whether vv. 20f. were an original elaboration of this, or
whether, as many commentators have argued, these two verses were
added later. The basic form is that of a psalm, but in this case adapted
to the context of an eschatological hope concerning the Jewish
people, rather than the situation calling forth a lament on the part of
an individual. The text is not in a very good state of preservation and
it is probable that some additions have been made. The form of the
whole composition is mixed, and contains some didactic Wisdom
elements. It is questionable, therefore, whether we can assume that
an original psalm has been adapted to a prophetic context. More
probably, with Kaiser and Wildberger, we must conclude that we are
presented here with a section which was composed from the outset for
its present setting. If, with Wildberger, we assign it to the Groundwork, then it belongs to the fifth century, although many commentators have viewed the much discussed v. 19 as of a much later
date than this. The section forms the continuation of 24:1-6, 14-20.

7. The way of the righteous is level: The verse provides a basic
affirmation of faith which introduces a lament. By establishing the
rightness of God's ways a worshipper could then proceed to set his
complaint before God, showing that such an affirmation of faith was
being set in doubt. The idea of the **way of the righteous** echoes the
imagery of Ps. 1, but was in any case a very common metaphor. The
author seeks to establish the principles by which God's government of

the world is to be understood. Whether any specifically didactic Wisdom influence is discernible is questionable in view of the wide range of such basic moral concerns. **thou dost make smooth the path:** The translation follows the LXX (cf. *RSV* margin) in omitting any counterpart for the Heb. word *yāšār* ('upright'), which is in MT. The rendering of *NEB* is to be preferred in taking *ṣaddîq* ('righteous'), not as a noun but as an adjective describing the nature of the **path**. Then 'Thou dost make clear (or 'dost mark out') the right way for the up-right'.

8. O LORD, we wait for thee: It is preferable to follow the reading of 1QIs[a] in omitting the Heb. suffix with the verb and to render: 'we wait for the path of thy laws (judgments, *mišpāṭîm*)'. The idea of 'waiting for' conveys the sense of longing for with expectancy, and here indicates a desire for the establishing of a just, law-abiding, order on earth. This verse, together with the first part of the one following, gives expression to the complainants' longing for the coming of the divine order of righteousness into human life. After having affirmed what the divine way is, the author asserts his own desire for it.

thy memorial name: It is better to take as 'thy name and thy reputation' (Heb. *zēker*).

9. My soul yearns for thee in the night: The language is the tra-ditional cry of an individual's lament, but here it is not a personal misfortune which is the occasion of the appeal to God for his action, but the condition of all Jewry. **my spirit within me earnestly seeks thee:** It is probable that we should read 'seeks thee in the morning' (Heb. *babbōqer* instead of *beqirbî*). This was the traditional time at which to expect God's help in the idiom of individual laments cf. Ps. 90:14; 143:8; J. Ziegler, *Festschrift F. Nötscher*, Bonn, 1950, pp. 281–8.

For when thy judgments are in the earth: Better 'when thy judg-ments prevail' (reading *ka'ašōr* instead of *ka'ašer*). Cf. *HTOT*, p. 184. With this and the following verse the author introduces a reflection on the ways of God into his lament.

10. If favour is shown to the wicked: *NEB* 'The wicked are destroyed'. The Heb. text as it stands is scarcely intelligible. Cf. G. R. Driver *JTS* 38 (1937), p. 43, who reads the verb as *yûḥan* (from *ḥûn*, 'was humbled, perished', cf. Arabic). Driver prefers the sense 'the wicked is humbled (but) has not learnt righteousness'. The reflection is on the inevitable fate of the wicked because he has paid no attention to God's way of righteousness. The clause **and does not see the majesty of the LORD** may be understood here in an eschatological sense of not seeing the end-time, when God will appear. In a tra-ditional lament context it had a more timeless significance, meaning 'does not enjoy the favour of God'.

11. O LORD, thy hand is lifted up: At this point the lament passes into a direct appeal to God for the destruction of the enemy. The meaning is that God is indeed ready to punish the wicked, even though they are unaware of the fact, and pay no heed to him. **Let them**

see . . . and be ashamed: The two verbs see and be ashamed should
be omitted as marginal glosses which have crept into the text. Then
thy zeal for thy people should be read as the object of the preceding
verb: 'but they do not see thy zeal . . .'

12. O LORD, thou wilt ordain peace for us: Vv. 12–15 contain an
expression of assurance that God, because he is righteous, will
respond to the pleas of his righteous people and will, in turn, punish
and destroy the wicked. The certainty of God's answer, which is a very
commonly found element in lament psalms (cf. H. Gunkel—J.
Begrich, *Einleitung in die Psalmen*, Göttingen, 2nd edn. 1966, pp.
132f.) is here evidently used as a further confirmation of the eschatological hope of judgment. Probably the word translated peace (Heb.
šālôm) should be emended to 'a recompense' (Heb. *šillûm*). Thou
hast wrought for us: We should emend to 'for thou hast wrought a
reward of our work for us' (Heb. *gᵉmûl* instead of *gam kôl*).

13. other lords besides thee have ruled over us: The Heb. is
strange and would appear to refer to the political overlords, both
Babylonian and Persian, who had exercised dominion over Jews. The
emendation to 'which we have not known' (*bal nēḏāʿ*) instead of besides thee (*zûlāṯᵉḵā*) is hardly an improvement and would take lords
to mean 'other gods'; i.e. by worshipping other gods Jews had become
subject to their power. but thy name alone we acknowledge: The
pious Jews affirm their desire to remain loyal to Yahweh alone, even
though the compulsion to live among aliens has imposed the strain
and temptation of being ruled by foreign powers.

14. They are dead, they will not live: The statement contrasts
rather strikingly with the context, and this has led some commentators to question its originality here. However, it does make sense as
a comment upon the 'other lords', who are pictured as having suffered
the fate of all mankind. They have gone the way of all flesh without
the hope of a final victory which the author looks forward to for
himself and his people. they are shades refers to the shadowy
existence of the departed after death as a 'shade' (Heb. *rᵉpāʾîm*; cf. R.
Martin-Achard, *From Death to Life*, pp. 34f.), which was a very
limited and insubstantial form of existence, unworthy to be compared
to life. Since the wicked are doomed to die it marks the end of everything for them. Cf. Ps. 49 : 10–14.

15. But thou hast increased the nation, O LORD: The nation is
Israel, which is frequently described as a *gôy*; cf. Dt. 4 : 6; Isa. 10 : 6,
etc. and see *TWAT*, II, pp. 965–73; *THAT*, II, cols. 290–325. The
idea of the author seems to be that the individual shares a hope
through his descendants, and especially through the knowledge that
they will come to vindication and great joy. The second thou hast
increased the nation should be deleted as a dittography of the first (so
one Heb. MS). thou hast enlarged all the borders of the land. The
past tense is striking, and must give expression to a certain hope of
the future, rather than to any immediate change in the political
fortunes of the post-exilic community in Judah. Perhaps the author
has been influenced by such promises as 54 : 1–3.

16. O LORD, in distress they sought thee: Cf. G. R. Driver, *JTS* 38 (1937), p. 43. It is preferable, with two Heb. MSS to read 'we sought thee' (*peqaḏnúḵā* in place of *peqāḏúḵā*). **they poured out a prayer** can scarcely be correct since Heb. *lahaš* does not properly mean 'prayer', but 'charm, incantation'. G. R. Driver suggests 'humiliating constraint'; cf. Akkadian *lahāšu*, 'to be bowed down'. Then 'Thy chastening has been a burden/humiliation for them' (or 'for us', reading *lānû*).

17. Like a woman with child: The picture continues the plaintive cry of distress and lamentation which comes to full expression in vv. 16–18. The simile used here is a common one to express distress and anguish, which is nonetheless deeply felt, in spite of the hoped-for joy that childbirth will bring. At this point the author gives vent to his feeling of complete and utter frustration.

18. we were with child, we writhed: The author pictures himself and his people as having experienced frustration and disappointment like a woman who undergoes a false pregnancy. By the use of such a simile the author hides the real cause of his present disappointment. Probably we should think of some anticipation of the final victory of the Jewish community over their enemies, which has not been realised. This leads him to seek further assurance from God that this victory will not be long delayed. **We have wrought no deliverance:** *NEB* 'We have won no success'. What exactly the writer had hoped to see achieved has evidently been frustrated, and this suggests that the time of the 'end' had been thought to be near, but has now become remote and uncertain again. **and the inhabitants of the world have not fallen:** This must refer to the wicked who abuse the faithful, and make life hard for them.

19. Thy dead shall live: The verse is a peculiarly difficult one and has been very extensively discussed. Cf. R. Martin-Achard, *From Death to Life*, pp. 130ff. J. F. A. Sawyer, *VT* 23 (1973), pp. 218–34. It stands in marked contrast of mood and content to the preceding lament in vv. 16–18, and several commentators have consequently regarded it as a later addition. So O. Kaiser, who regards it as an assurance of a resurrection of the righteous after death, and would therefore place its origin in the Hellenistic age, probably from Maccabean times. Cf. Dan. 12:2. However, both Fohrer and Wildberger regard the verse as quite authentic to its present context, but see in it an assurance of the rebirth of the Jewish community; cf. Ezek. 37:1–14. Its language, is, therefore, highly poetic and symbolic, not a promise of a resurrection for individuals. Within it we can discern some highly traditional and evocative imagery such as that of the **dew**. The contrast with the lament that precedes is then deliberate and consciously contrived by the author to emphasise the note of assurance for the community given here. This 'collective' interpretation as a promise of the resurrection of the community, and not of individuals, is probably to be sustained, and, on these terms, its originality here may be defended. Certainty is scarcely possible in the matter, however. **their bodies shall rise:** Heb. has 'my body', which

suggests some influence from Ps. 49:15, and points to a later reading
of the verse in reference to the resurrection of individuals. Some
commentators have sought to understand it as 'my corpse' taken in a
collective sense. Duhm, Marti, and now Wildberger, regard 'my body'
as a later insertion. **O dwellers in the dust:** The appeal is to those who
are dead, and this makes best sense if it is taken as a metaphorical
reference to the Jewish community. Instead of the imperative **awake
and sing for joy.** 1QIs^a, with LXX, Syr. and Targ, read the third person
plural indicative, 'they shall awake'. **For thy dew is a dew of light:**
The suffix must refer to God and the language seems to reflect, if only
metaphorically, the ancient belief that the **dew** had a fertilising, life-
giving, power. As each dawn reveals a fresh fall of dew, with all its
life-giving potency, so God will give new life to the dead community.
The difficulty in explaining how, or exactly when, the great turning
point in Israel's fortunes would come has encouraged the heavy use of
pictorial imagery. The **dew of light** (Heb. *ṭal'ôrōṯ*) is a rather obscure
expression, but apparently contrasts the sparkling brightness of a
fresh fall of dew with the shadowy gloom of the land of the dead
(**shades**).

20. Come, my people, enter your chambers: It is better to regard
this verse and that following as a later addition to the original lament
(vv. 7–18), followed by an oracle of assurance from God (*Heilsorakel*)
in v. 19. The anxious reader may still ask how soon the longed-for
salvation promised in v. 19 will come. These two verses have then
been added in order to explain that the days of Yahweh's **wrath** with
Israel must last for a little longer, but will then be totally past. That is
the moment when God will act decisively to punish all the wrong-
doings of earth (v. 21). The exhortation in v. 20 must be understood
metaphorically and be taken to point to a time of waiting, when
nothing could be done except to pray for God's action. Certainly when
v. 19 came to be understood as a reference to the resurrection of
individuals then v. 20 could be understood in line with this. Death
would be followed by a short time of waiting (in **chambers**) in expectation of a subsequent resurrection to a time of judgment; cf. 2 Esd.
7:32, 80, 95. Possibly the imagery here has been influenced from the
tradition of the exodus from Egypt, when the Israelites hid in their
homes whilst God slew the firstborn of Egypt (Exod. 12:21–36. So
now they were invited to stay in their homes **until the wrath is past.**
The implication is that loyal Jews were to remain patient under
oppression for a little while longer, and not to undertake direct
political action against their oppressors because the time would
shortly come when God would undertake this for them.

21. For behold, the LORD is coming forth: This is a reference to
the work of God at the end-time (24:1ff.) when he would act to bring
about a full and final judgment upon the earth. All the crimes of
violence—**the blood shed upon her**—would then be disclosed and
punished. This would include even such crimes as had until then
remained undetected and consequently unpunished. Cf. Gen. 4:10
for the idea of the earth reacting to a violent crime leading to the

shedding of blood. For such a time of just judgment the suffering
Jews were to wait confidently, and not try to exact vengeance of their
own prematurely (cf. I C. 4 : 5).

THE SLAYING OF THE DRAGON

27 : I

The concluding chapter of the Isaianic 'Apocalypse' contains a series
of four 'eschatological impressions'. The first of these in 27 : I stands
by itself and affirms that at the end-time Yahweh will overthrow the
power of evil. This is conveyed by the use of imagery drawn from the
ancient myth of a great combat between a divine being and a monster,
or **dragon**, which represents the powers of darkness and chaos. Cf. M.
K. Wakeman, *God's Battle with the Monster*, Leiden, 1973. This
monster is here named as **Leviathan** (cf. Pss. 74 : 14; 104 : 26; and see
C. H. Gordon, 'Leviathan, Symbol of Evil', *Biblical Motifs*, ed. A.
Altmann, Cambridge, Mass., 1966, pp. 1–9), but instead of describing
a conflict which takes place in primordial time at the creation of the
world it here describes a conflict of the end-time. The verse has
certainly been added to the Groundwork of chs. 24–27 at a late stage,
and offers a kind of summary interpretation of God's final triumph
over evil.

27 : I. In that day the LORD . . . will punish Leviathan: The use of
the common joining formula signifies that this is an addition by a
later hand, and one which has almost certainly been made in order to
sum up the message of assurance given in 26 : 19. It is, therefore, a
further response to the lament of 26 : 7–18. The eschatological victory,
when it comes, will mark the final overthrow of all evil, which is here
embodied in **Leviathan** (Ugaritic *Lôtān*). This was a title given to the
mythical **dragon** of chaos who represented the powers of the **sea** and
of the deep. He has a very similar role to that ascribed to Rahab (Isa.
30 : 7, etc.). The two dragons, therefore, scarcely have entirely
separate identities. By slaying the dragon of the deep, the god (Baal in
Ugarit, Yahweh in Israel) created an ordered world, but such a victory
was one that needed to be repeated each year in the seasonal cycle (cf.
O. Kaiser, *Die mythische Bedeutung des Meeres (BZAW 78)*, 2nd edn.
1962, pp. 74ff.) Here in this eschatological development of the image
the dragon expresses the power of evil and oppression throughout the
world. **he will slay the dragon that is in the sea:** By doing this
Yahweh would remove the cause of social disorder and silence the
voice of oppression and contempt which threatened the lives of Jews.

THE NEW SONG OF THE VINEYARD

27 : 2-6

In the context of the eschatological hope of a final judgment of the
nations and the exaltation of the faithful of Israel to a new position of
peace, eminence and prosperity the threat contained in the original
Song of the Vineyard of Isa. 5 : 1–7 had become obsolete. In the second

of these final eschatological impressions, therefore, the poet introduces a totally new song which describes the frustrations and failures of the Jewish people as Yahweh's vineyard. For the New Song of the Vineyard, cf. E. Jacob in *Wort-Gebot-Glaube. W. Eichrodt Festschrift zum 80. Geburtstag*, Zürich, 1970, pp. 325–30. The composition is a piece of late theological reflection upon prophecy and its message which basically develops, and ultimately reverses, the verdict of Isa. 5:6. In the old 'Song' Yahweh had found it necessary to punish his vineyard for its failure to produce a useful vintage. Now this threat is called in question and finally rescinded (v. 6). It is questionable, however, whether v. 6 belonged to the original composition, and the meaning of v. 4 is very uncertain. In this case the original New Song would appear to be a reflection upon the earlier one, made in a time of stress, which has subsequently been extended in a very positive fashion.

The assurance of v. 6 goes very much beyond the uncertainty and sense of conflict which pervades vv. 2–5. Whether, with Jacob, we should see the background to this conflict in the growing tension between the Jewish and Samaritan communities in the fourth to first centuries BC, is unclear. Undoubtedly such a conflict appears as the most likely context for the following section in vv. 7–11. The text of vv. 2–5 is far from clear, and this contributes to the general difficulty in arriving at a full understanding of the message of the composition as a whole.

2. In that day: 'A pleasant vineyard, sing of it!': Possibly an introductory verb 'In that day one will say' (Heb. *wᵉʾāmar*) has dropped out, since the beginning of the song comes very abruptly. The allusion to 5:1 is clear and certain, so that the understanding that the **vineyard** is Israel-Judah is taken for granted. Nevertheless the author has dropped all the romantic overtones about a 'lover' and his 'vineyard' (beloved). Some MSS read 'a vineyard of wine' instead of **pleasant vineyard** (Heb. *ḥemer* instead of *ḥemeḏ*). As it is, the description of the vineyard as **pleasant** points in the direction of a very positive and favourable expectation of its fate.

3. every moment I water it: The particular emphasis upon the constant care which God lavishes on it points to the conclusion that the time of his wrath has passed, as is then explicitly spelt out in v. 4. Even so this leaves some element of tension between the present providential care which Yahweh bestows on his people and their waiting for the time of eventual release and triumph. The best understanding is that Yahweh is watching over his faithful people until the time of the ultimate blessedness. **Lest any one harm it**: The Vulg. takes the verb (Heb. *yipqōḏ*) as passive (Niph 'al *yippāqēḏ*), which *BHS* follows. *NEB* adopts the passive understanding, but takes the verb in a different sense 'be missing, fail', and construing *ʿālehyā* not as the preposition *ʿal* (with suffix), but as 'its leaves' (Heb. *ʿāleh*, 'leaf, foliage', Lev. 26:36, etc.). This is a preferable rendering. The original parable (Isa. 5:2) records the ineffectiveness of the owner's care.

4. I have no wrath: The entire verse is difficult and obscure, and

NEB offers a preferable rendering which differs considerably from
that of *RSV*. Instead of **wrath** we should read *ḥēmāh* as 'wine', and
take this with the last three words of v. 3. *NEB*: 'Night and day I tend
it, but I get no wine'. The author of the new song takes up the major
theme of the old Song of the Vineyard of 5 : 1–7, which is that Israel
has become unfruitful. This is precisely the metaphor which he feels
describes the condition of the Jews of his day. **Would that I had**
thorns and briers to battle: The **thorns and briers** are mentioned in
5 : 6, where they form part of the picture of the original parable. They
have also become a major theme of the developmental exegesis which
later redactors have applied to the original song; cf. 7 : 23–25; 10 : 17.
The phrase **to battle** then belongs with the following line: 'I would
set out against them in battle'. The author envisages God wishing to
encounter the 'briers and thorns' which signified the enemies in the
original song, because it is Israel itself which has become the cause of
the frustration now. **I would burn them up together**: This follows an
emendation to *'aṣṣîṭennāh* instead of *'ᵃṣîṭennāh*.

5. Or let them lay hold of my protection: *NEB* 'Unless it grasps
me'. The time has come when Israel has got to turn back to find its
protection and **peace** in God, instead of seeking it in ways which turn
them against him; i.e. they must turn away from their submission to
foreigners for protection.

6. In days to come Jacob shall take root: The Heb. MT has simply
'those that are coming', and we should restore *bayyāmîm* at the
beginning. *BHS* achieves the same general sense with a slightly
different emendation. The verse must be regarded as a later addition
to the original composition, giving it a very much more positive note
of hope and certainty of world-wide power and blessedness in the
future. Israel, like a vine, will **blossom** and fill the world. The sense
must be that Israel will become very numerous, and will attain great
power whilst being scattered among the nations, rather than that
members of these nations will come to join Israel. Evidently a later
editor felt that the new song of the vineyard should give expression to
a more positive note of hope for the future than that which was
originally contained in it.

THE DESTRUCTION OF THE FORTIFIED CITY

27 : 7–11

Commentators are agreed that this represents a most difficult text,
which makes clear and very precise observations about certain people
and a **fortified city** (v. 10), neither of which is clearly identified. The
most attractive and convincing solution of the difficulty is that
proposed by Duhm, and followed by Marti, Rudolph, Fohrer, Plöger
and Wildberger. This is to refer the **fortified city** to Samaria, and to
take the references to **Jacob** (v. 9) and the **people without discern-**
ment (v. 11) as referring to the population of the Northern Kingdom.
Cf. O. Plöger, *Theocracy and Eschatology*, Oxford, 1968, pp. 71–5,
and for the broader problems regarding the Jewish-Samaritan conflict,

A. Alt, *Kleine Schriften*, III, pp. 258–302; R. J. Coggins, *Samaritans and Jews. The Origins of Samaritanism Reconsidered*, Oxford, 1975. If this link with the Samaritan controversy is followed it is, however, unlikely that the section should be dated after the destruction of Samaria by John Hyrcanus in 108 BC. Such a date is far too late for the probable time of origin of this section. Great uncertainty surrounds the time when the sharp rift between Jews and Samaritans occurred, and this might well, in any case, indicate a time of origin of this section in the Hellenistic age. Vv. 7–8 then describe in historical retrospect the fate that had been meted out to the Northern Kingdom, and v. 9 explains this as a consequence of its idolatry. Vv. 10–11 then pass sentence on the Samaritans and their city for their lack of spiritual discernment. The heirs of the old Northern Kingdom of Israel, which had itself been under a cloud of guilt because of its idolatry (cf. 2 Kg. 17 : 7ff.), had persisted in the ways of their ancestors and so had in turn needed to be punished and rejected by God (v. 11).

7. Has he smitten them as he smote those: The subject is indefinite in the Heb. but must be God, as *NEB* correctly interprets. Similarly, **them**, which is singular in Heb. and should be understood as collective, is undefined but must refer to Israel-Jacob as in v. 9. This points to the inhabitants of the old Northern Kingdom of Israel, in whose territory Samaria lay. The rhetorical question then means: Has God punished Israel as resolutely as he has punished Israel's attackers? The implied answer is 'no', with the suggestion that the time for a more adequate punishment had now come. However, *NEB*'s rendering would apply the question to Israel's attackers. Have they yet been punished as they deserve? Again the answer would appear to be 'no'; but in order to sustain this sense *NEB* is compelled to rearrange the verses and to place v. 8 after v. 10a. It is possible in any case that v. 9 should be regarded as an interpolation, elaborating upon the nature of Israel's guilt. **Or have they been slain as their slayers were slain?** The Heb. is difficult and *NEB* interprets slightly differently, 'Has the slayer been slain as he slew others?'. Cf. LXX, Syr. and 1QIs^a. This would refer the line to Israel's enemies, who have been used by God to punish Israel, but who have not yet suffered the just punishment of their own sins.

8. Measure by measure, by exile. The words **by exile** should be removed as a gloss on the preceding words which had become unintelligible. *NEB* reads as 'in brushing her away'; cf. *HTOT*, p. 185. **thou didst contend with them:** The tense of the verb (Heb. impf.) suggests rather a present sense, and 3rd. fem. sing suffix in Heb. ('her' rather than **them**) most plausibly refers to Judah-Israel. **Contend** (Heb. *rîb*) is to be taken in its normal legal sense of 'prosecute a case'. God has continued to fight his case against Israel for its sins by sending her away into exile. **he removed them with his fierce blast:** God has brought desolation to Israel and driven the people out of their land by a **blast** like that of the east wind. The most probable reference is to the political destructions wrought by Assyria and Babylon in 722 and 587.

9. Therefore by this the guilt of Jacob: The verse is best understood as an interpolation designed to soften the sense that Israel's banishment into exile is a permanent punishment. The sense is then that, once Israel turns away from idolatry, then its **guilt** will be removed, and its punishment revoked. **the full fruit of the removal of his sin:** The words **full fruit** (Heb. *kol pᵉrî*) give an overcrowded line and should probably be omitted (cf. *NEB*); they are to be regarded as the work of a glossator who wished to stress still further the need for the avoidance of idolatry. **when he makes all the stones of the altars:** The meaning is that Israel will not have cleared itself of guilt until it has abolished every cultic site outside Jerusalem, reducing them to rubble like powdered chalk. If the reference is to the community of Northern Israel, we must assume that they had been tempted into new forms of idolatry as a result of the confused political and social situation prevailing in that kingdom. **no Asherim or incense altars will remain standing:** The **Asherim** were wooden poles set up beside altars and dedicated to the goddess Asherah. Cf. *BHH*, I, cols. 136f. The **incense altars** (Heb. *ḥammānîm*) appear to have been small altars, cut from soft limestone and used in illicit cult-practices. Cf. 17:8; Ezek. 6:6, *BHH*, I, col. 64.

10. For the fortified city is solitary: Kaiser would regard vv. 10–11 as unconnected with the preceding, whereas Wildberger (and *NEB*) seek a sense connected with vv. 7–8(9). If Plöger and Wildberger are correct in seeing the context to lie in tensions between Jews and Samaritans, then the **fortified city** can best be identified with Samaria. However, we cannot place the verses as late as is required to make their picture of this city's destruction relate to the action of John Hyrcanus in destroying Samaria in 108 BC. If they are to be understood, not as a description of what has happened but of what is going to happen to Samaria, then they may emanate from a much earlier period. The alternative interpretation would be to take the reference as indefinite, and applicable to any of Israel's fortified cities, which are in such a state of ruin that they offer no protection to their inhabitants.

11. When its boughs are dry: The implication is that the city lies in ruins, but no one cares about this parlous condition, so that the inhabitants can scarcely deserve any better fate. **For this is a people without discernment:** This clause makes the allusion to the inhabitants of Samaria most plausible as a basis for the interpretation of the entire section. This description is in line with other expressions of Jewish disdain for the Samaritans, and bears close comparison with Ben Sira's description of them (Sir. 50:26). It could, admittedly, apply more widely than this, however, although the connection of vv. 6–11 with the incipient Samaritan problem remains the most attractive interpretation in view of earlier interest in the fate of the Northern Kingdom in Isaiah (cf. 17:1–6, and see below on 28:1–6). **therefore he who made them:** The emphasis upon God's creation of these people shows that they are to be regarded as Israelites—Jews who have become apostate, and now no longer receive the love and compassion that they might have expected from their Creator.

THE GREAT RETURN

27 : 12–13

That ch. 27 marks the close of a very distinctive redactional section of the book of Isaiah is shown by the fact that it has been rounded off by the inclusion here of a picture of the ultimate eschatological hope. We may compare 11 : 12–16; 35 : 1–10. The picture given here refers to the return of exiled Jews from Egypt and Assyria, and their return to Jerusalem. There is no indication at this stage that a very much wider Diaspora is envisaged, suggesting that this hope has been set out during the Persian, rather than the Hellenistic, period. We should not doubt that this short section has been intended to round off the whole eschatological hope given in chs. 24–27, and provides one of the important redactional touches which seek to give a unified message to the book as a whole. Cf. further, below, on 35 : 1–10.

12. **In that day from the river Euphrates:** The territorial region described represents the very 'idealised' limits of the Holy Land. Cf. 2 Kg. 24 : 7 for this region as controlled by the king of Babylon. **the Brook of Egypt** was the *Wadi 'El 'Arish* which marked the border between Israel and Egypt (Num. 34 : 5; Jos. 15 : 4, 47). The *RSV* rendering **will thresh out the grain** requires a slight emendation of the Heb. text (cf. *BHS*). The meaning is that Yahweh will shake out the loyal Jews from the apostates and Gentiles throughout the entire area once ruled by David (cf. Gen. 15 : 18; 1 Kg. 8 : 65; Ezek. 47 : 15ff.). It will then become a faithful and God-fearing kingdom, and nothing is said about the fate of the Gentiles. The implication is that they will be removed. **and you will be gathered one by one:** i.e. from the countries of exile to which you have been banished.

13. **And in that day a great trumpet will be blown:** V. 13 is evidently dependent on v. 12 and marks a separate redactional addition, as the repetition of the connective formula **and in that day** shows. The intention is evidently to bring out the spiritual and cultic side of the significance of the Great Return. It will not be simply a return to the political independence and greatness of the kingdom of David, but will be a spiritual return to worship the true God in his temple in Jerusalem. With this strong note of hope the various assurances for Israel's future among the nations contained in chs. 24–27 is brought to a close.

Prophecies Regarding Judah: chapters 28–33

With chs. 28–33 we return to an important collection of Isaianic prophecies which are, for the most part, to be regarded as authentic to Isaiah, and most of which relate to the later period of Hezekiah's reign and to the revolt against Sennacherib in the years 705–701. Their main theme, therefore, is that of Judah's rebellion against Assyria, and the reliance upon Egypt for political and military support in maintaining this revolt. Thus there is a pronounced anti-Egyptian element present in a number of sayings. The opening prophecy in 28 : 1–4 derives from an earlier period, being addressed to the Northern Kingdom of Israel, and its capital Samaria. It must therefore refer to the time before the fall of Samaria to Shalmaneser V in 722. The section also contains some important additions from the 'Josianic Redaction' of the seventh century BC. These are to be found in 29 : 5–9; 31 : 4–5, 8–9 and 32 : 1–5, and a few even later redactional additions appear, which were added after 587 BC; so 28 : 5–6, 13, etc. Overall, however, there is little doubt that we are presented in chs. 28–33 with a basic kernel of Isaiah's prophecies relating to the time of Hezekiah's revolt against Sennacherib. They have been combined, as an independent collection, with the Isaiah prophecies of chs. 1–23, and there can be little reason for disputing the claim of H. Barth (pp. 211–15) that 32 : 1–8 originally formed the conclusion of the 'Josianic Redaction' of the collection of Isaiah's prophecies.

THE DRUNKARDS OF EPHRAIM

28 : 1–6

The prophecy of vv. 1–4 is addressed to the **drunkards** of Ephraim, by which must be meant the citizens, and primarily the political leaders, of the Northern Kingdom of Israel. *Ephraim* must here indicate the rump state left by the Assyrians after the ending of the Syro-Ephraimite war in 732, so that this prophecy is to be dated between this event and the eventual siege and fall of Samaria to Shalmaneser V of Assyria in 722. Since there is no indication of any military conflict between Judah and Ephraim, but only a sense that Samaria is itself now threatened, the prophecy belongs to the period shortly before Samaria's eventual downfall. The date suggested by Donner, p. 77, of 724 BC, therefore, is most probable. The allusion in v. 2. must then be a reference to the Assyrians, and vv. 3–4 present a clear threat of its destruction.

What is unexplained about the prophecy is its occurrence in the collection of chs. 28–32. Vv. 7–13 also deal with drunkenness, but in this instance of the priests and prophets of Jerusalem at the time of Hezekiah's rebellion against Assyria. It is unlikely that the present prophecy was simply left over from the 'foreign nation' prophecies of chs. 13–23, or that the rebuke of drunkenness alone (as Fohrer) provides the reason for its placement here. More plausibly the redactor has sought to establish an indictment of 'all Israel' by prefacing this threat against Ephraim to a sequence of subsequent threats against Judah during Hezekiah's reign.

Vv. 5–6 form an additon, offering assurance and hope to the remnant of 'his people'. This must certainly be a post-587 expansion setting out the message of hope for the restoration of all the survivors of the kingdoms which had been shattered by Assyria, both Judah and Israel. It probably derives from a late sixth, or early fifth, century time when the hope of restoring a new united kingdom of Israel was still at its height.

28 : 1. Woe to the proud crown of the drunkards of Ephraim: The **proud crown** is certainly an allusion to the city of Samaria which stood at the head of a valley (cf. K. Elliger in *BHH*, III, cols. 1655–60). The prophet likens this to a garland of flowers (*ʿᵃteret̲*, 'garland, coronet', rather than **crown**) on the head of a reveller. Whether, in making the prophecy, Isaiah was able to address directly political leaders from the North, or whether he was simply informing the citizens of Judah of what he now saw as the inevitable fate of Ephraim can only be guessed at. **which is on the head of the rich valley:** The double use of the image of a garland of flowers, as a sign of a reveller's rejoicing and as a portrayal of the capital Samaria set at the head of a fertile valley, has occasioned difficulty for many commentators (cf. also v. 4). Fohrer would therefore remove the clause in both instances, whereas *NEB*, following the reading of 1QIsᵃ, would read 'dripping with perfumes' (Heb. *gē 'š̲ᵉmānîm*). Cf. G. R. Driver, 'Another Little Drink – Isaiah 28 : 1–22', *Words and Meanings. D. Winton Thomas Festschrift*, Cambridge, 1968, pp. 47f.

2. Behold the Lord has one who is mighty and strong: Several MSS and 1QIsᵃ read *yhwh* instead of *ʾᵃd̲ōnāy*, which is certainly to be accepted. The reference is undoubtedly to the Assyrians whom Isaiah prefers not to name overtly, but to describe by forceful imagery. The veiled language has presumably been chosen in order to retain the skilful effect of a *double entendre* of a rainstorm sweeping down the valley and ruining the flower garlands. We may compare 8 : 7ff. for a similar powerful, and artistically very carefully chosen, use of metaphor to describe a military threat. **he will cast down to the earth with violence:** The language retains the picture of the fate of the flower garlands with a more insidious warning of the fate that awaits those who wear them. Donner would omit **with violence** (Heb. *bᵉyād̲*) as a gloss. There is sufficient bitterness expressed against the rejoicing to suggest that the prophet may have been intentionally castigating revellers whom he, imaginatively, pictures celebrating their decision to withdraw their allegiance to Assyria.

3. The proud crown of the drunkards of Ephraim: The threat that has been made allusively in v. 2. is now made firm and clear. Samaria and its leaders are both doomed.

4. and the fading flower of its glorious beauty: It is probable that the second clause **which is on the head of the rich valley** should be deleted as a glossator's addition (so Fohrer, who removes it also from v. 1). *NEB* would read differently. The image of the **flower** which quickly fades is extended by that of the **first-ripe fig**, which quickly tempts the person who sees it, so that it is eaten the moment it is noticed. Just as quickly will Assyria destroy Ephraim.

5. In that day the LORD of hosts: In this and the following verse a redactor has interpolated a message of hope, which both makes use of the image of **a crown of glory** (better, 'garland of glory') as applicable to God's relationship to his people, and concerns itself with the fate of **the**

remnant of his people since this is to include survivors of the Northern Kingdom (cf. 10 : 20–23). The saying most probably dates from after the Babylonian exile, but gives little indication how it envisages the change in Israel's situation taking shape. If it were to be referred to a 'remnant' (Heb. *šᵉār*) of the Northern Kingdom only, it might possibly be dated earlier. It is certainly not (as Schoors) to be regarded as the 'community of the end-time', but neither (with G. F. Hasel, *The Remnant*, pp. 301–9) can its Isaianic origin be defended. Most likely here it is the broad mass of dispersed Jews who form the remnant of both Israel and Judah (cf. 11 : 16).

6. and a spirit of justice to him who sits in judgment may be a reference to the restored Davidic king who is to re-establish a righteous social order (cf. 11 : 1–5), or simply to the leading citizens responsible for the well-being of society, a duty which the drunkards of Ephraim had so blatantly neglected. **those who turn back the battle at the gate:** *HTOT* p. 185, would insert the preposition *l* before **those who**, although Schoors would achieve such a sense by regarding the *l* in *layyôšeḇ* as a 'double-duty' prefix. The redactor's purpose is to show that God is able to give the strength to the people's leaders which will enable them to fulfil the tasks demanded of them, which Ephraim's drunkards had been both unable and unwilling to do.

THE GODLESS PRIESTS AND PROPHETS

28 : 7–13

From time to time we find the great prophetic figures coming into conflict with other of the religious leaders of their people, either priests or prophets (cf. Am. 7 : 10–17; Hos. 6 : 9; Mic. 2 : 11; 3 : 6). Here Isaiah found himself in sharp conflict with certain priests and prophets of Jerusalem who had eaten and drunk too much at one of the great festival occasions of Jerusalem. Whether the celebration was a specifically cultic one, or whether it was held in celebration of a new political venture is not clear. Most probably the latter is correct, since, in their uncontrolled revelries, the priests and prophets mock Isaiah and his preaching (vv. 9–10). Isaiah then turns back their drunken mockeries upon their own head by warning of the way in which God himself will punish them (v. 11). The beginning of v. 7, which connects the rebuke with the preceding vv. 1–4 (but not vv 5–6) is certainly redactional. V. 13 also, which runs as a parallel to v. 11 and draws from 8 : 15, must also be the work of a redactor.

The occasion of the original threat can only be inferred, but there can be no doubt that v. 11 alludes to the coming of the Assyrians, so that the background is that of Hezekiah's rebellion against Sennacherib. Fohrer would place it earlier at the time of the Ashdodite rebellion (713–711), thereby linking it with ch. 20. However, we can much more plausibly relate the prophecy to the time of Hezekiah's revolt (so Donner, Eichrodt, Kaiser, Wildberger), but evidently not too close to 701, since there is no imminent danger to Jerusalem. Wildberger suggests that it may be the earliest of Isaiah's sayings condemning Hezekiah and the alliance with Egypt upon which his rebellion against

Sennacherib was based (Wildberger, III, p. 1057). Certainly a date about 703 BC appears likely.

7. These also reel with wine: The introductory **These also** connects the theme of the drunkenness of the priests and prophets of Jerusalem with that of the leaders of Ephraim in vv. 1–4. Almost certainly, therefore, the first line of v. 7 is the work of a redactor designed to connect together the threats against Ephraim and Jerusalem. **the priest and the prophet reel:** The linking together of the two religious offices suggests strongly that they were both accepted and accredited members of the Jerusalem temple personnel. In this case the prophets would have been official professional figures (cult-prophets) who were expected to give oracular utterance when called upon to do so. **they err in vision, they stumble in giving judgment.** The Heb. is uncertain, so that the *RSV*'s rendering rests on a rather questionable interpretation of the text. As it stands it implies that these officials are unable to perform their professional tasks competently. The prophets cannot properly interpret visions (Heb. *rô'ēh*), nor are they able to secure **judgment** (better, 'intercession', Heb. *pᵉlîliyyāh*; cf. P. A. H. de Boer, *Oudtestamentische Studiën* 3 (1953), p. 132). *NEB* margin, 'lose their way through tippling,' interprets differently and seeks to avoid reference to professional prophetic duties at all. Cf. G. R. Driver, *Words and Meanings*, p. 52. It is possible that *RSV*'s understanding may be supported if it is granted that Isaiah had been incensed by the content of certain prophecies given by these men. Since the occasion was that of Hezekiah's proposed withdrawal of allegiance to Assyria, backed up by the promise of Egyptian support, we may conjecture that these prophets had foretold a favourable outcome to this, and were now celebrating. In any case it seems unlikely that drunkenness alone occasioned Isaiah's rebuke, and what the drunken prophets said of Isaiah would support this (vv. 9–10).

8. For all tables are full: The tables were usually simple mats or rugs laid on the floor to provide a place on which food could be set. Their deplorable state is effectively described by Isaiah, which may have been all the more shocking if it took place in the courts of the Jerusalem temple.

9. Whom will he teach knowledge: This and the following verse represent a quotation by Isaiah of what the drunken priests and prophets are saying about him. Perhaps Isaiah even mimicked their slurred speech. The indication is clearly that Isaiah had already delivered some warning to them, either on account of their drunkenness, or more probably their prophecies, and now they are mocking him. Who does he think they are – little children? **and to whom will he explain the message:** Better 'Who will he make understand what they hear (Heb. *šᵉmû'āh*)?' The meaning is that Isaiah is simply wasting his time because those he is speaking to are too drunk to care. **Those who are weaned** retorts back at the prophet that the priests and prophets he is addressing are not children to be spoken to in this way. He is not entitled to speak to them as though they were so young as to need instruction about public behaviour.

10. For it is precept upon precept . . . line upon line: The meaning of the verse has been much discussed, and *RSV* is scarcely correct. The Heb. text repeats each of two short monosyllables four times (*ṣaw lāṣāw ṣaw lāṣāw qaw lāqāw qaw lāqāw*) which *RSV* translates as **precept** (*ṣaw* from *ṣwh*, 'to command') and **line** (*qaw* from *qwh*, 'to extend, stretch out'). *NEB* has 'harsh cries and raucous shouts', taking the words as onomatopoeic and representations of the din made by the revellers (cf. G. R. Driver, *Words and Meanings*, pp. 53f.). Several alternative suggestions have been made. The LXX understood the words to mean 'oppression' (Heb. *ṣar*) and 'hope' (from *qwh* in this sense). Others have suggested the words for 'filth' (Heb. *ṣēʾāh*) and 'vomit' (*qîʾ*). More plausibly Fohrer suggests the words are the sounds used for teaching children the letters of the alphabet (*ṣ* and *q*), so that the mocking revellers imitate the repetitive chanting of teacher and children together learning their alphabet. Thereby they hope to make Isaiah's rebuke sound foolish and childish. **here a little, there a little** is taken by *NEB* to be the cries of people calling out for more drinks. If the reference is to children learning, then it reflects their slow progress in the elementary stages. Kaiser's 'Boy, be careful', follows an earlier suggestion by G. R. Driver in *Semitic Writing from Pictograph to Alphabet*, p. 90, note 1.

11. Nay, but by men of strange lips: The reference is clearly to the harsh-sounding Assyrian language which the members of **this people** (cf. on 6 : 9) would soon be hearing. Oppressive and vindictive masters would soon be teaching them a lesson, and God's judgment on them would be their sufferings at the hand of these Assyrian invaders. Quite clearly the arrival of the Assyrians had now become a distinct possibility in view of the political situation which forms the background of the confrontation between prophet and prophets.

12. to whom he has said, 'This is rest.': The word translated **rest** (Heb. *mᵉnûḥāh*) is used in Dt. 12 : 9 as a description of the promised land as Israel's 'resting-place', which Schoors sees as the intended reference here. However, the allusion must be to Yahweh's policy of staying quiet under Assyrian vassaldom (cf. 30 : 15), and of maintaining a determined neutrality in the face of pressures to join an alliance against Assyria. Israel had been shown the way of **rest** and **repose** (Heb. *margeʿāh*), which would secure them against further bloodshed and destruction. Isaiah had consistently advocated such a policy of non-alignment, yet now the king had rejected it, and these priests and prophets had encouraged him in doing so. **yet they would not hear.** The comment marks the prophet's own consciousness that his message had been rejected yet again. Kaiser regards v. 12 as the work of a glossator, working between 598 and 587, but this is not necessary.

13. Therefore the word of the LORD will be to them: The verse is made up of a repetition of v. 10, coupled with a quotation from 8 : 15. It is the work of a later redactor who has applied the warning that God will speak to Judah through the language of foreigners in another direction. He has taken it to mean that God's word of prophecy will be treated by the people as a foreign language so that they will not heed it and consequently will fall and be snared by events. It is clearly a comment made *post eventum*, and must have been added after 587 to show why the people failed to heed the warnings that such a disaster would come.

THE REFUGE OF LIES

28 : 14–22

The section in vv. 14–22 is closely related in circumstance and subject matter with that which precedes in vv. 7–13, so that Donner (pp. 146–53) would take the two units together, although he clearly recognises a break after v. 13. However, this section should be regarded as addressed to a different group from that of the preceding. Here it is those **who rule this people in Jerusalem** (v. 14) who are the subject of Isaiah's threat. This must refer to the political leaders who are congratulating themselves on their successful negotiation of a treaty with a neighbouring power which will support them in their bid to throw off the yoke of Assyria. Cf. above on chs. 18–19. This treaty will lead only to defeat and disaster (v. 18). The treaty is described by the prophet as **a covenant with death** and **with Sheol** (vv. 15, 18), and this has led Kaiser, among others, to think of some kind of mysterious rite in which the political leaders believed themselves to have secured immortality by negotiating with, and warding off, the powers of death. Admittedly there were some rituals involving necromancy and such like, current in ancient Israel (cf. I Sam. 28), and Mot, the god of Death, figured prominently in Canaanite religion. Yet it is very unlikely that this is the prophet's meaning here. Rather he is using heavily satirical language to characterise the political treaty upon which the leaders pride themselves as an act of political folly which will lead to their doom and death. Who precisely this neighbouring power was cannot be satisfactorily determined, but most probably it was Egypt. Exactly why Egypt could be meaningfully described metaphorically as 'Death' (Mot) is not clear unless it was the apparent religious preoccupation of that country with death and the care of the dead. In any case it suited Isaiah's purpose to affirm that the treaty which promised military support to Judah was nothing other than a promise of doom.

This threatening aspect of the section is challenged to some extent by the interpretation of vv. 16–17*a* which appear to offer hope and assurance to Judah by asserting that God has set a sure foundation in Jerusalem. These verses appear to be affirming a promise, therefore, rather than a threat. Yet the difficulty here can be overcome by recognising that the prophet's purpose is to contrast God's way of salvation with the false way chosen by the leaders of Judah. The implication is that God had offered his security to Judah, but by seeking a foreign alliance, this had been decisively rejected. The very rock of their foundation, therefore, would become a rock of 'testing' (see below on v. 16). We may compare 8 : 14–15 for a similar turning by the prophet of the metaphor of a rock, used of God, into a warning of judgment.

The question of the authenticity of the section can only be decided once it is recognised that certain glosses have been made. V. 19 consists of two separate glosses, easily identifiable, which attempt an extended meaning of the prophet's words. Similarly v. 22 is a gloss which interprets the threat in an apocalyptic eschatological fashion as a warning of judgment coming upon the whole earth (rather than **land**). V. 20, which consists of a proverbial saying, is more difficult to evaluate, since it could be regarded as a kind of proverbial comment on the situation threatened in v. 18, emanating from the prophet himself. More probably it is a redactor's comment. So too v. 21, which comments upon the strangeness of God's act of judgment, may not derive from Isaiah, although Wildberger points out that no completely compelling reason exists for denying either vv. 20 or 21 to the prophet. For the rest the complex use of metaphor in vv. 14–18 is typically Isaianic and its authenticity to him cannot be in doubt. The question of date is impossible of certain resolution, and J. Lindblom, 'Der Eckstein in Jes. 28, 16', *Festschrift S. Mowinckel*, Oslo, 1955, pp. 123–32, would place the section early in Isaiah's ministry. However, much greater likelihood exists in linking the prophecy with the revolt against Sennacherib in 705–701, and most probably to the early negotiations with Egypt and other powers for the withdrawal of allegiance to Assyrian suzerainty.

14. Therefore hear the word of the LORD, you scoffers: The **scoffers** are evidently not the priests and prophets of v. 7, and it is a redactor who has linked the two sections together by adding **Therefore**. Those addressed are the political leaders **who rule this people in Jerusalem**. Once again the term **this people** contains a hint of divine rejection and rebuff. Fohrer's suggestion that 'rulers' should be read as 'proverb-makers' (*mšl*, II, 'to speak in proverbs') is ingenious, but unconvincing. It is the leaders who are pleased with themselves because they regard their treaty promising military aid as a boon to the citizens they represent.

15. We have made a covenant with death: The prophet is putting words into the mouths of the rulers in a heavily ironic fashion. What they say is full of assurance; the treaty is a 'cast-iron guarantee' of protection and security. In reality, however, the prophet sees it as precisely the opposite – a sentence of death. It is most likely that the reference is to the treaty with Egypt, condemned elsewhere by Isaiah (e.g. 30 : 1–5), but possibly with some other neighbouring power. The prophet's meaning would not be lost on his hearers who would be full of talk about their **covenant** (treaty). Popular association of Egypt and Egyptian religion with the cult of the dead may have been widely spoken of in Judah. **With Sheol we have an agreement:** The word **agreement** (Heb. *ḥôzeh*) is a unique occurrence, but its meaning cannot be in doubt (cf. *K–B*, I, p. 289, and *ḥāzût* in v. 18). An emendation to the more common *ḥesed* ('steadfast love') is therefore not to be followed. **when the overwhelming scourge passes through:** The **overwhelming scourge** (Heb. *šôṭ šôṭēp*; *Qᵉre'* and 1QIsᵃ) was the desert rainstorm, which Canaanite tradition identified with the stormgod Hadad. Cf. H. Gese, 'Der strömende Geissel des Hadad und Jes. 28, 15 und 18', *Festschrift K. Galling*, Tübingen, 1970, pp. 127–34. **for we**

have made lies our refuge: By putting such words in a purported quotation of what the rulers claimed, the prophet was caricaturing their trust, but hinting also at the disastrous consequences it would have. To rely upon a shelter which is inadequate is to expose oneself to the full fury of the storm. The **lies** are apparently the assurances of support and protection contained in the treaty which had been made.

16. therefore thus says the Lord GOD: The words are taken by Kaiser to be part of the original prophetic saying, linking up with v. 17*b*, where the pronouncement of Yahweh's punishment is made. What then comes in vv. 16, 17*a* establishes the condition which makes such a sentence inevitable: '*Because* I am laying in Zion . . . *then* hail will sweep away . . . '. **Behold I am laying in Zion for a foundation:** The ptc. *yôsēd* is to be read with the ancient versions of 1QIs[b]. **a stone, a tested stone:** The metaphor has given rise to a very extended discussion over the question of what type of **stone** is actually meant. For discussion cf. M. Tsevat, *TWAT*, I, p. 591; J. Lindblom, *op. cit.*, p. 126, and H. Wildberger, *comm.* II, pp. 1066f. Suggestions have ranged between 'capstone', 'foundation stone' and 'testing stone'. Both etymologically and on the grounds of context the last seems the most probable. It is a stone by which the measurements and shape of other stones is tested. *BDB* suggests 'tested stone', whereas LXX has 'costly stone'. The prophet's meaning would then be that God has already established in Jerusalem himself as the 'rock' and defence of his people (cf. 8, 14f.) by which all other guarantees of security are to be tested. Since the treaty cannot comply with this condition, it stands rejected by God and becomes a source of false trust. **He who believes will not be in haste:** Better 'will not waver' (*NEB*). The prophet appears to be citing an inscription cut into such a stone, with an intentional *double entendre* on his part: 'He who builds firmly ('has faith') will not waver.'

17. And I will make justice the line: The prophet extends his architectural imagery by introducing two further metaphors of the measuring **line** and the **plummet**. This is preferable to seeing here (with Kaiser) a secondary exegesis of the 'line' of vv. 10, 13. By showing how God tests the firmness of his people's building, the prophet makes it very plain that they will not be able to pass so stringent a test (cf. Am. 7 : 7–9). They stand condemned by the very security (God) whom they have so foolishly rejected for a worthless treaty.
and hail will sweep away the refuge of lies: The prophet now pronounces his judgment against his people, returning to the imagery of the rainstorm of v. 15. Just as a violent storm sweeps away all flimsy shelters, so will this treaty be shown up as a lie when the storm (the king of Assyria) comes.

18. Then your covenant with death will be annulled: The verse is made complex by the combining of two images, that of a **covenant with death** and of a rainstorm, but the threatening intent of the message is perfectly clear. His people have looked for protection in the wrong place, and they will find out its inadequacy when the time comes to use it.

19. As often as it passes through: The first half of the verse is a gloss which endeavours to generalise upon the specific content of the

Isaianic warning. The **scourge** (rainstorm = Assyria) will pass through regularly, but is here understood as any kind of misfortune to which the people will be continually subject, and from which they will have no protection after having rejected God. **and it will be sheer terror to understand the message:** This is a second gloss, aimed at warning the reader that the content of the message (Heb. *šᵉmûʿāh*) will be awe-inspiring and fearful. Evidently the **message** is an allusion back to v. 9, but is here applied to the prophetic word as a whole, interpreted as an apocalyptic disclosure of God's plan.

20. For the bed is too short to stretch oneself on it: The saying is obviously a simple proverbial one to the effect that in certain conditions, there can be no rest. Whether it is from Isaiah or not is almost impossible to establish, and it merely comments upon the threat of v. 18. Most likely it is a further attempt at drawing more generalised conclusions from the prophet's message to a specific situation.

21. For the LORD will rise up as on Mount Perazim: Wildberger would defend the authenticity of this verse to Isaiah, although this cannot be regarded as certain. The references are to David's defeat of the Philistines **on Mount Perazim** (2 Sam. 5:17–25) and to Joshua's victory in the **valley of Gibeon** (Jos. 10:10–15). **to do his deed – strange is his deed:** God's action will be 'foreign', or **strange** (Heb. *zār*), because it will involve his punishment of his own people.

22. Now therefore do not scoff: This is a late redactor's comment addressed to the reader not to **scoff** at God's word as the rulers became 'scoffers' (v. 14). The message that is deduced from the prophecy is that God has issued a decree of destruction upon the whole 'earth' (rather than **upon the whole land**), which must ring strangely on human ears. Yet this apocalyptic eschatology is how the later post-exilic age discerned prophecy as still having a message for it.

THE WISDOM OF THE FARMER

28:23–29

The parable of the work of the farmer, used as an analogy to explain the action of God, has aroused a great deal of discussion, and has witnessed wide dissension among commentators regarding its authenticity. A considerable number of scholars have acclaimed its authenticity, including Duhm, Skinner, Schoors, Wright, R. B. Y. Scott, Fohrer, and also the special studies of J. W. Whedbee, *Isaiah and Wisdom*, pp. 51–68 and W. Dietrich, *Jesaja und die Politik*, pp. 124–6. Most recently Wildberger (II, p. 1087) has defended its Isaianic origin. Against this, T. K. Cheyne, K. Marti, R. H. Pfeiffer, and more recently O. Kaiser and H. Barth, p. 211, have denied it to the prophet, Barth ascribing it to the work of the 'Assyrian Redactor' of Josiah's reign, whilst Kaiser sees in it a piece of apocalyptic eschatology. In view of such dissension it is obviously necessary to proceed cautiously. The fact that the parable is set out in a didactic form, reminiscent of Wisdom compositions, cannot, of itself, be used to support, or weaken, the claim to an Isaianic origin. Similarly arguments based on vocabulary, especially when used in such a distinctive context as this, can have no substantial weight. The issue must depend ultimately on questions of content, and the relevance of this to Isaiah's own preaching.

On this basis the interpretation of the parable can be considered first, and its relationship to the preaching of Isaiah deduced from this. The theme of the parable of the farmer's actions during the agricultural seasons is quite clear. The farmer, in working his fields, has a time for ploughing, a time for sowing and a time for harvesting; there is great variety in his actions. The implication is that this is also true of God, who does not always judge and punish his people, but has a time to heal and restore them. The parable is therefore levelled against critics of Isaiah's preaching who complain that it is inconsistent. God does not always act towards his people in a uniform manner. However, it is not only the inconsistency that is complained of, but the parable is quite explicitly aimed at showing that the time for judgment is past (ploughing, crushing, vv. 24, 28). The purpose, therefore, is to argue from the farming analogy that God's message is not only of judgment but also of salvation. In fact the parable seems to be directly designed to soften the implication of v. 21 that God will execute a **strange work** of judgment against his people. It shows that this must come to an end, and in turn be followed by a time of salvation. Wildberger, Barth and Kaiser are, therefore, all in agreement on this point, even though they disagree about assigning it to Isaiah. Wildberger would so so and would align the parable with the claim that, after having threatened Hezekiah for his rebellion against Sennacherib, Isaiah came subsequently to affirm that the Assyrian attack on Jerusalem would fail (14 : 24–27; 17 : 12–14; 29 : 5–8, etc.). The parable, therefore, belongs to the time of 701, and serves to defend Isaiah's change of attitude at that time. Yet we have seen that these passages which threaten the Assyrians do not come from Isaiah himself, but from the Josianic Redactor of the prophecies (Barth's AR). There is therefore much plausibility in linking, as Barth does, this parable also with the work of the Josianic Redactor. It is designed to show that God can both judge and save his people as part of a single consistent purpose. It is impossible, however, to place the emphasis upon salvation, which forms the basis of this parable, into the known pattern of Isaiah's preaching. It already presupposes their compilation into a written collection and serves to elaborate upon their meaning.

23. Give ear and hear my voice: The author adopts the distinctive idiom and didactic approach of the Wisdom teacher.

24. Does he who ploughs for sowing plough continually: We should delete **for sowing** (cf. *BHS*) as a rather superfluous addition. The force of the parable rests on the analogy between certain farming actions: ploughing, harrowing, threshing, and judgment. Isaiah's prophecies appear to be full of warnings of judgment and threat against God's own people (cf. especially 28 : 14–22). The point of the parable is to show that these actions have their place, but are necessary for a time only. Thus both of the questions in this verse are rhetorical and imply the answer 'No!'.

25. does he not scatter dill: The various crops mentioned – **dill, cummin, wheat, barley** and **spelt**—were the most common in use in the small peasant farming communities of Judah. **and put in wheat in rows:** The words **in rows** are omitted by LXX, which also lacks **in its proper place** after **barley**. Both omissions are probably original, since the line is over-long. For agriculture in Old Testament times, cf. E. W. Heaton, *Everyday Life in Old Testament Times*, London, 1956.

26. his God teaches him: This comment provides an interesting sidelight on the belief that the age-old wisdom of agriculture, the sources of which lay far beyond the horizons of remembered history, were to be traced back to God. Like the gift of the secret of fire from heaven, so the knowledge of agriculture was considered as bestowed by God. In Canaanite religion it is abundantly clear that agriculture and religion were closely intertwined so that many agricultural acts had a ritual-cultic significance. Cf. F. F. Hvidberg, *Weeping and Laughter in the Old Testament*, Leiden/Copenhagen, 1962, pp. 50ff.

27. Dill is not threshed with a threshing sledge: The parable moves on to argue that even specific actions like threshing have to be undertaken with due regard for the crop, so that this is not spoiled by too heavy an action. Just as there are different seasons for the growing of crops, so also are there different techniques for dealing with them.

28. Does one crush bread grain: The use of rhetorical questions in relation to the harsher actions of farming shows that the softer, gentler tasks are also needed.

29. This also comes from the LORD of hosts: The meaning of the various questions is clear: there is a time for gentler, 'saving' work on the farm, and so also is this true of God in his dealings with Israel.

THE SIEGE OF THE CITY OF DAVID

29 : 1–8

The address of this prophecy to **Ariel** has occasioned much comment on account of the precise explanation and origin of this name, by which Jerusalem is certainly meant. It pictures God himself laying siege to the city, as once before David had done, and reducing it to abject weakness and helplessness (v. 4). Then suddenly the picture changes with v. 5, and the foes are no longer the agents of Yahweh, but have become his enemies. They are to be threatened and shattered by him, when he visits them with thunder, earthquake and storm. How this change is to be accounted for has occasioned very great difficulty. Fohrer sees it as a conditional change, affirming what would happen if Jerusalem repents and trusts Yahweh, whilst Wildberger defends its integrity and authenticity to Isaiah by arguing that, when Jerusalem was besieged by Sennacherib in 701, then Isaiah turned his message round to affirm the overthrow of the Assyrian attackers (cf. 14:24–27; and see below on chs. 36–37). However, such a view of a sudden and dramatic change on Isaiah's part must be rejected, and the recognition made that only vv. 1–4 are an authentic prophecy of Isaiah's. It must derive from the period 705–701, probably not too far from 701 itself, when the possibility of an Assyrian siege of Jerusalem began to appear likely. The prophet is then affirming that Yahweh will be the chief actor behind this siege, working through the Assyrians to punish his people for their faithlessness. Vv. 5–8 have then been added by the Josianic Redactor, who has built them up out of traditional imagery of a divine theophany in a storm. It is pointless to speculate whether the original Isaianic threat has been shortened to make room for this new redactional ending. The aim of the redaction has been to interpret the failure of Sennacherib to take Jerusalem in 701 as a victory for Yahweh and a mark of his providential purpose for Jerusalem, Judah and the Davidic monarchy. See below on chs. 36–37. More than this, the redactional addition develops out of its interpretation of what happened in 701 a broader theme, or doctrine, of the inviolability of Mount Zion, which will be invincible, not just against Assyria, but against 'all the nations' that dare to threaten her (v. 7). This provided the basis for the short-lived 'Zion Tradition', which proved so disastrous a hope in the face of the later threat from Assyria (see below on chs. 38–39). Only vv. 1–4 come from Isaiah, therefore, and vv. 5–7(8) are from the redactor, or more probably redactional school, which edited and developed a contemporary message on the basis of Isaiah's prophecies during Josiah's reign (640–609 BC). V. 8, which is in prose, appears to have been added later still.

29 : 1. Ho Ariel, Ariel, the city where David encamped: The oracle begins with the cry 'Woe . . . ' (Heb. *hôy*), and immediately identifies the subject threatened. *RSV*'s **Ho** is therefore misleading and ambiguous, since the intention is explicitly to threaten Jerusalem. The name **Ariel** evidently refers to Jerusalem, and the most probable interpretation is that it is a reference to the altar of burnt-offering in the temple. Cf. 2 Sam. 23 : 20; Isa. 33 : 7 and Ezek. 43 : 15f., and see W. F. Albright, *JBL* 39 (1920), pp. 137–42 and *Archaeology and the Religion of Israel*. 2nd edn, Baltimore, 1953, p. 151. The name, which 1QIs^a reads *'ᵃrû'el* appears to mean 'altar hearth' (cf. Akk. *arallu*). In any case the reference is to David's capture of Jerusalem from the Jebusites (2 Sam. 5 : 6–10). Kaiser interprets **encamped** to mean no more than 'took up his abode', but more probably a more explicit allusion to David's siege and capture of the city is intended. Jerusalem had not fallen in battle since David's time, and the prophet now intends to affirm that the city, which was proud of its strong defences, was not impregnable. The reference to **Ariel** ('altar-hearth') may also have had a deliberately threatening overtone. **let the feasts run their round:** The meaning is that, no matter how zealously the inhabitants attend to their religious services and duties, they will not succeed in buying off God's hostility towards themselves.

2. Yet I will distress Ariel: Better, 'Now then I will lay siege to . . .'. The adversative translation of the Heb. *waw* as **yet** is misplaced, since v. 1 is already threatening. God will 'lay siege to' (Heb. *ṣûq*) Jerusalem through the armies of Sennacherib. The prophetic identification of God with a human agency is a common idiom, which is contrasted with the image of v. 6, where God is portrayed as acting more directly through natural phenomena. How close the situation en-visaged was to that of 701 is not made evident, but probably the possi-bility of an Assyrian siege of Jerusalem had now arisen. In fact only the initial preparations for such a siege appear to have been made before Hezekiah surrendered. **and she shall be to me like an Ariel**: Probably we should read 'And you shall be . . . ' (cf. *BHS*). The prophet makes a grim play on the threatening aspect of the mystery of the name **Ariel** by warning that the entire city will become an altar-hearth (*NEB* 'fiery altar'), in which the inhabitants will become the sacrifice.

3. And I will encamp against you round about: This marks a further development in the idea of 'encamping' by threatening siege. Instead of **round about** (Heb. *kaddûr*) some MSS and LXX read 'like David' (*k^{a}dāwîd*), but the allusion is in any case sufficiently clear. **and will besiege you with towers**: The techniques of a military siege are described quite fully, and suggest that the prophecy comes from a time when the Assyrians were already in Judah, so that the probability of an attack on Jerusalem was evident. Nevertheless a siege was almost inevitable against a fortified city like Jerusalem, so that Isaiah was not only concerned that it would happen, but that his hearers should recognise that it was God who was bringing it about.

4. Then deep from the earth you shall speak: The verse is cryptic in its meaning, and yet remains central to the understanding of the relationship of vv. 1–4 to 5–7. Fohrer understands it to express the situation of humbled penitence which will be forced on the inhabitants of Jerusalem, so that vv. 5–7(8) convey the form which the deliverance could take, but which will be conditional upon this penitent attitude. Barth, pp. 184–90, however, takes vv. 5–7 in quite a different way, with the inhabitants inside Jerusalem being Yahweh's enemies whom he will attack. We must, however, reject the attempt to understand vv 5–7(8) in a threatening sense, and, with this, recognise that it is an addition to vv. 1–4. V. 4 itself then conveys the threat of humiliated devastation which will be inflicted on Jerusalem as a result of the siege. The inhabitants of the city will be reduced to grovelling ghosts of their former selves. They will be brought down (*špl*) and humbled (*šḥḥ*), which can only be understood in an adverse sense. **your voice shall come from the ground**: The currency of various necromantic rites may have encouraged the prophet to use such a simile. In any case there is a subtle allusion to death and abject weakness and humiliation in such a comparison. However the siege was finally resolved, the prophet makes clear that it would be disastrous for the inhabitants of Jerusalem. It must be considered possible that the prophet's original threat may have elaborated more fully on the ruin that would come to Jerusalem. If so, this has been curtailed to make room for a more positive estimate of the outcome now given in vv. 5–8.

5. But the multitude of your foes: The MT has 'foreigners' (Heb. *zārayik*), but this must be read with IQIs^a and the ancient versions as **foes** (Heb. *zēdayik*). Vv. 5–7 derive from the Josianic Redactor of Isaiah's prophecies and look back upon what took place in 701 BC, as a sign of God's plan to protect Jerusalem 'for his own sake and for the sake of his servant David' (cf. 37 : 35). v. 7 then establishes from this a broader doctrine of the 'inviolability' of Jerusalem in the face of a threat from all nations, and this has been further elaborated in v. 8 in a semi-apocalyptic fashion. **like passing chaff:** Cf. 17 : 13 for a similar comparison. **And in an instant, suddenly:** Just how the overthrow of the Assyrian attackers would be brought about is not made clear, but the emphasis upon the divine action which would accomplish this has led to great stress upon the extraordinary suddenness of the event.

6. **you will be visited by the LORD of hosts:** The imagery of God's action is taken from the traditional imagery of theophanies. Cf. J. Jeremias, *Theophanie. Die Geschichte einer alttestamentliche Gattung* (*WMANT* 10), Neukirchen–Vluyn, 1965, p. 71. The use of this theophanic imagery here is to stress that the action will be the direct work of God, not mediated through human agents.

7. **And the multitude of all the nations:** Vv. 5 and 6 have been composed as a retrospective interpretation of the preservation of Jerusalem from destruction in 701 as a result of Hezekiah's surrender. Now v. 7, which may have been added later, broadens this into a future assurance that all nations that threaten Jerusalem will be confronted by Yahweh, protecting his city and people. This gave rise to a central feature of what has come to be called the 'Zion Tradition' (cf. J. Schreiner, *Zion-Jerusalem. Jahwes Königsitz*, pp. 191ff.), but which must be seen rather as a special development of a feature of the ancient royal Davidic traditions. Cf. J. J. M. Roberts, *JBL* 92 (1973), pp. 329–44. **all that fight against her and her stronghold:** Better read 'all their garrisons' (reading *muṣṣābeyha*, or *ṣubbeyha*; cf. *HTOT*, p. 185) and 'siege works' (*mᵉṣūrṭeyhaā*; cf. Vulg. and 1QIsᵃ). They will disappear as suddenly as a dream passes out of the mind.

8. **As when a hungry man dreams he is eating:** This elaboration of the comparison with a dream comes rather prosaically after the vivid imagery of vv. 5–7 and is a secondary elaboration of it by a later redactor (so Marti, Fohrer, Schoors, Wildberger, Barth, p. 186). Barth would identify this with his 'Assyrian Redaction' of Josiah's time, but it must probably be regarded as of later origin than this. It is set out in prose (*RSV* attempts to adapt to a poetic form), and is most probably to be seen as a post-exilic eschatological reinterpretation of the protection theme of v. 7, asserting that ultimately **Mount Zion** would be triumphant over all nations.

THREE SHORT SAYINGS CONDEMNING JUDAH

29 : 9-16

There now follow three short independent sayings in vv. 9–10, 13–14 and 15–16, the first of which has been expanded by a later redactor in vv. 11–12, as the prose character of the verses confirms. The authenticity of all three of the sayings from Isaiah has been widely maintained by almost all commentators, and this is to be followed. They condemn the leaders of Jerusalem for the pursuit of policies which are contrary to Yahweh, and this must certainly be taken to refer to the protracted

series of negotiations between Hezekiah, Egypt, and other neighbouring powers, in the period 705–701. Most probably they come from an
early stage of such negotiations, and sharply condemn the Jerusalem
politicians for their arrogance and lack of discernment in what they
propose. They have been blinded, and all their senses numbed, by
Yahweh (v. 10); their minds are closed to any understanding of God (v.
13), and in their folly and embarrassment they even think that they can
hide their plans from God (v. 15).

(i) 29:9-12 *The Spirit of Deep Sleep.*

9. Stupefy yourselves and be in a stupor: The text requires a slight
emendation. Cf. Hab. 1:5 for the verb (Heb. *tmh* in hithpa'el) meaning
'to be dumbfounded'. The imperative is heavily ironic, and the idea is
of men making decisions which only lead them on into greater confusion and disaster. Cf. 6:9. The people addressed are not identified,
but must be the political leaders of Jerusalem, no doubt including the
king himself. The occasion is the negotiations with neighbouring
powers for rebellion against Assyria. **Be drunk, but not with wine:** The
MT reads the verbs as indicatives, but these must be emended to
imperatives, as *RSV* and cf. *HTOT*, p. 185.

10. For the LORD has poured out upon you: The policy is viewed as
so disastrous that the prophet avows that its only explanation must be
that God himself has deprived these people of their senses, and induced
in them a deep intellectual torpor. Possibly by such bitter words the
prophet hoped to awaken in his hearers an awareness of the consequences of what they proposed. The two explanatory appositions, **the
prophets** to **your eyes** and **the seers** to **your heads**, are explanatory
glosses introduced by a later redactor who has mistakenly understood
the imagery as allegorical. He has made the original rebuke of the
political leaders into a rebuke of Jews who do not pay attention to the
(mysterious) message of the prophets.

11. And the vision of all this: Vv. 11 and 12 are clearly dependent on
vv. 9f. and come from a redactor of the post-exilic age (Wildberger
suggests fifth century BC). They urge greater attention to the message
that the prophet had given by complaining that the people neither
listen to it, nor understand it. It has become like a book that is sealed,
which a literate person refuses to unseal and which is in any case
useless to the illiterate. The **vision of all this** must refer particularly to
the promise of Jerusalem's deliverance in the face of a threat from 'all
nations'. This was evidently now interpreted eschatologically as a
promise of the final exaltation and triumph of the city (as in v. 8). Those
who refuse to accept this eschatological interpretation of the **vision**
(message) are accused of having succumbed to the 'spirit of deep sleep'
(v. 10). The addition is an instructive illustration of the way in which
prophecy was revitalised and re-interpreted in the post-exilic age, and
increasingly understood in an apocalyptic eschatological fashion.

(ii) 29 : 13–14 Lip-service.

13. Because this people draw near with their mouth: Vv. 13 and 14
form an independent saying from that of vv. 9–10, but from a closely
similar time and situation. Their derivation is almost entirely uncontested. They add yet a further perspective to the knowledge of the deep
gulf which separated Isaiah's advocacy of continued submission to
Assyrian rule from Hezekiah's intention of attempting to break free
from it. The king and people evidently reasoned that, if they trusted in
Yahweh and remained loyal to him, he could then be relied upon to
uphold their cause. Isaiah firmly rejects such hopes by denouncing
them as a false piety. No matter how earnestly they prayed and performed their religious duties, because their intentions were opposed to
God, they could not expect his help. The whole of v. 13 rebuts the claim
that the cultus of Jerusalem, including that of its temple, could save the
people from the wrath of God if they disobeyed him. It is important,
however, to note the context in which such a criticism of cultic religion
appears. It is not a criticism of religious rites *per se*, but as a cloak to
hide a deeper moral disobedience. **while their hearts are far from
home:** The heart was not the seat of the emotions, but of the intellect,
in Hebrew thought. Cf. H. W. Wolff, *Anthropology of the Old Testament*, London, 1974, pp. 40ff; F. Stolz, *THAT*, I, cols. 861–7. The
precise occasion in which this saying was given can only be guessed at,
but it must belong to the period 705–701. W. Dietrich, p. 174, would
locate it at a time close to the actual siege of Jerusalem in 701, when the
people were beginning to consider their fate after the Assyrian army
had entered Judah.

14. therefore, behold, I will again do marvellous things: The
words **with this people** are almost certainly a later addition, although
they accurately interpret the reference. The actions of God are 'marvels'
(Heb. *pele'*) and he 'acts marvellously' (Heb. *haplē'*) – descriptions
which Israelite tradition associated with God's might acts of deliverance for Israel, Cf. Jos. 3 : 1; Ps. 98 : 1, etc., and see *THAT*, II, cols.
413–20. It could also describe his actions through individuals like
Abraham (Gen. 18 : 14). This saving significance of God's action is now
entirely turned round by the prophet to affirm its opposite effect. God
will act, but instead of leading to Israel's deliverance and freedom from
the yoke of Assyria, it will lead to their destruction and further submission to it. **and the wisdom of their wise men shall perish:** The **wise
men** here must be a reference to the counsellors and political advisors
of the king who had encouraged him to undertake his anti-Assyrian
policy. Only when it failed, totally and tragically, would men come to
realise that it was not based on true wisdom at all, but was merely the
misguided gamble of irresponsible men. Cf. W. McKane, *Prophets and
Wise Men (SBT* 44), 1965, pp. 70f.

(iii) 29 : 15–16 Hiding from God

15. Woe to those who hide deep from the LORD their counsel: Vv.

15-16 form the last of the sequence of three Isaianic sayings condemning the ruling classes in Jerusalem for their revolt against Sennacherib.
V. 16 carries echoes of 10:15 and simply comments upon the invective
of v. 15 without adding any additional threat. Vermeylen (I, p. 404),
therefore regards v. 16 as a redactor's expansion of v. 15, which is
complete in itself. This may indeed be so, although there is nothing
that decisively precludes the acceptance of v. 16 as Isaiah's own comment upon the mentality of the rulers he condemns in v. 15. The
political leaders had sought to keep hidden from the general public,
and therefore from Isaiah also, the policies they had agreed upon.
Kaiser relates the rebuke to the time when the Assyrian armies were in
Judah and Hezekiah sent a mission to the Egyptian Pharaoh Shabako to
ask for assistance against Sennacherib. Such a plan necessarily required
secrecy, which would have been hard to maintain. The action is seen by
Isaiah as a further sign of the folly of such a policy, and even hints that
the secrecy is a mark of the shamefacedness of those who have originated the plan. **whose deeds are in the dark:** The prophet hints at the
nefarious nature of what had been planned by such a description of the
secrecy surrounding it. However much they try to hide their decision,
they must know that they cannot hide it from God, to whom all things
are known.

16. You turn things upside down: The Heb. is obscure and has
occasioned uncertainty. *RSV* follows MT, taking the noun as *hepek*,
'perversity, contrariness'; cf. Ezek. 16:34. (1QIs[a] reads slightly differently). Various emendations have been put forward: Ehrlich,
Randglossen, IV, p. 105, proposes 'Is he (i.e. God) like you?'
(*he^{e}kākem*), whereas *BHS* follows T. H. Robinson, *ZAW* 49 (1931), p.
322, in suggesting 'as flasks?' (*hak^{e}pakkim*). It is preferable to retain
MT, although recognising the uncertainty. The verse elaborates upon
the folly of the politicians and leaders in desperately trying to bolster
up their policy of rebellion, when it is that policy itself which is wrong.
They cannot devise plans contrary to God. **Shall the potter be regarded
as the clay;** The argument occurs earlier with reference to the Assyrians. Man is a creature, and he must obey the laws imposed by his
creatureliness. He cannot act independently of God, or still less in
defiance of him. What folly, therefore, to imagine that secrecy could
improve the chances of their disastrous plan. **that the thing made
should say:** Instead of a repetition of **should say** (Heb. *'āmar*), 1QIs[a]
reads 'clay' (*hēmer*); i.e. 'that a thing of clay should say', which is clearly
correct.

THE COMING AGE OF SALVATION

29:17-24

These verses present a marked contrast to the threats which have
preceded it and set out a broad picture of reassurance and hope, focus-
ing on a coming age of salvation. In this the poor and oppressed will
find joy and freedom; the ruthless and tyrannical will be restrained, and
the survivors of Israel will maintain a glad and unwavering piety. In

spite of a few attempts to defend an Isaianic, pre-exilic, origin
(Eichrodt, Hertzberg would seek to trace an Isaianic nucleus), the
whole section must be ascribed to the post-exilic age. Vermeylen, I, p.
406, finds in it traces of elements from chs. 40–55 and 56–66, as well as
from Deuteronomy, but more certainly than this the whole perspective
is that of the great eschatological turning-point which was awaited at
the end-time. The affinities are with chs. 24–27, and this is an expression of post-exilic eschatology, closely bordering on apocalyptic. The
precise date of its origin is difficult to define, but most probably it is
that of the early fifth century, when the immediate hopes of a political
restoration after the exile were being couched in more and more
extreme forms. The section has been included here in order to round
off the threatening import of chs. 28–29, and the specific threat to
Jerusalem and its leaders, with a more enduring word of hope. For
those living under judgment, in which ancient prophecies had been
fulfilled, the message was not one of ultimate condemnation, but a call
to repentance in expectation that a great turning-point would soon
come in which the ancient hopes of Israel would find fulfilment. Cf. my
essay 'Patterns in the Prophetic Canon', *Canon and Authority*, ed. G.
W. Coats and B. O. Long, Philadelphia, 1977, pp. 42–55.

17. Is it not yet a very little while: Cf. 32 : 15 for a similar emphasis
upon the extraordinary fertility of the earth in the time of salvation. Not
only will the political frustrations for Israel be removed when God acts
to deliver her, but the entire order of nature will reflect the divine
blessing and goodness. Ancient ideas concerning God's power as the
giver of life and fertility have been adapted to an eschatological perspective. **until Lebanon shall be turned into a fruitful field:** Probably
here **Lebanon** should be understood as more than just the high
wooded mountain range to the north of Israel, and be seen as representative of all forest land. The emphasis upon the reversed roles of
woodland and grassland is strange; cf. *NEB*'s 'Lebanon goes back to
grassland'; but the intention would appear to be to stress the increased
fertility of the earth in the time of salvation. Cf. 35 : 2.

18. In that day the deaf shall hear: The words should probably be
taken in their literal sense that, when the age of salvation dawns,
physical handicaps will be overcome so that the **deaf** will hear and the
blind see. It will be a kind of 'new creation'. J. Skinner, however,
would take it metaphorically of the spiritually blind and deaf; cf. 43 : 8,
whilst Kaiser would link it directly with the warning of 29 : 10f. concerning those who do not accept the eschatological interpretation of
prophecy. Certainly 35 : 5, in a section which has many affinities with
that here, understands the removal of deafness and blindness literally,
but it may be that the present author has adapted this promise in a
metaphorical way. In any case it must be borne in mind that the theme
of 'deafness' and 'blindness' in the Isaiah tradition may have originated
with 6 : 10 and subsequently been adapted in more than one sense.

19. The meek shall obtain fresh joy in the LORD: The **meek** (Heb.
ʿaⁿāwîm) are the afflicted and oppressed, rather than those who simply
do not assert themselves. It becomes an almost technical term for the

afflicted pious community of the faithful, who suffer under oppressors and 'violent men' (Heb. *ʿarîṣîm*). **the poor among men** Heb. *ʾebyônê ʾādām*) are the economically impoverished, but increasingly in the post-exilic age the factors of economic impoverishment and oppression of the pious appear to have become linked together.

20. For the ruthless shall come to naught: The **ruthless** is literally the 'tyrant, oppressor' (Heb. *ʿārîṣ*) who takes advantage of the poor. The **scoffer** (Heb. *lēṣ*) is the arrogant and haughty person who acts in total disregard of others and disdains any piety. Cf. Prov. 13 : 1. **and all who watch to do evil:** *NEB* 'quick to see (Heb. *šôqēd*, cf. Jer. 1 : 12) mischief'.

21. who by a word: The Heb. (Hiph 'il ptc. of the verb *ḥāṭāʾ*, 'to sin') would normaly mean 'to lead a person into sin' (Exod. 23 : 33, etc.), but must here have the sense 'to lay false charges against a person'. The whole verse is concerned with the perversion of justice. **and lay a snare for him who reproves in the gate:** The meaning is of frustrating the evidence of, and even using violence against, an honest citizen who brings a valid case against another. In this way the prosecution of justice is perverted. **And with an empty plea** (Heb. *tōhû*, 'what is empty, confused') refers to the perversion of justice by giving deliberately misleading evidence. The verse as a whole reveals the deficiencies of the legal system as it was experienced in ancient Israel, and which have proved perennial problems for juridical institutions.

22. Therefore thus says the LORD, who redeemed Abraham: Vv. 22–24 stand rather apart from vv. 17–21, and some commentators have regarded them as a separate unit. Vermeylen, I, p. 406, takes vv. 19–21 as a later addition to the section. However, vv. 22ff. must be interpreted against the background of the preceding verses, since the great eschatological turning-point which these describe is presupposed. They may represent an expansion of the original section, therefore, but must be interpreted as belonging to it in subject matter. The reference to God's action in 'redeeming' Abraham, i.e. rescuing him from the pagan world in which he lived and calling him to a divine purpose, is a mark of the re-awakened interest in this patriarch in the post-exilic age. Cf, my **Abraham and David** (*SBT*, Second Series, 3), London, 1967, pp. 70ff. Instead of **concerning the house of Jacob**, we should read 'the God of . . .' (Heb. *ʾēl* for *ʾel*). **Jacob shall no more be ashamed:** The phrase conveys a far greater benefit than the total failure and frustration of a person's way of life. Cf. M. A. Klopfenstein, *Scham und Schande nach dem A. T.* (*ATANT* 62), Zürich, 1972, pp. 58ff., and *THAT*, I, pp. 269–72. Hence the meaning is that when the time of salvation dawns Jews will no longer experience failure and the frustration of their ambitions.

23. For when he sees his children: We should emend to 'When his children see . . .' (cf. *HTOT*, pp. 186). The reference then is to Jacob's children seeing God's action of salvation in their midst and returning wholeheartedly to him in piety and devotion.

24. And those who err in spirit: In a warm note of assurance the author describes the final age of Israel's salvation as one in which the

wrongdoers – **those 'who err in spirit'** — will come to see the folly of
their ways and, by repenting, turn to accept the wisdom and instruction
of God. The allusion must be to erring Jews, rather than to Gentile
oppressors.

WOE TO THE REBELLIOUS CHILDREN

30 : 1–5

In this section Isaiah develops his sharp criticism of Hezekiah's withdrawal of allegiance to Assyria on the basis of the expectation of
military aid from Egypt. Similar warnings of the folly of trusting in
such a treaty are to be found in 18 : 1–7, as well as in 28 : 14–22
and 29 : 1–16. The authenticity of the present section to Isaiah cannot
seriously be set in question, and the main issue of location is whether it
is to be linked with the Ashdodite rebellion of 713–711 or to the
negotiations and rebellion of 705–701. Wildberger favours the first
alternative, as also for 18 : 1–7 (and 19 : 1–15). Certain criteria for establishing the date are not present, but the general context of chs. 28–29
would encourage the conclusion that it is built up from an Isaianic
collection relating to the rebellion of 705–701. This is the view of
Donner, p. 133, and Dietrich, p. 137. Hezekiah had sent emissaries to
Egypt, to the Pharaoh Shabako, seeking military aid, and this is referred to in v. 4. Both Donner, p. 132, and Kaiser would strike out v. 3
as a gloss, but this appears neither necessary nor probable. Dietrich, p.
140, would accept that a short interval separates vv. 4–5 from 1–3, so that
the former represent a rejoinder by the prophet to objections from his
hearers. The sending of emissaries from Judah to Egypt (v. 4) may
indicate a relatively late stage of the revolt of 705–701, when the
Assyrian threat to Judah was imminent, and when the promises of
military assistance from Egypt had become desperately urgent. This
would help to illuminate the sharpness of the prophet's strictures on
the uselessness of such promises. Even if the Egyptians attempted to
fulfil their pledges, their help would be worthless (so v. 5 and also vv
6–7).

30 : 1. Woe to the rebellious children: The **rebellious children** are
the king and government of Judah, but since the entire country was
involved in the decision to rebel against Assyria, the rebuke inevitably
applied to all. There is a deliberate *double entendre* on the adjective
rebellious, which primarily refers to rebellion against Sennacherib,
but carries also a hint that it is rebellion against God. Isaiah appears
surprisingly restrained in not singling out Hezekiah for individual
condemnation, whilst correspondingly sharply condemning the
political leaders of Jerusalem. This may well indicate the pressure
exerted by the pro-Egyptian party, which Hezekiah may have endorsed
only reluctantly. **who carry out a plan, but not mine:** The **plan** (Heb.
'ēṣāh) must indicate generally the policy of rebellion, but may refer
here to a more immediate decision to send emissaries to Egypt to
secure the promised aid. **and who make a league:** The Heb. (*wᵉlinsōk
massēkāh*) means literally 'to pour out a drink offering' (so Wild-

berger, III, pp. 1147f.). Such a cultic ceremony solemnized the making of a covenant, so that *RSV*'s **make a league** conveys the sense.

2. who set out to go down to Egypt: 18 : 1-7 clearly refers to Egyptian (Ethiopian) emissaries in Judah, so that the negotiations with Egypt cannot all be linked with a single situation. Probably 18 : 1-7 refers to the period of 713-711, but in any case, the decision to send envoys to Egypt here may reflect a more pressing state of emergency of the year 701, when Judah's virtual defencelessness was all too evident. The initial gamble in the policy of rebellion—that Assyria would be too preoccupied to reassert its authority—had already failed. Now the promise of Egyptian assistance was all that was left to fall back on. We should probably locate the departure of the Judean emissaries before the defeat of the Egyptian forces at Eltekeh, but the precise sequence of events in 701 cannot be reconstructed with certainty. **to take refuge in the protection of Pharaoh:** This requires reading the verb *lā'ûz*, instead of the noun *lā'ôz*.

3. Therefore shall the protection of Pharaoh: The assertions overlap to some extent with the implications of v. 2, but there is no need on this account to remove v. 3. as an addition (as Donner, Kaiser). **turn to your shame** conveys a very much stronger sense than that of embarrassed disappointment, and points to total failure and ruination. Cf. on 29 : 22.

4. For though his officials are in Zoan: The suffixes to **officials** and **envoys** (= 'his') have no proper antecedent. Either they must be taken to refer loosely to Hezekiah, whose involvement is assumed, or they should be deleted (as Wildberger). In any case v. 2 makes clear that it is envoys from Judah that we are concerned with. Zoan was in the lower Nile region of the Delta, the Tanis of the Greeks (modern *Sān 'el-Hajar*) and Hanes was Heracleopolis, close to present-day Fayyum. The point of making the geographical reference may be that Shabako, the Ethiopian Pharaoh, had only secured his position in this lower Nile region after 715, or less dramatically, that these provincial centres provided suitable (secret?) meeting-places for the Judean emissaries.

5. every one comes to shame: Reading, *hôbîš* with *Q*^e*re'* and 18 MSS. The prophet is absolutely clear that the belief that Egyptian military aid can be of any help to Judah is ill-founded and unjustified. Once again **shame and disgrace** imply complete political ruination.

WORTHLESS HELP

30:6-7

Wildberger describes these two verses as 'an Eldorado for the imagination of exegetes' (III, p. 1157), and certainly they contain many unresolved obscurities, although their main intention is clear. See further, K.-D. Schunck, *ZAW* 78 (1966), pp. 48-56. Undoubtedly they belong to the same general situation as that presupposed by vv. 1-5. Their authenticity to Isaiah, and to the situation of 705-701, cannot therefore be in doubt. The allusion to the desert of the Negeb region in v. 6, and to the passage of caravans through it, is most directly to be explained as a portrayal of the route that the emissaries of 30 : 2 would take. If so, it is possible, as Kaiser and Wildberger suggest, that the Assyrian forces were already in Judah and had cut the coastal route to Egypt. This short saying would therefore belong to a slightly later time than vv. 1–5.

6. An oracle on the beasts of the Negeb: This heading, which is couched in the form used for the foreign nation prophecies of 13–23, must be the work of a redactor. The **Negeb** was the desert region to the south of Judah through which overland travellers to Egypt would pass. **Through a land of trouble and anguish** describes the harsh physical contours and conditions of the terrain, rather than any immediate political turmoil envisaged by the prophet. Presumably this route had been chosen as politically safer at the time. **from where come the lioness:** Better 'of the lioness and growling lion' (reading *mēhēm*, 'growling', instead of *mēhem*). **the viper and the flying serpent.** The inhospitable nature of the route is exemplified by the creatures that roam and live there. The **flying serpent** must be regarded as a mythical creature, although possibly some form of long-tailed bird, misidentified, had given rise to the concept. The prophet's meaning is that a risky journey will have been undertaken—for nothing! **they carry their riches on the backs of asses:** The description suggests caravan traders who would normally be the main travellers of the region, and possibly the intention is to suggest that they would be forced to flee from the Assyrians. Eichrodt thinks of Arabian tribes whose help was also being sought by Hezekiah, but more likely the Judean emissaries are themselves compared to caravan traders, loaded with gifts to impress the Pharaoh.

7. For Egypt's help is worthless and empty: Isaiah appears willing to concede that Egypt would attempt to make good its assurances to Hezekiah, but insists that it would be entirely powerless to fulfil them. **I have called her 'Rahab who sits still':** Rahab (Strong One) was the name of a mythical monster which personified the powers of chaos and misrule. Cf. Isa. 51:9; Job 9:13; 26:12; Ps. 89:10. Why the name is used here in specific reference to Egypt (cf. also Ps. 87:4) is not entirely clear, but may well have been encouraged by the many huge images of animals of mixed and part-human form. Cf. the Sphinx. In any case the fundamental concept is that of a creature that looks fearsome, but is in reality powerless. K.-D. Schunck, (*op.cit.*, pp. 48ff.) suggests that the use of the name indicates a time of political chaos in Egypt, but this is to read too much symbolism into the name. The precise meaning of **who sits still** (Heb. *hēm šēbet*) has been much discussed. Donner, p. 159, and Kaiser would keep MT and translate rhetorically 'Rahab are they?—Inactivity!' More plausibly, however, we should follow the widely advocated emendation (cf. *BHS*, Fohrer, Schoors, Wildberger) and read 'Rahab that is stilled' (*rāhāb hammošbāt*). In any case the intention is perfectly clear.

THE WRITTEN TESTIMONY

30:8-11

The precise delineation of the sections that follow between vv. 8 and 17 is difficult to determine, and has been variously estimated. Eichrodt would take v. 8 by itself, whereas Wildberger prefers to link it with vv. 9–11. Duhm and Kaiser treat the unit as comprised of vv. 8–17. The impression is created of various short sayings from Isaiah, all to be linked with the situation of 701, which have been coupled together by a redactor. The separate sayings in vv. 8, 9–11, 12–14 and 15–17 all appear to be self-contained, and to present different images of the certainty and awesomeness of the judgment which Judah had heaped upon itself. We may follow Wildberger in taking vv. 8–11 together.

8. And now go, write it before them on a tablet: The situation must be compared very closely with that in 8:1, 16. The prophet is very conscious that he has faithfully delivered his message, but it has been rejected by those who had the power to act upon it. He is therefore commanded by God to set out this message in a written form so that generations to come will know that the rulers who chose the path of rebellion had done so in defiance of God. They were the agents of their own destruction. It seems improbable that what was written here was a single word, or phrase, as in 8:1, although this cannot be entirely discounted. At the same time neither can the written document be identified with the memoir of 6:1–8:18*. More satisfactorily it must be linked with the events of 705–701, and have provided a nucleus of Isaianic prophecies relating to these events, and which are now preserved in chs. 28–31. Hence Kaiser suggests that a scroll containing a collection of Isaianic prophecies was in mind, although we cannot altogether rule out that initially a much shorter inscription **on a tablet** was envisaged, as in 8:1. **as a witness for ever:** Reading *le'ēd* for *lā'ad* with Aquila (cf. *BHS*, *HTOT*, p. 186).

9. For they are a rebellious people: Cf. 1:2, and the further development of such a title in Ezek. 2:3, 7. The people had rebelled against God, whose will had been made known to them by his prophet, but the substance of this rebellion lay in the political act of withholding allegiance from Assyria. The prophet has consciously associated the two meanings of the term. **who will not hear:** Reading *lišmôa'*, with 1QIs[a]. The **instruction of the LORD** refers to the preaching of the prophet, and it is instructive that the title *tôrat yhwh* could here be applied to the contents of prophecy. For *tôrāh* here, cf. P. Jensen, *The Use of tôrâ by Isaiah*, Washington, 1973, pp. 112ff.

10. who say to the seers, 'See not': LXX adds 'for us'. Cf. 29:10 for the indictment, although there it is undoubtedly a very secondary elaboration which may have been inspired by the passage here. **Speak to us smooth things, prophesy illusions:** The prophet means that the people would only listen to him if he told them what they wanted to hear, thereby making a nonsense of prophecy and its claim to be a word from God. Mic. 3:5–6 shows that there were 'false' prophets active during this time in Judah, who had undoubtedly been busy in

supporting the disastrous politics of rebellion against Assyria. Such
'illusions' were all the more dangerous because they had the specious
plausibility of appearing to be patriotic.

11. leave the way, turn aside from the path: Such words were
obviously not actually a quotation of what the people said, but the
prophet puts into their mouths the true implication of what they
wanted. By rejecting the messages of Yahweh which had been given
through Isaiah, they had given evidence that they wanted nothing
more to do with him.

THE SUDDEN CRASH

30 : 12–14

This short section is concerned to elaborate upon the threat which
faced Judah as a result of its rebellion by insisting upon the suddenness and devastating completeness of the ruin that will come. It
achieves this by drawing two comparisons, the first with the collapse
of a high wall and the second with the smashing of a pot, which is
quickly reduced to fragments so small that they no longer have any
use whatsoever. The authenticity of the verses from Isaiah is not in
doubt, and they must be placed close in time to the threat to Jerusalem from Sennacherib's army, perhaps when it was already in Judah.

12. Therefore thus says the Holy One of Israel: This introductory
formula is lacking one LXX text and *BHS* would delete. Donner, p. 160,
prefers to retain it as original. **and trust in oppression and perverse-
ness:** The specific condemnation appears to relate to general corruption
and violence on the part of the citizens of Judah, rather than to the act
of rebellion against Assyria. Perhaps the prophet saw the two as linked.
Moral perversity in life has led to political folly.

13. therefore this iniquity shall be to you: The **iniquity** must refer
to the rebellion against Assyria, and the effect that it will have upon
Judah is then compared to a crack appearing in a high wall. The point
of the comparison lies in the sudden dramatic nature of the collapse,
even though the weakness which caused it will have been developing
over a long period. So in Judah's case it must have seemed a long time
since the first actions of withdrawal of allegiance to Assyria had taken
place (705), but much later (701) would their terrifying consequence
be seen. The present prophecy must come from a time close to the
threat to Jerusalem in 701, when Isaiah was concerned to make clear
why this threat had come about, and how consistently he had opposed
the actions which had led to it.

14. and its breaking is like that of a potter's vessel: The initial **and
its breaking** should be deleted as a repetition of a similar word
at the end of v. 13. By the use of a vivid simile Isaiah brings out
still further the awful completeness of the destruction which he
envisaged was about to overtake Judah and Jerusalem. Although the
nation was engulfed by calamity, it is evident that Hezekiah's surrender to Sennacherib (2 Kg. 18 : 13–16) did manage to secure Jerusa-

lem from a terrible fate, so that the capital did not experience the complete disaster Isaiah had feared. **not a sherd is found:** The use of sherds of broken pottery was evidently extremely commonplace, and the kind of uses to which they might be put is well illustrated here. In addition we know that such sherds provided a cheap and common writing material.

THE REJECTION OF THE WAY OF PEACE

30:15-17

Several scholars would regard these three verses as the continuation of the preceding verses (so Duhm, Kaiser, Donner, pp. 159ff., who all take vv. 8–17 as forming a single unit). However, the combining of the material would appear to have been secured by a redactor, and there is no clear indication that the separate units were not uttered on separate occasions. Nevertheless the subject matter makes it plain that these verses also belong to the period of Hezekiah's rebellion against Sennacherib, and in this instance from a time when military action by Assyria was imminent. Kaiser is isolated in disputing their authenticity to Isaiah and in ascribing them to a post-exilic author. This is most improbable, and we must rather see in the section a very clearly expressed contrasting of Isaiah's understanding of Yahweh's will with the actual policy chosen by Hezekiah and the Judean leaders.

15. For thus said the Lord GOD: The new introduction both marks a new prophecy and also serves to give added emphasis to the divine authority which stands behind the policy now set forth. **In returning and rest you shall be saved:** A very substantial discussion has arisen over the precise meaning of the terms **returning** (Heb. *šûbāh*) and **rest** (Heb. *nahat*). See F. Huber, Exkursus II, pp. 140–7, and Wildberger, III, p. 1181, besides R. F. Melugin, *CBQ* 36 (1974), pp. 303–4. Fohrer understands **returning** to mean 'turning away from (a military alliance with Egypt)'. Others prefer the sense 'returning (to Yahweh)', whilst M. Dahood, *CBQ* 20 (1958), pp. 41–3 would take the verb from the stem *yšb* meaning 'to sit, be still'. Cf. also G. R. Driver, *JSS* 13 (1968), p. 51. This follows a suggestion which goes back to W. Gesenius and gives a meaning 'staying still' (Dietrich, p. 149) or 'staying quiet' (G. R. Driver). The point would then be on making no alliance with Egypt and remaining submissive to Assyrian domination. Similarly **rest** may be taken to mean 'fidelity to a treaty' (cf. O. Eissfeldt, *Kleine Schriften* III, ed. R. Sellheim and F. Maass, Tübingen, 1966, pp. 124–8). Undoubtedly the emphasis is upon rejecting the alliance with Egypt and not resisting Assyrian rule, but the exact understanding of the terms is somewhat dependent upon the point of time at which this prophecy was given. The prophet recognises that it has already become too late for this policy to be implemented, since he affirms **and you would not** at the end of the verse. Most probably 'returning (to Yahweh)' and 'staying quiet' (i.e. not resisting Assyrian rule) give the correct sense, but it should certainly be considered that, if the prophecy dates from 701 when Judah had been in a state of rebellion for three years, what Isaiah was advocating was 'returning' to accept allegiance to Assyria and 'staying quiet' (i.e. submissive) to the consequences of this. A similar ambiguity attaches to the parallel line **in quietness and in trust shall be your strength** which could allude to a submissive trust in God, or to a submissive attitude of renewed loyalty to Assyria.

16. but you said, 'No! We will speed upon horses': The allusion is particularly to the treaty with Egypt and its promise of military aid. Prominent among the latter was Egyptian cavalry and chariotry, as well, most probably, as a promise of **horses** from Egypt for use by Judah. The Heb. contains a marked poetic assonance (*'al sûs nānûs*) which the prophet then proceeds to interpret in a negative fashion: **therefore you shall speed away** (in flight). The point of the sharp contrast is not that military power is always useless, but rather that Hezekiah's particular trust in military assistance from Egypt would prove quite inadequate to the threat which now faced him.

17. A thousand shall flee at the threat of one: The verse should most probably be regarded as an addition (cf. Schoors, Fohrer), and its address—**till you are left**—would point to Jerusalem, rather than to Judah as a whole, which is threatened in vv. 15–16. To this extent the sharpness of the threat in the preceding two verses is alleviated by the picture of Jerusalem's isolation. Cf. 1 : 8 which may well have influenced the author here. Possibly we should link this verse with the Josianic Redaction, in which great stress was placed upon the uniqueness of the role of Jerusalem in the face of the threat from Assyria. The **threat** (Heb. *gᵉ'ārāh*) refers to 'shouting, rebuke', so that the hyperbole of the addition rather overpresses Isaiah's own more realistic warning. This was concerned, not with the fact that Judeans and Egyptians made poor soldiers, but rather with the hopeless inadequacy of the attempt to resist the power of Assyria by such means. The comparison with a **flagstaff on the top of a mountain** retains the military context, but suggests that somehow Jerusalem will be spared whilst the rest of Judah is overrun. The comment must certainly have been made *post eventum*, in the light of what eventually transpired in 701.

THE COMING SALVATION

30 : 18–26

V. 18 is certainly an isolated promise which rounds off the threats and admonitions of 30 : 1–17 with a note of assurance that Yahweh's salvation has not been entirely forgotten and will eventually come (so Procksch, Kaiser). The verse is in poetic form, and can most convincingly be placed after 587 BC, when the threats to Judah and Jerusalem had acquired a new meaning with defeats inflicted by Babylonia. This restrained word of assurance has then been more extensively amplified in vv. 19–26 by a more general promise of salvation which compares very closely with that of 29 : 17–24. It promises a dramatic change in the natural order, warns of the renewed need to forsake idolatry (v. 22), and concludes with a quite extreme assurance that the light of the sun and the moon will be increased to an extraordinary degree. The overall impression is of promises which contain an eschatology bordering an apocalyptic in which a totally new world-order is envisaged. Clearly the section is not from Isaiah, and is only marginally related to Isaiah's prophecies as a late (probably fifth century BC—so Wildberger. Kaiser would place it as late as the time of Antiochus Epiphanes) expression of the hope which would witness the reversal of all the threats which Isaiah had delivered. It is couched in a form of elevated prose (cf. *RSV*, although *BHS* prints as poetry).

18. Therefore the LORD waits to be gracious to you: Judgment is already assumed to have fallen (in fulfilment of the threats of vv. 1–17), and Judah is envisaged as suffering as a punishment for its sins. Yet this is not the end of Yahweh's will for his people, which must endure till the time of punishment is over. Then Yahweh's deeper feelings of love and compassion will assert themselves, establishing a new hope for the future. Clearly the situation presupposed is that of the Babylonian exile which was interpreted as a necessary judgment upon Judah's sins. **For the LORD is a God of justice:** The meaning is more positive than *RSV*'s rendering would suggest, since **justice** (Heb. *mišpāṭ*) indicates 'good order' and implies that God will eventually be gracious to those who have repented and are looking to him for a renewed life and nation.

19. Yea, O people in Zion who dwell at Jerusalem: The identification **in Zion** is superfluous beside **at Jerusalem** and should be deleted as a gloss. The concern specifically with the inhabitants of Jerusalem must be taken as a reflection of the political situation of the post-exilic, Persian, period. **you shall weep no more.** The phrase assumes that the author's time is one of adversity which will soon come to an end. **He will surely be gracious to you:** We should insert 'the LORD will . . .', with 1QIs[a]. The assumption behind the promise is that the hoped-for renewal has been long delayed, but will now surely come.

20. And though the Lord give you the bread of adversity: The Heb. is difficult and Kaiser, following Marti, would delete **of adversity** and **of affliction** as yielding no proper sense. With *BHS* we should possibly insert the preposition *min* before both nouns, meaning 'instead of'. As it is the sense could only be metaphorical: you have been living on trouble long enough. *RSV*'s and *NEB*'s introduction of a concessive sense **though** attempts to secure such a meaning. The identity of **your Teacher** (Heb. *môreykā*) is very obscure. Possibly we should emend to 'early rain' (Heb. *môreh*), cf. Joel 2:23. The verb **will not hide himself** (Heb. *yikkānēp*) is obscure and adds to the difficulty. *BDB* suggests a meaning 'thrust aside', and if this is extended to mean 'withhold' we could read 'and your early rain will not be withheld'. The second **your Teacher** must be deleted as a gloss on **eyes**; cf. 29:10.

21. This is the way, walk in it: Way must here be understood in a metaphorical sense of the right moral and religious path revealed through the Torah. God would not allow his people to go astray again, as had happened in the past. He himself, therefore, would guide them personally and spiritually, so that they would not face the risk of downfall and suffering again as they had done in the past.

22. Then you will defile your silver-covered graven images: Better, 'treat as unclean'; cf. *NEB* 'reject, as things unclean'. Idolatry is here regarded as the greatest sin which had been the cause of leading Jerusalem astray in the past. Cf. 2 : 20, which may directly have influenced the passage here, and which may itself be regarded as an expansion of the reference to turning aside from 'the way' in v. 21. **You will scatter them as unclean things:** Possibly we should emend to 'as filthy water' (Heb. $k^e m\hat{e}$ instead of $k^e m\hat{o}$; cf. LXX).

23. And he will give rain for the seed: When the great turning-point comes in the fortunes of Israel-Judah it will be accompanied by a marvellous improvement in the fertility and richness of the natural order. Cf. 29 : 17. We may note also the assumption in Hag. 1 : 6 that a lack of fruitfulness reflects a lack of true worship.

24. and the oxen and the asses: As a mark of the return of conditions like those which were believed to have pertained at the beginning of time, there will be such a rich harvest that even domestic farm animals will be fed with great abundance. **which has been winnowed:** Reading *zôrāh*; cf. *BHS*.

25. And upon every lofty mountain: On the very locations which had been the scene of the idolatrous high-places where earlier generations of Israelites had sinned, there would be streams of water to make the land fertile. **in the day of the great slaughter, when the towers fall;** This can refer only to the great eschatological day of God's victory when he overthrows all that opposes him and his people. Cf. 25 : 1–5; 26 : 5. Instead of **towers**, *NEB* more plausibly reads 'highest in the land' (*m^e ḡuddālîm*), thereby understanding the eschatological age as the final Day of the LORD. Cf. 2 : 12. Even so, the grim violence of the reference introduces a somewhat jarring note into the idyllic portrayal of the New Age.

26. Moreover the light of the moon will be as: The final promise affirms that a complete transformation of the cosmic order was expected in the age to come, in which all that was beneficial to man would be greatly magnified in power. The imagery is rather bizarre and pointless, but reflects a certain sense of exuberance about the hope of Judaism. It contains an element of hyperbole, but must be understood as intended literally, rather than as a poetic metaphor of the new era of **light**. Concern with the light of the sun and moon became a popular theme of later Jewish apocalyptic imagery. Cf. Jub. 1 : 29; 19 : 25; Enoch 91 : 16. A softer note is given in the promise that the dawning of the New Age would be a **day when the LORD binds up the hurt of his people:** Ultimately the new world order was to be a reflection of the new experience of the people of Yahweh.

THE ANGER OF THE LORD AGAINST ASSYRIA

30:27–33

The fact that this picture portrays Yahweh's punitive action against the Assyrians has contributed to the great difficulty that it has occasioned to commentators in assessing its authenticity. We may summarise the three main views regarding it. O. Kaiser, as earlier K. Marti and H. Donner, pp. 162–4, regards it as inauthentic to Isaiah in its language, theophanic imagery and general content. He understands **Assyrians** (v. 31) to refer to the Seleucid power of the second century BC. In contrast with this Wildberger, who examines the question of its possible Isaianic origin with great care (II, pp. 1210–15), concludes that none of the arguments against this can be regarded as decisive, and avers, therefore, that it is from Isaiah, although with the recognition of two additions in vv. 29 and 32. A third alternative is advocated by H. Barth, pp. 92–103. This is to see in the section a part of the Josianic Redaction (Barth's Assyrian Redaction) of Isaiah's prophecies, which he would link with 10 : 16–19. The *terminus a quo* for the time of its composition would then be 621 BC, and a basic assumption of this view would be that the historical (pre-exilic) power of Assyria is referred to.

We may certainly follow Barth in seeing the section as not original to Isaiah and as forming part of the Josianic Redaction of his prophecies. A close counterpart for it is to be seen in 10 : 24–27 (which Barth would date later). Its primary message is that God will appear in great power to terrorise the Assyrians, and heap utter and total destruction upon them (v. 33). The bitterness and hatred that pervades this reflects the depth of animosity that the Assyrians aroused, and the joy with which their final defeat was anticipated. Undoubtedly the present section must have been composed before the fall of Nineveh in 612 BC.

27. Behold, the name of the LORD comes from far: Duhm, Fohrer and Wildberger would all delete **name** (Heb. *šēm*) as an obvious Deuteronomic theologoumenon. Cf. G. von Rad, *Studies in Deuteronomy* (*SBT* 9), 1953, pp. 37ff. This is no doubt correct, although the authors of the Josianic Redaction of Isaiah's prophecies were evidently closely linked with the origins of the Deuteronomic movement. However, the accompanying description makes it very clear that an appearance of God himself in a theophany is being referred to. Whether **from far** intends to suggest 'from his heavenly dwelling-place' or 'from Zion', as Barth affirms, makes little difference, and was probably not intended to be firmly pinpointed in such fashion. **and in thick rising smoke:** It is doubtful if the Heb. *wᵉkōbed maśśā'ah* can mean this, and *NEB* takes *maśśā'* to have its normal meaning of 'burden, doom', cf. *HTOT*, p. 186. The language and imagery is traditional of a theophany. Cf. J. Jeremias, *Theophanie*, pp. 56ff. It adapts thunder- and storm-phenomena to the divine punitive action. Hence **his tongue** must be a reference to lightning.

28. his breath is like an overflowing stream: The language takes up the imagery used by Isaiah of Assyria in 8:7. In particular the phrase **that reaches up to the neck** is drawn directly from 8:8, but is turned in a totally new direction. It is a recurrent feature of the Josianic Redaction that it makes use extensively of words, images and themes from authentic Isaianic sayings, but often applies them in quite different ways from those in which they originally appeared. **to sift the nations with the sieve of destruction:** Heb. *nāp̄āh* is a *hapax legomenon:* BDB 'sieve'; *NEB* 'yoke'. The corresponding verb is clearly a denominative.

29. You shall have a song as in the night: The imagery turns to that of celebrating a festival, most probably that of Passover on account of its nocturnal features; cf. 2 Kg. 23:21–23, for the celebration of Passover in Josiah's time at the Jerusalem temple, instead of in a more domestic environment. The overthrow of the Assyrians is to have the character of a cultic event, but both the nocturnal setting and the great rejoicing are themes which have almost certainly been taken by the author from 9:2–3.

30. And the LORD will cause his majestic voice to be heard: The verse combines together various traditional elements of theophanic accounts: thunder, lightning, torrential rain, tempest and hail. The **flame of devouring fire** appears to go back to the 'light' theme of 9:2 combined with the 'fire' of 9:5. Cf. 10:16–17, which also belongs to the Josianic Redaction.

31. The Assyrians will be terror-stricken: The emphasis throughout the Josianic Redaction upon the manner of the overthrow of the Assyrians is to stress that it will be the direct and personal action of God, unassisted by men. The arousing of terror and panic is one of the ways in which this is envisaged. **when he smites with his rod** alludes back to the theme of the 'rod' of 10:5, where it is Assyria itself which is the rod of the divine anger. The picture is now reapplied so that Assyria is smitten by the rod.

32. And every stroke of the staff of punishment: Reading **punishment** (Heb. *mûsārāh*) instead of MT *mûsādāh*. The staff of punishment develops further the theme of Yahweh's 'rod' from 10:5 (although the noun here is *maṭṭeh* against *šēbeṭ* in 10:5), and the combination of the themes of a cultic celebration with the infliction of punishment gives rise to a rather grotesque overall picture. Almost certainly the phrase **which the LORD lays upon them** is a secondary addition. **battling with brandished arm he will fight with them** should be emended to read 'and with sacred dances of an offering', Heb. *ûbim^eḥôlōt t^enûp̄āh*). So Gressmann, Procksch.

33. For a burning place has long been prepared: Donner, p. 163, comments that the text is hopelessly disturbed. *RSV*'s rendering of **burning place** (literally 'Topheth') is based on LXX. Topheth was the place used for burning rubbish outside Jerusalem, which had ancient associations as a place where human sacrifices were offered (2 Kg. 23:10; Jer. 7:31f.). The picture brings to a kind of conclusion the extensive use of light and fire imagery in this section, which originated in Isaiah's own language. **yea, for the king:** It is preferable to follow the marginal note and read 'for Molech', cf. 1 Kg. 11:7; 2 Kg. 16:3; 17:31. Molech, or Moloch, was the deity to whom human sacrifices were dedicated, although O. Eissfeldt, *Molk als Opferbegriff im Punischen und das Ende des Gottes Moloch*, Halle, 1935, would understand this as meaning 'for an oath'. Cf. further, M. Weinfeld, *Ugarit-Forschung*–4 (1972), pp. 133–54; *THAT*, cols. 918f. So bitter does the author feel regarding the Assyrians that he regards a great heap of burning rubbish, which had acquired notoriety as a place of pagan sacrifice, as the fitting location for their end. The text is very obscure, however, and it would scarcely be justified on the basis of this verse to conclude that the Josianic Redaction expected the final destruction of the Assyrians to take place outside Jerusalem. See further below on 31:5–9. In any case many commentators (Duhm, Marti, Gressmann, Procksch, Donner) take the whole clause **yea, for the king it is made ready** as a gloss on the name Topheth. **its pyre made deep and wide:** It is preferable to follow Targum and read as imperatives, 'Make ready . . .' **with fire and wood:** Better 'with coals of fire', since some burning material is evidently required. **the breath of the LORD . . . kindles it:** The assertion reaffirms that the final destruction of the Assyrians, which the authors of the Josianic Redaction saw as an imminent event of their own day, would come about as a result of the direct action of God. Such an overthrow was viewed by them as foretold by Isaiah (Isa. 10 : 5ff.), and was held to mark the final stage in the encounter between Israel and Assyria which formed the basic context and subject of Isaiah's preaching.

THE USELESSNESS OF EGYPT'S HELP

31 : 1–3

Ch. 31 is a complex structure, since it is evident that vv. 6–9 are secondary to, and in some way related to, the warnings and threats of vv. 1–3, whilst vv. 4–5 have been very differently interpreted by different commentators. Furthermore, the additions in vv. 6–9 are not all from the same hand or the same time, so that the relative consequence in which they were added remains a matter to be considered. As to the authenticity of vv. 1–3 from Isaiah there can be no serious doubt. The verses deal with the situation already covered by the prophecy of 30:1–5 and provide further warnings of the threat to Judah from Sennacherib and of the uselessness of the promises of help from Egypt. Wildberger places them at a slightly later time than 30:1–5, and suggests that they emanate from a time after the battle of Eltekeh had taken place, and when the military situation in Judah had become desperate. In a last pleading bid to ward off the consequences of his own rebellion against Assyria, Hezekiah had sent emissaries to Egypt begging for their further military intervention. Isaiah could rightly point out how useless now were all the promises of Egypt and how misplaced had been the Judean confidence in their help. Nothing any longer stood between Jerusalem and the forces of Sennacherib, and the retribution they would exact for Hezekiah's folly.

31:1. Woe to those who go down to Egypt for help: The general situation envisaged is closely similar to that of 30:1–5, although news of the defeat of the Egyptian forces at Eltekeh may already have reached Judah. The use of the present participle **who go down** suggests that a further deputation was being sent to Pharaoh Shabako, but quite possibly this is simply an additional comment on the fruitlessness of the mission that had left earlier. Whatever aid the Egyptians proffer it would never be enough. **but do not look to the Holy One of Israel** contrasts the inadequacy of military aid with the sure and certain power of Yahweh and his purpose. By having rejected the latter Hezekiah had been forced into a greater and greater reliance on the former. The prophet's criticism is not of militarism as such, nor a Utopian objection to all foreign alliances out of any rigidly conceived dogma that they betrayed a lack of faith, or involved an observance of foreign cultus. The criticism belongs to a specific historical situation in which Hezekiah had embarked on a risky policy of rebellion in open opposition to Isaiah's (and God's) word. Now that the full consequences of this rebellion had to be suffered, it was all too clear that the assurances from Egypt which had served to bolster it up were worthless. The defeat of their forces at Eltekeh, assuming that this had already taken place, was eloquent testimony to their inadequacy. It is very possible that Isaiah has made use of the language and ideology of the 'Holy War' in Israel (cf. Dt. 20:1–4), but, if so, it has been applied prophetically in a concrete historical situation, rather than developed as a broad dogma. Cf. P. D. Miller, *The Divine Warrior in Early Israel*, Cambridge, Mass., 1973, pp. 64ff. The real basis of the prophet's contrast is between man and God, which no one could contradict, rather than between two types of political, or religious, ideology. **or consult the LORD:** The phrase refers to the enquiring (Heb. *drš*, 'to seek') of God by means of a prophet, or less plausibly, by the use of a sacred oracle.

2. And yet he is wise and brings disaster: Childs, pp. 33–35, and Donner, pp. 135f. would remove v. 2 as an addition, but this is to be rejected (so Barth, p. 80, Wildberger). With biting irony Isaiah affirms that God also has a political 'Wisdom', by which he has arrived at a decision as to what he must do. In contrast with Hezekiah's frantic efforts to find a way of avoiding defeat, Yahweh had determined that his plan was to inflict it. 1QIs[a] reads the perfect 'has brought' instead of the present **brings**, and this may well be correct. **but will arise against the house of the evildoers:** The threat follows the customary Isaianic, and prophetic, convention of describing what is about to take place as the direct intervention of God. Both the prophet and his hearers, however, clearly understood that this would be through human agents, in this case the Assyrians. This sharply contrasts with the understanding given later by the redactor in v. 8.

3. The Egyptians are men, and not God: The traditional contrast between **man** and **God** and **flesh** and **spirit** serves to reinforce the prophet's warning. No one could deny the validity of such a contrast, yet in fact Hezekiah's policy had relied for its efficacy on the human element in opposition to God. For **flesh** as a part of man's make-up, cf. H. W. Wolff, *Anthropology of the Old Testament*, pp. 26ff. and G. Gerleman, *THAT*, I, cols. 376–9. For **spirit**, see H. W. Wolff, *idem*, pp. 32ff., and R. Albertz-C. Westermann, *THAT*, II, cols. 726–53.

When the LORD stretches out his hand: Yahweh had only to act (through the Assyrians) and both parties to the disastrous treaty would come to grief. Egypt (**the helper**) and Judah (**he who is helped**) would be overthrown. **and they will all perish together.** The final pronouncement is the sentence of death upon both Judah and Egypt. Now nothing lay between Hezekiah and the certainty of Assyrian retribution, because the hoped-for promise of Egyptian military intervention could be seen as worthless.

THE FATE OF JERUSALEM AND THE DEFEAT OF THE ASSYRIANS

31:4–9

The verses which follow have occasioned not a little difficulty to commentators and have been extensively discussed as to both their meaning and possible authenticity to Isaiah. A major crux centres upon v. 4 and the question of a threatening, or re-assuring, interpretation of it. We may attempt to deal with the most obvious and certain features first. Vv. 6–7 are quite clearly an expansion from a later, post-exilic, time as their close similarity to 2:20 and 30:22 shows. V. 6 understands Judah to be in a state of rebellion against God, and appeals to the reader to repent from this. These verses must represent two separate additions, the first appealing for repentance and the second elaborating upon this by showing that it must entail the abandonment of idolatry.

The question then remains concerning the authenticity of the remainder of vv. 4–9. Wildberger would defend their Isaianic origin, once vv. 6–7 have been removed. He sees in them an expression of how, at the last moment, Isaiah did come to assert that Yahweh would protect and deliver Jerusalem in 701. Yet we have already had occasion to reject this view as not substantiated by the other evidence of the book. H. Barth, pp. 83ff., would interpret only vv. 4 and 8*a* as from Isaiah, seeing the unit as comprised of vv. 1–4, 8*a*, and discerning in it a threat against Jerusalem, which is subtly turned by the prophet into a threat against Assyria as well (vv. 4, 8*a*). This view is rather surprising in view of Barth's overall recognition of the Josianic origin of much of the material referring to a defeat of the Assyrians (Barth's AR). Certainly he then goes on (pp. 83ff.) to argue that vv. 5 + 8*b*–9 are from this Assyrian (our Josianic) Redaction. With this latter point we must concur, save for the modification that v. 8*a* also belongs to this redaction. Only v. 4, therefore, can be held to have an authentic origin from Isaiah. In order to understand this Isaianic setting, it must also be held that this verse has a consistently threatening content, entirely in line with the threatening tone of vv. 1–3. Isaiah did not, even at the last, turn to assert that Yahweh would, after all his warnings, protect Jerusalem and rescue Hezekiah from his predicament. The attempt to find a measure of ambiguity in v. 4 must be held to be quite impossible. It is a dire warning that now Jerusalem's fate is sealed, and that nothing can rescue the city from its tormentors. In fact Hezekiah surrendered to Sennacherib before the siege of Jerusalem was fully enforced (2 Kg. 18 : 13–16), and the Josianic Redaction in vv. 5, 8–9, has sought to take account of this fact and to link Isaiah's quite authentic threat against Assyria (especially 10 : 5–15*) with this event.

4. For thus the LORD said to me: The use of the first person form by the prophet is striking, and may indicate Isaiah's own recording of his message in writing (cf. 30 : 8). The fresh introduction marks off v. 4 as a short prophetic oracle which stands by itself. Its theme is that of the sealing of the fate of Jerusalem. **As a lion or a young lion growls over his prey:** The point of the simile is quite clear and straightforward. Jerusalem is the **prey** and Yahweh is the **lion** who has seized it. Once this has happened nothing can rescue the victim from its attacker. The stress is on the fact that Jerusalem's fate is now sealed. Whatever hope there may have been of some distracting intervention by Egyptian forces had now passed. Although Yahweh is the **lion** it is understood within the prophetic imagery that Yahweh will act through his human agents—the Assyrian army, as in v. 3. There is no intention therefore of suggesting that the Assyrians are **the band of shepherds**, who are in some way interfering in God's action, and who might therefore themselves be subjected to his punishment. The elaboration of the picture by **is not terrified by their shouting** is designed to show that, once the prey is seized, the fate of the victim is certain. If any allegorical interpretation of the **shepherds** is to be sought it could only be in the Egyptians, but none is necessary at all. The figure of speech is self-explanatory. What we have here is Isaiah's last utterance in Jerusalem, isolated and besieged by Sennacherib's forces, before Hezekiah surrendered.

so the LORD of hosts will come down to fight upon Mount Zion: For the interpretation of **to fight upon**, see B. S. Childs, p. 57. The Heb. (*liṣbō' 'al*) must be understood in a hostile sense. Yahweh is not coming to rescue Jerusalem, but to attack and take it (cf. 29 : 1–4). It is only the addition of the Josianic Redactor's elaboration in vv. 5, 8–9, which has encouraged the opposite understanding that Yahweh will suddenly intervene to rescue Jerusalem.

5. Like birds hovering, so the LORD of hosts will protect Jerusalem: This verse belongs with vv. 8–9 to the Josianic Redaction, although it cannot be assumed that they all come from a single hand, or contain a uniform conception of how Yahweh would act against the Assyrians. There are certainly indications of a process of 'building-up' and of developmental elaboration of basic themes, beginning with the affirmation that Yahweh thwarted the Assyrians in 701 and extending this to encompass the idea that he directly overthrew their army then (see below on v. 8 and on 37 : 36). The present imagery (**like birds hovering**, which fits awkwardly with that of Yahweh like a 'lion' in v. 4) is to be explained from the Isaianic language of 10 : 14, where a boast is put into the mouth of the king of Assyria. The present verse refutes that boast, and throughout it there is no suggestion that a miraculous defeat will occur to humiliate the Assyrians, but only that Jerusalem will be protected and rescued. Various hints occur in the narrative accounts (see below on chs. 36–37) to suggest how this happened.

6. Turn to him from whom you have deeply revolted: This, together with the following verse, represents two separate glosses from the post-exilic era, aimed at offering further reflection on the fate of Jerusalem. Jerusalem is understood to be in ruins, or at least to have suffered setbacks, so that, in order to claim the promise of the city's protection given in v. 5, the reader is enjoined to a new act of penitence and returning to God. We may compare 2 : 20 and 17 : 7–8, as well as 30 : 22. **you have deeply revolted** requires an emendation from the third to the second person (cf. *RSV* margin).

7. For in that day every one shall cast away his idols: The fresh introduction marks this out as a further expansion to v. 6, intended to stress that the foremost feature of any act of repentance must be the rejection of idolatry. Increasingly in the post-exilic age idolatry appears to have been regarded as the worst form of sin, and as the major cause of the frustration of Israel's hopes. **which your hands have sinfully made for you:** The ancient versions omit **sinfully**, which is in any case superfluous.

8. And the Assyrian shall fall by a sword, not of man: V. 8 must be taken as a single whole, and not as two separate threats, one of a defeat of the Assyrians outside Jerusalem and the other of their flight from the city. The manner and location of the final overthrow of the Assyrian army is deliberately left vague, and two separate fates—death by the hand of God and flight from the field of battle—are described. This is then further supplemented by the case of the treatment of prisoners of war: **and his young men shall be put to forced labour.** The Josianic Redaction appears to have shared a variety of convictions about Yahweh's intentions regarding the punishment of the Assyrians. First, the redactors insist that Yahweh had deliberately protected Jerusalem in 701 from the destructive intent of Sennacherib (as in v. 5 here); secondly, Judah no longer had anything to fear from Assyria (as in 10 : 24–27); and thirdly, Assyria would shortly be destroyed by the direct action of Yahweh (as in 10 : 16–19; 30 : 27–33). This event was expected in the near future when considered from the perspective of the redactor's day in Josiah's reign. As a kind of 'final development' the belief appears to have emerged that what took place in 701 constituted a remarkable defeat for the Assyrians inflicted by the action of God (as in 37 : 36, on which see below). There is therefore a process of heightening of the tradition in which the event of 701 came to be seen as a part of Yahweh's action in overthrowing the Assyrians. What is described in vv. 8–9 here appears to belong to this latter category and to envisage a shattering military defeat of the Assyrians by the appearance of God himself in Jerusalem. Possibly the reinterpretation of v. 4 in this sense has contributed to such an idea and has linked such a threat with the events of 701.

9. His rock shall pass away in terror: The noun **rock** is awkward and unexpected, so that G. R. Driver, *JSS* 13 (1968), p. 52, would see in it a word meaning 'officers, staff-officers'; cf. *NEB.* **says the LORD, whose fire is in Zion:** The saying brings out very forcibly a fundamental feature of the theology of the Josianic Redaction—that Yahweh has a special unique association with Jerusalem, and that this has a major military significance, since he will protect and guard it. The much-used 'light' and 'fire' imagery is here understood in a cultic sense.

THE RIGHTEOUS KINGDOM

32:1–8

The picture of the righteous kingdom given in 32:1–8, in which the king and princes will reign justly, protecting the innocent and weak and enriching the life of the whole community, presents an almost idyllic hope. It clearly falls into two parts, with vv. 1–5 forming the main section, and vv. 6–8 representing a later expansion of this. These latter verses are particularly preoccupied with the bad behaviour of the fool and scoundrel. The broad affinities with some prominent aspects of the Wisdom tradition are evident. What is especially striking about the basic section is that the introduction of the king ruling justly in v. 1 does not foretell his advent, as is usual in the case of the promises of the restoration of the Davidic monarchy (cf. 11:1–5), but simply describes him as a present figure. The features are strongly idealised, but are applicable to almost any age. In spite of a few attempts to defend the Isaianic origin of vv. 1–5 (so Duhm, Skinner) that must certainly be abandoned. R. B. Y. Scott, Fohrer and Kaiser ascribe the section to a post-exilic Wisdom writer who has outlined a picture of good government to contrast with the sharpness of Isaiah's strictures upon the princes and leaders of his own day. Most recently Wildberger (III, pp. 1253–4) has argued that vv. 1–5 belong to the time shortly after Haggai and Zechariah, probably *c.* 500 BC.

Against all these views, however, we must set the greater conviction created by H. Barth's contention (pp. 213–15) that these verses belong to the Josianic Redaction (Barth's AR) of Isaiah, and are intended to round off the series of condemnations of Judah's leaders by a picture of the true nature of godly government. Similarly 32:15–20 presents this Redaction's view of the future hope of Israel. The strongest of the arguments in favour of such a setting for vv. 1–5 is the clear assumption that they make of an actually reigning king, which must then present an idealised picture of Josiah. The verses belong to the era of the monarchy, before 587 put an end to a reigning Davidic ruler. Both sections (vv. 1–5 and 15–20) are then to be seen as a summarising conclusion to the Josianic collection of Isaiah's prophecies.

32:1. Behold, a king will reign in righteousness: There is no indication to suggest that the **king** referred to will re-establish the monarchy after a period in which it has lapsed. Since the section, vv. 1–5, is to be ascribed to Josiah's reign, then the king referred to here must be Josiah. The presupposition is that Assyrian control over Judah has now relaxed to minimal proportions so that the truly Israelite ideal of kingship can re-assert itself. On any reckoning the circles from whom the Josianic Redaction emanated were strongly pro-monarchic. There is no justification whatever for following W. H. Irwin, pp. 118ff, in casting the whole verse in a timeless didactic form: 'If a king reigns with justice . . .' **and princes will rule in justice:** Much of chs. 28–31 has been concerned with a strong condemnation of 'those who rule this people in Jerusalem', so that the redactor must have been consciously seeking to provide a contrast to this with his portrayal of a just and righteous political and social order. The **princes** (Heb. *śārîm*) were not only the royal sons at court, but the governing classes more generally, hence *NEB*'s 'rulers'. The preposition *l* should be omitted from MT before 'princes'.

2. **Each will be like a hiding place from the wind:** The verse is self-explanatory and gives four word-pictures of protection drawn from the natural order, which are taken to be applicable to the rulers of a just government. Instead of exploiting and oppressing their subjects, their wealth and wisdom will be entirely used to watch over their interests for the betterment of men's lives.

3. **Then the eyes of those who see:** It is attractive to view the assurance here as a deliberate allusion back to the warning given to Isaiah at his call (6:10). Isaiah's prophecies failed to elicit the response that they deserved because the eyes and ears of his hearers were closed. In a godly and righteous age men will always listen to the word of God, so that the promise here should clearly be understood metaphorically. We should probably regard 30:19f.; 42:18–20 and 43:8 as further developments of the tradition from 6:10 (and also 35:5?). The verb **will not be closed** must be pointed as hoph'al instead of qal.

4. **The mind of the rash:** The reference is to hasty and panicky decisions, which are likely to be unfair and dangerous. We may compare 29:15; 30:1–2 for examples of such ill-judged actions from the Isaiah tradition. The reference to **the tongue of the stammerers** must be an allusion back to 28:9f.

5. **The fool will no more be called noble:** The fool (Heb. *nābāl*; cf. M. Saebo, *THAT*, II, cols. 26–31) was the 'dull', or 'thick-headed' person. Probably the major emphasis here is upon political folly, but a more general picture also presents itself that, under bad government, moral values quickly become distorted and even perverted. **nor the knave said to be honourable.** The knave (Heb. *kîlay*) was the unscrupulous opportunist who could quickly exploit his talents in a time of weak and inadequate government.

6. **For the fool speaks folly:** Vv. 6–8 must be regarded as a short didactic homily that has been added to vv. 1–5, probably in the fifth century BC. Their intention is to elaborate more extensively upon the different ways in which the **fool** and the 'knave' can exploit society to their advantage. The verses betray a sense of disillusionment with the

assurances of vv. 1–5, and concentrate their attention more fully on
the ways of the wicked. **and his mind plots iniquity** follows the
reading of 1QIs^a in reading **plots** (MT has 'works'). **to practise ungodliness.** For **ungodliness** (Heb. *ḥōnep̄*), cf. R. Knierim in *THAT*, I,
cols. 597–9. The unscrupulous and unfeeling way in which such
wrongdoers operate is well shown by the claim that they even **deprive
the thirsty of drink.**

7. The knaveries of the knave: The Heb. has a deliberate alliteration; 'knaveries' is from Heb. *k^{e}lē* = 'weapon, tool', but is evidently
intended to be taken metaphorically. The evil person always has his
own lack of scruple as a sure means of defence. When one trick fails,
another is ready at hand. **he devises wicked devices:** Better, 'plans
crafty schemes'. **to ruin the poor:** The description refers to the abuse
of the processes of law and justice in the courts by making false
charges, or giving false evidence. **even when the plea of the needy:**
The Heb. is very terse and can better be rendered 'and by what they
say to deny justice to the impoverished'.

8. But he who is noble: This final summing up brings out very
characteristically the essential Hebrew understanding of the relationship between the inner, psychological, aspects of the human make-up
and the outer, active, side of life. Cf. H. W. Wolff, *Anthropology of the
Old Testament*, p. 8.

AGAINST THE WOMEN WHO ARE AT EASE

32:9–14

The authenticity of this section has been a repeated point of contention among scholars, with a number of significant claimants leaning
towards ascribing it to Isaiah. So Fohrer, followed by Schoors, en-
titles it 'The Last Words of Isaiah', and regards it as Isaiah's last
prophecy, a threat and call to lamentation delivered after the sparing
of Jerusalem in 701. He would locate it shortly after 22:1–14*.
Against this, earlier scholars (e.g. K. Marti), and more recently O.
Kaiser, have argued that it cannot be shown to be authentic to Isaiah,
and must be dated to the post-exilic age. The question of authorship
is very extensively examined by Wildberger (III, pp. 1265–6), who
decides finally against ascribing it to Isaiah. Its theme is the
threatened destruction of Jerusalem, and he would place it shortly
before the threat to Jerusalem from the Babylonians either in 598 or
587, most probably the latter (p. 1266). This view would appear to be
most likely, with the modification that, although couched in the form
of a threat and a lament, it can better be regarded as having been added
post eventum. It is a lament over the fall of Jerusalem in 587, an event
which may be presumed already to have happened. Once this is seen,
it explains the powerful lament form of vv. 11–13 especially, and also
reveals why a redactor, working after 587, has felt it necessary to add
such a note here. Originally 32:1–5, 15–20 formed the conclusion of
the Josianic Redaction of Isaiah's prophecies, providing a compre-

hensive interpretation of the fate of Israel, Judah and Jerusalem under the threat from Assyria. Yet the hope that had burned so brightly in the period of Josiah had been shattered and frustrated after Josiah's death and the arrival of the Babylonians (see further, below, on chs. 38–39). It was appropriate, therefore, to separate the immediate expectation, relating to Josiah, of vv. 1–5, from the longer term and more ultimate hope of vv. 15–20. Since Josiah's death the dire calamity and grief of the fall of Jerusalem, and the ending of the Davidic reign in the city, had come about. The present section has been designed to point to this, to interpret it, and to leave room for the hope still ultimately to be fulfilled. By placing this section here the post-exilic redactor has deliberately separated the shorter from the longer term aspects of Israel's hope for the future. Very possibly the content of the lament, which begins with concern for the failure of the crops and goes on to the far more serious portrayal of the destruction of **the populous city** (v. 14) was traditional. With this agrees the fact that the city is unnamed, although its relevance to Jerusalem and the fate of this city in 587 is clear. The redactor, therefore, has adapted part of an old lament, or typical lament themes, to his specific purpose of interpreting the fall of Jerusalem.

9. **Rise up, you women who are at ease:** The address to the **women** was traditional for laments, as those who would be deeply affected by the suffering that was envisaged. The fact that they are described as being **at ease** should not be taken here as a mark of rebuke for their complacency, but rather as a basis for the contrast that is to come when they begin their grieving and lamenting. So **you complacent daughters** (Heb. *bōṭᵉḥôṭ*; cf. E. Gerstenberger, *THAT*, I, pp. 300–5) rather over-interprets. The meaning is rather 'happy, carefree'.

10. **In little more than a year;** The meaning is unclear, and *RSV* can hardly be correct in understanding so long an interval. The Heb. literally reads 'days over a year'. Delitzsch took as an idiom, meaning 'at most a year', which Schoors follows. However *NEB* is more convincing in taking the sense as 'when the year is out', i.e. when the vintage and fruit-crop, which mark the end of the agricultural year, will have passed. The intention is to begin by pointing to a traditional and very evident fact of life that disaster, however caused, will ruin the harvest. There is then a threat of famine for an unknown time.

11. **Tremble, you women:** Once again **at ease** and **complacent** introduce a pejorative note which is not truly present in the Heb. The intention is to contrast the present happy state with the grievous one which is so soon to come.

12. **Beat upon your breasts:** The MT reads the participle (masc.!), which should be emended to the imperative with 1QIsᵃ. The whole phrase is probably a secondary insertion, occasioned by a misreading of *śᵉḏê*, 'fields', as *śᵉḏê*, 'breasts'.

13. **for the soil of my people:** The devastation of the agricultural land was an inevitable consequence of war. The phrase **growing up with thorns and briers** picks up once again the 'thorns and briers' theme from the Song of the Vineyard (5:6). Cf. further 7:23–25; 27:4.

yea, for all the joyous houses: The Heb. *kî* (yea) is taken as asservera-tive by *RSV*, but should probably be deleted along with the preposi-tion *'al*. Cf. LXX and *NEB*, 'in every happy home'. The contrast is deliberate between the present happiness and confidence and the coming misery and distress. The **joyful city** (Heb. *qiryāh 'allîzāh*) must be a reference to Jerusalem, and it is the traditional stereotyped language which has left it unidentified.

14. For the palace will be forsaken: The imagery is very stereo-typed and is not designed to present a graphic description of what actually befell Jerusalem in 587. The reason why the city will become deserted is not stated, but the redactor has made use of a traditional lament form in order to point to the disaster that overtook Jerusalem in 587, and which so decisively put an end to the hopes of good government and social justice set out in vv. 1–5.

THE SPIRIT FROM ON HIGH

32 : 15–20

This short section marks the ending of the Josianic Redaction of the collection of Isaiah's prophecies and expresses the future hope of the people of Israel. As such it is eloquent testimony to the strong and eager hopes that arose at that time. Most commentators have preferred to assign it to a later, post-exilic, age (so Fohrer, Schoors, Kaiser, Wildberger). However, we may follow H. Barth, pp. 211–13, in locat-ing it in an earlier time. It provides a very beautiful and fitting con-clusion to the message of Isaiah, and looks to the future as a time of peace, security and general well-being. It offers a far more satisfactory conclusion to the book than the present gruesome Isa. 66:24.

15. until the Spirit is poured upon us from on high: The *RSV* unduly personalises the concept of **spirit** (Heb. *ruaḥ*) by printing it with a capital letter. However, earlier Israelite thinking linked the spirit closely with the activity of God. Cf. Jg. 6:34 and see R. Albertz—C. Westermann, *THAT*, II, cols. 726ff. Its special signi-ficance here is stressing the divine origin of the new life that will be lived by the people of God. The source of human righteousness is in the power and righteousness of God. Cf. 11:1–5. **and the wilderness becomes a fruitful field:** The language is traditional and should not be understood in the dramatic eschatological sense of 30:23–26. The new age of peace will also be an age of plenty.

16. Then justice will dwell in the wilderness: This picks up the theme of 32:1 and recognises that prosperity without justice is a worthless acquisition. Throughout vv. 15–20 there appears to be an intentional sequence established: prosperity—justice—peace—happi-ness.

17. And the effect of righteousness will be peace: Significantly the verse recognises that peace must be the crowning gift of other de-sirable features of the age of salvation, and that a major condition of this is stability and a context of security. Hence it is to be a lasting condition: **quietness and trust for ever.**

18. My people will abide in a peaceful habitation: The emphasis upon **my people** (cf. also v. 13) indicates that what is promised here is the future deliverance and well-being of Israel. The **peaceful habitation** and **quiet resting places** are then understood to be in the land of Judah, and no hint is given that the people have been in exile and must first return to the land. The pre-exilic (Josianic) origin of the passage is certainly the best explanation of this assumption.

19. And the forest will utterly go down: The verse, which is threatening in tone, reads strangely in this context. Several commentators have consequently taken it to be a gloss, or to be misplaced. Duhm and Marti would insert it between vv. 14 and 15. However, the translation is probably in error, and *NEB* understands differently: 'It will be cool on the slopes of the forest then, and cities shall lie peaceful in the plain.'

For this interpretation, cf. G. R. Driver, *JSS* 13 (1968), pp. 52f. Instead of **will utterly go down** this takes the initial verb (*brd*) to mean 'be cool' (cf. Arabic *baruda*). The second hemistich is then read in line with this by understanding the verb *špl* ('to be low, levelled') in the sense 'lie peacefully'. Undoubtedly the interpretation of the verse in a reassuring sense is required by the context.

20. Happy are you who sow beside all waters: The sense is that in the coming age men will be able to go about their business unmolested and untroubled by the thought that they will not be able to reap the reward of their labours.

THE ATTACKER IS THREATENED

33 : 1–6

It must be accepted that the major collection of Isaianic prophecies has been made in chs. 1–32 and that chs. 33–35 have been added as a supplement to this. Whether these latter chapters contain any authentic Isaianic prophecies at all has been much debated, but has generally been answered in the negative by all but the most conservative of scholars. Certainly chs. 34–35 form what has sometimes been called the 'Little Apocalypse' of Isaiah in contrast with the 'Great Apocalypse' of chs. 24–27. Some defence has been made of the contention that short fragments of Isaianic sayings are embedded in ch. 33 (so J. Vermeylen on 33 : 1), but even this claim must be rejected. In fact no part of chs. 33–35 can convincingly be shown to derive directly from Isaiah himself, although extensive use has been made of Isaianic themes and images. There are therefore several allusions back to prophecies and themes which occur earlier in the book.

Ch. 33 has been widely acclaimed as a prophetic liturgy. So G. Fohrer, A. Schoors and earlier S. Mowinckel, *Psalmenstudien* II, Oslo, 1923, pp. 235–8; H. Gunkel, *ZAW* 42 (1924), pp. 177–208. Such liturgical elements are to be found in several parts of the prophetic literature and cannot of themselves point to a specific origin in cult-prophecy. Isa. 33 falls into four clearly identifiable units: vv. 1–6, the threat against the 'destroyer'; vv. 7–9, a lament; vv. 10–13 an oracle;

vv. 14–16 a Torah-liturgy; vv. 17–24 the Promise of Salvation. The structure is evidently deliberate, although no clear connection can be shown between the threat to the 'destroyer', which remains unidentified in vv. 1–6, and the following sections. It is preferable therefore to take these two parts separately. The question of date is hard to determine, although it may be assisted by considering the actual literary processes of redaction by which the present book was formed. Duhm, Marti, and more recently Kaiser, have pointed to the Maccabean age, and in particular to the attack on Jerusalem by Antiochus Eupator in 163/2 BC. Yet there is nothing to give positive identification for such a setting, and, on other grounds, it must be regarded as far too late. Much more convincingly the whole of ch. 33 must be assigned to the age of the Babylonian exile (cf. H. Barth, pp. 46f, 287f., 292–4). What we have here are two summarising prophecies dating from the sixth century BC, the first in vv. 1–6, threatening that Israel's attacker will shortly be destroyed, and the second, in vv. 7–24, addressing the survivors of Judah concerning their present plight and future hope. Ch. 33 therefore is a reflection on the message of Isaiah in the light of the fall of Jerusalem and the Davidic monarchy in 587 BC.

33:1. Woe to you, destroyer: The familiar 'woe'-form has appeared frequently in Isaiah's prophecies. Here the **destroyer** is left unidentified and it is the presumed historical context alone that can identify this as Babylon. There may be some deliberate intention of associating earlier threats against Assyria with this, so that Babylon and Assyria together represent a common Mesopotamian enemy. More probably Babylon alone is in mind as the world power that has destroyed Judah and Jerusalem. J. Vermeylen, I, pp. 429ff., would defend v. 1 as an authentic threat from Isaiah against the Assyrians given in 701, but such a view must be abandoned as nothing more than conjecture. The further description **who yourself have not been destroyed** points to a time before the fall of Babylon in 538. The age of Cyrus, and of the prophecies of chs. 40–55, is still not yet. **you treacherous one** picks up the language of 21:1, which has clearly influenced the author here in his description. **When you have ceased to destroy:** The bitterness against Judah's enemy is strong, but the time of retribution cannot now be long delayed. No hint is given of any political basis for such an expectation. Rather the expectation arises out of a deeper moral conviction that justice must eventually be done.

2. O LORD, be gracious to us; we wait for thee: After the basic pronouncement of the threat against the 'destroyer', the author turns to consider the case of his own people, who await God's action as necessary before their own time of salvation can come. God alone is the basis for his people's hope. The author is presumably in Judah itself, rather than among the exiles in Babylon, although even this cannot be firmly made out.

3. At the thunderous noise peoples flee: There appears to be a conscious allusion back to 17:12 with its reference to the **thunderous**

noise (Heb. *hāmôn*) of the peoples. God is greater than the power of even the greatest of nations, and the earlier threats of his action provide an assurance that he is now about to act again to rescue his people from their oppressors. W. H. Irwin, p. 139, takes the noun to mean 'army', and follows this by reading **at the lifting up of thyself** as 'at the sound of your soldiers' (following a suggestion of M. Dahood's). The sense, however, would appear to be 'at the raising (of your voice)'. Cf. Isa. 13:2, where the verb *rûm* is used in the sense of 'to raise the voice'.

4. and spoil is gathered: The verse is difficult, and must have suffered some disturbance. Its imagery is that of the severity and sharpness of war, which God is about to unleash against the 'destroyer' of v. 1. **as the caterpillar:** Better 'grasshopper' (Heb. *ḥāsîl* is a near synonym of **locusts**). When the battle is over soldiers strip the spoil from the slain, like locusts stripping foliage from a forest.

5. The LORD is exalted: Ultimately Yahweh's will asserts itself, and vv. 5-6 appear to pick up the imagery of hope presented in 32:1-5. **he will fill Zion:** Heb. has imperative, 'fill Zion', which is preferable.

6. And he will be the stability of your times: I.e. the LORD will bring about conditions of prosperity and security, cf. 32:15-20. **abundance of salvation:** The Heb. *ḥōsen* (**abundance**) means 'treasure, wealth', so that the meaning is of the wealth and prosperity which will come through salvation, wisdom and knowledge. Cf. Prov. 15:6. Vv. 1-6 appear to be quite self-contained, threatening the destruction of Judah's enemy, and reaffirming that soon the age of salvation will come. They mark the period of transition from a broad prophetic hope to a quite distinctively eschatological one.

ISRAEL'S LAMENTATION AND GOD'S ANSWER

33:7-24

The liturgical form of this section has already been noted above. It falls into four distinct units, each marked by a firmly kept liturgical form: Lament (vv. 7-9); Oracular Response (vv. 10-13); Torah-liturgy (vv. 14-16) and Prophetic Promise (vv. 17-24). It is possible that separate units have been woven together into a liturgical whole, but against this there are evident marks of the resumption and development of earlier Isaianic themes, especially in the final section. On the whole it appears that an exilic redactor has compiled the section in order to round off the prophecies, adapting some of their themes to a liturgical form. There is no suggestion that the section ever formed an independent liturgical composition. The age of composition would still appear to be that of the Babylonian exile, before the collapse of Babylon in 538.

7. Behold the valiant ones cry without: The Heb. is obscure. For the word translated **valiant ones** (Heb. *'er'ellām*) K-B, p. 80, notes three possibilities: 'heroes', 'priests' or 'inhabitants'. W. H. Irwin, p. 144, proposes 'leaders'. The parallel with **envoys** indicates that important figures in the community are meant. The description of a land suffering distress given by vv. 7–9 would appear to refer to the conditions in Judah after 587, when the ravaged countryside lay desolate. To this extent they describe the fulfilment of the Isaianic threat given in 6 : 11. **the envoys of peace weep bitterly:** The reason for the mission of the **envoys** can only be conjectured. Possibly the meaning is that 'messengers' (Heb. *mal'āḵ*), who report that the battle is ended, can only weep over the devastation it has left.

8. The highways lie waste: All the various features in the breakdown of normal life and prosperity in the community constitute a situation to which God's gracious intervention can provide the answer. The imagery is traditional for the aftermath of war. **Covenants are broken** must refer to the cessation of normal business life, where **covenants** (Heb. *bᵉrîṯ*) provide the natural basis of agreement. Similarly **witnesses** (Heb. *'ēḏîm*, instead of MT, *'ārîm*, 'cities'), are witnesses to commercial transactions.

9. The land mourns and languishes: All the richest and most luxuriant parts of the Holy Land—**Lebanon . . . Sharon . . . Bashan . . . Carmel**—are pictured as withered and decaying. The language must be regarded as metaphorical, rather than as a description of a time of drought, and is intended to reflect the total ruination of Israel—its land, social structure and political fortunes.

10. 'Now I will arise,' says the LORD: In vv. 10–13 Yahweh speaks in the first person in an oracular formulation. This has been adapted from cult-prophecy which must at one time have formed a significant feature of Israel's cultic life. Cf. A. R. Johnson, *The Cultic Prophet in Israel's Psalmody*, Cardiff, 1979, esp. pp. 92ff. God is pictured as reasserting himself and reaffirming his will to act to remedy the conditions described in the preceding lamentation. This action must, however, be regarded as imminent, but still future, from the author's perspective. **now I will lift myself up:** Heb. *'ērômām* is Hithpolal with the *t* assimilated; but cf. 1QIs[a] for a more regular form. The threefold repetition of the same basic idea with the reiterated **now** creates a dramatic note of certainty of imminent divine action.

11. You conceive chaff you bring forth stubble: The language must be regarded as highly stylised. It is addressed to Yahweh's enemies, but there is no reason to follow Kaiser in regarding the identification of them as 'peoples' in v. 12 to mean that a great cosmic battle is envisaged. Rather, all that men can do is no better than produce **chaff** before God, so that man's will cannot for long thwart that of God. The reference is deliberately vague and general. When God acts no men will be able to stand against him, and their efforts to do so will look ridiculous. **your breath is a fire that will consume you:** I.e. anything that you (the enemy) do to try to stop God will do more harm to you yourself. *BHS* follows the ancient versions in emending to 'a wind like fire'.

12. And the peoples will be: The imagery asserts the frailty of man and of all his efforts to stand in God's way. For **as if burned to lime**, cf. Am. 1 : 2.

13. Hear, you who are far off: The final appeal to everyone, near and far, is to recognise who God is, and then to accept that he can be relied upon to act soon, as he has warned. It is improbable that **far off** and **near** are intended to refer to the Babylonian exiles and the community in Judah respectively, as each having an interest in God's intended action. Cf. Dan. 9:7.

14. **The sinners in Zion are afraid:** Vv. 14-16 follow the pattern of a Torah-liturgy. Cf. H. Gunkel, *ZAW* 42 (1924), pp. 177ff.; K. Koch, 'Tempeleinlassliturgie und Dekaloge'. *G. von Rad Festschrift 60. Geburtstag*, Neukirchen, 1961, pp. 45-60; and my book *God and Temple*, pp. 73ff. The closest parallels are to be found in Pss. 15 and 24:3-6. The form is based on a question-and-answer pattern used between pilgrims seeking entrance to the temple and a priestly response to this. This response sets out, in a highly stylised way, the qualities of life required of those who would worship Yahweh. Here the author has adapted the pattern to deal with the question of **the sinners in Zion**. The presupposition would appear to be that Zion (= Jerusalem) still has not learnt all the lessons of its past, and that many of those who live (and rule?) there are still to be regarded as sinners. Will they not thwart the plan of God to restore his people and to give them a secure and prosperous future? The reply takes the form of a fresh application of the ancient Torah-liturgy affirming that Yahweh will test the inhabitants of the city, so that those who cannot live alongside his presence there will be doomed and cast out. The city will then be purified. Cf. 1:24-26. How closely this section reflects a knowledge and disapproval of those who had risen to authority and leadership in Jerusalem during the exilic age can only be conjectured. Cf. Ezek. 33:23-29 for prophetic opposition to the survivors in Jerusalem.

Who among us can dwell with the devouring fire: The familiar prophetic device of putting hypothetical words in the mouths of those addressed is followed here. God is a **devouring fire**, and so those who want to live in Jerusalem will have to live with his presence there. They answer their own question by couching it in these terms.

15. **He who walks righteously and speaks uprightly:** The particular qualifications follow closely those traditionally set out in such Torah-liturgies. Cf. Ps. 15:2-5; 24:4. Great emphasis is placed upon those actions and attitudes which lay outside the scope of the law to deal with, or which could seriously undermine the application of the law such as bribery. **who stops his ears from hearing of bloodshed** does not mean refusing to hear that crimes have been committed, but rather that the person refuses to take part in plots and schemes which intend, or may involve, violence against other people. Similarly, **shuts his eyes from looking upon evil** refers to a refusal to contemplate becoming involved in an evil plan, and not a refusal to act when evil can be seen to be taking place. A refusal to risk personal injury through intervention against evil was certainly not in mind.

16. **he will dwell on the heights:** The language is traditional and metaphorical. To **dwell on the heights** appears to have been an expression meaning 'to worship in the sanctuary'; cf. Ps. 148:1, and its

metaphorical sense as a place of protection has been elaborated in the succeeding imagery. Already the language here appears to offer an extended, metaphorical, understanding of enjoying the blessing of God's presence (in a sanctuary). Thus the meaning becomes simply 'he will live his life in security.' **his bread will be given him:** I.e. he will not lack the necessities of life, which is a development of the older idea that God's presence in the sanctuary was a source of blessing and prosperity for the life of the worshipper.

17. Your eyes will see the king in his beauty: The concluding section in vv. 17–24 sets out Yahweh's promises to his people once again, and describes the triumphant Israel living in Jerusalem under a righteous king, and with no further fear from external enemies. The parallel with 32 : 1–5 is very close, and the latter passage must have influenced the author here. The original fulfilment of that promise had been shattered by the Babylonian exile, and so now it needed to be reaffirmed in the new situation that had arisen since 587. In this glowing portrait of the final age of Israel's blessedness vv. 17–19 stand by themselves with their special interest in the role of the king, and may once have been composed separately. Schoors goes so far as to suggest that they may be based upon an original Isaianic saying referring to the ending of Assyrian oppression. However, this is only true in a very extended sense, for these verses mark the renewal of the Isaianic promise by way of the interpretation given to it in the Josianic Redaction, especially in 32 : 1–5, 15–20. The concern with the kingship is especially interesting and must here allude to the hope of restoring the Davidic monarchy, a hope which flourished during the Babylonian exile and for a short time after it. Cf. Jer. 33 : 14–26; Ezek. 37 : 24–28. The king's **beauty** (Heb. $y^o\bar{p}\hat{i}$) is praised in Ps. 45 : 2. **a land that stretches afar:** The Heb. *'ereṣ marḥaqqîm* means 'distant land', rather than 'broad land', an allusion which could otherwise be referred to the Abrahamic promise (Gen. 15 : 18–21). Possibly the situation of the exiles is already envisaged here.

18. Your mind will muse on the terror: The reference is clearly to foreign oppressors, first the Assyrians and then the Babylonians. The allusion to the counting and weighing of tribute may well point back specifically to the action of Hezekiah in Isaiah's time (2 Kg. 18 : 14ff.). More probably, however, the meaning is that the days of submission, and payment of tribute, to a foreign suzerain power will be at an end. Possibly the word **terror** is a gloss, since the sense is clearer without it, but if it is retained, it must refer to the horror of foreign domination. **Where is he who counted the towers:** G. R. Driver, *JSS* 13 (1968), p. 53, would understand **towers** (Heb. *migdālîm*) as 'piles, store-chests' cf. Ca. 5 : 13.

19. You will see no more the insolent people: We may compare 28 : 11 for a reference to the Assyrians as a people with an 'alien tongue', a verse which may directly have influenced the author here. The meaning has been broadened, however, to affirm that the strange-sounding speech of foreign oppressors and rulers will no more be heard in Judah.

20. Look upon Zion: The use of the title **Zion** to refer to the entire city of Jerusalem, instead of to the temple quarter only, reflects post-exilic usage. Cf. G. Fohrer, *TDNT*, VII, pp. 292ff; *THAT*, II, cols. 543ff. With this must be linked the increased concentration in the post-exilic period upon the restoration and rebuilding of Jerusalem as the central focus of hope, rather than upon the restoration of all Israel. Cf. 62:1–12. The description of Jerusalem as **the city of our appointed feasts** points to the cultic role of the city as its most important function.

21. But there the LORD in majesty: The meaning appears to be that God's presence will give to Jerusalem the beauty and elegance which other cities acquire by having great rivers running through them. The verse is certainly a strange one since it introduces a totally unrealistic feature into the description of a city which has no major waterways at all. Two possibilities of explanation present themselves. Either a deliberate contrast has been made between Jerusalem and Babylon, famed for its river traffic, with the intention of showing that Jerusalem will not spiritually lack the beauty which other cities enjoy, or alternatively we may conclude that some traditional mythological symbolism has been associated with Jerusalem, perhaps encouraged by the identification of the spring Gihon in Jerusalem (1 Kg. 1:33, etc.) with one of the rivers of paradise (Gen. 2:13). Most probably the former is correct, and in this case the particular imagery used would suggest that the author of the section was very conscious of Babylon, if not by experience at least by its reputation. **a place of broad rivers and streams:** Probably we should delete **rivers** (Heb. *nehārîm*) as a gloss on **streams** (Heb. *ye'ōrîm*). The reference to a **galley with oars** appears to associate such vessels with war, rather than with trade.

22. For the LORD is our judge: Because he is **judge**, Yahweh can be relied upon to look after the welfare of his people and to guard them against the unjust actions of hostile nations. The affirmation **the LORD is our king** may quite directly reflect the experience of Isaiah at his call in seeing God as 'King'. Cf. Isa. 6:5. Increasingly in the post-exilic age the idea of a theocracy came to oust and replace the desire for a human king who would adminster God's rule. This cannot be the meaning here, however, since v. 17 would appear quite clearly still to anticipate the restoration of the Davidic monarchy.

23. Your tackle hangs loose: V. 23*a* is certainly misplaced (*NEB* sets it in square brackets), but it can hardly be a conventional gloss since it sheds no useful light whatsoever upon the preceding verses. It describes a ship in distress, and the only way that this can make sense in the present context is to regard the ship as a metaphor for Jerusalem. However, this is a counsel of despair, and it is preferable to associate it with the dirge over Tyre in ch. 23, where it could possibly fit, although not very well. Beyond this we can only conclude that the verse is entirely misplaced, and makes no real sense.

Then prey and spoil in abundance: The sense is difficult, but may be an allusion based on v. 4. Targ. reads 'the blind (Heb. *'iwwēr* instead of '*a̲d*) will divide the spoil', which is preferable. Cf. *NEB*. Possibly 2 Sam. 5 : 6 has influenced the expression here, although the allusion there to 'the blind and the lame' must be proverbial.

24. And no inhabitant will say: This concluding verse must be a redactor's addition which has been introduced because the reference to the blind and lame in v. 23 was felt to jar with the portrayal of the coming age of salvation and happiness in Jerusalem. It 'corrects' the previous impression that there will be sick people in the city, and further hints at the ancient association of sickness with sin by asserting that all iniquity will be forgiven the people. The root cause of sickness will therefore be removed.

The Coming Judgment and Salvation: chapters 34–35

The section comprised of 34 : 1—35 : 10 is recognised by almost all critical scholars to be a unity, and to derive from some time after the Babylonian exile. It is therefore certainly not from Isaiah, but rather shows very close similarities with the 'Apocalypse' of chs. 24–27. Both A. Schoors and J. Vermeylen, I, pp. 439ff., would describe it as the 'Little Apocalypse' of Isaiah. Cf. further, W. Caspari, *ZAW* 49 (1931), pp. 67–86; M. H. Pope, *JBL* 71 (1952), pp. 253–43 and D. R. Hillers, *Treaty Curses and the Old Testament Prophets*, Rome, 1964, pp. 44–54. C. C. Torrey, *The Second Isaiah. A New Interpretation*, Edinburgh, 1928, pp. 53ff. argued that chs. 34–35 were to be linked with 'Deutero-Isaiah' of chs. 40–46 (cf. also M. H. Pope). Yet these latter chapters were not placed by Torrey in the Babylonian Exile, but to a much later time (cf. also J. D. Smart, *History and Theology in Second Isaiah*, London, 1967, pp. 41, 292–4). That there is an affinity between much of the content of chs. 34–35 and 40–55(66) is fully to be conceded, but it appears highly improbable that this is to be explained as a consequence of common authorship. Rather, they result from a dependence of chs. 34–35 upon the prophecies of 40–55. Fohrer, II, p. 138, would describe the author of chs. 34–35 as belonging to the 'school' of Second Isaiah, and would place them in the sixth century BC, shortly after the close of the Babylonian exile. They are therefore to be compared closely to the contents of chs. 56–66, which also date roughly from this period.

The material content of chs. 34–35 shows a dependence on 40–55, and certainly has a proto-apocalyptic character, very similar to that of chs. 24–27. A date some time in the fifth century would appear to be more plausible than one in the sixth, but certainty on this point can hardly be achieved. Their character is thematic, drawing out the implications of earlier prophetic hopes and themes, rather than directly historical, relating to specific situations and persons. However, their general background is that of the tensions, frustrations and expectations of the attempts to reestablish a stable religious and social life in Judah under Persian government. A period after the work of Haggai and Zechariah would therefore appear to be most probable. The common authorship of the chapters is supported by the appearance of a common structure: judgment on the nations, especially Edom, in 34:1-17, followed by the triumphant vindication and exaltation of Judah in 35:1-10. Common features which are to be found throughout the whole include a coherence of vocabulary and style, and a strong measure of dependence on earlier prophecy.

THE GREAT JUDGMENT

34:1-17

The major part of ch. 34 is concerned with the threat of a fierce judgment upon Edom (34:5-17), to which is prefaced a threat of Yahweh's judgment upon all nations (vv. 1-4). The case of Edom, therefore, is seen as a special application of the coming eschatological world-judgment. Feeling against Edom became very sharp among Jews after the time of the Babylonian destruction of Jerusalem in 587, as is shown by Obadiah, Jer. 49:7-22 and Ezek. 25:12-17.

34:1. Draw near, O nations, to hear: The prophet begins by addressing the nations, since his message concerns the fate of all of them. That these nations were not actually present to hear what the prophet had to say made no difference to its efficacy. However, it is clear from the content of the message of judgment that it had a special relevance for Israel-Judah, since already there is an assumption that Judah's destiny is to be different from that of the nations. In the eschatological age, which the prophet-author is concerned with here, the distinction between 'Jew' and 'Gentile' would be a decisive one. The address to the **nations**, therefore, must be understood rhetorically, for in reality the author wishes to encourage his own immediate hearers by disclosing a knowledge of what the fate of the nations is to be. The contrasting fate of the faithful among God's own people is brought out in 35:1-10.

2. For the LORD is enraged against all nations: No specific reason, or explanation, is given for this divine anger, but it becomes a commonplace assumption of eschatological apocalyptic expectation that the entire world has shown itself to be in rebellion against God, especially on account of its treatment of God's people, so that what man needs to know is not 'whether', but 'how soon', judgment will fall upon them. **he has doomed them.** The Heb. $heh^e r\hat{\imath}m\bar{a}m$ takes up the ancient language of the Holy War ideology. Cf. *THAT*, I, cols. 635-9. In this the captives and booty were destroyed as forfeit to God, who was believed to have led the battle.

3. Their slain shall be cast out: The gruesome picture envisages no respectable burial for those slaughtered in such a fearful conflict. The imagery and expectation appears as a further extension of that foretold in Hag. 2:22, and the present passage must be dated shortly after the time of this prophet.

4. All the host of heaven shall rot away: Here the eschatological expectation has been expanded to embrace the entire created order.

Cf. 24:23. The language is extravagant, but must be understood as more than poetic hyperbole and to reflect a genuine expectation of a dramatic change in the whole cosmic order. IQIs^a reads differently, and many commentators would emend **host of heaven** (Heb. $ṣ^eḇā$' *haṣṣāmayim*) to 'hills (Heb. $g^aḇā'ô_t$). However, this is not necessary, and MT can stand. Cf. *NEB*, 'All the host of heaven shall crumble into nothing'.

5. For my sword has drunk its fill: The threat against all nations (vv. 1–4) is set out as a background, and now the author proceeds to deal with the people whom he regards as the more immediate threat to the wellbeing of the people of Yahweh in Judah. Little is known of the actual historical situation which aroused such deep bitterness and rivalry between Judah and Edom in the 6th–5th centuries BC, but quite evidently the gravely weakened state of Judah under Babylonian control had allowed the Edomites to expand their territory and control at the expense of the native Judean population. Instead of **my sword**, *NEB* reads 'sword of the LORD'. Cf. *NEB* margin and *HTOT*, p. 187. This then requires a further change at the end of the verse to 'the people he has doomed' (Heb. $ḥer^emô$). Instead of **has drunk its fill**, IQIs^a reads 'appears' (Heb. *tērā'ēh*), which is preferable.

6. The LORD has a sword: The coming destruction of Edom is compared to a sacrificial slaughter, and this particular image is elaborated extensively by reference to features of the sacrificial practice applied to animals. **a sacrifice in Bozrah: Bozrah** was the chief city of the Edomites. Cf. Jer. 49:13, 22, situated 27 miles south of the Dead Sea; modern *el-Buṣēra*. All aspects of the joyous situations in which sacrifices were customarily offered have been ignored in stressing the fact of physical slaughter.

7. Wild oxen shall fall with them The point would appear to be that nothing is to be spared among men and beasts. Along with the Edomites themselves all types of cattle, **wild oxen, young steers** and full-grown **bulls**, are all to be slaughtered.

8. For the LORD has a day of vengeance: The sense of grievance against Edom comes right to the fore, and all the past misdeeds against Judah are to be avenged. **a year of recompense for the cause of Zion:** Literally to 'contest the case' (Heb. *rîḇ*). *NEB* takes the Heb. noun as a participle (cf. *BHS*) and renders 'for the champion of Zion', i.e. Yahweh himself. This establishes a better parallelism between the two hemistichs.

9. And the streams of Edom: Heb. has literally 'her streams'. The imagery must be understood metaphorically and conveys the idea that the countryside of Edom will become as barren and desolate as the slopes of an active volcano. An association with the traditional picture of the divine judgment inflicted upon Sodom cannot be overlooked (Gen. 19:24–29).

10. Night and day it shall not be quenched: The hyperbolic imagery becomes somewhat overstretched in describing the permanent smoking ruin that will mark the site where Yahweh inflicted his judgment upon Edom.

11. But the hawk and the porcupine shall possess it: The imagery of a ruined city inhabited by nothing more than wild animals is a common theme of prophecy; cf. 32:14. D. R. Hillers, *Treaty-Curses and the Old Testament Prophets*, pp. 44ff., sees in it a particular point of connection with the curse formulations of vassal-treaties. Here, however, it introduces a word-picture which fits badly with what has preceded it, and indicates that the author's intensity of feeling has outrun his poetic control of style. The reference to **the line of confusion** (Heb. *bōhû*) and **the plummet of chaos** (Heb. *tōhû*) contains a deliberate reference back to the description of the formless void of the world before God imposed his created order upon it (Gen. 1:2).

12. They shall name it No Kingdom There: The finality of Edom's end is to be preserved in the new name which will be given to the desolate land where it had once been.

13. Thorns shall grow: Once again the rather stereotyped image of the waste-land, where once a city had stood, is used. **an abode for ostriches:** The rendering **abode** (Heb. *ḥāṣēr*) follows 1QIs[a] and the ancient versions.

14. the satyr shall cry to his fellow: The satyr (Heb. *śā'îr*, literally 'hairy ones') may mean 'goat'; cf. *NEB*, 'he-goat'. **yea, there shall the night hag alight.** The **night hag** (Heb. *lîlît*) became a familiar figure of semi-religious mythology in later Judaism, but the context scarcely supports the idea of an uncanny and powerful supernatural creature. Hence *NEB* is more probably correct in reading 'nightjar'.

15. There shall the owl nest: The multiplying of examples of the wildlife to be found in the ruins of Edom is designed to illustrate the complete and lasting abandonment of the land by men and its return to a wild state.

16. Seek and read from the book of the LORD: The reference would appear most probably to be to an earlier prophecy found in the book of Isaiah, such as Isa. 13:21–22. This might especially be linked with the description of the overthrow of Sodom and Gomorrah in 13:19. Otherwise we might think of references more explicitly to the threatened downfall of Edom in Jeremiah and Ezekiel, in which case a larger prophetic collection than that in the book of Isaiah is referred to. D. R. Hillers, *Treaty-Curses*, p. 45, argues that the 'book of Yahweh' must refer to an inscription relating to a treaty between Judah and Edom, sanctioned by Yahweh, which would be the 'covenant-document' of Yahweh. However, this is certainly to read into the prophetic text too much from the situation appropriate to treaties, which is not otherwise evident here. **and his Spirit has gathered them:** I.e. God has ordained that they should come to inhabit the ruins, because their doing so is in fulfilment of his purpose of judgment upon Edom.

17. He has cast the lot for them: The meaning is that God has taken the land away from the Edomites and given it to the wild animals instead. The allocation of cultivable land by means of a socio-legal rite of casting the **line** is referred to in Ps. 16:6; Mic. 2:5.

THE BLESSING OF THE LAND OF JUDAH

35:1-10

In sharp contrast with the preceding section, with its threat of a dire and fearful fate awaiting the people of Edom in the eschatological age, the following picture describes the blessedness which will be conferred on Judah. Its future will be one of unprecedented prosperity, security and contentment. The imagery is drawn from other parts of the book of Isaiah, especially from chs. 40–55, which has given rise to the mistaken contention that this chapter once formed a part of the same collection. Yet the secondary nature of the references here is unmistakable. The theme of the **highway** is taken from 40:3, and that of the **streams in the desert** from 43:19; 44:3. Moreover, the fundamental promise of the return to Zion of all the **ransomed** of God's people (35:10) takes up the promise of 51:11. However, the concept has now been extended to encompass the return of all scattered Jews from the Diaspora, and not simply the Babylonian exiles. That the imagery in 35:1-10 has been drawn from the prophecies of chs. 40–55 cannot be seriously in question. Possibly this indicates that the composition of 35:1-10 took place when the material in chs. 40ff. had already been linked with the earlier chapters. More likely, however, it is the use of such imagery and assurances in chs. 35 which has occasioned the joining of the prophecies of chs. 40ff. to the earlier material. Then the narrative section of chs. 36–39, which originally belonged to the books of 1 and 2 Kg, was inserted at a late stage, thereby separating the different collections. In any case ch. 35 must be interpreted as a 'concluding summary' of the message of hope that was built upon and added to the prophecies of chs. 1–33, rather than as a preface, or introduction, to chs. 40ff. (as Torrey, Pope).

35:1. The wilderness and the dry land shall be glad: Just as surely as Edom will be judged, so also is it sure that a great transformation will take place in the natural order. The understanding is of a great change that will take place when the end-time comes, but the basic promise appears to have been drawn from 43:19f. At the same time there has no doubt been some poetic recollection of the dramatic way in which the desert is changed after a rainstorm. **like the crocus:** I.e. the 'desert crocus', probably asphodel. Cf. Ca. 2:1.

2. The glory of Lebanon shall be given to it: The most barren parts of the land would become as rich and covered with luxuriant growth as the forest of **Lebanon**. Cf. 29:17. Similarly the lush pastures, **the majesty of Carmel and Sharon**, would be seen covering regions that had hitherto been found infertile and unsuitable for agriculture. There can be no doubt that the author here has broadened and generalised the picture given in chs. 40–55 and developed it into a promise of the richness of life in the new age. **They shall see the glory of the LORD:** The promise is taken over directly from 40:3, 5; 60:1, but has become detached from the specific historical situation of the return of the exiles from Babylon to which it originally applied. Essentially there has entered a great shift of emphasis from a historical event, interpreted as a manifestation of God, to a change in the natural order as bringing about such a revelation.

3. Strengthen the weak hands: Cf. 40:29-31; 41:17, from which the author appears to have taken his injunctions here. The joy of the new age is to act as an incentive in the present to be strong, and to endure oppression, because the time of such sorrow would soon be past.

4. Behold, your God will come with vengeance: Cf. 40:9. The consciousness that the readers were still living under the oppression of foreign rule, and had not yet received the promise of salvation, leads to a new patience in looking for the time when God will appear. The prophetic poetry of chs. 40-55 has been interpreted in terms of a radical eschatology, with the consequence that the poetic imagery has become apocalyptic expectation.

5. Then the eyes of the blind: The reference is back to the prophecy of 42:18f., where 'blindness' and 'deafness' are used as metaphors of the spiritual condition of Israel in exile. Here, however, the language appears with a literal sense and refers to the removal of all physical disabilities in the coming age of salvation.

6. then shall the lame man leap: This develops further the theme that a new healing and life-giving energy will be given to God's people. Cf. 33:24 for the belief that there would be no sickness in the final age. **For waters shall break forth:** The promise of rivers in the desert, taken from chs. 40ff., provides a foundation assurance of the new world order that is expected.

7. the burning sand shall become a pool: The theme drawn from 41:18f. is here developed still further. Possibly we may detect a sense of economic weakness and the experience of poor harvests to lie behind the author's intense pre-occupation with this promise from 'Second Isaiah'. In origin the promise was used to show the exceptional measures that Yahweh would take to enable his people to cross the desert in returning from Babylon to their homeland. Here it has become an expectation of the miraculous abundance of life and of luxuriant vegetation which would mark the eschatological age. Ideas of a wonderful paradisal age, which would be established at the end of time, may have influenced the general understanding, and undoubtedly become a prominent feature of later apocalyptic.

8. And a highway shall be there: The reference back is to 40:3-5. Cf. also 11:16 for a parallel development of the same theme. Here the picture has been much enlarged, even beyond that of 11:16, and has taken on a metaphorical significance. After **highway** MT adds 'and a way', which must be a scribal error for a reference to the character of the way. After **the unclean shall not pass over it** MT has four additional words, but the Heb. is obscure. *BHS* suggests 'and the foolish man shall direct his way', whereas *NEB* emends to 'it shall become a pilgrim's way' (cf. *HTOT*, p. 188). The concluding clause **and fools shall not err therein** is a glossator's addition, who has further developed the idea of the 'way' as a metaphor for *tôrāh*.

9. No lion shall be there: Cf. 11:6-9 for a comparable picture of the removal of any threat from wild creatures in the coming age of salvation.

10. And the ransomed of the LORD shall return: The promise of the **return** goes back to 'Second Isaiah's' prophecy in 51 : 11, but has now acquired a much extended meaning. From referring initially to the return of the exiles from Babylon it has come to be understood as a promise of the return of all Jews from the Diaspora, cf. 11 : 12; 27 : 12–13. This time of the great 'Return' is to herald the final age of Israel's blessedness in which all that had been promised to the nation's ancestors would be realised. It would be an age of peace, prosperity and national greatness for Israel. There can be little question that the presentation of this hope here was intended by a redactor, probably working sometime in the fifth century BC, to mark the conclusion of his expanded collection of Isaianic prophecies. Subsequently the large collection of chs. 40–66 has been added to this, and at a subsequent stage the connection has been broken off to allow of the insertion of the narratives of chs. 36–39.

The Isaiah Narratives: chapters 36–39

The four chapters of Isa. 36–39 are repeated, almost word for word, from 2 Kg. 18 : 17—20 : 19. The only really major addition is in the psalm attributed to Hezekiah in 38 : 9–20. Aside from this, the character of the minor variations between the two accounts leaves no doubt that their setting in 2 Kings is original and their inclusion here a secondary carrying-over by a redactor. An editor has evidently sought to bring together an important sequence of narratives which related to Isaiah, so as to provide a relatively complete compendium of traditions about him and his activity. Since it becomes evident from an examination of their contents that the narratives were not complete until some time in the sixth century, this implies that their incorporation into the book of Isaiah took place at quite a late stage in the formation of the book. In any case this should no doubt be inferred from the way in which the inclusion of the narratives makes a separation between chs. 35 and 40, which are otherwise closely related in content. It must be held as possible that chs. 40ff. had already become associated with chs. 1–35 prior to this time, although whether this can be taken to imply that the two collections had become joined must be left in uncertainty. Probably the inclusion of chs. 36–39 into the book of Isaiah was one of the latest steps to occur in its formation, so that we may deduce that a redactor has quite consciously sought to use these narratives to form a bridge between the 'Assyrian' background of chs. 1–35 and the 'Babylonian' background of chs. 40–66, with ch. 39 forming a key transition unit. Certainly the understanding and interpretation of the narratives of chs. 36–39 can be best guided by their place in the account of 2 Kg., rather than their setting here. In fact, it is evident that their primary point of focus is that of the fate of

Jerusalem under the Assyrians, especially when contrasted with the fate of the Northern Kingdom, and the special role that Hezekiah, the ruling king of the house of David, was to play in the divine purpose for Judah and Israel. The work and preaching of Isaiah are in fact quite peripheral to the main themes of the narratives, and his role is simply that of acting as God's mouthpiece in a series of critical situations concerning Jerusalem and the kingship. Even so, the appearance of the material in a vigorous narrative form has meant that these accounts have tended to exercise a very powerful influence on the interpretation of the message of Isaiah.

The chapters should be considered as a whole, forming a trilogy of stories concerning Isaiah, Jerusalem and the Davidic kingship. A very full discussion of them is offered by B. S. Childs, *Isaiah and the Assyrian Crisis (SBT Second Series* 3), London, 1967, and my own forthcoming study, *Isaiah and the Deliverance of Jerusalem*, ch. 3. Earlier specialist studies are to be found in J. Meinhold, *Die Jesajaerzählungen. Jesaja 36–39. Eine historisch-kritische Untersuchung*, Göttingen, 1898, and L. L. Honor, *Sennacherib's Invasion of Palestine. A Critical Source Study*, New York, 1926. In all of these treatments fuller details and bibliography can be found. Since the problem is a very important one for the understanding of Isaiah's message a summary of the various views may be noted here.

In the first place it is clear that the major groundwork of the trilogy of stories is to be found in 36:1—37:38, which is usually described as narrative B, to distinguish it from the account of Hezekiah's surrender to Sennacherib in 701 in 2 Kg. 18:13–16, which is described as narrative A. This latter was taken from the royal chronicles of Judah and incorporated into the Deuteronomic History (Jos.—2 Kg., cited as DtrG). However, narrative B is made up of two separate accounts which have been woven together (B^1, consisting of 36:1—37:9a, + 37:37–38; B^2, consisting of 37:9b—36). It is evident that these two narratives were combined together into a whole as the end result of an extended process of growth, and they are remarkable for their portrayal of a dramatic defeat of Sennacherib's army by 'the angel of the LORD' outside Jerusalem. This comes into conflict with the picture of Hezekiah's surrender given in narrative A. Three major possibilities of reconciling the accounts have been proposed:

(1) The narrative of account B (the combined B^1 and B^2) represents a highly elaborated account of the sparing of Jerusalem, written long after 701, but which essentially refers to the same event as narrative A.

(2) The narrative of account B refers to a later incident than the surrender of Hezekiah to Sennacherib, and implies that, after accepting Hezekiah's submission, Sennacherib came back to Jerusalem later in 701 in a subsequent attempt to take the city, regretful of his earlier leniency. So J. Skinner, *Isaiah i–xxxix*, Cambridge, 1915, pp. 276ff.; H. H. Rowley, 'Hezekiah's Reform and Rebellion', *Men of God*, London/Edinburgh, 1963, pp. 98–132.

(3) The narrative of account B refers to a subsequent attempt on the part of Sennacherib to take Jerusalem, not in 701, but in a later cam-

paign, perhaps as late as 688 BC. So R. W. Rogers, 'Sennacherib and Judah', J. *Wellhausen Festschrift*, ed. K. Marti, Giessen, 1914, pp. 317–28; J. Bright, *A History of Israel*, 2nd edn., London, 1972, pp. 296–308. The view adopted here is that (1) is correct and that the narrative now set out in Isa. 36–37 (narrative B) is a highly theologised reflection back upon the events of 701, which culminated in Hezekiah's surrender, made sometime during Josiah's reign. It contrasts the fate of Jerusalem with that of the rest of Judah, and even more with that of the Northern Kingdom, which had suffered frightful deportations and harassment under Assyrian rule. The closest literary affinities of this narrative, therefore, are with the Josianic Redaction of the prophecies of Isaiah, which has developed, by a form of elaborate 'developmental exegesis', a promise of the overthrow of the Assyrians. The final redactor of narrative B has come to accept that a first major step in this overthrow of the Assyrians took place in 701 (especially 37:36; see below). It is only in an extended sense, therefore, that the picture of events, and of Isaiah's preaching, given in chs. 36–37 can be said to reflect accurately his actual message. It is rather his preaching seen and interpreted in the light of subsequent events.

From this perspective regarding the form and character of the narrative of chs. 36–37, we can proceed to see how the two following narratives in chs. 38–39 relate to them. It is in any event very clear that the view of the importance of Jerusalem and of the Davidic monarchy expressed in narrative B was closely related to the basic ideas of the reform movement of Josiah's reign which was associated with the production of the Deuteronomic literature. The account of Hezekiah's sickness (Isa. 38) and that of the Babylonian envoys' visit to Jerusalem (Isa. 39) have been introduced to modify and particularise more closely the very high, and even exaggerated, estimate of the divine protection assured to Jerusalem in the narrative of chs. 36–37. Their intention is quite clearly to show that such protection as had been given against Sennacherib related to a very special king (Isa. 38), and that already the forewarning had been given that Jerusalem would not be similarly protected from the Babylonians (Isa. 39). The three narratives together (chs. 36–39), therefore, form a connected presentation concerning the role of Jerusalem and its Davidic kingship for the life and destiny of Israel and Judah. Whether all three narratives were already combined together when they were incorporated into the Deuteronomic History, as W. Dietrich, *Prophetie und Geschichte* (FRLANT 108), Göttingen, 1972, argues, is a more open question. Certainly we must dismiss the idea that the incorporation took place as late as Dietrich argues (second half of 6th century), as I have shown in my essay in the *I. L. Seeligmann Festschrift*, Jerusalem, 1979. Either all three narratives were incorporated together during Zedekiah's reign (598–587 BC), or the major narrative (2 Kg. 18:17—19:37 = Isa. 36:1—37:38) was incorporated into the first draft of that history during Josiah's reign. (For such an origin of the Deuteronomic History, cf. F. M. Cross, *Canaanite Myth and Hebrew*

Epic, Cambridge, Mass., 1973, pp. 287ff.). The second and third narratives (2 Kg. 20:1–19 = Isa. 38:1—39:8) were then incorporated later, probably during Zedekiah's reign.

THE DELIVERANCE OF JERUSALEM
36:1–37:38

The narrative of Isa. 36–37 is made up from two separate accounts (B¹ = 36:1—37:9a + 37:37–38; B² = 37:9b—36). There is a considerable difference of emphasis, since it is only the B² account which refers to any dramatic defeat of the Assyrians outside Jerusalem. B¹ simply affirms that Sennacherib will return to his own land without destroying Jerusalem (cf. 37:7) and will die there. Similarly, the main basis of the B² narrative also makes the return of Sennacherib to his own land without attacking Jerusalem or pressing a siege against it the major feature (cf. 37:33–35). It comes as a surprise, therefore, that in describing the fulfilment of these threats the physical destruction of Sennacherib's army is included (37:36; B²). Quite clearly this represents a heightening of the miraculous and dramatic elements of the account at a late stage in the growth of the tradition, quite possibly after B¹ and B² had been combined. Apart from this, the narratives follow a strikingly parallel structure with Sennacherib challenging Hezekiah and the inhabitants of Jerusalem, by an emissary—the Rabshakeh—in B¹ and by letter in B². Hezekiah is distressed by this, and turns to Yahweh for help. Isaiah then brings a reassuring message from God that Sennacherib will be unable to fulfil his threats and will not succeed in taking Jerusalem. The prophecies attributed to Isaiah do not relate directly to any recorded prophecies from the prophet himself, and we must conclude that they have been composed freely for incorporation into the narratives. However, the narratives as a whole, when taken separately, have a very marked 'disputation theme', which recalls the boast put into the mouth of the king of Assyria in Isa. 10:5–15* (especially vv. 8–9, 13–14). Since this important prophecy has provided a very basic text for the development of the Josianic Redaction, there seems no reason whatsoever to doubt that it has also provided the basic source for the growth of the narratives here. The whole is a piece of narrative theology, therefore, which has been developed on the basis of a specific prophecy, and interpreted retrospectively in the light of contemporary and subsequent events.

36:1. In the fourteenth year of King Hezekiah, Sennacherib king of Assyria: This year is 701 BC, as the Assyrian record confirms (cf. *ANET*, pp. 287f.), which must have been the twenty-fourth year of Hezekiah's reign, if he came to the throne of Judah in 725 (see Introduction, pp. 8f.). How the error arose is not clear, although there may have been some confusion with the Ashdodite rebellion of 713–711 BC.

2. And the king of Assyria sent the Rabshakeh: The title of the Assyrian officer translates as 'chief cup-bearer', according to H. Zimmern *ZDMG* 53 (1899), pp. 116ff. Possibly the title had acquired a

specifically military significance, with the meaning 'officer', or perhaps it was simply an Assyrian title known to the author, and therefore deemed suitable. The extent of the Assyrian destruction of Judah
('forty-six cities . . .') is fully reported in Sennacherib's Annals (cf.
ANET, p. 288), and the capture of Lachish is brutally portrayed in
Assyrian wall-reliefs.

3. And there came out to him Eliakim: Cf. 22:20 for **Eliakim** and
22:15 for **Shebna. the son of Asaph the recorder.** (Heb. *mazkîr*);
better, 'the herald'. Cf. T. N. D. Mettinger, *Solomonic State Officials*,
pp. 52ff.

4. And the Rabshakeh said to them: The Rabshakeh's speech is a
free creation by the author of the narrative, but appears to rest on a
knowledge of an authentic collection of Isaiah's prophecies, especially 10:8–9, 13–14; 19:1–15; 30:1–5.

6. Behold, you are relying on Egypt: The saying reveals a familiarity with Isa. 30:4f.

7. But if you say to me: 2 Kg. 18:22 uses the plural, whereas the
second person singular is used here. The traditions regarding
Hezekiah's religious reforms are reported in 2 Kg. 18:3–7 and serve to
indicate that the author of B¹ must have been closely associated with
the Deuteronomic circle of Josiah's reign. At the close of the verse 2
Kg. 18:22 adds 'in Jerusalem'.

8. my master the king of Assyria: *BHS* regards **of Assyria** as a gloss,
both here and in v. 16.

9. when you rely on Egypt for chariots and for horsemen: there is
an allusion to Isaiah's prophecy recorded in 31:1.

10. Moreover, is it without the LORD: The proud boast, put into the
Rabshakeh's mouth, that Yahweh has incited the Assyrians to this
action, is clearly drawn from Isaiah's portrayal of Assyria as the 'rod' of
Yahweh's anger (10:5). **against this land:** 2 Kg. 18:25 reads 'against
this place', drawing closer attention to the city itself and to its temple.

11. Pray, speak to your servants in Aramaic: Aramaic was the
common diplomatic language of the period in which negotiations
could be conducted, but which would not have been intelligible to the
ordinary citizens of Jerusalem. The composition of the speeches in the
account, and the fact that they are presented as being addressed openly
to everybody, builds up the tension towards the final moment of divine
dénouement in which everything of which the Rabshakeh had boasted
is confounded by what Yahweh does. The narrative, therefore, is
primarily designed around a theological assertion that Yahweh is the
true God who demonstrates this fact by fulfilling his word through
events.

12. and not to the men sitting on the wall: The contemptuous and
threatening way in which the people of Jerusalem are referred to
intensifies the sense of blustering arrogance on the part of the Assyrians. Quite probably the author was familiar with certain Assyrian
edicts and inscriptions in which such an arrogant tone was present.
Certainly the Assyrian royal Annals reveal such a tone in full measure.

15. Do not let Hezekiah make you rely on the LORD: The author skilfully uses the Rabshakeh's speech to put his finger on the central issue that is at stake in the entire episode covered by the narrative: faith in Yahweh. Once the outcome is known, then everything points back to show that it is faith in Yahweh alone which has made the deliverance of Jerusalem possible.

16. Make your peace with me and come out to me: The picture presented by the verse—that the citizens will suffer no harm—contrasts with the warning of v. 17 that they will eventually be deported. The introduction of a delay between surrender and eventual deportation must reflect what happened to the citizens of the Northern Kingdom of Israel, who were still being taken from their homes and land as late as Esarhaddon's time (680–669 BC). Cf. Ezr. 4:2.

18. Beware lest Hezekiah mislead you: The repetition of essentially the same warning already given in vv. 15 and 18 is for added emphasis. It brings out very forcibly the idea that the satisfactory outcome for the citizens of Jerusalem is entirely due to the work of Yahweh. **Has any of the gods of the nations:** Cf. 10:9, which has evidently influenced the author here. Once again the content of the speech serves to bring out the theological emphasis of the entire narrative sequence of chs. 36–37: Yahweh is superior to all other gods—even the god of Assyria—and the proof of this is that Sennacherib was unable to take Jerusalem in 701.

19. Have they delivered Samaria out of my hand: Cf. 10:9. The emphasis is interesting since it indicates a sense of the apostate worship of the people of Samaria, who could not rely on Yahweh's protection as could those of Jerusalem.

21. But they were silent: The issue is to be decided not by words, but by actions, so the silence of Hezekiah's officials lifts the controversy from the level of a disputation to that of a 'trial by events'. Who controls history, the king of Assyria or Yahweh?

37:1. When Hezekiah heard it: The king's personal reaction of humble submission to God forms an important part of the theological structure. Hence the fact that **he went into the house of the LORD** must be interpreted as a mark of his own piety and trust in God. The B² account introduces a prayer on the part of the king at this point (37:15–20). Hezekiah's turning to God, and his acts of contrition and mourning, serve to demonstrate his personal weakness when confronted by Sennacherib, and his willingness to submit totally to God. Possibly the author was also conscious that Isaiah had sharply rebuked the king for his folly in rebelling against Assyria, and so wished to make clear that Hezekiah had now fully repented from the folly of such an act.

2. And he sent Eliakim ... to the prophet Isaiah: The role of Isaiah in the three narratives of chs. 36–39 is quite secondary. He acts as the mouthpiece of God to interpret his actions, but the focal point of the stories is more directly to be found in the king (and Yahweh himself) than in the prophet.

3. children have come to birth, and there is no strength: This is evidently a proverbial expression, which is used here to highlight the weakened condition of Judah.

4. It may be that the LORD your God heard the words: Yahweh had clearly been blasphemed by what had been said, so he could certainly be looked to in the hope that he would act to vindicate his name, a type of appeal familiar in psalms of lamentation. Cf. Ps. 10 : 1ff. **lift up your prayer for the remnant that is left.** This displays an interesting development of the remnant theme from 7 : 3 in which Jersualem is interpreted as the **remnant** of Israel. Cf. further 37 : 30–32.

7. Behold, I will put a spirit in him, so that he shall hear a rumour: There is nothing dramatically miraculous, in the popular sense, about the way in which Sennacherib is thwarted from taking Jerusalem, according to the account B¹. Nor is this significantly true of B², save in the one striking assertion of 37 : 36. Whether the author had available a tradition which showed that Sennacherib had been influenced in his dealings with Jerusalem by a report of action from Egypt, or elsewhere, is quite unclear. Most likely this seemed a plausible explanation of why Jerusalem had not suffered the same fate as Lachish and other towns of Judah. **and I will make him fall by the sword in his own land:** This points forward to the conclusion recorded in v. 38. Sennacherib's death did not in fact take place in 682, some considerable interval after the attack on Jerusalem.

8. The Rabshakeh returned: After the capture of Lachish Sennacherib's camp had moved to Libnah, the precise location of which is uncertain.

9. Now the king had heard concerning Tirhakah king of Ethiopia: This **Tirhakah** did not become ruler of Upper and Lower Egypt until 690/689. He could not have been king in 701 therefore. However, he may well have participated in action against the Assyrians at this period, so that it would be an understandable assumption to describe him by his later title. For Tirhakah, cf. K. A. Kitchen, *The Third Intermediate Period in Egypt* (1100–650 BC), Warminster, 1973, pp. 154–72, 387–93; J. M. A. Janssen, *Biblica* 34 (1953), pp. 23–43. The reference to a move from the Egyptian side against Assyria most probably reflects a knowledge of the battle at Eltekeh in which the Egyptians were defeated. It is not clear that any subsequent Egyptian action took place in 701, and, from the Assyrian records, their defeat had already occurred when Sennacherib began to prepare for the siege of Jerusalem.

And when he heard it, he sent messengers to Hezekiah: Instead of **heard** (Heb. *wayyišma'*), LXX and the counterpart in 2 Kg. 19 : 19 read 'and he turned back' (Heb. *wayyāšoḇ*), which is certainly original. The text here marks the beginning of the B² account, which extends as far as v. 36. In large measure it runs parallel in structure and character to B¹. Instead of a speech by the Rabshakeh, Sennacherib makes his boast by means of a letter sent to Hezekiah. The B² account also has more extended citation of prophecies ascribed to Isaiah. As the combined narrative now reads it appears that the B² account reports a subsequent series of negotiations between Sennacherib and Hezekiah, but it is evident from an examination of the structure of the two accounts that they are basically parallel reports of a single confrontation. The existence of the two accounts therefore (B¹ and B²) cannot be said to strengthen the case for arguing that Sennacherib subsequently reneged on his acceptance of Hezekiah's surrender (2 Kg. 18 : 13–16), or mounted a second campaign against Judah at a later time.

10. Thus you shall speak to Hezekiah: For the arrogant boasting of the Assyrian king and the highly theological form of his ultimatum to Hezekiah, see above on 36 : 14, 18. It is evident that 10 : 8f. has provided a basic source for the presentation.

11. Behold, you have heard what the kings of Assyria have done to all lands: The recounting of Assyrian achievements appears to reflect quite reliably the bombastic note that characterised their official Annals. Whether it also accurately reports their attitude in negotiations can only be surmised, but may well be correct. **And shall you be delivered:** The singling out of Jerusalem in this way is a very marked feature of both the B¹ and B² accounts. The point is made that no other city had escaped from the grip of the Assyrian king in the way that Jerusalem did. Although this has led to a considerable theological heightening of the historical picture, it was basically a true one, especially when viewed in the retrospect of more than half a century. The reason for this special divine protection of Jerusalem is given in v. 35.

12. Have the gods of the nations delivered them: By such a question the historical issue is turned into a theological one, concerning the identity of the true God.

13. Where is the king of Hamath: With this verse the belief in the unique character of the divine support for the Davidic kings of Jerusalem is brought into the discussion. It is not simply 'Which nation?', or 'Which god?', but 'Which king?' which will affect the determination of events.

15. And Hezekiah prayed to the LORD: The prayer which follows in vv. 16–20 bears a stamp and character which are very markedly Deuteronomic. At other great turning-points in the history of Israel the authors of the Deuteronomic History (DtrG) introduce prayers spoken by kings. Cf. 2 Sam. 7 : 18–29 (David) and 1 Kg. 8 : 23–53 (Solomon). The use of a prayer at such a point in the account greatly strengthens the theological interpretation relating to the situation described.

17. Incline thy ear, O LORD, and hear: God himself had been mocked by the claims inherent in the Rabshakeh's speech, so he is here invited to defend himself. Both the political and military foundations of Hezekiah's defence had collapsed. Now there remained only the theological defence that Yahweh his God was alone the true God of all nations.

18. the kings of Assyria have laid waste all the nations: 1QIsᵃ omits **and their lands**. Once again the historical fact of the unchecked might of Assyria provides the background to the startling fact that Jerusalem alone appeared to have escaped such a fate.

19. and have cast their gods into the fire: The Assyrians did not normally actively suppress the religions of subject states. Cf. M. Cogan, *Imperialism and Religion, Assyria, Judah and Israel in the Eighth and Seventh Centuries B.C.E. (SBL Monograph Series* 19), Missoula, 1974, pp. 15ff. However, they did claim that their enemies' gods had abandoned them, and the author's point here is that the very defeat of the nations who worshipped them had discredited the gods themselves.

20. that all the kingdoms of the earth may know: The formula *that . . . may know* becomes a prominent literary formulation, popular in the exilic and early post-exilic age as the 'Recognition Formula'. Cf. W. Zimmerli, *Erkenntnis Gottes nach dem Buche Ezekiel (ATANT* 27), Zürich, 1954, pp. 16ff.

that thou alone art the LORD: Read, with 1QIs^a and 2 Kg. 19:19, 'that thou alone, O LORD, art God'.

21. Then Isaiah . . . sent to Hezekiah: Isaiah figures rather more prominently in the B^2 account than he does in B^1. Both accounts report a surprisingly indirect manner of communication between Isaiah and Hezekiah in which they do not actually meet. **Because you have prayed to me:** LXX adds 'I have heard'. As Kaiser notes, it becomes evident on examination that the B^2 account did not originally contain the oracle of vv. 22–32, which has been interpolated subsequently. Thus we may deduce that the narrative originally disclosed what Isaiah had to say to the king in vv. 33–35. The message is clear and concise: Sennacherib would not lay siege to Jerusalem, nor attack, but would return home 'by the way that he came'. All of this represents a substantially factual knowledge of what took place in 701. Hezekiah surrendered before a full siege was enforced, although Sennacherib began preparations for one. What is 'foretold' in Isaiah's original prophecy is therefore a highly onesided, but basically factual, report of how Jerusalem was spared in 701. The important point omitted is that Hezekiah surrendered and paid a heavy indemnity to save his capital.

22. this is the word that the LORD has spoken: Alongside the original prophecy recounted in the narrative (vv. 33–35), two further prophecies have been interpolated. The first of these is addressed to Sennacherib (not to Hezekiah) and extends from v. 22 to v. 29. The second interpolation (vv. 30–32) is addressed directly to Hezekiah. Both additions must have been made not long after the time of composition of the original narrative, but possibly after B^1 had been combined with B^2. The whole of this first interpolation contains essentially the same message as that of the original prophecy, but elaborated in a more extensive poetic form (see especially v 29). **She despises you, she scorns you:** I.e. the city of Jerusalem, pictured as a young woman of spirit and courage, in elaboration of the metaphor of the city as **the virgin daughter of Zion.** The unwelcome advances made to her by Sennacherib are sharply rebuffed. There are certainly a number of similarities of style between the language of vv. 22–29 and that of chs. 40–55, but it seems unlikely that the time of composition for these verses can have been as late as the Babylonian exile.

23. Whom have you mocked and reviled: Once again the theological element in the threat to Jerusalem, and its deliverance from Sennacherib, is prominently brought out. It is not simply a historical event that is the subject, but a theological interpretation of it which is intended to demonstrate the unique power of Yahweh the God of Jerusalem.

24. I have gone up the heights: The image of Assyria as a fruitful forest is used in 10:18f. to tell its downfall. Since this is part of the Josianic Redaction it may well have suggested the imagery here. **I felled . . . I came:** Reading the past tense with LXX.

25. I dug wells and drank waters: 1QIs^a adds 'of foreign lands'. Cf. 2 Kg. 19:24. **I dried up . . . all the streams of Egypt:** The claim is certainly a poetic hyperbole, apparently designed to put into the mouth of the king of Assyria a claim which only a god could perform. Cf. Isa. 51:10; Exod. 7:17-24; 14:21-25.

26. that I determined it long ago: I.e. the Assyrian conquests were simply the outworking of Yahweh's plan which he had determined long before. The argument is in accord with the claim of Isa. 10:5 that Assyria is simply a rod in the hand of God. **crash into heaps of ruins:** The Heb. is obscure and 1QIs^a reads 'rubble' (Heb. $n^e\d{s}\^orim$).

27. blighted before it is grown: Better, 'blasted before the east wind', with 1QIs^a; cf. *HTOT*, p. 188. The image is the quite picturesque one of grass growing on housetops which has insufficient depth of soil to survive when the hot east wind comes.

28. I know your sitting down: Better, with 1QIs^a 'your rising up and sitting down'.

29. Because you have raged against me: These words are omitted in 1QIs^a and should be deleted as a variant of the last line of v. 29. **I will put my hook in your nose:** I.e. like a wild animal that has been captured (cf. Ezek. 19:4), although possibly also reflecting the cruel treatment of prisoners of war by the Assyrians (cf. also Ezek. 38:4). **and I will turn you back:** Cf. below v. 34. Sennacherib's returning home without success is seen as a mark of poetic justice in that, for all his arrogant boasting, the king of Assyria was entirely under the hand of Yahweh, the God of Israel.

30. And this shall be the sign for you: V. 30 begins a second interpolation, evidently made after the first, which is addressed to Hezekiah, rather than to the king of Assyria. Vv. 30-31 must originally have formed an independent saying, and v. 32, with its reference to the 'remnant', a further appendage to this. Both parts of the prophecy represent exegetical developments of the Isaianic prophecy concerning Shear-jashub—the Remnant who returns—in 7:3. We may compare also 10:20-23. For the significance of a **sign**, see above on 7:11. The sign here is a relatively simple one: the processes of agriculture, so adversely affected by the Assyrian ravaging of the countryside, will be overcome within three years, and this will then serve as a sign of the restoration of the community. Very probably vv. 30-32 have been added after 598, and almost certainly before 587 BC.

31. And the surviving remnant of the house of Judah: Although the situation envisaged is that which developed after 701, it seems likely that the author here has been influenced by his knowledge of what transpired after 598 (see further below on ch. 39). For the development of the idea of a **remnant**, it is noticeable here that it is specifically applied to Judah.

32. for out of Jerusalem shall go forth a remnant: The saying reads like a fixed doctrine as a result of its direct impersonal formulation. It may come from a different hand from vv. 30–31, but undoubtedly from a similar time, between 598 and 587. Soon after 587 the idea of the **remnant** came to be applied to the Babylonian exiles; cf. 11 : 16.

33. He shall not come into this city, or shoot an arrow there: Vv. 33–35 mark the original 'prophecy' which resumes from v. 21. The 'message' is a *post eventum* reflection on what took place in 701, but adheres reasonably closely to the external facts of the situation then. It says nothing about the miraculous destruction of the Assyrian army, which is subsequently reported in v. 36.

34. By the way that he came: Cf. v. 29 for a similar sense of poetic justice in the failure of Sennacherib's arrogant boasting to fulfil its claims.

35. For I will defend this city to save it: God's affirmation that he will protect Jerusalem brings out a central theological feature which governs the author's entire approach to what he has described. God is in a very special relationship to the Davidic dynasty, and he has established his own temple in Jerusalem. These two factors mean that he will not allow Jerusalem to be treated like other cities, but will instead assert his own will to protect. Jerusalem and its king, therefore, are the subjects of a very special providence.

36. And the angel of the LORD went forth: The **angel of the LORD** represents God himself in his direct activity on earth. Cf. R. Fickner, *THAT*, I, cols. 904f. The work of the angel of the LORD, therefore, is a mark of God's own personal action, and nothing is said concerning a plague among the Assyrian soldiers or the hearing of a rumour of Egyptian military activity. It is entirely unsatisfactory to attempt to explain the reference here as a shorthand way of referring to some natural disaster. Rather, the belief that such a miraculous destruction of the Assyrian army took place outside Jerusalem must be a direct reflection into the historical narrative of the belief that Yahweh would overthrow the Assyrians by his own hand (cf. especially 29 : 6; 31 : 8). Originally the Josianic Redaction of Isaiah's prophecies had foretold that a remarkable and overwhelming destruction of the Assyrian power would be inflicted by Yahweh. This was initially in the (near) future, according to the Josianic Redaction, but it appears that this belief has been allowed to reflect back upon 701 to foster the idea that what took place then was a part of such a defeat by the hand of Yahweh. The verse here stands quite isolated, even in the B² account, which otherwise only expects Sennacherib to be sent home without conquering Jerusalem (vv. 29, 34). It is very possible that this verse did not belong even in the original B² account, but has been added subsequent to the combining of B¹ with B². Certainly its literary isolation shows fully that it cannot be used as evidence for a second attempt by Sennacherib upon Jerusalem in which some untoward misfortune to his army prevented his capturing the city.

37. Then Sennacherib king of Assyria departed: This and the following verse form the conclusion of the B¹ account, which was broken off at v. 9*a*. The historical perspective is foreshortened since, after departing from Judah, Sennacherib reigned a further twenty years. However, from the perspective of the author of the B¹ account, Sennacherib's failure to take and destroy Jerusalem fully substantiated the theological point that he wished to make that Yahweh was in control of the events of history, and was using the Assyrians as his tool.

38. And as he was worshipping in the house of Nisroch his god: The final end of Sennacherib, and the unseemly circumstances surrounding it, all appeared as a fitting judgment upon such a tyrant. The name of the deity **Nisroch** has so far defied satisfactory explanation. *BHS* suggests emending either to Nimrod (Ninurta) or to Merodach (Marduk), the name of the great god of Babylon, but neither suggestion is accepted by R. Borger in *BHH*, II, col. 1316. The murder of Sennacherib is referred to in the Annals of Ashurbanipal (cf. *ANET*, p. 288), with a mysterious allusion to his being crushed by the statues of protective deities. The year of his death was 681 BC. **And Esarhaddon his son reigned in his stead:** This ruler, according to Ezr. 4 : 2, was responsible for introducing a large element of alien population into the territory of the old Northern Kingdom of Israel, and presumably inflicting corresponding deportations on the indigenous population of that country.

HEZEKIAH'S SICKNESS AND RECOVERY

38 : 1–22

This account of Hezekiah's sickness and recovery is taken from 2 Kg. 20 : 1–11. However, some changes have been made, notably by the introduction of a psalm of thanksgiving in vv. 9–20, in which Hezekiah looks back upon his closeness to death and gives thanks to God for his deliverance. The assisting of the recovery by Isaiah, with the treatment consisting of the application of a cake of figs to a boil (v. 21) occurs between vv. 6 and 7 in the 2 Kg. account. *NEB* has consequently transposed the reference to this earlier position. As a result of the relegation of the account of the healing to a later point, Hezekiah's question about a sign (v. 22) comes too late, and must quite properly be understood to belong before v. 7. Almost certainly the reason for this alteration is to be found in the assumption that in the original text of Isa. 38, neither vv. 21 or 22 were at first a part of the text, but have subsequently been restored by a redactor at the wrong place.

There are certain features of the narrative forming the basis of the chapter which are comparable to prophetic sign- or miracle-stories, such as are told about Elisha. Cf. 2 Kg. 2 : 19–25; 4 : 1–44. The sign that the healing will be effected is itself of a miraculous nature, consisting of the going back of the shadow of the sun on the steps leading to an upper room (or perhaps a sundial?). The action of the prophet in applying a cake of figs to a boil, which is not otherwise mentioned as the nature of the illness, must be understood as a form of medical treatment, and not a sign in the true sense. It seems very doubtful whether either feature had more than a loose association with the prophet Isaiah. Rather, it appears likely that the sign-story was a popular legend about a prophet, which became linked with Isaiah, and thereby with the story of Hezekiah's sickness and recovery. This illness must represent the kernel of fact in the story, and the remainder has been built up from this in two stages. First, the king's recovery has been interpreted as a mark of his devotion and piety, and this in turn has become associated with the deliverance of Jerusalem from Sennacherib in 701 BC (see below on vv. 1 and 6). The king's recovery was then seen as a further confirmation of the belief that Yahweh acted out of a special regard for David and his dynasty (v. 5; cf. 37:35). When the story had been developed this far the simple inference was drawn that the prophet who had foretold the king's recovery was Isaiah because of his known connection with Hezekiah and the events of 701. Properly, therefore, the narrative is a story illustrating the piety and blessedness of a good king, and must be compared with the genre of the royal *Novelle*. The fact that the editor who has added to it the story of Jerusalem's deliverance in 701 saw it as shedding some light on this event is significant. It comes to form the second of the trilogy of Isaiah narratives, which could more accurately be described as 'Hezekiah' narratives, and is, like the third such story (Isa. 39), intended to illuminate the major narrative dealing with Jerusalem's deliverance. From this it is not difficult to determine what the author's intention was, for throughout the emphasis is upon Hezekiah's remarkable piety (see especially v. 3). By drawing attention to this the author has served to modify the very strong note of assurance present in the assertion of 37:35. That God will protect Jerusalem 'for the sake of his servant David' is shown to apply only when the king is a loyal and obedient servant, such as Hezekiah is portrayed. Most probably, therefore, we should infer that this story has been added to that of Jerusalem's deliverance at a time when the high confidence which permeates that story was being set in question. An origin, in its present form, during Jehoiakim's reign (609–598 BC), or even during that of Zedekiah (598–587) seems most probable.

38:1. In those days Hezekiah became sick: The time reference is rather vague, and it is v. 6 which explicitly links the recovery of Hezekiah from his illness with the deliverance of Jerusalem from Sennacherib. Evidently the author has seen a connection between the two events, but not to the point of regarding them as more than roughly contemporaneous. **And Isaiah the prophet . . . came to him:** The direct intervention of the prophet with such a sombre message is unexpected, and quite striking. Within the story the fact that Hezekiah's death had been foretold, but was subsequently replaced by a promise of a further fifteen years of life, serves to show that God had acknowledged the pious king's prayer and act of submission. For a similar threatening intervention by a prophet, we may compare 1 Kg. 21 : 19, 21. The whole account is scarcely historically reliable, but nevertheless reveals very vividly the Israelite conception of providence in relation to prayer and prophecy. Even the 'true' prophecies of such a figure as Isaiah did not announce an irreversible fate. Rather, they remained themselves subject to the openness of history to the personal will of God.

2. Then Hezekiah turned his face to the wall: I.e. he turned away from life to commune with God.

3. Remember . . . how I have walked before thee in faithfulness: The prayer is very remarkable since it contains no element of penitence, nor of remonstrance with God. Hezekiah submits totally to the divine will which has been disclosed to him by Isaiah. The author's emphasis is clear: to show that Hezekiah was a pious and obedient servant of God, who had nothing to repent of, even when faced with the prospect of his own imminent death. The king simply reminds God of the faithfulness in which his life had been lived. By showing such exemplary piety on the part of the king, the author makes plain that the subsequent recovery from illness was no ordinary act of providence. So similarly, the deliverance of Jerusalem from Sennacherib (v. 6) was no ordinary act of divine protection for the city, but a very special one appropriate to such a godly ruler. By such means he expresses consciousness that the assurance implicit in the narratives of chs. 36–37 (especially 37 : 35) was not one that would always apply. We may contrast the same generalised note of assurance in the Josianic Redaction (29 : 7).

5. Go and say to Hezekiah . . . I have heard your prayer: The form which the prophet's message takes is interesting, and corresponds to what J. Begrich has identified as the 'oracle of assurance' (Ger. *Heilsorakel*; cf. J. Begrich, *Gesammelte Studien zum Alten Testament*, ed. W. Zimmerli (*TB* 21), Munich, 1964, pp. 217–31. The reference to **the God of David your father** draws out once again an awareness of the special relationship which was believed to exist between Yahweh and the Davidic dynasty, and which forms a central feature in the explanation of why Jerusalem was saved in 701. **I have heard your prayer, I have seen your tears:** The words must be regarded as a stereotyped formula common to such oracles of assurance. **I will add fifteen years to your life:** The date appears to have been calculated on the assumption that Hezekiah reigned twenty-nine years (2 Kg. 18 : 2), and that the deliverance of Jerusalem took place in his fourteenth year (2 Kg. 18 : 13 = Isa. 36 : 1). The reference here has assumed that the illness occurred at the same time as Sennacherib's threat to Jerusalem, but does not provide any independent evidence for this.

6. I will deliver you and this city: The reference to the Assyrian threat comes entirely unanticipated, and reveals how the author has linked the protection of Jerusalem with the healing of the king.

7. This is the sign to you from the LORD: The prophet's announcement of a **sign** follows the king's request for one, which has now become misplaced and is to be found in v. 22. For the character of a **sign** (Heb. '*ôt*) as a confirmation that a prophetic word would be fulfilled see above on 7 : 11.

8. Behold, I will make the shadow: Many commentators, in company with the *RSV* translators, have accepted that the sign was to take place on a specially constructed sundial (hence *RSV* reads **dial** for Heb. 'steps') in the palace courtyard. This may have been the case, but it is not a necessary inference, and the Heb. *maʿᵃlôt* means simply 'steps'. It would then refer to an outside staircase leading to a balcony or upper room. Instead of the normal course of the shadow declining as the day lengthened, it was to go back ten steps. For *RSV*'s rendering **cast by the declining sun**, cf. *BHS*. The legendary character of the story defies clear explanation as to its origin, and it would be gratuitous to attempt any association with an eclipse of the sun (calculated to have taken place on 11th January 689 BC). The idea of such a miraculous 'sign' is probably much older than its connection with the story here, or with Isaiah, although the latter's use of such 'signs' may have encouraged the association. The 'miraculous' healing of the king has been embellished to the extent of acquiring a 'miraculous' sign to support it. The Heb. is obscure at several points, and both *RSV* and *NEB* are forced into reconstructing the original intended sense.

9. A writing of Hezekiah: The title **writing** (Heb. *miktāb*) may be a scribal error for *miktām*, perhaps meaning 'lament psalm', but S. Mowinckel, *The Psalms in Israel's Worship*, ET by D. R. Ap-Thomas, Oxford, 1962, II, p. 42, would retain *miktāb* meaning 'inscription'. It is very improbable that the psalm, which does not appear in the original narrative of 2 Kg., was actually composed by Hezekiah, since it contains no specific details that would relate personally to the king. It is a typical psalm of thanksgiving for recovery from illness which the author, or possibly a later editor, has introduced at this point because of its general appropriateness. **after he had been sick:** Although the psalm contains many expressions of lamentation, the triumphant note of assurance in vv. 19 and 20 shows that the time for such lamenting was past when the psalm was intended to be sung. It evocatively reflects back on the distress in order to emphasise the sense of the renewal of salvation that came with recovery from illness.

10. In the noontide of my days: Literally 'half of my days', which *NEB* would capture with its 'in the prime of life'. Death itself, and with that a descent to Sheol, would come anyway, but it was the anguish of premature death that was felt as such a cruel fate.

11. I shall not see the LORD: For **LORD** Heb. has *yah, yah*, but there can be no doubt that the fuller form of the divine name is to be restored with LXX and two Heb. MSS. The verse specifically refers to the fact that death would rob the speaker of any further opportunity to worship Yahweh in the temple. Cf. Pss. 42 : 5; 43 : 34. 'Seeing God' was to worship him in a sanctuary. **The inhabitants of the world:** Reading *ḥeled* (**world**) instead of *ḥedel* ('cessation'); cf. *BHS*.

12. My dwelling is plucked up: The imminence of death is described with the aid of two telling metaphors: that of a tent being pulled up and of a piece of cloth suddenly cut off from the loom, once it is finished (cf. *NEB*'s rendering). The images are of objects which suddenly disappear from their expected place. **I have rolled up my life:** Better, 'thou hast cut short my life', reading *sippartā*. Cf. IQIs[a] and *HTOT*, p. 189. **thou dost bring me to an end:** The Heb. is obscure and *NEB* suggests 'thou tormentest me'. Cf. G. R. Driver, *JSS* 13 (1968), p. 56.

13. I cry for help: The Heb. has 'I wait', and *RSV* rests on an emendation to *šiwwa'tî*. IQIs[a] reads *šappôtî*, which *NEB* takes as 'I am racked with pain'. **thou dost bring me to an end:** Once again *NEB* renders as 'thou tormentest me', as in v. 12.

14. Like a swallow or a crane: For **crane**, *NEB* margin suggests 'wryneck'; but in any case we should omit the alternative bird name with LXX. **My eyes are weary with looking upward:** The Heb. is very obscure and J. Begrich, *Der Psalm des Hiskia (FRLANT* 42), Göttingen, 1926, pp. 51f., emends **are weary** (Heb. *dallû*) to 'grow faint' (Heb. *kālû*). **with looking upward** is literally 'to the height'; i.e. looking to heaven (or to the temple?).

15. But what can I say: Once again the sense is difficult, and we should probably emend **For he has spoken to me** to 'that I might speak (to him)'. Cf. *BHS*. The words **he himself has done it** mean that God is assumed to be the cause of the illness as was taken to be true of all illnesses. Cf. Job 2 : 10. **All my sleep has fled:** *NEB* renders as 'I wander to and fro all my life long', which requires only a minor emendation of the Heb., based on IQIs[a]. However, it scarcely makes a very much better sense in this context. The text of vv. 15–17 is seriously disturbed, and a wide range of emendations have been proposed, as is shown by *BHS* and J. Begrich, *op.cit.*, p. 52. Even so, little confidence can be placed in the proposed restorations.

16. O Lord, by these things men live: The Heb. is unintelligible and *RSV* is an attempt at a literal translation. For *NEB*'s rendering 'Yet, O Lord, my soul shall live with thee', cf. *HTOT*, p. 189.

17. Lo, it was for my welfare: Better. 'Bitterness has been mine, instead of prosperity'; cf. *NEB*, and reading the preposition *l* in the sense of 'instead of.' **but thou hast held back my life:** The clause introduces a change of perspective in which the worshipper reveals that all his troubles are now in the past, and that he has experienced a recovery which he can attribute to the love of God. **for thou hast cast all my sins:** The assertion reveals the intimate connection which was believed to exist between sin and disease, so that the worshipper could readily assume that his being ill implied that he had in some way sinned against God. This was so, even when it was not clear exactly what his sin may have been.

18. For Sheol cannot thank thee: I.e. those who are dead have no further opportunity of thanking God, so that, by his premature death, the speaker would have ceased to be among God's worshippers who could offer thanks to him. **for thy faithfulness:** Literally 'truth'. The reference is to a demonstration on God's part that he had shown regard for the loyalty and trust of those who worshipped him, and had heard their cries.

19. The living, the living, he thanks thee: The joyous sense of exultation at recovery from illness reverberates out as the worshipper expresses publicly his sense of indebtedness to God. It is God who has healed him, so that every other worshipper who hears the psalm of thanksgiving is encouraged to trust in him on the strength of the testimony that this brings.

20. The LORD will save me: Better, 'is at hand to save me', since the sense is not that deliverance is still to come, but that every confidence now exists for accepting that God can always be relied upon to save those who trust in him.

21. Now Isaiah had said: The notice of a very simple aid to healing in the form of a compress of figs belongs after v. 6, as the parallel in 2 Kg. 19:7 shows. Cf. the transposition in *NEB*. The use of various simple forms of medical treatment as a means of assisting recovery was clearly not ruled out by the more fundamental belief that healing and recovery could come only from God. Almost certainly the redactor who carried over the story into the book of Isaiah from 2 Kings omitted the reference, but a later editor has restored it.

22. Hezekiah also had said: This properly belongs before v. 7 (cf. *NEB*) and has become dislocated as a consequence of the earlier omission of Isaiah's instruction regarding the cake of figs.

THE AMBASSADORS FROM BABYLON

39:1–8

The narrative which brings to a close the series of accounts in which the prophet Isaiah was involved with Hezekiah has been taken over, along with the previous two narratives, from the Second Book of Kings. Its original form, therefore, is to be found in 2 Kg. 20:12–19, and there are only minor changes in the 'Isaianic' version. It concerns the visit to Jerusalem made by envoys from the Babylonian ruler Merodach-baladan (Marduk-apla-Idinna). Thematically, however, its purpose and character is quite clear: it is intended to explain why the miraculous deliverance of Jerusalem, so vividly portrayed in respect of the events of 701 when the Assyrian armies threatened the city, was not repeated in respect of the Babylonian threat in 598. There can be no question, therefore, that the date of composition of the present narrative is after 598, and that it has been quite consciously composed to serve as an *apologia* for the painful experience which Judah and Jerusalem received in that year. This explains a feature of the account which is immediately striking in that, although it now appears after the story of Jerusalem's deliverance from Sennacherib, it must relate to an incident which took place before this. Cf. P. R. Ackroyd, *SJT* 27 (1974), pp. 329–52, and my essay in *Studies in Ancient Narrative and Historiography* (I. L. Seeligman Anniversary Volume), ed. A. Rofé and Y. Zakovitch, Jerusalem, 1979. Further discussion is to be found in my study, *Isaiah and the Deliverance of Jerusalem.*

Merodach-baladan occupied the throne of Babylon in 721–710 BC, but was then forced to flee from the city. He subsequently returned and helped to foment further rebellion against his Assyrian overlords in 703. There is no independent confirmation of the sending of envoys to Jerusalem, but it can most probably be dated in the year 703, when it occurred as a part of the plan to co-ordinate the withdrawal of allegiance to Assyria. An alternative date would be earlier, in the period 713–711, at the time of the Ashdodite rebellion against Assyria. It can hardly have taken place after 701 on any reckoning, and has been placed in its present position for a theological rather than a historical reason. Like the narrative concerning Hezekiah's sickness it offers a modification and toning down of the high doctrine of assurance for Jerusalem which underlies the present account of how the city was delivered in 701. It is concerned to show that, already in Hezekiah's time, events had taken place which had determined long in advance that a similar protection would not be afforded against the Babylonians.

So far as the date of the narrative is concerned, one point is of overriding significance. This is that v. 6 describes the carrying-off to Babylon of all the treasures of Jerusalem and must be a reference to what took place in 598 BC. More strikingly still, nothing at all is said about the destruction of the temple or the ending of the rule of the Davidic dynasty in Judah. Both of these events occurred with the second Babylonian attack on Jerusalem in 587, and were quite clearly concerned with institutions which mattered very greatly indeed to the circles from which the three 'Isaiah' narratives have come. These were themselves closely connected with the authors of the Deuteronomic History, as can be seen by the many similarities of theological outlook and vocabulary. We must conclude, therefore, that the present narrative dealing with the Babylonian envoys was written after 598, but before 587 BC. The prophecy concerning the carrying-off of the treasures of Jerusalem to Babylon has been composed *post eventum*, and is in reality an attempt at accommodating the harsh facts of 598 to the 'doctrine' of the promise of the divine protection of Jerusalem given in the basic account of Jerusalem's deliverance in 701 BC (Isa. 36–37). Overall, therefore, the story of the visit of the Babylonian envoys to Jerusalem is a further piece of narrative theology, designed to tone down the high doctrine of providence which emerged with the Josianic Redaction of Isaiah's prophecies. It endeavours to modify this belief, which related centrally to Jerusalem and the Davidic kingship, in the light of the experience of 598 without abandoning it altogether.

39:1. At that time Merodach-baladan: For this Babylonian ruler, cf. R. Borger in *BHH*, II, col. 1195. According to cuneiform sources, he was king of the land *bit yakin*, which was a region on the northern coast of the Persian gulf, and ruled in Babylon from 721 to 710 BC, when he was driven out by Sargon II. With Elamite assistance he briefly regained control of Babylon in 703, but was then forced to flee by Sennacherib. He died *c.* 695 BC. **he heard that he had been sick:**

The statement must be an inference drawn by the author from the fact that the story of ch. 38 was already coupled with that of Jerusalem's deliverance from Sennacherib, and has been used to provide a connecting link between all three stories.

2. And Hezekiah welcomed them: The account of the arrival of the envoys in Jerusalem must relate to an actual event of Hezekiah's reign, most likely occurring in the period *c*. 703, when both Judah and Babylon shared a common enmity against Assyria. The author, writing after 598, now looks back bitterly on the aftermath of the friendship. The erstwhile friend had been turned into a bitter enemy. **and he showed them his treasure house:** The emphasis upon the royal treasures effectively reveals the *post eventum* nature of the prophecy which follows in vv. 6 and 7. The specific content of the penalty which Hezekiah would suffer at the hands of the Babylonians is given with considerable precision. At the same time, the action appears as a gesture of courtesy, and nothing of a distinctively 'sinful' nature appears in regard to it. All that can be deduced from the fact that Isaiah is said subsequently to have condemned the king's action is that the display of the treasures produced a bad result. There is a hint that the Babylonians coveted such treasures, but nothing to suggest that Hezekiah was guilty of any misplaced pride in his possession of them.

3. Then Isaiah the prophet came to King Hezekiah: Having already described very fully the extent of the royal treasures in v. 2, the author proceeds to use the occasion of the interview of Isaiah with the king in order to bring out the fact that all the treasures were shown to the envoys. Quite evidently all were now destined to be lost, once the Babylonian envoys had cast a covetous eye upon them.

5. Hear the word of the LORD of hosts: The formula for the introduction of a prophetic message is adapted to suit a pronouncement couched in an impersonal form. The style of such a prophetic address was undoubtedly ancient, but has clearly been found very useful in narratives where God is spoken of in the third person. In this case the saying which follows consists entirely of a pronouncement regarding the fate of the royal treasures and future sons of the royal (Davidic) line, without offering any motive or explanation for the threat. The implied reason is 'because you have shown them these things', but nothing is said as to why this is wrong. Almost certainly the author himself felt puzzled by the severity of the loss of the royal treasures and the deportation of the princes which took place in 598, and could offer no full explanation for such a disaster.

6. Behold, the days are coming The 'prophecy' of Isaiah reflects quite accurately the humiliating terms of surrender imposed upon Jehoiachin in 598, as recounted in 2 Kg. 24 : 10–17, especially v. 13, with its connecting hint with the narrative here 'as the LORD had foretold'.

7. And some of your own sons: The term **sons**, of course, clearly included grandsons and other descendants. The reference is primarily to Jehoiachin's deportation and imprisonment in Babylon, but also to the other princes mentioned in 2 Kg. 24 : 14, who were taken with him. For the subsequent hopes of a restoration of the Davidic monarchy through these sons a hint is given in the genealogy of I Chr. 3 : 17. **who are born to you:** IQIs^a reads 'born from your loins' (Heb. *mimmē°eykā*). The fact that nothing is said about the subsequent removal of the Davidic kingship from Jerusalem altogether, which took place in 587 BC, must indicate that this event had still not happened in the author's time, for it is scarcely credible that he would have failed to mention it, if it had.

8. **Then said Hezekiah:** The reply of Hezekiah to the disturbing disclosure from Isaiah is strangely non-committal. The affirmation that **the word of the LORD ... is good** means no more than that it is a reliable message which can be taken to be assured. The king's acquiescence here contrasts interestingly with his unwillingness to accept the message of his own imminent death in 38 : 1, and this would appear to have provided a reason for introducing a comment concerning what the king thought. **For he thought, 'There will be peace and security in my days.':** The comment appears to reflect adversely upon the king and to suggest a note of complacency and self-interest, which conflicts with the earlier emphasis upon his piety. However, it appears unlikely that this was the author's real intention, which was rather to explain why, since the coming threat from Babylon was known this far in advance, no acts of penitence and contrition had been offered to God to avert the disaster to the royal house. With such a grievous warning, and a pious submission to its words of censure, the first part of the book of Isaiah comes to a close. The prophecies which occupy the remainder of the book are then concerned with the Babylonian period, and with the hope of the restoration of the life and worship of Jews in Jerusalem which this brought.

INDEX OF AUTHORS

GENERAL INDEX

Aaron, 117
Abraham, 31, 242
Ahaz, 6, 8f., 10, 14, 16f., 29, 39, 43, 47, 49, 55, 58, 60, 69, 71ff., 76, 79ff., 90, 98ff., 105ff., 112, 118, 121, 148
Amos, 15, 29, 60, 130
Apocalypse of Isaiah, 2f., 8
apocalyptic, 21f., 53f., 98, 113, 133, 196ff., 264ff.
Arabia, 179ff., 245
Ark, 73
Ashdod, 11, 173ff., 189, 243
Asherim, 159, 222
Ashurbanipal, 288

Babylon, 3, 7, 21, 43, 54, 61, 103, 131ff., 176ff., 180, 182ff., 192, 209, 261f., 265, 293ff.
bribery, 65

council of Yahweh, 72f.
covenant, 59, 201, 229f.

Damascus, 4, 79, 81, 94ff., 156ff.
Davidic kingship, 6f., 10, 14, 16f., 36, 41, 54f., 57, 67, 78, 80ff., 103ff., 115, 117, 121ff., 153ff., 188ff., 223, 235, 259f., 265, 269, 278ff.
Day of Yahweh, 45f., 135f.
death, 209, 216
Deutero-Isaiah, 2, 8, 21
Deuteronomy, 241
diaspora, 125, 275, 277
disciples, 4
drinking, 63

Edom, 180, 272f.
Egypt, 11, 54, 90, 107, 116f., 129ff., 163ff., 169, 173ff., 224, 229ff., 243, 254f., 281, 283
Elephantine, 171
Esarhaddon, 192, 282, 288
Ethiopia, 163ff., 244
Ezekiel, 8, 13

Galilee, 79

Gentiles, 223
Gideon, 107
glory, 55
God, Holy One of Israel, 16, 74
God, prophetic conception of, 71

Hezekiah, 2, 8f., 11, 17, 19, 30, 35, 39, 43, 49, 58, 90, 103ff., 110f., 118, 120ff., 148, 150, 161, 163ff., 182ff., 188ff., 224, 226, 238f., 243, 245, 247ff., 254ff., 277ff.
holy war, 14f., 272
Hosea, 29
host of heaven, 205f.

idolatry, 7, 44, 46, 111f.
Immanuel, 8off., 92f., 97f.
Isaiah, as person, 12, 70ff.
Isaiah, name, 29

Jeremiah, 8
Josiah, 5ff., 103f., 106, 108, 115ff., 253
Jotham, 8f., 10, 29, 73

Leviathan, 218
Little Apocalypse of Isaiah, 3, 8

memoir, of Isaiah, 4, 55, 70ff.
Merodach-baladan, 294
messiah, 54, 87, 103ff., 124f.
Micah, 7, 15
Midian, 107, 116f.
Moab, 130, 150ff., 209f.
Moloch, 154

Nahum, 130
Nathan, 57f., 109
Nebuchadnezzar, 182, 194
Nehemiah, 44
Nineveh, 6
Noah, 201

Obadiah, 130

Passover, 30